LOUIS XIV

VINCENT CRONIN is well known for his historical biographies and for his two-volume history of the Renaissance
("Probably the best book that has ever been written on the
Renaissance" *Times Educational Supplement*). His other historical biographies include *Louis and Antoinette, Catherine,
Empress of All the Russias* and *Napoleon*, the last of which has
been translated into eight languages and is a standard
biography both in Britain and in France ("To present
Napoleon plausibly . . . takes nerve, originality, prodigious powers of research and a true historical imagination"
Michael Foot, *Standard*). His most recent book is *Paris on
the Eve 1900–1914*, a collective portrait of the key figures
in art, literature, science and politics in the cultural capital
of Europe on the eve of the First World War. His dual
biography of *Louis and Antoinette* ("an impressive addition to
the small list of biographies that are neither journalism nor
Christmas pudding", Robin Lane Fox) and his biography of
Catherine, Empress of all the Russias ("A quite overpowering
portrait of a great and admirable woman", *Spectator*) are also
available as Harvill Paperbacks.

Vincent Cronin

LOUIS XIV

THE HARVILL PRESS

LONDON

For Chantal

First published in Great Britain 1964 by Collins Harvill

This paperback edition first published 1996
by The Harvill Press,
84 Thornhill Road,
London NI IRD

1 3 5 7 9 10 8 6 4 2

© Vincent Cronin 1964

Vincent Cronin asserts the moral right to be
identified as the author of this work.

A CIP catalogue record for this book
is available from the British Library.

ISBN 1 86046 092 5

Printed and bound in Great Britain by Butler & Tanner
at Selwood Printing, Burgess Hill

Contents

Illustrations

Louis XIV, King of France by Hyacinthe Rigaud (*Louvre*)

Louis as a young man. Anonymous engraving in the Bibliothèque Nationale

Louis XIII, by Philippe de Champaigne (*Louvre*)

Anne of Austria, engraving by Morin after a portrait by Philippe de Champaigne (*British Museum*)

Jean-Baptiste Colbert, by Philippe de Champaigne (*Metropolitan Museum, New York*)

Cardinal Mazarin, by Pierre Mignard (*Chantilly*)

The interview between Louis XIV and Philip IV, 6th June 1660. Tapestry after Le Brun (*Versailles*)

Mademoiselle (Anne-Marie-Louise de Montpensier), by Henri de Beaubrun. Painted in 1655 when Mademoiselle was twenty-eight.

Marie Mancini, by Pierre Mignard (*Versailles*)

Maria Teresa, Infanta of Spain, later wife of Louis XIV, by Velasquez (*Museum of Fine Arts, Boston*)

Louise de La Vallière, attributed to Pierre Mignard (*Musée de Marseille*)

Louis aged fifteen, in the role of 'The Sun'. Contemporary engraving (*Bibliothèque Nationale*)

Louis, by Robert Nanteuil. The engraving is dated 1664, the year of Louis's twenty-sixth birthday (*British Museum*)

Louis, by Bernini (*Versailles*)

Athénaïs de Montespan, as Iris. Anonymous contemporary painting (*Versailles*)

ILLUSTRATIONS

Louis at the crossing of the Rhine, by A. Van der Meulen (*Versailles*)

The Parterre d'Eau in the Gardens of Versailles, by Jean Cotelle (*Versailles*)

Louis receives the Doge of Genoa, by Charles Le Brun (*Versailles*)

Madame de Maintenon and her niece, by F. Elle (*Versailles*)

Louis visiting the Gobelins. Tapestry after Le Brun (*Versailles*)

Louis, his son the Grand Dauphin, his grandson the Duc de Bourgogne, his great-grandson the Duc de Bretagne, with the latter's governess the Duchesse de Ventadour, by N. de Largillière (*Wallace Collection*)

Marie Adélaide, Duchesse de Bourgogne, in hunting costume, by P. Gobert (*Versailles*)

Marly, by P. D. Martin (*Versailles*)

Louis in 1706, aged sixty-seven, by A. Benoist (*Versailles*)

Maps

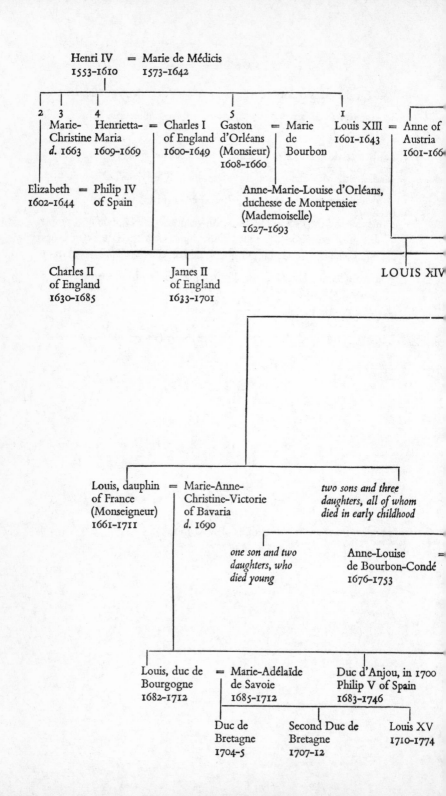

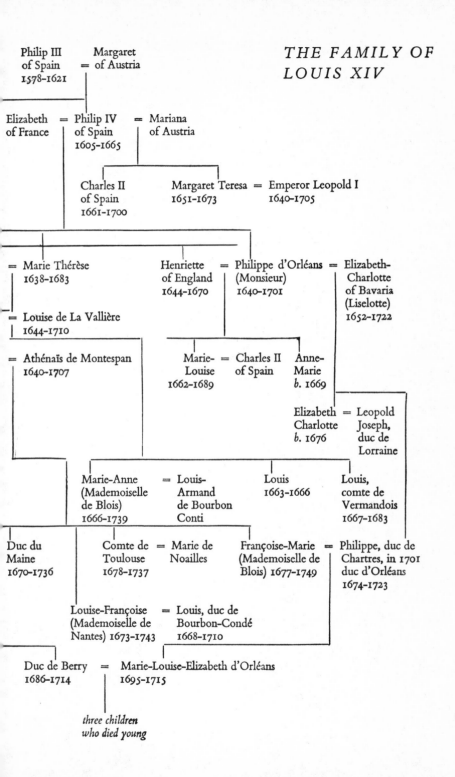

THE FAMILY OF
LOUIS XIV

Philip III
of Spain
1578-1621

Margaret
= of Austria

Elizabeth
of France

= Philip IV
of Spain
1605-1665

= Mariana
of Austria

Charles II
of Spain
1661-1700

Margaret Teresa = Emperor Leopold I
1651-1673   1640-1705

= Marie Thérèse
1638-1683

Henriette
of England
1644-1670

= Philippe d'Orléans
(Monsieur)
1640-1701

= Elizabeth-
Charlotte
of Bavaria
(Liselotte)
1652-1722

= Louise de La Vallière
1644-1710

= Athénaïs de Montespan
1640-1707

Marie-
Louise
1662-1689

= Charles II
of Spain

Anne-
Marie
b. 1669

Elizabeth
Charlotte
b. 1676

= Leopold
Joseph,
duc de
Lorraine

Marie-Anne
(Mademoiselle
de Blois)
1666-1739

= Louis-
Armand
de Bourbon
Conti

Louis
1663-1666

Louis,
comte de
Vermandois
1667-1683

Duc du
Maine
1670-1736

Comte de
Toulouse
1678-1737

= Marie de
Noailles

Françoise-Marie
(Mademoiselle de
Blois) 1677-1749

= Philippe, duc de
Chartres, in 1701
duc d'Orléans
1674-1723

Louise-Françoise
(Mademoiselle de
Nantes) 1673-1743

= Louis, duc de
Bourbon-Condé
1668-1710

Duc de Berry
1686-1714

= Marie-Louise-Elizabeth d'Orléans
1695-1715

*three children
who died young*

CHAPTER I

Birth of a Dauphin

ONE AFTERNOON in early December, 1637, a party of horsemen with an escort of guards rode out of the main gate of a small country house at Versailles-au-Val-de-Galie. One of the horses was caparisoned with white fleurs de lys on blue brocade, while the bridle and saddle were fitted with silver. But the man who rode it was dressed simply, with no lace at his wrists or neck. He wore a plain military cape and jackboots; on his head was a black plumed hat. He might have been taken for an army officer except that the others addressed him as Sire.

After riding eight miles through flat, wooded country with apple trees and ponds the horsemen entered Paris through a gate overshadowed by two grey stone buildings: the new abbey of Port-Royal, and the Benedictine convent of Val de Grâce, a favourite retreat of the Queen of France. They rode up the Rue St. Jacques, past the Luxembourg, the palace built by the exiled Queen Mother, Marie de Médicis, and crossed the Seine by a wooden bridge laden with houses. At the Hôtel de Ville they turned east into the district known as the Marais, or Marsh. Under the late King, Henri IV, this had been reclaimed and was now the most fashionable part of Paris. The horsemen clattered down the Rue St. Antoine, which was paved and lined with smart new brick houses. Near the end of the street, within sight of the eight-towered Bastille, they stopped at one of the houses, similar to its neighbours save that across its windows were iron bars. A horseman dismounted and knocked at the door. Presently the door opened slightly and a woman's face appeared. The horseman gave her the visitor's name. The man dressed like an army officer dismounted and entered the brick building. He had been here several times and knew his way to the sparsely furnished parlour on the ground floor at the end of which was a latticed grille. Here he waited, surrounded by his courtiers.

He was a handsome man, with a long face, big brown eyes, a straight nose and "the Austrian lip," a slightly protruding lower jaw which he had inherited from his mother, Marie de Médicis. He wore a long straight pointed moustache and a tuft of hair on his chin. His long black curly hair fell to his shoulders. For all his air of authority, he looked unhappy and tired. He was now thirty-six. At the age of nine he had inherited the crown—but not the kingdom of France. That he had had to win for himself, and still it was not certainly his. Nearly all his life had been spent in the saddle, fighting France's enemies, Spain and Austria, fighting the Huguenots at home, fighting ambitious noblemen, fighting his father's bastards, defending himself against his brother's plots and his mother's intrigues.

Yet this man who dressed like a soldier and had fought most of his life was not by temperament a soldier. He was just the opposite of Henri IV, his father, who had been a jolly, back-slapping fellow, physically strong and a born leader. Louis XIII was a gentle, quiet, reserved, extremely sensitive man, neither quick nor very intelligent and rather inclined to suspicion. He loved working with his hands; he loved doing and making. At any time of day, when not campaigning, he could be found in his own forge, gun-room, printing press or carpenter's shop. He could make a pair of shoes better than most cobblers. He could draw an accurate map. He liked cooking and invented a dish consisting of hard-boiled eggs chopped up with bacon. One day he took it into his head to shave the whole Court himself, leaving only a tuft of hairs on the chin. He had an ear for music, played most of the string instruments and composed several motets. Besides these hobbies he had one real passion in life: falconry. He who found it so difficult to keep the confidence and loyalty of men had a rare gift for imposing his will over birds of prey, even over the eagle. He was never happier than when out in the fields, a hawk on his gauntleted fist. He hunted wild duck with the peregrine, quail with the sparrow-hawk and merlin, partridge with the goshawk. Against crows and rabbits he flew the gerfalcon or kite. A clever fellow at anagrams turned *Louis treizième roy de France et de Navarre* into *Roy très rare estimé dieu de la fauconnerie*. He and his taloned birds lorded it over the game of France.

The son and grandson of kings, Louis was bred brave. Though not robust, he feared no physical danger. But morally he had many fears. He was over-scrupulous. He disliked hurting people. He hated executing traitors. Moreover, being moody, he found it difficult to evolve and follow a continuous line of policy. He had the sense to realise these shortcomings and to remedy them by taking as his chief Minister Cardinal de Richelieu.

Richelieu was the King's other self. He supplied the intelligence, the will of steel and three guiding principles: crush the nobles, crush the Huguenots, crush the house of Austria; while it was the King, sword in hand, who put these ideas into action. The people of France accepted the partnership without much enthusiasm. It was one thing to obey their local lord or their King, for these men, they believed, owed their exalted position to God and, so to speak, took His place; quite another to obey a politician whose family were merely bourgeois lawyers. Yet so far the partnership had worked. The King and his Minister were linked so closely that it was difficult to say who was master. To-night, as almost every night, the King would write affectionately to Richelieu, describing the day's events. Perhaps not all of them, for the Cardinal disapproved of the visit he was making.

Presently, on the other side of the latticed grille a young girl appeared. She had blue eyes and dark brown hair, cut short. The King went to the grille and began to speak to her, intently and with feeling. The courtiers edged discreetly to the other end of the room. But they knew quite well what the conversation was about.

The girl on the other side of the grille used to be called Louise de La Fayette. She had come to Court as maid of honour to the Queen. She sang well, she danced well, and before long her bright, happy nature attracted the King. He did not fall in love easily, but he fell in love with Louise and asked her to be his mistress.

Louise was a more than usually pious girl. Not only did she decline the King's offer; she believed she had a vocation. She felt drawn to a gentle Order, the Visitandines, recently founded by Jeanne Françoise de Chantal, Madame de Sévigné's grandmother. Seven months ago, in May, Louise de La Fayette had entered the Visitandine convent of Sainte Marie as a novice. She was not yet twenty. The King had wept and been ill for five days.

Since then the King had visited Sister Angélique several times. Once he had stayed three hours. After each visit his health improved. He was still in love with her, but his visits were not prompted by sensuality. He came to cool his feverish nerves in the silence and peace which she had found, and for which he too sometimes sighed. As he told his confessor, he longed to retire from the world, escape the servitude of kingship, the ceaseless intrigues and cabals, and the obligation to punish. He also came to tell Sister Angélique his troubles and listen to her advice, for she was a sensible girl and quite disinterested. His latest trouble was the Queen. For years now she had been retiring at regular intervals to the corner apartment, marked with a stone pelican, in the convent of Val de Grâce: she too felt the need to escape from a world torn by intrigue and war. There she prayed and read St. Teresa of Avila. She also wrote letters, which were slipped to a secretary in the English embassy, who smuggled them out of France. Richelieu, alerted by his spies, had recently had her apartment raided. Letters were found to her brothers, the King of Spain and the Cardinal-Infante, commanding Spanish troops in the Netherlands. They were fairly harmless letters, but in one she warned against a certain monk whom Richelieu was sending to Spain as an agent. Richelieu made the most of this "treacherous. correspondence with the enemy." The King was made to feel that he who had been betrayed by so many friends—by Saint-Simon, Luynes, Toiras and Barradas—by his mother and by his brother—had now been betrayed by his own wife.

From the other side of the grille a girl's voice pleaded with the King. She begged him to soften towards the Queen, to give to the Queen the affection he insisted on turning towards herself. The Queen was worthy of his trust—more so than Richelieu. As for

State affairs let him reverse Richelieu's foreign policy, abandon Protestant Holland and the German princes, and make peace with the house of Austria. Let him also recall his mother from exile. The advice was familiar—even at Court she had been urging it on the King—and somewhat idealistic: politics as a form of Christian morality. But even if it were sound advice, how could he ever follow it? Richelieu hated and feared the influence of women, "Women have no say in the Church; they should have no say in politics either." And to the King Richelieu was indispensable.

After talking about these matters for much of the afternoon the King said good-bye to Sister Angélique and accompanied by his courtiers left the convent parlour. Outside, in the Rue St. Antoine, it was already dark and rain had begun to fall. The King took shelter, hoping the weather would clear. But the rain became heavier and, lashed by a cold wind, turned to driving sleet. The King had planned to spend the night at Saint-Maur, eight miles south-east of Paris: his bed, furnishings, linen, clothes and plate had gone ahead that morning. His servants and the officers in charge of his table were there awaiting his arrival. But it would be difficult now either to reach Saint-Maur or to return to Versailles, for the sleet would put out his guards' torches. Moreover, the King's health was poor—he suffered from rheumatism, insomnia and gout—and an hour's ride drenched to the skin would certainly bring on fever. As for his apartment in the Louvre, it was not furnished. He did not know where to pass the night.

His suite noticed the King's embarrassment. Among them was Guitaut, captain of the guard, who had served in the daring expedition of 1629, when the King led an army across the snowbound Alps to relieve the town of Susa. Being an old and trusted friend, Guitaut was accustomed to speak freely. He pointed out to Louis that the Queen was living in the Louvre and that he could sup and lodge for the night in her apartment. No, replied the King, they must wait for the storm to clear. And wait they did, though the driving sleet showed no sign of stopping. Guitaut again suggested that the King should spend the night in the Louvre, which lay only a mile off. Louis replied curtly that the Queen supped and went to bed too late for him. There the conversation might have ended, had not Guitaut felt so strongly on the matter. He was not thinking of the King's comfort. Like any loyal Frenchman, he was thinking of the future of his country. The heir presumptive to the throne was Louis's brother, Gaston d'Orléans, an odd-looking man with thick black eyebrows and gaping mouth: conceited, stupid, weak—worse than weak, dangerous. For eleven years Monsieur, as Gaston was called at Court, had been working with Louis's enemies to obtain the crown. As Richelieu put it, "He entered into the conspiracies because of lack of will, and he always crept shamefully out of them because of lack of courage," —while eagerly revealing the names of his accomplices, who in due course went to the scaffold. In 1636, for instance, he had joined a conspiracy to kill Richelieu. The conspirators surrounded the Cardinal in the courtyard of a house in Amiens. Hands on their sword hilts, they watched Monsieur's face for the agreed signal: a wink. But Monsieur could not even bring himself to wink. He slowly backed away to the nearest staircase, then took to his heels. Monsieur was a puppet, a weather-vane, a scarecrow : even on the throne of France, he would never be a king, merely an excuse for civil war. That was why Guitaut, like any good Frenchman, longed for Louis to have a son. That was why he continued the present conversation.

Guitaut pointed out to Louis that the Queen would gladly change her programme, that she would sup and go to bed whenever it suited His Majesty. So persuasive was he, and so well did his argument chime with Sister Angélique's pleas that Louis finally yielded. Before the King could change his mind the delighted Guitaut rode off at full gallop to tell the Queen that His Majesty would be supping with her that evening, and that he wished supper to be served early.

Through streets thick in mud the King, followed by his suite, rode to the palace of the Louvre. As he crossed the dank moat bearded Swiss guards, in goffered ruffs, puffed sleeves and white-plumed hats, snapped to attention. He went to an apartment on the ground floor of the half-completed courtyard and there was met by his Queen. She was a handsome woman of thirty-seven, tall, with a rather full figure, fair hair, large eyes, a nose a shade too long and a small red mouth. She was said to have the most beautiful and whitest hands in Europe. She dressed well but simply, without gold or silver.

The Queen was Spanish. She belonged to the house of Hapsburg, which for over a hundred years had provided kings of Spain and Austria, and was known by the courtesy title of Anne of Austria. But she had long been a patriotic Frenchwoman. On the day she was hailed queen she insisted on wearing ear-rings in the shape of fleurs de lys: "I want everything to be French"; and she had acquiesced when Louis asked her to send away her Spanish maids, confessors, cook and doctors. She did a lot for the people of Paris. Dressed as an ordinary lady or even as a servant, she would tend the sick poor and, according to Madame de Motteville, her lady-in-waiting, "since she did not have enough money for alms, she robbed herself of jewels and chains, pretending she had lost them accidentally, in order to give them to the poor."

The Queen did retain one Spanish custom. She liked to sup about ten or eleven, whereas the King kept to the French habit of supping at seven or eight. To-night the Queen ordered an early supper, which they ate together.

They had not seen each other for several weeks, but the King was not much of a talker. When he spoke it was slowly, in order to avoid a stammer. He was also a light eater, whereas the Queen had a hearty appetite. She talked easily and to-night she had every reason to try to hold her husband's interest. For seven years he had not slept with her, and the Queen desperately wanted a child.

Theirs had been a curious life together. They were distant cousins, married at the age of fourteen. For a long time Louis showed no sign of wishing to consummate the marriage. As the years passed his mother became anxious and made him dance with Anne in amorous ballets. As the Demon of Fire in a flame-like costume Louis had to declare a "burning love"; but his passion continued merely allegorical.

When Louis was seventeen his illegitimate half-sister was married to the Duc d'Elbeuf. The couple invited Louis to the marriage chamber, where, according to the Venetian ambassador, "the act was repeated more than once, to the great applause and particular pleasure of His Majesty. It is thought that this example has excited the King to do the same. It is also said that his half-sister, Mademoiselle de Vendôme, encouraged him, saying, 'Sire, you do the same with the Queen, and you will be the better for it.' " Later that month his intimate older friend, Charles de Luynes, came to his bedroom at eleven one night and begged Louis to go to the Queen. Louis, at first annoyed, then moved, began to cry. But he could not bring himself to go. Finally Luynes took the King from his bed and carried him in his arms down the corridor, struggling and crying. And since protocol never waived its rights, this odd procession was headed by M. de Beringhen, first *valet de chambre*, gravely carrying a candle. Luynes finally landed Louis within the Queen's apartments, where he remained until two in the morning. That night the marriage was consummated.

Three years later the Queen became pregnant for the first time. Returning from a party at midnight, she went romping "like a schoolgirl" in the Louvre. The Duchesse de Luynes and Mademoiselle de Verneuil held her by the arms and urged her to run down the long gallery. She slipped on the polished floor and fell. As a result she had a miscarriage. Louis ordered the two ladies to leave Court and towards the Queen his fury became a persistent grudge. For the past fifteen years he had slept mostly in his own bed. Only once again, in 1630, had the Queen been pregnant, and that too had ended in a miscarriage.

The grudge, like the charge that Anne was betraying his secrets to Spain, seems to have been an expression of a deep-seated fear of women and feeling of shame at sexual relations. Even as a boy of five Louis had shown abhorrence (unusual at that period) of coarse language and gross gestures. "No naughty thoughts," he would often warn his courtiers, wagging a finger, and he would show disapproval of a low neckline by pulling his hat-brim over his eyes. For the fast-living Princesse de Conti his nickname was "Sin." Hand in hand with this went a desire for purity and simplicity, which came out in the King's laws forbidding luxurious dress, his love of birds and his love of baths—sometimes he would spend an hour and a quarter in his morning bath.

What was the cause? An extremely sensitive modesty wounded as a child? An over-strict mother who had brought him up on a black mixture of cassia, senna and rhubarb? A trait inherited from his puritanical grandmother, Jeanne d'Albret? No one knew. But to Anne it had brought much unhappiness, borne for the most part patiently. Only once, twelve years ago, had she had a little adventure. The handsome, dashing Duke of Buckingham arrived for a week's stay in Paris with twenty-seven suits, one spangled with diamonds. Anne found him attractive and flirted with him. On his way home in the gardens of a house in Amiens he tried to make love to her. Anne got control of herself in time, called for her equerry, then took to her bed with the vapours. Buckingham continued to Boulogne, then dashed back to Amiens to have a last few moments with Anne. To the Court's amazement, he forced his way into her bedroom, knelt at her bed and told her that he loved her. Apart from that one flirtation Anne had been an exemplary wife to the King.

After supper the question of sleeping arrangements arose. There were half a dozen royal country houses and palaces, but only one set of royal furniture. This went ahead of the King on his journeys, like the props of a touring company; to-night it was set up at Saint-Maur. The Louvre was a cold, damp stone building, empty and bare save for the Queen's apartment and the small rooms occupied by her ladies. The only comfortable bed in the place was the Queen's big curtained four-poster.

As the King had told Guitaut, he and the Queen had different habits. Louis, an early riser, liked to go to bed soon after supper, while Anne enjoyed talking late to her ladies, until midnight or one. But on this occasion, as Guitaut had predicted, she renounced her candlelight conversation. She even ordered a long bolster to be put on her bed, for the King liked a bolster. And so that winter night in 1637, because of a storm, the pleas of a novice and the wily perseverance of an old soldier, the King and Queen of France slept together.

Next morning the King left for Saint-Maur, but invited the Queen to pay him an early visit. Almost at once he seems to have regretted his action, for on 10th December he dismissed his confessor, a friend of Sister Angélique and an enemy of Richelieu. On 13th January he danced in the Ballet des Nations, for which he had composed the music, at Richelieu's country house, Rueil. "On the 30th," according to Renaudot's *Gazette*, the recently founded first French newspaper, "all the princes, lords and people of fashion went to congratulate their Majesties at Saint-Germain on their hopes of a happy event, which, with God's help, we will tell you about soon." On 15th March, 1638, *Le Mercure François* announced that "France has hopes of her greatest happiness so far in this august and marvellous reign, namely the birth of a dauphin, destined by God to take place this year." After twenty-two years of childless marriage the news caused a sensation and all France shared Anne's hopes for a son, since a daughter could not succeed to the throne. As the months passed special novenas were said for a male child, while Anne wore the girdle of the Blessed Virgin, lent by the Capuchins of Notre Dame du Puy. Because the mud and rubbish of Paris made the Louvre unhealthy in warm weather, she moved to apartments in Saint-Germain, a dozen miles west of the capital. The old castle had been built by François I, and bore the mark of his tasteful hand: a square-cut pentagon of brick and grey stone, relieved from grimness by graceful arcades. Close by Henri IV had added a much smaller pleasure-house of brick. This "new castle" had panelled rooms and was more comfortable. It was here that Anne prepared to have her child.

At first Louis was delighted and unusually tender for his wife, but this lasted only a few weeks. Soon he was off hawking and visiting his armies. On 22nd April the Queen felt her child stir for the first time; in celebration a firework display was held at the Arsenal. A layette of softest wool, silk and lace was prepared, and a cradle hung with white muslin. Anne's slightest symptoms were gravely discussed by the royal doctors. Bishops were summoned to offer Mass in the palace. Wet-nurses were chosen with meticulous care. The royal accoucheur took up his post, with midwives in attendance. It was as though no child had ever been conceived before.

As the ninth month drew on, all France was wondering what the royal child would be like. On paper, at least, its heredity was brilliant. Of fourteen immediate ancestors, all but two had worn crowns. Farther back were the Emperors Charles V and Maximilian. From the Médicis the child might inherit a taste for the arts, but also perhaps a touch of violence. Hapsburg blood would come to it from Anne of Austria, who was the daughter of two Hapsburgs, and from Marie de Médicis, whose mother was the Archduchess Joanna of Austria. Bourbon blood would come through the child's grandfather, Henri IV, who, through his father, Antoine de Bourbon, was a direct descendant of Robert de Clermont, sixth son of St. Louis. It was the Bourbon character the French loved: open, gay, sensual, enjoying life, whereas Hapsburgs tended to be narrow-minded, shut in and inclined to religious bigotry. The French wanted Anne to have a son, but a Bourbon son.

Shortly after midnight on the morning of Sunday, the 5th of September, Anne entered labour. The King's brother, Monsieur, and the highest ladies in France, including the Princesse de Condé, the Duchesse de Vendôme and the Comtesse de Soissons, were wakened and summoned to the Queen's room. Witnesses to hereditary monarchy, it was their duty to watch every moment of the birth and testify later should charges be made that another child had been substituted for the royal infant. Anne continued in labour throughout the night and early morning. In a neighbouring room three bishops, having said Mass, remained kneeling in prayer.

The birth took place at twenty-two minutes past eleven on Sunday morning. The child was a big, well-formed boy, weighing forty-eight marks—nine pounds. According to custom, he was at once washed in wine and oil of red roses. Louis, who was at dinner, came up immediately to the bedroom. "Unused to such occasions," he had to be prompted to kiss his wife. Then Dame Péronne, midwife in charge, handed him his son and proudly pointed out that the child had been born with two teeth.

Salvoes were fired from the palace cannon. The bridge at Neuilly happened to be down, but an agreed signal was at once transmitted across the Seine to Paris. Messengers were sent galloping north, south, east and west. One reached Toulouse, four days' journey by post, on the evening of the seventh. News at that time usually meant heavier taxes, or losses in the Thirty Years' War, but here at last was cause for rejoicing.

In the arms of his governess, the Marquise de Lansac, the infant was carried to the palace chapel, where the first almoner, in the presence of the King, Monsieur and Pierre Séguier, Chancellor of France, poured a few drops of holy water over his head to make him a Christian. At a christening ceremony later he would be given his full name: for the moment he was called simply Louis. This was one of the most auspicious names in French history. The first Louis, Charlemagne's son, had been born in 778; King of the Franks and Emperor of the West, he was known as Louis the Débonnaire or Louis the Pious. Another Louis, the Lion, had won much of France from the English, and his son, the Crusader, was a canonised saint; Louis XI had laid the foundations of national unity, while Louis XII, the Father of the People, was one of the best kings France had ever had.

The newly named Louis was carried back between two rows of guards to an apartment hung with white damask. There he was handed to Dame de La Giraudière, wife of the King's attorney in the Treasury at Orléans, chosen by seven learned doctors to give suck to the royal child.

For six days Paris celebrated with *Te Deums*, musket and cannon salvoes and dancing in the streets. The rich distributed hams and patés, and vied to provide the best illuminations. The official firework display on the Place de Grève showed a vast rock, its summit covered with clouds through which shone the rays of a rising sun. Below was the emblematic ship of Paris: "You will not founder through sedition Because on the banks of the Seine A dauphin is playing with halcyons."

At Saint-Germain an obelisk was set up with free wine spouting from four silver dolphins. At Lyon so many fireworks were set off "that the air, infected by the plague which had recently swept this powerful city, was cleansed of impurities." Even in Rome regattas were held and *Te Deums* chanted in the church of Our

Lady of Loretto, to which Anne donated a gold statue of her son nine pounds in weight.

The royal astrologer, present at Saint-Germain, noted that the dauphin had been born under Virgo: a specially happy coincidence in view of Anne's devotion to the Blessed Virgin. The astronomer Campanella, letting loyalty get the better of science, announced that on the fifth the sun had moved closer to the earth, "in order to share in the happy event."

When the boy was two days old the red-robed members of Parlement came to pay their respects. Behind a gilt balustrade he lay sleeping on a white pillow in Madame de Lansac's arms, and when the lawyers' heads bowed in homage "Monseigneur le Dauphin opened his eyes in order to see his most faithful servants." Day and night his head was covered with a cap and his body swaddled tight as a mummy. Swaddling babies was considered very important: as a certain Dr. François Mauriceau explained, "this gives its little body an upright bearing, the most decent and suitable for a man, and accustoms it to stand on its feet; otherwise perhaps it would walk on all fours, like most other animals."

It was soon remarked that the child had an unusually big appetite. This was a Bourbon trait and therefore caused satisfaction. So big was its appetite that after three months Elizabeth de La Giraudière no longer had sufficient milk and was relieved of her office as wet nurse. Peasant women were now recruited—there was no class distinction in this matter—sturdy mothers with sturdy names: Jeanne Potier, Marguerite Garnier, Marie Mesnil, Anne Perier. They succeeded one another at intervals, but none could satisfy the infant's lusty appetite. In six months Louis went through no less than seven nurses. "When they did not have enough milk to satisfy him," wrote the surgeon Dionis, "he would bite their teats."

At last the doctors found an exceptionally strong peasant woman, Perrette Dufour, wife of Etienne Ancelin, a carter at Poissy, who could satisfy the royal appetite and support the two royal teeth. She was appointed *nourrice du corps* at £400 a year. A second nurse named Marie de Segneville, an auxiliary, Marie Lebas, and a woman to rock the cradle, Marguerite Robert, were each paid £200 a year. When the dauphin slept, six women kept watch under the direction of the first chambermaid. Two pages, two handymen, a washerwoman and a cook brought the dauphin's suite to seventeen.

Anne was overjoyed with her son. For one thing, now she could never be sent back to Spain on the pretext of sterility. She scarcely left the dauphin a moment, and when the weather grew warmer took him out in his pram to the garden. The royal mint struck a medal with her portrait; on the reverse was the lys of France, with the words: "It takes its birth from a goddess"—in allusion to a legend that the lily of France was made of Juno's milk. Her baby was already being called Hercules. Another medal showed the rising of the Sun of France: official as well as popular hopes for a brighter future were centred on this one small child.

Gifts for the dauphin began to arrive from abroad. Pope Urban VIII sent Cardinal Sforza with consecrated swaddling clothes, sheets, pillow-cases, bonnets and a large piece of silver lamé on which was worked in gold needle-point figures of St. Louis and Pope St. Urban. The Cardinal touched the child's hands with the swaddling clothes "as a sign that His Holiness recognised him as the eldest son of the Church." In the log cabins of New France Indians decided that as "our good King has given us clothes, we will now send a gift in return," and there arrived at Saint-Germain for the heir apparent the beaded outfit of a Redskin papoose.

It was at Saint-Germain that Louis cut his milk teeth, learned to crawl and took his first steps. When he was sixteen months old he performed his first official function: at dinner on 6th January, 1640, he received a napkin from the *maître d'hôtel* and handed it to the King. About that time his mother again found herself pregnant. On 21st September, 1640, she gave birth to a second son, whom she named Philippe after her father the King of Spain. He was given the title of Duke of Anjou. According to Madame de Motteville the King showed more joy at Philippe's birth than at the dauphin's, "because he did not expect the happiness of having two children, after fearing he would never have any." She also relates that when the dauphin was three the King came to see him wearing a nightcap. The child was frightened by the nightcap and began to cry; at this the King became very upset, complained to Anne that she was responsible for bringing up the boy to dislike him, and threatened to take away both children from her.

This was the outburst of a tired man whose nerves were on edge and who was fighting a losing battle against illnesses, the latest being tuberculosis. In March, 1643, the King took to his bed, and on Maunday Thursday it was the four-year-old dauphin who washed the feet of the poor. Richelieu had died the previous year and Louis felt sure he was going to die too. He summoned his councillors to his bedroom at Saint-Germain and made provisions for a long minority. His sons' education he entrusted to Anne, but not the control of France. In defiance of custom he made her Regent in name only, subject to a council of five. "The Queen must be bridled," he said. He still did not trust his Spanish wife.

Louis also decided that the dauphin's solemn baptism, usually held at the age of seven—the age of reason—should take place at once. So on 21st April, 1643, the dauphin, dressed in long silver taffeta, was escorted to the chapel royal by his godparents, the Princesse de Condé—in her fifties now, but still the beautiful Charlotte de Montmorency with whom Henri IV had been madly in love—and Jules Mazarin, Richelieu's protégé, resplendent in scarlet silk and the Cardinal's hat which Louis had recently obtained for him. The Bishop of Meaux anointed the prince with holy oil and placed a few grains of salt in his mouth. To the question whether he renounced Satan and all his works and pomps, the boy replied "with wonderful assurance": "*Abrenuncio.*" He was given the name Louis-Dieudonné. The fact of having been an answer to prayer set him apart from all other bearers of the name: he was Louis the God-given.

When he returned to his father's bedside, the King kissed his son and asked, "What is your name?"

"Louis the fourteenth, Papa."

"Not yet, not yet," said the sick King. "But you will be soon, if that is God's will."

The King's illness was a painful one: tuberculosis of the digestive tract with acute tubercular peritonitis. He bore his suffering bravely and even composed, one quieter day, a fresh setting of the *De*

Profundis, to be chanted over his tomb. On 13th May the dauphin was taken to the King's bedroom. "The King is asleep," said the *valet de chambre*. "Look at him well, so that when you grow up you'll remember him." The child gazed at the long thin pale face and seemed deeply moved. When he came out into the corridor, he was asked by the gentleman usher on duty:

"Monseigneur, if God took away your daddy, would you like to be king in his place?"

"No, I don't want to be king," replied the dauphin, bursting into tears. "If he dies, I'll throw myself into the moat."

His governess, alerted, watched the boy carefully all that day.

On the 14th, Ascension Day, the King went into delirium. Suddenly he sat up and called for his swords and pistols. "Don't you see the Duc d'Enghien fighting the Spaniards? Good God, how bravely he charges. They're all beaten, dead or prisoners!" With that he fell back on his pillows. The doctors felt for his pulse and listened for his heart-beat, but Louis XIII was dead. At the news Anne, who knelt beside the ruelle of his bed, burst into tears. "She loved the King more than she had imagined," and her ladies-in-waiting had to escort her sobbing from the room.

A note on currency values appears on p. 355.

Anne, Regent of France

LATER THE SAME AFTERNOON, after praying in her oratory, Anne went to the nursery to hail on bended knee the four-year-old Louis, "her son and her King." Finding the nursery crowded with noisy courtiers, Anne asked François de Beaufort to make everyone leave. Beaufort was a young war hero with long blond curls who looked like a Viking. He was the best pistol shot in France and had lately led the capture of Arras by swimming the Scarpe. Anne liked him and had asked him to guard the royal children in case one of the princes tried to kidnap them. Beaufort turned first to Monsieur and asked him to leave the room. Monsieur, as usual, did as he was told. Then Beaufort asked the grey-haired Prince de Condé to leave. Now the Condés, a collateral branch of the Bourbons, were princes of the blood, whereas Beaufort was merely a son of one of Henri IV's bastards. Condé replied coldly that the Queen's wishes should be given him by the captain of the guards. Beaufort, who hated the rival Condés, calmly repeated the request to leave the room. Condé flared up and refused. Eyes blazing, both men reached for their swords, and just in time Anne intervened. So the new reign began.

The first duty of a king after his proclamation was to show himself to his people in his capital city. Next day Louis was perched on cushions in a coach drawn by six white horses, and escorted by his bodyguard and musketeers set off for Paris. In order to line the route Parisians got up early and walked the seven miles to Nanterre, birth-place of St. Geneviève, an earlier saviour of France. They cheered and tried to kiss the clothing of the small alert figure with light chestnut hair as his coach clattered past, into the garlanded streets where church bells rang and waving figures shouted from every window, *"Vive le roi!"* The Parisians remarked on Louis's striking good looks, his precociously serious expression and his dignity: they felt certain that a new era of happiness and prosperity was about to begin.

While the late King was laid to rest in the basilica of Saint-Denis, Louis went to live in the Louvre with his mother and two-year-old Philippe. Anne chose the Louvre because behind its towers and moat Louis would be safe from ambitious nobles. She was well aware that whoever had the person of the King was master of France. And it was from the Louvre, three days after his entry to Paris, that the young King crossed to the pepper-pot towers of the Palais de Justice, where the two hundred and twenty members of Parlement, councillors in scarlet robes, High Court presidents in ermine cloaks, each holding his square cap, sat waiting to receive him. Preceded by two heralds with the sceptre and mace, the King, wearing violet mourning, was carried into the hall and lifted on to his throne. When the captain of the guards had called for silence the solemn grey-bearded lawyers watched a boy of four stand up and address them in words he had learned by heart:

"Gentlemen, I have come to see you in order to express my affection and goodwill towards my Parlement. My Chancellor will tell you my will."

For the moment Louis's will was Anne's will. Anne had asked her fellow councillors, Condé among them, to waive their control over the Regency; and all had agreed, each hoping to gain sole ascendancy over the susceptible, still beautiful Queen. The Chancellor rose and asked approval for this modification of the late King's testament. Now Parlement looked favourably on Anne; she, like them, had suffered from Richelieu's despotism and—a wild but attractive hope—perhaps she would end the expensive war with her Spanish kindred. Having declared that "the royal authority should be one and indivisible"—words which before very long their actions would belie—the members of Parlement voted in favour of abolishing the Regency council. It was then announced that the King was pleased to give his mother "free, absolute and entire administration of the affairs of his kingdom during his minority." Anne left the hall sole ruler of France.

But she knew that she could not rule France alone. She was aware of her own weaknesses. She was inclined to be lazy, she acted from the heart, not from the head, she was too easily swayed by good looks or a shapely leg. Then again, she was naturally kind and straightforward, incapable of dealing alone with the intrigue that hummed around her, of waging war or bargaining for peace. She knew nothing of taxes, lobbying, spies, codes or bribery. For these she needed a man by her side. Who should it be?

Her late husband's younger brother, Monsieur, should have been that man. He was thirty-five now, wore his hat like a swash-buckler, and with hands deep in his trouser pockets swaggered about whistling some of the hundred drinking songs he knew by heart. In the last five years Monsieur had changed little—he was still plotting, still sending his accomplices to the scaffold—the latest was Cinq-Mars. Most tiresome of all, he lacked a will of his own. According to his wife, Monsieur laboured longer to make a decision than she did to have a child. He could never be of any help to Anne.

The Prince de Condé? He cared only for his prerogatives and money: indeed he spent whole days checking his cook's accounts. The Duc de Vendôme, Henri IV's bastard? Not intelligent enough, and like his son Beaufort concerned more with his family's advance-ment than with the unity of France. The same held true of all the great nobles: what they wanted was more provincial governorships, more estates, more servants, carriages, horses and jewels. Someone from the petty nobility? The princes and dukes would consider that an insult and never obey him. The Chancellor? A dry lawyer, lacking in energy and courage. And what of Cardinal Mazarin? Richelieu's secretary, according to report he was likely to become another Richelieu, an enemy rather than an ally. But was this so? Richelieu had been austere and a woman-hater, while his former secretary seemed to enjoy life and whenever Anne met him tried to please her.

Jules Mazarin he was called since entering the service of France, but he had been born Giulio Mazzarini, at Piscina in the Abruzzi, in 1602, which made him a year younger than Anne. He was the son of a servant: his father, a Sicilian, had been major-domo in the Colonna household in Rome. The Colonnas had paid for the young Mazarin's education at the Roman College and the University of Alcala, where he had learned Spanish. After taking a doctorate in law he entered the Papal diplomatic service.

Mazarin first made his name as a peace-maker, and a peace-maker he was to remain all his life. In 1630 the French garrison at Casale, a key town in North Italy, was hard pressed by Spanish and Imperial troops. Mazarin hurried to the spot and began conversations with both sides. Five weeks later, just as a relieving French army attacked the Spaniards, Mazarin galloped up amid the bullets, waving a paper. "Stop! Peace! Peace!" Sure enough, at the last moment he had worked out a clever compromise treaty. Richelieu, who had met Mazarin earlier that year and found him well disposed to France, brought him to Paris as nuncio, then as his secretary. In 1640 he received the Cardinal's hat, but he did not claim to be a religious man and was never ordained priest.

He was above middle height, burly but not robust, auburn-haired, with a broad forehead, large nose and large greyish-blue eyes. His beard was carefully curled, his hands well formed, small and white. People said that he resembled the Duke of Buckingham, and that was why Anne noticed him. He was the best dressed man of his day, his favourite colour the rich blue which bears his name. Indeed he was something of a dandy; he perfumed himself and was said even to perfume his pet monkey. He was highly cultivated, loved objets d'art, drama and opera—which he introduced to Paris; but he also liked hunting and was a good man to hounds. His handwriting, beautifully round and even, shows a well-balanced nature. His manner was gentle and unassuming, full of kindness, but rather reserved. He always seemed to be smiling.

Anne asked her friends what they thought of Mazarin. The Marquis de Liancourt and the Marquis de Mortemart assured her that he was intelligent, reliable and devoted to France. Then she asked the advice of an Englishman who stood outside the cabals, the Abbé Walter Montagu, who had started his career as the Duke of Buckingham's secret agent in France. Montagu told her that Mazarin "was the opposite in all things of Cardinal Richelieu." Few recommendations could have pleased Anne more. Another point in Mazarin's favour was that he spoke fluent Spanish. For a little while she studied the young Cardinal, then took her decision. Summoning him to the Louvre, she invited him to help her govern France. Mazarin replied in his flowery way that the honour overwhelmed him, that he was quite unprepared for it, but that nevertheless he would be pleased to serve Her Majesty for a short time, until she could find a less unworthy adviser.

Louis, meanwhile, was more than ever the people's idol since news had arrived of the battle of Rocroi, in which the Duc d'Enghien, Condé's son, had defeated the Spaniards, "the only general in history to have won a great victory for a King of four on the fourth day of his reign": this was the battle Louis XIII had foreseen on his sick bed. The young Louis was still in the nursery, being looked after by women. His first governess, Madame de Lansac, a relative of Richelieu appointed by his father, had been replaced by Marie Catherine de La Rochefoucauld, Marquise de Senécé, but the kind-hearted Anne allowed Madame de Lansac to keep the rank of her office and to draw her salary. Madame de Senécé, an old friend of Anne's, was sensible, worldly-wise and very much the great lady. She saw that Louis was impeccably turned out in satin or brocade ankle-length dresses (boys wore dresses until their seventh birthday) on which lay the pale-blue sash of the Order of the Holy Spirit. He was growing up a healthy, vigorous boy. What struck people most were his extraordinary good looks. He had large hazel eyes and chubby pink cheeks; his hair was still light chestnut and very curly. When it was trimmed, Court ladies fought for the curls, which they mounted in silver lockets.

With France at war Louis's favourite toys were naturally soldiers. A goldsmith of Nancy had made him an army all in silver: pikemen, halberdiers, musketeers, troopers, gunners with their model pieces of ordnance of the six calibres used in France, pioneers with their tools, all correct in every detail. He also had a tiny set of gold cannon drawn by a team of fleas. But at this age even more than soldiers Louis loved his bedtime story. His favourite was *Peau d'Ane*: about a princess who has to flee the Court, her face disguised with soot, and with an old ass's skin for dress. She lives alone in a hovel and there she sometimes comforts herself by secretly resuming her beauty and gay clothes. On one of these occasions a prince who is out hunting looks from curiosity through the keyhole and discovers her. He inquires who lives there and is told "Peau d'Ane." He falls ill from love of her, and nothing will cure him but he must have a cake made by Peau d'Ane. His whim is humoured, but as he eats the cake he comes upon a ring which has slipped off Peau d'Ane's finger. The prince will now only marry the woman whose finger the little ring will fit. All the women of the kingdom try it on in vain. Finally Peau d'Ane is brought in, amid the derision of the courtiers. The ring fits her finger, she becomes once more a beautiful princess, and her royal birth is revealed.

While this and other fairy stories were initiating the young King into the world of make-believe, his mother was being initiated into the world of politics. At first Anne was popular with the nobles, recalling former friends like the Duchesse de Chevreuse, who had been exiled by Richelieu, and distributing favours: one courtier remarked that the French language had been reduced to five words: "The Queen is so kind." But when it became clear that she intended to rely on an Italian upstart and—unexpected paradox—to continue the absolutist policy which her arch-enemy Richelieu had enforced for eighteen years, some of the nobles began to jib. Beaufort organised a plot to kill Mazarin and the plot was discovered; Anne, showing unexpected strength, locked up Beaufort in the prison of Vincennes and banished his accomplices to their estates.

Louis was too young to realise the danger, though doubtless he noticed the sudden disappearance of familiar faces, like those of Beaufort, Vendôme and the Bishop of Beauvais. All things considered, his life at this time was extremely calm and secure. At home he was easy to handle—indeed according to Madame de Sénécé's first report while the young King's conduct was satisfactory, he was too humble and submissive for his station, and according to the priest who taught him his catechism he was "docile as a lamb."

By the time of his sixth birthday, however, Louis had become less docile and more self-assertive. According to the Venetian ambassador: "His Majesty Louis XIV has a lively and attractive nature, which gives promise of virtue. His body is strong, his eyes bright and rather severe, but this severity is full of charm. He seldom laughs, even at play. He insists on being respected and obeyed by his brother the Duc d'Anjou, aged three. He knows that he is King and wants to be treated as such. If the Queen Mother sometimes takes him to task he replies that one day he will be the master. When the ambassadors speak to the Regent, he does not listen. But when they address him, he is very attentive, and later has their speeches repeated to him. In short, if he lives and receives a good education, he gives promise of being a great King."

The following year Louis signed his first decree with his own hand. It was occasioned by continued war with the house of Austria, taxes for which were causing hardship. Peasants in the Rouergue and some of the nobles in the Aunis and the Saintonge rose in protest, whereupon the Marquis d'Aumont was sent to crush them. Heads would have rolled in Richelieu's day, but the new Cardinal was made of milder stuff, and so the decree Louis had to sign was a merciful decree, proclaiming a general amnesty: "the speed with which the said provinces have been brought to submission has led me to forget their faults, on the advice of the Queen Regent my mother." Below, a small boy scrawled a painstaking but lopsided Louis, the great green seal was affixed and the decree became law.

On his seventh birthday Louis, like other French boys, was held to have attained the age of reason. He exchanged his long dresses for breeches and hose and was entrusted to two *valets de chambre*, Dubois and La Porte. At first he missed his fairy stories and would not go to sleep unless La Porte read to him from a history book and laid his head on the pillow next to his. Louis was also given a squad of teachers, whose payment was scaled to the importance of their subject. Hardouin de Péréfixe, an historian, received the highest salary, £2000. The teacher of mathematics received £1500—this was the century of spectacular progress in mathematics, especially in geometry. Next in rank came the dancing master, at £1000, for it was part of a king's duties to dance publicly. Then came a drawing master, a master for Italian and Spanish, a writing master, a reader, a riding master, and two music-masters, one for the guitar, the other for the lute. Controlling them all Anne had appointed as Superintendent of the Education of the King, Cardinal Mazarin.

This was a mark of Anne's increasing confidence in her Minister and in their joint policy. Another mark of confidence was her decision to move from the fortress palace of the Louvre to the modern, comfortable house which Richelieu had built nearby and bequeathed to the Crown: formerly the Palais Cardinal, it now became the Palais Royal. It was to be Louis's town house for the rest of his boyhood. For Anne there was a gold-fitted bathroom, for Louis a school-room dominated by a map of "French Europe," showing all the places ever governed by members of the royal family: France, Naples and Sicily, Portugal, Navarre, Poland, Jerusalem, the German Empire, Constantinople. The implication was that all these places belonged by right to Louis.

Every day Péréfixe read aloud a few pages of a Life of Henri IV which he had specially written for his royal pupil. It was probably the book which most influenced Louis as a boy. It made much of Henri's virtues: how he had loved his people and won their love, how during his two illnesses all Paris had seemed to be ill too; how he had been a man of his word, which his enemies trusted more than anyone else's signature, what a brave soldier he had been—under arms from fifteen to forty-five—and what a great builder—witness the Place Royale and the new castle at Saint-Germain. He had reduced the nobles' power by prohibiting private armies; he had kept watch on the exchequer and known how every hundred écus were spent. In everything except his love affairs—with their consequence, trouble-making princes like Ven-dôme and his son Beaufort—Henri was to be the young King's model. Further edification was provided for Louis by a pack of cards representing the good and bad kings and queens. The queens were divided into the brave, the wise, the clever, the unchaste and the saintly—Anne being placed in the last suit.

In accordance with his text-book *The Education of a King*, every morning Louis had to remind himself that he was about to act God during the day, and to ask himself every evening how far he had succeeded. His writing master, Jean le Bê, set him to copy such texts as "Homage is due to kings, they act as they please."

But his mother took good care that Louis did not act as he pleased. Once, hearing him swear, she locked him up in his room for forty-eight hours. At least until he was nine she used to spank him when he was naughty. She made him accompany her on visits to churches—an increasingly favourite habit: one Whitsun she visited no less than thirty-seven—and even to lay the foundation stone of the new domed church of Val de Grâce, a thanks-offering for what she considered his "miraculous" birth. She herself had been strictly brought up by the Clarisse nuns of Madrid and precisely because she loved him so much disciplined rather than humoured her son. When she felt herself weakening, Mazarin was there to play a father's role.

For recreation Louis would go shooting sparrows in the Tuileries gardens with a small arquebus, light and very accurate, forged, filed and mounted by the late King. In summer at Fontainebleau he was allowed to bathe in the Seine. "The Queen and her suite wore voluminous shifts of grey linen, which trailed on the ground, and as the young prince and his governor—the Marquis de Villeroi—wore the same sort of thing, modesty was never offended."

Louis's favourite game was still soldiers. He would march through the Palais Royal deafening people with his drum. When he was nine, Mazarin had a miniature fort built in the garden, the small outworks being furnished with scale-model guns which could fire blank cartridges. Louis and chosen friends like the Comte de Brienne and the Marquis de Villeroi's son used to play at storming the fort. One day the blanks caught fire and exploded: that put an end to siege warfare. More exciting still, Louis was occasionally allowed to review his own soldiers, in Paris or nearer the fighting on the vulnerable northern frontier, dressed in a gold-laced coat and diamond-buckled hat with ostrich feather, mounted on a white horse, real pistols at his saddle. Once at Dieppe he watched a mock naval battle and saw two fire-ships run aground.

When he was nine Louis caught smallpox at Fontainebleau and fell very ill. Anne never left his bed, administering tablets prepared from pearls and sugar dissolved in oxytriphyllon water or decoctions of hartshorn. The doctors preferred the lancet, indeed a well-known physician of the day, Guy Patin, would bleed himself up to seven times merely for a cold in the head. So, to get rid of Louis's "impurities," his "noxious humours," the doctors bled him three times, and on each occasion he held out his arm "like a brave soldier." On the eleventh day he fell into a coma lasting three-quarters of an hour, whereupon he was purged, but that did not help either: according to his chief doctor Vallot, "his toes became infected, which might have necessitated amputation, had they not been lanced and smeared with balm." Three days later the news was whispered across France that the King's life was despaired of. Then quite suddenly he began to recover. He asked to see his favourite English pony, a present from Mazarin, and the little white pony was led whinnying into his bedroom. Scabs formed on the pustules, and in due course fell off. The only after-signs were a few small scars taking some of the smoothness from his round cheeks. In the precious Court language of the day, "Cupid gave way to the young Mars."

The King's illness, and the fever of the Queen which followed, were only two anxieties in an anxious year. The Duc d'Enghien, who had succeeded to the princedom of Condé in 1646, suffered the one reverse of a brilliant career before Lerida, and had shaken the reputation of the French throughout Catalonia: in the Spanish Netherlands (Belgium) and in Italy too the French cause had suffered reverses. "Mazarin has grown pale," wrote the Venetian ambassador, "and his hair has turned white." The nobles began to murmur, and during Louis's illness friends of Monsieur had dared to drink toasts to King Gaston I.

While the nobles murmured, it was Parlement which stirred and, seeing its chance in these setbacks to the King's armies, finally took action. But what exactly was Parlement? What were its functions?

It had been originally and still chiefly was a supreme court of justice—a group of lawyers, one of whose functions was to register all acts emanating from the King and thus to make them law. Sometimes Parlement entered protests under the guise of respectful observations, and occasionally declined to register a particular financial measure of which it disapproved. But Parlement wanted to do more than this. For three centuries it had been trying to have a say in policy and administration. In 1641 Richelieu had dealt what seemed a decisive blow at its political pretensions, forbidding it to take any part in State, as opposed to financial affairs. Paul Scarron had compared its reduced role to that of the Roman senate under Domitian, its chief function to decide the kind of sauce to be served on the imperial turbot—a *mot* for which Richelieu promptly sent him into exile.

Ever since Richelieu's death Parlement had been looking for a chance to salve its wounded pride, to reassert itself, to become an altogether more important force in the country, in short, to act —no two members agreed quite how. All around, examples seemed to exhort them to limit the royal power. In less than twelve months the people of Naples had driven out their viceroy, the Low Countries successfully thrown off Spanish rule and been recognised as a republic, and in England Parliament had captured Charles and were drawing up plans for the Commonwealth. "The constellations were terribly against Kings."

If some check on the royal power was the magistrates' negative aim, they found it difficult to agree on a positive one. They were rich men who formed a group apart, with their own name, *gens de la robe*; they were scholars who admired the formula *Senatus Populusque Romanus* and gravely warned that Caesar must not be allowed a second time to cross the Rubicon: they were flowery orators who declared that France must have "temperate political rule, befitting its climate," that despotism belonged "to deserts and countries baked by the sun" or "among the Lapps or other northern islanders who have nothing human about them except their faces." They lived in a bookish world. They liked to win applause from the public gallery by defending the rights of the people, but the vast majority were completely out of touch with the people and refused to share their burdens. Each seat in Parlement had cost its holder—or his forebears—£33,000, and they wanted more value for their money, more power. But they lacked a cause.

In May, 1648, the paulette came up for renewal. The paulette was an arrangement whereby office-bearers paid an annual sum to the Crown to ensure that their office would pass to their heirs. The King, that is to say Anne and Mazarin, now decreed that the sum to be paid by office-holders in the sovereign courts should be slightly increased, whereupon the courts appealed to Parlement. Parlement, mindful that the last meeting of the States General in 1614 had demanded the suppression of the paulette altogether, not only made common cause with their fellow lawyers in the sovereign courts but decided to send thirty-two delegates to a newly established Chambre Saint Louis set up by the courts "for the reformation of the Government, and the better ordering of the realm." In defiance of the Queen Regent, who described the Chambre Saint Louis as "a kind of republic within the monarchy," the delegates met in June and drew up a charter of constitutional rights, including a form of Habeas Corpus, control over taxation and abolition of Richelieu's intendants—officials appointed by and responsible to the King—whose powers sometimes encroached upon the jurisdiction of Parlement.

Anne never forgot that she was a great-granddaughter of the autocratic Charles V: moreover, she had been brought up in a country where, at the King's approach, the bourgeois must shut the leather flaps of their carriages, lest their gaze fall on his august person. At first she refused absolutely to whittle down the royal power. Then Mazarin explained to her that the military situation had taken a sudden turn for the better. Peace talks with the Emperor were going on: one more decisive victory and Mazarin believed the war would be over. Let Parlement win this first skirmish. "Time and I": Mazarin had made the Spanish maxim his own.

After tearful scenes in her little grey salon, at some of which Louis was present, Anne swallowed her pride and removed all the intendants except those in the Lyonnais, Champagne and Picardy. But this concession did not satisfy Parlement, and the Chambre

Saint Louis continued its sittings. Then, in the second half of August, came news of Condé's decisive victory, with fewer men, over the Spanish army at Lens. Six thousand prisoners and several generals were captured. "At last heaven has declared in our favour," said Mazarin. The nine-year-old Louis clapped his hands with joy. "Parlement," he said, "will be very sorry."

Knowing now that peace was certain, and that the King's armies would soon be freed to deal with the King's enemies at home, Anne acted boldly—this time on her own initiative, against Mazarin's advice. On the very day when at Notre Dame, hung with seventy-three Spanish standards, a *Te Deum* was being chanted in thanksgiving for Lens, she ordered the arrest of three trouble-makers in Parlement, the most prominent of whom was Pierre Broussel.

Broussel was a tall bony figure in his seventies with a white moustache and brush beard. He had a grudge against the Queen because his son had been refused command of a company of guards. He never lost a chance of annoying her. For instance, when the Duc de Beaufort escaped from prison by means of a silk cord smuggled to him in a savoury pie, Broussel insolently demanded an inquiry into the circumstances of Beaufort's arrest. Though his speeches were heavy with Latin tags and audacities veiled in Latin (*Junonem iratam habemus*—we have against us the wrath of Juno, meaning Anne), he was popular because he lived frugally with only two servants in a small house and went on foot to the Palais. When a passer-by said, "Bonjour, Monsieur Broussel," he would smile and return the greeting.

Learning that this "Father of the people" had been arrested, Parisians shut up shop and marched through the streets shouting "Broussel! Freedom!" Armed crowds surged round the Swiss guards outside the Palais Royal, giving way only to a small figure in scarlet cape and rochet: Paul de Gondi, the thirty-five-year-old nephew and assistant of the Archbishop of Paris. Monsieur le Coadjuteur, as he was called, had a dark ugly face, peering, near-sighted eyes—he could not even button his cuffs—and an awkward body with bandy legs. He had entered the Church only because he was a younger son, and boasted openly of his duels and love affairs. By nature unsatisfied and an intriguer, he wanted power, in particular a Cardinal's hat. His means to power were his seat in Parlement—where he would appear with a dagger ostentatiously stuck in his soutane belt—and the people of Paris, whose goodwill he had won with eloquent promises and alms from his uncle's fortune.

The Coadjutor blinked his way into the Queen's grey salon while a courtier quipped, "Your Majesty is so sick at heart, he is bringing you Extreme Unction!" He drew a threatening picture of a hundred thousand angry, armed Parisians. For a woman it was all very terrifying, and it says much for Anne's courage that when he slyly began to predict further rioting she cut him short.

"It is sedition even to imagine sedition," she cried.

Quite so, said the Coadjutor. He was a man of peace and all he wanted was to help Her Majesty. He alone had sufficient prestige with the Parisians to prevent further rioting. He would do so— provided Broussel was handed back.

"I would rather strangle him with these two hands," cried Anne, brandishing her beautiful white hands in front of the Coadjutor's peering eyes. She rejected all his proposals for bargaining and then dismissed him very coolly indeed.

Later in the day Anne ordered Maréchal de La Meilleraye to disperse the crowd. Pelted with stones, he and his troop of light horse managed to clear a way to the Pont Neuf. There to his surprise he found a cassocked figure in front of the statue of Henri IV gravely making the sign of the cross over the rebellious crowd, who thundered approvingly, "Long live the Coadjutor."

That night angry Parisians reassembled outside the Palais Royal, shouting that they wanted to see Louis and keep him safe in the Hôtel de Ville. Meanwhile the Coadjutor, furious that Anne had not treated him better, sent out agents to fan the rebellion. Next morning twelve hundred barricades—chains, barrels, flagstones, old furniture—criss-crossed the streets of Paris.

At ten in the morning on this Day of the Barricades a deputation from Parlement petitioned for Broussel's release. Again the Queen refused. The red-robed lawyers started back to the Palais, only to be stopped at the second barricade. A cook's apprentice thrust out his halbert at Molé, the first president, shouting, "Back to Madame Anne. We'll kill you unless you bring us Broussel, or Mazarin, or the Chancellor as hostage." Back went the five presidents and twenty-five councillors to the Palais Royal, again to implore the Queen. All day talks continued. Hearing the laughter of Louis and his friends in the garden, Molé observed darkly, "That young prince playing down there is in the process of losing his crown."

At last the cautious, compromising Mazarin persuaded Anne to yield. That evening she signed an order releasing Broussel, who was welcomed home like a hero. "Long live Broussel and the King!"; "Down with Mazarin!"; then the city became "as quiet as on a Good Friday." But darkness hatched a new and ugly rumour: that the royal troops planned to fire on the people. More barricades went up, the Palais Royal was alerted and Mazarin, in travelling cape and boots, ordered his fastest horse to be saddled. The seven-year-old Duc d'Anjou began to cry. Louis did his best to reassure him, and even flourished his little sword, patting and taking his brother in his arms, and cheering him up, "but without alarming him, with the air of a general in an emergency who encourages his troops with a stirring speech. Finally he had the kindness to take Monsieur into his own room to pass the night."

Next day Paris was calmer, but Mazarin, shocked by Parlement's "affront" to the King—some magistrates had even offered the Regency to Gaston d'Orléans—wrote to Condé, the conqueror of Rocroi and Lens, urging him to ride south at full speed. The Day of the Barricades had shown that Paris was no longer safe. On 13th September the Queen announced that the Palais Royal required one of its periodic cleanings and went with the King to the Château du Rueil.

Life for the ten-year-old Louis had suddenly become very exciting and also very bewildering. Why did a King have to flee his capital? The people shouted that they loved him and wanted him by them but only—so his mother said—to make him their hostage. Everyone seemed to want him—for their own ends. And why were they hateful to Mazarin and his mother, whom he loved and who were acting to save the Crown? The result was that Louis drew even closer to his mother, partly to protect her, partly to be protected, while the reserved and serious side of his nature became more marked.

When Condé arrived at Rueil, Anne gave him a very warm welcome. Condé was just twenty-seven, a Duke six times over and a Governor three times over. He had a thin face, fierce eyes, a large mouth with buck teeth and immense aquiline nose—the face of an eagle. His body was small but well proportioned and pulsated with nervous energy. Once at a party an usher caught his wand in Condé's hair, which he wore long, thick and dishevelled. Condé promptly snapped the wand in two and gave the usher a public birching. As well as being liable to such outbursts of rage, Condé was proud, argumentative and stubborn.

One of Condé's titles was Grand Master of France and in 1648 this was a strictly accurate description, for Condé was the man on whose help Louis now depended. Whether Condé would in fact help was by no means certain. As a prince of the blood he considered himself above the law and free to choose his own allegiance —or strike out for himself. At any rate Anne told Louis to be specially nice to his difficult namesake, for Condé too was called Louis de Bourbon. Louis did as he was told, behaved amiably, praised Condé's victories and called him "cousin."

M. le Coadjuteur also behaved amiably to Condé. He painted the glory to be gained from siding with Parlement—Condé would supplant Mazarin, become "master of the Council, and arbiter in the State." Condé listened and seemed convinced. He was jealous of Mazarin and despised his lack of physical courage. Once, on parting, he tweaked the Cardinal's chin: "Good-bye, Mars." But at heart he also despised "those devils in square caps," greybeards "who will either drag me with them into a civil war, or force me to put that damned Sicilian over their heads and mine." He took a haughty tone to members of Parlement, and they in their turn became cool. Condé concluded: "My name is Louis de Bourbon; I can do nothing to shake the power of the Crown." Thereupon—for greed was the family failing—he named his price to Anne: the lordship of Dun, the town of Clermont in Argonne and the rich abbey of Varenne to round off his possessions in Champagne. He got them, but Anne's eyes were opened and she began to cling more closely than ever to Mazarin.

For Anne and Louis humiliation followed humiliation in that autumn of 1648. Parlement demanded further reforms: reduction of taxes, a say in financial policy, no more arrests on the strength of a *lettre de cachet.* "If I gave in to these demands," Anne retorted, "my son would be little better than a cardboard king." But again Mazarin persuaded her to make concessions, explaining that when peace came they could be retracted. The concessions were drawn up in a Declaration signed on 22nd September.

Two days later the peace on which Mazarin had been pinning his hopes was signed. By the treaty of Westphalia the Thirty Years' War was brought to an end: France gained Alsace, secured her eastern frontier and nullified Austria's attempt to unite Germany. Spain continued to fight, but with a small, demoralised army. Overnight Mazarin's policy had been justified, taxes could be cut and the army, if necessary, used to silence Parlement's demands. But the peace had come just too late. So many passions and ambitions, protests and intrigues, so much resentment and bitterness could not suddenly be damped down. Louis and his mother had barely time to listen to the bells of peace. A four-years' civil war was about to begin.

CHAPTER 3

The School of War

ON THE LAST DAY OF OCTOBER the Queen felt sure enough of
Condé to return to Paris with the young King and the Court. But
"ill-feeling flared up in a St. Martin's summer, and people seemed
drunk with the fumes of the grape harvest." The Queen was
hooted in the streets and Parlement refused to let the Crown borrow
much-needed money. The chief target of popular hatred was
Mazarin. They blamed him for heavy taxes and failure to pay
interest on State loans; and now he had had the insolence to build
a palatial town house, with murals by Romanelli and Grimaldi,
who had decorated the Vatican, filling it with tables of lapis lazuli
and mother-of-pearl, gold, ebony and tortoise-shell cabinets,
alabaster and porphyry figures and a carved ivory bed. His stables
alone had seven inner courts and a façade with Ionic columns. He
sent to Italy for his carriages, also for perfumes and a special cream
"to whiten his plebeian hands." That was where the people's taxes
went! Parlement and the bourgeois were determined to get rid of
Mazarin, and even if necessary depose the Regent. To this end the
Coadjutor went so far as to ask help from the Spaniards.

"It was impossible," says Madame de Motteville, "for France
to continue long like this. Either the King must reassert his authority
or his subjects would strip him of what remained. The King had
little power, the princes had too much; the Minister was discredited
and Parlement was too bold in its demands from the Government.
Everything had gone beyond its normal limits. Order was over-
thrown and the French people, because they had too many masters,
recognised none."

As the year 1648 ended, no longer able to govern without the
money which Parlement declined to vote, Anne and Mazarin

decided on a show of strength. Condé's troops would surround Paris and cut off food supplies, notably bread, which came from Gonesse, ten miles to the north. But meanwhile what of the boy King?

It was Twelfth Night, 1649. In every French home a cake containing a bean was being cut, and whoever got the bean was proclaimed king: a custom which this year had a grim irony. "I went to the Queen," says Madame de Motteville, "and found her in her little room watching the King at play, and apparently thinking of nothing else. Madame de La Trémoille, who was sitting beside her, whispered to me very softly, 'It is rumoured that the Queen is leaving Paris to-night.' . . . I shrugged my shoulders at an idea which seemed to me fantastic. . . . The Queen seemed livelier than usual. The Princes and Mazarin paid their respects, but did not stop, as they were going to supper with the Maréchal de Gramont, who always entertained splendidly on this night. . . . To amuse the King, the Queen cut the cake and got the bean herself. . . . We ladies-in-waiting supped as usual in the wardrobe room on the remnants of the Queen's supper . . . and so well deceived were we all that we laughed heartily with the Queen at those who had spread the rumour that she was leaving Paris that night. . . .

"Maréchal de Villeroi let the King sleep till three o'clock, then got him up, and also the little Monsieur, and put them into the carriage which was waiting for them at the garden gate. The Queen went with the King and Monsieur . . . They came down by the secret staircase which runs from the King's room to the garden, and when all had arrived at the Cours la Reine, the Queen halted there to await the rest of the royal family." The streets were unlighted and she carried only one small lantern.

Joined by Gaston d'Orléans and Condé, the royal party set off for Saint-Germain. It was still dark when their coaches drew into the palace courtyard, to find not a bed nor a chair nor a carpet. The sending of furniture might have aroused suspicion. Windows were unglazed and the weather piercingly cold. "Even the King and Queen lacked what was necessary for their sacred persons," wrote Jean Vallier, the *maître d'hôtel*, in tones of horror, forgetting that a boy of ten loves this sort of adventure.

Louis, moreover, had a young companion in his first cousin, twenty-one-year-old Anne Marie Louise, daughter of Gaston d'Orléans. Mademoiselle, as she was called, was the richest princess in France, granddaughter of Henri IV, daughter of the blood royal, accustomed to a household staff of sixty—"larger than any one of my three aunts, the Queen of Spain, the Queen of England, or the Duchess of Savoy had had before their marriage." But that night she spent shivering on a palliasse with one of her half-sisters, who kept seeing ghosts. "I had no change of linen: my nightdress was washed during the day and my vest at night. I had no maids to dress me or brush and comb my hair, which is very inconvenient. I took my meals with Monsieur, who keeps a very poor table. But that didn't stop me from being gay, and Monsieur admired me for not complaining. . . . Discomfort never ruffles me, and I'm quite above trifles." The same was true of the Queen. "Never have I seen anyone as gay as she: one would have thought she had won a battle, captured Paris, and hanged everyone who displeased her." Anne found it a relief after so many months of concessions to be able to take a brave line. So, doubtless, did Louis.

Parlement was furious at Louis's surprise departure, for the person of the King outweighed all other political factors. They ordered the city gates closed and the guard doubled. Ten thousand infantry and four thousand horse were levied, which was tantamount to declaring civil war. Madame de Motteville and her sister escaped arrest by fleeing to the Capuchin church near the Porte Saint Honoré. Others who tried to join the Court had their houses pillaged and furniture burned.

The rebellious Parisians and members of Parlement had come to be called frondeurs. This was the name given to boys who played the forbidden game of slinging stones in the dry moat outside the walls of Paris: hiding their slings when a patrol appeared, then taking them out again when the patrol passed. The name had been given in scorn, but now a new connotation was found—David with his sling—and the rebels proudly proclaimed themselves the Fronde. They wore blue scarves embroidered with a gold sling.

The Fronde protested that it was fighting Mazarin, not the King. Their general, the Prince de Conti, was called "Commander-in-chief of the Army for the release of the King." One day a herald, wearing a velvet tunic with the fleurs de lys, arrived from Saint-Germain with a message for Parlement. The lawyers decided that the message certainly contained stern orders from the King; if they disobeyed them, that would be rebellion. So they refused to let the herald enter the city, on the grounds that a herald-at-arms can be sent only to a sovereign or to an enemy: since the Parlement was neither, it could not receive his message "out of respect." Unconsulted, playing in the gardens of Saint-Germain, it was the ten-year-old boy King who dominated every move.

The Fronde won a first success by capturing the Bastille and installing as governor the son of their hero Broussel. Condé's army, numbering 15,000, was too small to besiege the city, but it cut off supplies from Gonesse and all traffic on the Seine. The Parisians made sorties waving banners inscribed "We seek our King," returning on one occasion not with the King but with a drove of pigs, which they herded triumphantly into the city.

It was a friendly war, almost within the family—for the Prince de Conti was Condé's younger brother, and his supporters included Condé's trouble-making sister, Geneviève de Longueville (she who once drawled, "I don't enjoy innocent pleasures"), her husband, and her lover, the future Duc de La Rochefoucauld, as well as the Duc de Beaufort. This explains why the royal furniture was permitted to be sent to Saint-Germain and, for Mademoiselle, a trunkful of her highly scented Spanish gloves, which caused the bourgeois guards who inspected the gloves at the city gate, "and who were unaccustomed to such strong perfumes, to suffer attacks of sneezing."

Despite an occasional gay moment, this first taste of civil war was bitter to a young boy more than usually conscious of his rights, and it marked Louis's character. It removed a tendency to complacency and provided an early but lasting lesson in the ill-effects of division, while reaction against the threatened loss of his inheritance set up in Louis a deep and possessive love of France.

As the war dragged into its third month for a few weeks in March a bitter wind blew from the east: Turenne, who with Condé was France's other brilliant general, sought to regain for his brother the principality of Sedan, which Richelieu had taken from him, and at the head of an army of German mercenaries was on the march to Paris. Mazarin found a few last oddments and offices to sell, and sent £170,000 in the hands of a secret agent to be used as bribes. The gold coins stamped with the image of the young Louis did their work: the German mercenaries refused to march farther, and Turenne hurriedly rode off to the Netherlands.

This setback, scarcity of food, divisions among the frondeurs, and the execution of Charles I of England, which shocked the moderate party in Parlement, led the Attorney-General in March to open negotiations for peace. In a treaty signed at Saint-Germain on 30th March it was agreed that the Parisians would lay down their arms and restore the Bastille to the Crown, while Louis on his side granted an amnesty and agreed to return to Paris "as soon as his affairs permitted." In short, this was a truce: Parlement's role in France still remained to be decided.

The expenses of war and civil war had reduced the royal family to poverty. Most of the crown jewels were in pawn. The leather on Louis's shabby old coach hung in tatters. According to La Porte, "the custom was that every year the King should receive twelve pairs of sheets and two dressing-gowns, one for summer, one for winter. But I have seen him use six pairs of sheets for three whole years, and a green velvet squirrel-lined dressing-gown summer and winter alike: in the second year His Majesty had grown so tall that it came only half-way down his legs. His sheets were so full of holes that I have found him several times with his legs through the sheets on the bare mattress." Sometimes—simply because courtiers were busy and preoccupied—the King went hungry. Here his schoolroom lessons in strategy came in useful. He and Philippe would intercept the Queen's meals on their way from the kitchen and run off with an omelette.

At ten years old Louis was a tall, plump, muscular boy with curly chestnut hair down to his shoulders. As other children pretend to be kings and queens, Louis's favourite game at this period was pretending to be a valet. One of his friends was the small daughter of the peasant servant who waited on his mother's ladies' maids. He called her Queen Marie because he always allowed her to take the part of queen and served her as a page and footman, holding her train, pushing her about in a little cart and carrying a torch before her.

He had begun to learn Latin as the Romans wrote it, not as it was spoken in the "barbarous" Middle Ages, and to translate Caesar's *Commentaries*. But Louis found the exciting life around him more to his taste than lessons, and the gentle Maréchal de Villeroi—"Monsieur Oui Sire," Louis had aptly nicknamed him—did not force his royal pupil.

"One evening," says La Porte, "the King, before getting into his bed, began to turn somersaults, and at last turned such a big one that he shot backwards right off the bed and fell on the platform with such a loud thump that I could not think what had happened. I ran at once to pick him up and, having carried him to his bed, it was found that he was only slightly hurt, as the carpet had softened his fall. But though His Majesty suffered less than he might have done, Monsieur le Maréchal was so terrified that he remained rooted to the spot for quarter of an hour. He could easily have spared himself this distress if he had forbidden the somersaults, as he ought to have done.

"One day, when the Court was moving about, the King insisted that Monsieur (Louis's brother Philippe) should share his bedroom, though it was so small that only one person at a time could walk through it. In the morning when they woke up, the King, without thinking what he was doing, spat on Monsieur's bed. Whereupon the latter spat on the bed of his brother, who, becoming angry, spat in the younger boy's face. At this, Monsieur jumped on to the King's bed and wetted it, and the King did the same thing on Monsieur's. Then they began a tug-of-war with the sheets and afterwards came to blows. I sent for Monsieur le Maréchal," adds La Porte, "who put a stop to it. I must admit that Monsieur lost his temper sooner than the King, but the latter was more difficult to pacify than Monsieur."

One characteristic that made a very favourable impression was Louis's generosity. One day from his window he was watching horses being exercised by the stable-boys. Leaning down, he called to them: "By the way, are you short of money? Yesterday evening

I played *petite prime* and won eight pistoles. Here they are. Share them between you." On another occasion Villeroi handed him a half-pistole to reward a soldier who had put on a fencing display. But Louis insisted on a whole pistole, saying that he disliked doing things by halves.

Louis's life at this period was one of adversity, penury and even at times of humiliation. But in June, 1649, he met a king even more unfortunate than himself. In that month Louis and the Court went to Compiègne to welcome Charles Stuart, recently pro-claimed King of England in Edinburgh if not in London, but still living in exile. Louis had already met him once three years before, when Charles could not speak a word of French: "Louis was prudent enough to say nothing for fear of not saying it well, and the Prince of Wales also kept silence." But now there was no language barrier, and Louis chattered eagerly to his cousin, a tall, dark-complexioned youth of nineteen, with black hair, brown eyes and full lips. Louis plied him with questions about hunting in Holland (Charles had just arrived from that country) and about the Prince of Orange's dogs and horses.

Queen Henrietta Maria had also come out to greet her son. She was living the hard life of a poor relation whose patrons were poor too. That winter her small pension from Anne had been six months in arrears. The Coadjutor, sensing an opportunity for new indignation, had paid her a visit and found her at the bedside of her little daughter. "You see, I am keeping Henriette company," the Queen had said. "The poor child cannot get up to-day for want of a fire." The Coadjutor sent a supply of wood, then rushed to Parlement, where he poured forth his shame and horror "that the granddaughter of the beloved Henri IV should have lacked a fire in the month of January, at the palace of the Louvre."

Henrietta Maria's hopes for herself and her son were pinned on a French princess who rode beside her at Compiègne. For three years now she had been trying to arrange a marriage between Charles and Louis's rich cousin Mademoiselle, the same who had spent Twelfth Night shivering on a palliasse at Saint-Germain. Mazarin and Anne, who had already unsuccessfully tried to marry Mademoiselle to the King of Spain and the Emperor of Germany, favoured the match. The question was, would Mademoiselle consent?

Mademoiselle was a strong-minded young lady, with all the will her father lacked. As a girl, if her governess irked her, she calmly locked her in her bedroom. She was tall and quite pretty, with a rather long face, blonde hair and healthy complexion. Her blue eyes were frank and unusually serious: "by nature I am totally opposed to the occupation known as flirting." She was very conscious of her exalted rank and wanted marriage to bring her an "establishment" greater than her own. Her future husband must be brave, sincere, witty—and a king.

Louis watched the meeting of his two cousins with special interest for he knew, as all the Court knew, that the king Mademoiselle really wanted to marry was the King of France. As a girl of eleven she had taken Louis out of his cradle, dandled him and called him "my little husband"; Anne had said, "You'll be my daughter-in-law." Even now, when the town of Paris gave a ball in Louis's honour, it was with Mademoiselle that he danced the first branle and courante.

Mademoiselle in her serious way began to question Charles about the military situation in England and his chances of regaining his throne. Embarrassed, suddenly feeling himself a helpless exile, Charles answered not a word, excusing himself at last by saying that he did not understand French. This displeased Mademoiselle: "I formed a very poor opinion of a king who at his age showed so little interest in affairs of State." At dinner Charles, famished after a long day's ride, "would not touch the ortolans but threw himself on an enormous piece of beef and a shoulder of mutton, as though he had never been accustomed to anything else: I felt ashamed that his taste was so unrefined." But Charles did not mind Mademoiselle's scorn, for he had brought with him his pretty mistress, Lucy Barlow. They lived together for three months at Saint-Germain while Henrietta Maria hastily explained to Mademoiselle that "with his marriage all other attachments would come to an end" and Charles "would love only his wife." Mademoiselle lifted her pretty nose in the air. Despite the difference in age, it was still Louis she wanted to marry.

In August Louis and his mother returned to Paris amid wild demonstrations of loyalty. Fickle fishwives, who had lately been begging for kisses from the Duc de Beaufort, whom they called "King of the Paris Markets," now fought to touch the King's clothes as he passed in his coach; at Notre Dame he was lifted on to the shoulders of the crowd, so that all might glimpse him. Church bells, triumphal arches, fireworks, banquets and an acrobatic display marked the public rejoicing.

In the front rank of these processions through Paris rode M. le Prince on a black horse, wearing dark green trimmed with gold. If the cheers were not for him Condé was well aware that only he had made them possible, and he began to assert himself in a manner bordering on insolence. He insisted that two officers of his guard should stand behind his chair at the King's Council. He demanded the title of Prince for his friends the Ducs de Bouillon, de La Rochefoucauld and de La Trémoille, although all had been frondeurs. He even forced his arch-enemy Mazarin to nominate generals, ambassadors and governors of provinces only with his consent.

All this made life very complicated for Louis. Mazarin tried to help but his rule of conduct tended to paradox. "The King must try to caress and humour M. le Prince. In Council meetings, His Majesty will declare that he intends the will of the majority to be carried out, and if M. le Prince raises his voice, he will say, *'Je veux.'*"

One day, at Compiègne, Condé passed through the room where Louis, with a tutor, was doing his lessons. At sight of the great man, Louis immediately rose from his seat, hat in hand. La Porte, the valet in attendance, was much perturbed and after vainly urging the tutor to protest, whispered to Louis to put on his hat.

"La Porte is right, Sire," said Condé. "Your Majesty should be covered. You do us enough honour by returning our salute."

Condé questioned the tutor and was pleased to learn that Louis was growing up an intelligent boy. "It would not do," he growled, "to serve a fool."

At the end of 1649 Condé over-reached himself. The Fronde

had now spread to the provinces, and the Parlement of Bordeaux rebelled against the governor of Guyenne. Condé not only supported the Parlement but sent his troops to their aid. His brother, the Prince de Conti, and his brother-in-law, the Duc de Longueville, did likewise in Berry and Normandy.

It was clear that the prince who had saved the monarchy was now through pride and ambition in danger of destroying it. On the evening of 18th January, 1650, Mazarin called an extraordinary meeting of the King's Council, to which Condé, Conti and Longueville were summoned. Though warned to keep away, they went. On the pretext of a headache Anne kept to her room, but Louis was present and knew what was going to happen. Suddenly Guitaut, the faithful captain of the guard, entered with two lieutenants, and courteously approached Condé. "In the King's name I am ordered to arrest you, together with M. le Prince de Conti and M. le Duc de Longueville."

It was touch and go whether the princes would make a fight for it. But Condé simply snorted, "This is what I get for my services!" Then, seeing the cavalry escort come to take him to Vincennes, "Comrades," he said, "this is not like the battle of Lens!"

That was Louis's first experience of the harshness of power politics and of the need for a king sometimes to dissimulate. The slightest excitement, even an anxious glance, might have alerted the princes. When the prisoners had been led away, Mazarin congratulated the King on having played his part so well.

"They have taken the lion, the monkey and the fox," commented Monsieur. But not their relations and friends. Normandy, Burgundy and Bordeaux immediately rose in revolt, and Mazarin deemed it necessary to set out on a protracted tour of the provinces with a small army—and with Louis. Having no money, he was obliged to pay the troops with the sight of their king.

This new revolt, called the *Fronde des princes*, was led in fact by a princess. As Mazarin once confessed to the Spanish Prime Minister: "You Spaniards are lucky. You have two sorts of women: plenty of coquettes and a few good women. The one wishes to please her lovers, the other her husband. They have no desire save for luxury and display, and they would be bewildered if you talked to them of politics. But in France it is not the same. Our women, whether chaste or gallant, young or old, wise or foolish, wish to have a hand in everything. A woman will not go to sleep until she has talked over affairs of State with her lover or her husband. They wish to manage everything, to embroil everything. We have three who are capable of governing or over-turning three great kingdoms: the Duchesse de Longueville, the Princess Palatine, and the Duchesse de Chevreuse."

It was the first of these three who now opposed Mazarin. Born in the tower of Vincennes, where her father had been imprisoned for revolt, Geneviève de Longueville had already played a trouble-some part in the first Fronde. A languorous beauty of thirty-two married to a gouty husband in his fifties whom she despised, she had picked up from cold-hearted literary ladies of the Hôtel de Rambouillet a belief that the highest end of beauty is to win power. With this in mind she now travelled through her husband's province of Normandy, calling the people to arms. She had a hair's-breadth escape from Dieppe in disguise, embarked on a fishing smack, was shipwrecked, half drowned, rescued, and finally reached Holland in an English boat. With the help of her lover, the Duc de La Rochefoucauld, she stirred up trouble in Poitou. She then took a new lover, the steely Maréchal de Turenne, and persuaded him to join forces with Spain. Turenne and Archduke Leopold, the Spanish commander, marched to within thirty miles of Paris before suffering a decisive defeat by Mazarin's troops.

All in all, 1650 was a year of frustration for Louis. France was in arms—but he was still too young to fight. During the siege of Bordeaux, he wept with rage before his friend, Loménie de Brienne, at the thought that a King of France was obliged to reconquer his heritage. "I won't be a child always," he warned. "Ssh! I don't want anyone to see me crying. Those Bordelais rogues shan't lay down the law for long! . . ."

Despite royalist successes in the field, Mazarin was growing more and more unpopular. At the Pont Neuf, on the Place Maubert and at the Croix du Trahoir framed oil portraits of the Cardinal were hung on gibbets, each with two holes at the neck, through which a rope was passed. Underneath was scrawled, "Cardinal

Mazarin, for having prevented a general peace settlement at Westphalia, for having used black magic to seduce and possess the
Queen's mind." Jingling rhymes were concocted, accusing
Mazarin of every imaginable abomination: some six thousand
different rhymes were printed and hawked in the streets, giving a
new word to the language: Mazarinade. One of the bitterest
attacked Mazarin's luxury—his two hundred dressing-gowns, his
musk and amber, his ballets and thoroughbreds; it was written by
Paul Scarron, a witty poet whose *Roman Comique* the young Louis
secretly read and enjoyed. Another, *Le Passe-Port*, alluded to
Mazarin's nieces:

> By the monkeys whom you love
> And whose scent is like your own
> By the lovely Mazarinettes
> And all your other marionettes;
> By the too-high price of flour,
> By the growing fear of famine:
> In short, by all the misery
> Which clouds the public memory:
> We tell you, "Go, and don't return."

At a more dangerous level Mazarin was vigorously attacked by
the Coadjutor, who coveted the Cardinal's hat, and by Parlement,
aided by the Princess Palatine and other partisans of Condé. On
4th February, 1651, Parlement, by 140 votes to 47, decided to
send a petition to the Queen asking her to dismiss Mazarin and
release the Princes. Knowing that Anne would never agree, and
aware that his continued presence was doing the King more harm
than good, Mazarin slipped out of the Palais Royal by night and
rode for Normandy.

Mother and son were now alone, and the danger greater than
ever, for they learned that Monsieur—Gaston d'Orléans—now in
command of the Fronde, planned to seize the King and proclaim
himself Regent. Again, whoever had the boy Louis would rule
France. Anne's control of Paris was slipping, so she decided to
leave the city secretly at 2.30 on the morning of 10th February.
On the eve of departure Louis ordered his velvet travelling suit
and black boots to be laid out. This started a trail of rumour and

by nightfall angry crowds had collected round the Palais Royal. They attacked with sticks and stones anyone suspected of aiding the King's departure.

Midnight struck. M. des Ouches, captain of Monsieur's guard, arrived at the Palais Royal and asked for an audience. Anne hastily told Louis to undress, to go to bed and pretend to sleep. Then she received des Ouches, who asked how she intended to restore order. Anne looked surprised: the only remedy was for Monsieur to proclaim that she had never intended to leave Paris, that she was ready to go to bed, and that the King and his brother were sleeping peacefully. Sleeping peacefully? In that case, said des Ouches, might he see for himself? Otherwise he declined to leave. Controlling her rage, Anne gave Maréchal de Villeroi the necessary orders and he, taking a candle, led des Ouches into a dark bedroom, lifted one of the embroidered curtains of a four-poster and held his flickering candle close to the face of a motionless boy apparently asleep. Des Ouches made sure it really was the King, then said he was satisfied.

As he left the Palais Royal, des Ouches told the crowd that the King was sleeping quietly and that they should go home and do likewise. But they suspected a trick. "We want to see the King," they chorused angrily. "We want to see the King." Then they smashed down one of the gates. Trusting in Louis's presence of mind, Anne gave orders that the doors should be unlocked and the crowd admitted. They clattered up the marble staircase, then tip-toed into the room where Louis lay still pretending to sleep, his face flushed, his long hair in disorder on the pillow.

"As they gathered round the bed—the curtains had been drawn back—their old feeling of love returned and they showered a thousand blessings on the King. For a long time they watched him sleeping and could not admire him enough. The mere sight gave them respect for him. They were all the more anxious now not to lose him, but they showed this by signs of loyalty. Their anger disappeared: and having stormed in like furies they left like gentle subjects, praying God with all their heart to preserve the young prince whose presence, even asleep, had brought them under his spell." It was a touching illustration of the bond between the monarchy and the ordinary man in the street. It was also Louis's second lesson in acting a part.

Mazarin, meanwhile, condemned by Parlement to exile, made a last attempt at appeasement by himself unlocking the cells and freeing the three princes from the prison in Le Havre to which they had been transferred. The gesture failed. Without so much as a word of acknowledgment the princes rode for Paris. "I had entered prison the most innocent of men," said Condé, enraged, "and had come out the most guilty."

Condé joined Monsieur in Paris, where he received a tumultuous welcome from the fickle crowd, who hailed him as "the hero and tutelary god of France." Mazarin settled near Cologne, but continued to direct Anne by letter. An Italian in Germany was now, through a Spanish queen, controlling the destiny of France. Back and forth went messages in code. Mazarin, from his favourite colour, was la Mer or le Ciel; l'Ami, l'Homme des Bois, l'Ambition, Gonorit, Sedan, or the Greek letter phi. The Queen was Seraphin, Zabaoth, les Anges, l'Espagnol, l'Assiégé, or Amiens. The King was le Confident, la Barque, les Galères, les Vaisseaux, le Patron. A star indicated Mazarin's feelings for the Queen, a cross with three strokes through it her affection for Mazarin.

Were Mazarin and the Queen lovers or even, as some claimed, secretly married? Anne gave the answer to Madame de Brienne: "I admit that I am fond—even very fond—of him. But my affection does not amount to love, or, if it does without my knowing, my senses play no part in it. Only my mind is charmed by the beauty of his." She added: "If there is even a shadow of sin in this love, I renounce it here and now before God." That this confession held true throughout their relationship seems clear from their characters. Anne was the proudest of queens, firm about the difference between royal and any other blood. She was also extremely pious—since 1643 she belonged to the third Order of St. Francis, and a eulogistic Carmelite, in dedicating to her the works of St. Teresa, had pointed to "the striking resemblance between the qualities and virtues of Your Majesty and those of St. Teresa." Mazarin, on his side, was not a passionate man: his ideals in private as well as in public life were peace and order. As for a secret marriage, since Mazarin wore the purple that would have required a dispensation from the Pope, no trace of which has ever been found. It was, as she confessed, Mazarin's mind the Queen loved, that balanced, subtle, diplomatic mind without which her impetuous Spanish will was powerless to protect her son's rights. For the relationship between the Queen and her Minister really hinged on Louis: it was for this boy in whom they both believed that they worked and suffered. He really was "le Patron."

Following the night when Parisians stormed the King's bedroom, Louis and his mother spent a very unpleasant month. The frondeurs would not let them out of the palace. Mazarin wrote to Anne, urging her to keep close watch on Louis, even in the garden. She herself was to play the martyr. In March Mazarin wrote to complain of a ballet having been danced at Court, in which Louis had figured as a knight in the suite of Cassandra: "All joy must be banished. Reports must be diligently spread of the Queen's grief, and of how the King and the little Duc d'Anjou weep to find themselves prisoners." No pains should be spared to win and hold Condé's adherence, "Insinuate to the Prince that once I am in power I will serve him in every matter he wishes." When Condé moved closer to the Fronde, Mazarin consoled himself and Anne: "I have no doubt that the pride and impetuosity of M. le Prince will soon lose him many followers." He wrote to Anne that he longed to see her, if only for two hours: that he would die unless they met soon, while Anne, on her side, urged him to return: she could not bear his absence. "I am having a difficult time. I haven't the strength to write a longer letter, indeed I hardly know what I'm saying. I have received your letters every day, otherwise I don't know what would have happened. Adieu, I can't go on!"

But she did go on. Patiently she foiled plot after plot by the arch-intriguers, Condé, Monsieur, the Coadjutor, Beaufort and the rest to depose her and seize the kingdom. She drove herself on with the thought that she had only a few months more as Regent. In September Louis would celebrate his thirteenth birthday and be of an age to rule. But the months until September proved painful. As Mazarin had foreseen, Condé began to alienate everyone. He demanded that Anne dismiss from the King's Council "Mazarin's creatures:" Servien, Lionne and Le Tellier. When Anne refused, he retaliated with insolence. For example, one day Louis was driving in his carriage along the Cours la Reine, with only a small bodyguard, for the main escort he had ordered to ride by the river, not in the main avenue, "lest they stir up dust and annoy the ladies." From the opposite direction a coach arrived with Condé and the Duc de Nemours. Etiquette demanded that both gentlemen should get out and present their respects. Instead, they remained in their carriage and merely bowed—an affront which angered the Parisians almost as much as Louis.

Like his mother, Louis was looking forward eagerly to his coming-of-age. He had had enough of the princes' insolence, of begging for favours, of weeks of virtual imprisonment. Lately, too, he had felt other restraints. That summer he had taken to riding with Mademoiselle and one of her friends, Madame de Frontenac. Anne, knowing Madame de Frontenac to be a flirt, forbade the rides. Louis tried to get round his mother by promising 100 pistoles for the poor each time he rode with Mademoiselle and her friend. When Anne declined, Louis retorted, "I'll be master soon, and then I'll go where I want."

At last arrived the long-awaited 5th September, 1651. Louis celebrated his thirteenth birthday and two days later rode in state to the Palais de Justice. In a steady voice he declared: "Messieurs, I have come to my Parlement to tell you that, following the law of the land, I intend to take the government myself; and I hope by the goodness of God that it will be with piety and justice." In a few simple words Anne resigned the powers she had exercised for eight years, and was then appointed by her son to be his chief councillor. From now on Louis alone, not his Spanish mother nor the exiled Italian Cardinal, would personify France and command Frenchmen's loyalty.

During the *lit de justice* Louis acquitted himself admirably, one courtier writing to Mazarin that "he has the bearing and intelligence of a man of twenty-five." Louis affixed his signature to two edicts, one against duels and blasphemy, the other declaring Condé innocent of recent charges that he had been treating with France's enemies. Condé's response to this gesture of friendship was deliberately to stay away from the dinner, play and concert which marked the King's majority. He was angry with Parlement, with Paris, with the King and Queen, with everyone. His imprisonment still rankled and somehow he was determined to take his revenge. Withdrawing to his house at Chantilly, he cast his eagle eye on France at large: "You shall have your way. I will make war! But remember what I tell you. I draw the sword now, against my will; and I shall be the last to sheathe it." He then set off for Bordeaux, the traditional Condé stronghold, which gave him a regal welcome, his aim being nothing less than to detach Navarre and Guyenne from France, and to make himself king of a separate kingdom.

Once again Condé's friends and allies stirred up the provinces and once again Louis rode out to calm them—this time without Mazarin as prompter. One army had to be sent to oppose the Spaniards in Champagne, while another under Harcourt faced Condé. They won success after success, for they were fighting now for a clear and steady image: their own King, now a man with a will of his own. Presently the King's position was so secure that Mazarin decided he could return to France with safety. At Louis's request he crossed the frontier with four thousand mercenaries in his own pay; in January, 1652, after a separation of eleven months, Louis and his godfather were reunited, with warmth of affection on both sides. At almost the same moment Turenne, alienated by Condé's selfishness and pretentiousness, joined the royal forces and for six months led them to a series of victories. Defeated in the provinces, Condé decided to stake everything on a last daring throw. He would seize Paris.

The leading spirit in Paris that summer was a young lady of twenty-five: Louis's first cousin and prospective fiancée, Mademoiselle. The first reaction of Mademoiselle when her father, Monsieur, had decided to help Condé against Mazarin was worry "lest he weary of the affair, and not carry it through to its conclusion." In March, when the town of Orléans had begged its Duke to come and take charge of its defences, Monsieur had wavered, as he always did, and sent his daughter instead. Mademoiselle had bravely bluffed and fought her way into the town and shut its gates on the King's troops. On her return to Paris she had been hailed so enthusiastically that she felt "ashamed"—though Henrietta Maria was heard to remark dryly that Mademoiselle resembled another saviour of Orléans, Joan of Arc, and like Joan she had driven out the English.

Mademoiselle still hoped to marry Louis. Like many of the unselfish great nobles she believed that helping Monsieur make war on Cardinal Mazarin was the best way of serving her king. It was also perhaps the best way of becoming Queen of France, for only Mazarin, she was convinced, prevented an alliance, political and matrimonial, between the King and his noble cousins. So when, in July, Condé sent word to Monsieur that he had been attacked at dawn between Montmartre and La Chapelle and asked for help, it was Mademoiselle who answered his appeal—her father, though up and dressed, claimed he was ill: "I'm not ill enough to be in bed, but too ill to go out."

First, Mademoiselle persuaded the municipal authorities to let Condé's now hard-pressed army, even its Spanish contingent, withdraw within the city walls if it wished. Then she hurried towards the fighting, past wounded frondeurs on makeshift stretchers of planks and ladders, past the dying and the dead; she was struck by one nightmarish sight: a dead man still riding his horse. She reached the Porte Saint-Antoine and made her headquarters in a house next to the Bastille. Condé, fighting just outside, was told she was there and rushed in to see her, "dust two fingers thick on his face, his hair tangled, his collar and shirt all bloody, his cuirass dented with blows, his naked sword in his hand." Entering Mademoiselle's presence, he respectfully handed his sword to her equerry, then burst into tears. "Forgive me," he murmured. "You see, I'm in despair. All my friends have been killed." He asked Mademoiselle to stay where she was: her presence would encourage his men. When she implored him to order his troops into the city, "What!" he cried. "Retreat from the Mazarins at noon?"

She watched him hurry out and continue the battle: five thousand against twelve thousand, Condé's men with yellowish-grey scarves, the King's troops in white. It was a blazing, dusty summer's day. As the afternoon wore on, half stifled in a buff-coat and cuirass, Condé turned aside into a field, let himself be disarmed and undressed, and rolled naked in the grass "as horses do," then was equipped again, and rejoined the fight. Asked if he had seen M. le Prince during the action, Turenne, the royal commander-in-chief, answered, "I saw a dozen of him—or more."

Inside Paris, despite her long skirts, Mademoiselle was almost as active. She sent wine to refresh Condé's troops, then entered the Bastille and climbed one of its massive towers. Through a telescope she surveyed the heights of Charonne, a mile to the northeast. "I saw a great crowd and the whole royal army in the distance, near Bagnolet; it appeared very strong in cavalry. I could make out the generals' position by their aides and attendants, but could not recognise their faces. I saw them divide their troops in order to drive a wedge between our men and the walls. I sent a page post-haste to inform M. le Prince. He was on top of the tower of the Abbaye Saint-Antoine and since my news confirmed his own suspicions, he hurried down to order a retreat."

The bulk of the frondeurs now wheeled round and withdrew to the Porte Saint-Antoine, but a rearguard under Condé, struggling to haul back their precious artillery, moved more slowly. Meanwhile the royal cavalry had begun to gallop down from the heights: in a matter of minutes Condé would be cut off before he could reach the safety of the walls.

Standing atop the Bastille were heavy cannon: the King's cannon, stamped with an L and the fleur de lys. If the Bastille stood for the King's authority, its cannon were the very symbol of the King's power. All day Mademoiselle, who believed in intuition and fate, had had the feeling that she was destined "to do something unexpected, as at Orléans." Now the moment had come. She ordered the commander of the Bastille artillery, M. de Richau, to have the cannon loaded. Powder was rammed down the iron barrels, then stone cannon balls. "Turn the cannon round." Richau's men strained at the thick oak mountings. "Aim at the royal cavalry." An amazing command: but Mademoiselle produced written instructions from Monsieur that her word was to be obeyed as his. Richau aimed at the galloping figures in white. "Fire!" Tapers were lighted and held to the firing-holes. The cannon roared in a cloud of smoke.

Louis and his Court, as Mademoiselle had supposed, were watching the battle from the heights of Charonne. They expected to see Condé's troops driven into the moat and smashed to pieces against the city wall. Suddenly puffs of white smoke appeared from the Bastille. Mazarin, at first, was delighted: his spies had told him that one of the colonels on duty that day was ready to help the royalists. "Good!" he said. "They're firing on the enemy."

But as the cannon thundered a second time, someone said, "No; they're firing on us."

"Perhaps Mademoiselle has gone to the Bastille," suggested another courtier, "and these are salvoes of welcome."

"If Mademoiselle is there," said the Maréchal de Villeroi darkly, "it's she who's firing on us."

Louis and Mazarin watched in dismay as twenty times the Bastille cannon balls crashed through the ranks of royalist cavalry, hurling horses and riders to the ground, among them Paul Mancini, the Cardinal's nephew and heir, who was mortally wounded. They watched Condé and his troops withdraw safely behind the walls of Paris; they watched the drawbridge outside the Porte Saint-Antoine being cranked up behind them. It was Mazarin who put the situation in a nutshell. "Elle a tué son mari," he said, pronouncing the third word "toué." "These cannon balls have killed Mademoiselle's husband."

The Battle of the Porte Saint-Antoine, for all its romantic deeds, revealed the paradox of the Fronde: you could not fight the King's Minister without fighting the King. It proved only a temporary setback to Louis, for two days later Condé defeated his own cause. He and the Princes, quarrelling once more with the municipal authorities, incited the mob to set fire to the Hôtel de Ville and killed several councillors. This act of violence irrevocably divided the Princes' party from Parlement and all moderate men. In their hats instead of a wisp of straw—emblem of the Fronde—more and more Parisians now sported bits of paper—white for the Court. Not only Paris but all France was weary of the war, even leading frondeurs. From Bordeaux the Duchesse de Longueville complained that she had almost no amusements and begged Chapelain to send her Gomberville's five-volume heroic romance of *Polexandre*. The truth was that as Louis grew to manhood and knit his subjects in loyalty, civil war stood less and less chance of success. In October, Condé fled from Paris, Mazarin bowed to Parlement's will and once more went into exile for a short period, whereupon Paris invited the King to take possession of his capital. On 21st October, 1652, Louis made his state entry and took up residence not in the Palais Royal, associated by Parisians with Mazarin and by the Court with riotous crowds, but in the ancient—and more easily defended—palace of the Kings of' France: the Louvre. As for Mademoiselle, Louis invited her to withdraw to one of her country estates. Next day Parlement renounced its claim to have any voice in political and financial affairs. After four years the Fronde was finished.

CHAPTER 4

Crowned King

AT SIX O'CLOCK on the morning of 7th June, 1654, the Bishops of Beauvais and Châlons, ecclesiastical peers of the realm, clad in full pontificals and preceded by canons of the chapter, gravely entered the palace of the Archbishop of Reims and stopped outside the bedroom where Louis had spent the night.

The preceptor tapped the door with his silver wand.

"Whom do you want?" asked the voice of the Lord Chamberlain.

"We want the King," replied the Bishop of Beauvais.

"The King is asleep."

This dialogue, so reminiscent of a less happy occasion during the Fronde, was repeated three times, the Bishop finally adding: "We seek Louis the Fourteenth of that name, son of the great King Louis XIII, whom God has given us as King."

At these words the door was opened wide and the two bishops were led by the Marquis de Rhodes, grand master of ceremonies, to the state bed where, surrounded by chamberlains, the fifteen-year-old King was lying, eyes closed. He wore a cambric shirt and a red satin tunic trimmed with gold, surmounted by a long robe of silver cloth. On his head was a diamond-studded black velvet cap with a white plume.

Louis opened his eyes as though awaking from sleep. Dipping a finger in holy water offered him by the Bishop of Beauvais, he made the sign of the cross while the bishop recited a prayer. Then he was helped from his bed by the two bishops, who accompanied him to the gate of the Archbishop's palace. Here a long procession had formed, ready to escort Louis to the cathedral of Reims for his sacring and coronation.

The coronation should have taken place soon after Louis had come of age. It had been delayed two years and nine months first by the Fronde, then by a flaring up of the war with Spain. Throughout 1653 Spanish troops from the Low Countries, brilliantly led by Condé, now officially a traitor and deprived of the name Bourbon, were driving deep into north-east France. The centre of the fighting was Sainte-Menehould, only forty miles from Reims. No one dreamed that Louis's coronation could take place anywhere but in Reims: the baptism of Clovis by the Bishop of Reims, St. Remi, in 496 had conferred this privilege on the town; and it was to Reims, almost a thousand years later, that Joan of Arc had fought her way for the crowning of Charles VII.

Through much of the summer and autumn Louis had been leading a soldier's life, fighting the Spaniards for his place of coronation. His teacher was Turenne, at forty-two the best general in Europe after Condé: beetle-browed, steady, serious almost to a fault and eager to expiate his brief period of disloyalty. While Mazarin — who had returned from exile in February, 1653 — watched carefully that he should come to no harm, Louis attended the briefing of officers, visited the trenches, ate army rations, slept under canvas and spent days on end in the saddle, refusing to rest even during a sharp attack of dysentery. According to his doctor, Vallot, "His Majesty told me several times that he preferred to die rather than miss the slightest opportunity of winning glory and putting the State to rights." After a month-long siege, Sainte-Menehould had fallen to the King's troops, the Spaniards had withdrawn from north-east France and Reims was now a place of safety and rejoicing, ready to play the role which not even Paris could usurp.

The sun shone, the bells rang, the people of Reims in their best clothes crowded the windows and lined the streets. Through the great west door of the Gothic cathedral, with its bas-relief of Christ enthroned, the procession slowly passed, at its head the grand Provost of France, followed by drummers and trumpeters, players of sackbut and flute, hautbois and musette, all in white taffeta; heralds from every province dressed in velvet, with white silk stockings, their tunics embroidered with fleurs de lys; the company of gentlemen called raven-beaks, carrying the halberds from which they took their name; the Marquis de Rhodes, and the Constable, Maréchal d'Estrées, flanked by two ushers carrying the gilt mace.

Then came the King—on foot—followed by his Chancellor, wearing crimson robes and a square gold hat, by Maréchal de Villeroi and by chamberlains and gentlemen-in-waiting. As the organ pealed, they entered the carpeted nave, between two ranks of Swiss guards. The congregation included the Queen, Mazarin and most of the high nobility. Louis walked up to the choir and knelt at a prie-Dieu covered in violet velvet, facing the high altar, on which lay the regalia, between reliquaries of St. Louis and St. Remi.

Before the officiating Bishop of Soissons Louis made a promise in Latin to defend and observe the rights of the Catholic Church. Then the Bishop asked the assembled company—peers, nobles and commoners—whether they accepted this prince as King: a question greeted by a respectful silence, the traditional way of showing assent.

Louis then pronounced the coronation oath: "I make this promise to the Christian people, and my subjects, in the name of Christ, first of all that all Christian people shall maintain the true Peace of the Church of God, at all times, by our Government. Also, that I will prohibit all violence and acts of injustice among all ranks of men. Also, that I will enjoin equity and mercy to be used in all judgments, that the merciful and gracious God may indulge his favour to me and to you."

After the oath the Lord Chamberlain put on the King's feet light shoes of violet velvet, to which Monsieur, Louis's brother, attached gold spurs set with garnets. The Bishop blessed the royal sword, called Joyeuse because it was used only on days of rejoicing. Louis kissed the blade, offering the sword to God and promising to use it in His service. The sword was then passed to the Constable, who held it point upwards beside the King.

The spurs and sword were not part of the regalia. With a mixture of realism and idealism, they asserted the fact that the King of France was a soldier, the man with the biggest army, and that his power was military power, whatever else it might be as well; but they also asserted that he was a chivalrous soldier who used his army only in the service of Christian ideals. These rites were now followed by one more important and mysterious.

Shortly after the King's arrival in the cathedral, the Grand Prior of the abbey of Saint-Denis, mounted on a white palfrey, had delivered the holy ampulla which all good Frenchmen believed had been sent from heaven for the baptism of Clovis, first Christian King of the Franks. Indeed, a medal had just been struck showing the ampulla being brought down in the beak of a bird. With a golden needle the Bishop of Soissons drew from the ampulla a drop of the holy balm the size of a grain of wheat and placed it on the golden paten which formed part of St. Remi's own chalice. Louis now lay face downwards on a length of velvet, not for a moment only but during the chanting of long litanies, in an attitude of utter humility before the high office he was about to assume.

After the litanies, he knelt. The Lord Chamberlain removed the King's silver tunic, and the Bishop, dipping his thumb in the little bead of balm, anointed the King in seven places: brow, chest, between the shoulders, right shoulder, left shoulder, bend of the right arm and bend of the left arm. The crosses of holy oil were left moist on the King's body.

While anthems and prayers hailed Louis as the anointed of the Lord, successor of Saul, David and Solomon, the King was clad in tunic, dalmatic and mantle of violet velvet. Their similarity to bishop's vestments was used by some to support the theory that the anointed king was layman and priest intermingled. But it could equally well have been argued that they resembled the robes of the Byzantine emperors, from whose coronation rites the sacring of Christian kings derived. The truth seems to be that all three stemmed from a common source, the official dress of the Roman republic.

Louis knelt again, to be anointed an eighth and ninth time, on the palm of each hand. The Bishop then blessed a diamond ring— the Treasury was so poor that Anne had lent one of her own rings —and placed it on the third finger of Louis's left hand: and so the King took *la France* to be his wedded wife.

Now came the moment when Louis received the symbols of sovereignty, equity and glory: the sceptre, six feet long, the gold and ivory hand of justice, and finally, while the peers hailed him with arms outstretched, the great crown of Charlemagne. The crown was of beaten gold, simply worked, with only a few jewels, still a little like the helmet from which it derived. It was rich in associations. Charlemagne had ruled not only France but also the Low Countries, Austria, half Germany and half Italy. Crowned Emperor of the West by the Pope himself, he had been the legitimate successor of Augustus, Trajan and Constantine. By receiving Charlemagne's crown, Louis made tacit claim to his predecessor's title and heritage.

Wearing his crown, carrying his sceptre and hand of justice, the King was led to the thousand-year-old throne of Dagobert, installed in the rood-loft so that all might see him. After the peers had paid homage and kissed his cheek, the officiating bishop hailed Louis with this remarkable phrase: "May the King live for ever!" The cathedral doors were opened; the crowd outside shouted and cheered, while the fowlers of Paris gathered in the vaulted galleries opened their cages and released forty dozen birds, which, after fluttering and circling, flew up to the stained glass, beating their wings against the Seraphim: "they were hardly able to escape, so dense was the crowd beside the windows."

As the *Te Deum* was chanted, guards in front of the cathedral fired three musket volleys to let the town know that Louis XIV had been crowned. Then Mass was celebrated, the King coming down from the rood-loft to offer wine, a loaf made of silver, a loaf made of gold, and a red velvet purse containing thirteen gold coins. The King's final acts in the cathedral were to go to confession and receive Communion in both kinds. After Mass, wearing a light crown ornamented with pearls and diamonds, he walked in procession down the nave to the west door, while bells rang and the organ pealed, to be seen and hailed by his subjects.

So imposing a ceremony doubtless made Louis deeply aware of the implications of his kingship. What did it mean in 1654 to be crowned King of France? First of all, Louis was now "the anointed of the Lord." He had received special graces and strength to fulfil his role as representative of divine law and order in the natural world. He was nothing less than God's representative on earth, vice-Dieu. The lawyer Omer Talon worded it like this: "Sire, the place where Your Majesty is seated represents for us the throne of the living God."

Secondly, Louis was now confirmed as absolute ruler of some eighteen million subjects. According to Claude Gousté, a sixteenth-century political theorist, a prince has a right to make his subjects till his soil, direct them to be farmers, gunsmiths or cartwrights, to employ some in the manufacture of unguents and perfumes, others as his concubines, commanding each and every one to work at the royal pleasure. "I had no doubt," writes Restif de La Bretonne, "that the King could legally oblige every man to give him his wife or daughter, and my whole village—Sacy in Burgundy —thought as I did."

That the King held these absolute powers by divine right was the general (though by no means uncontested) opinion of the period: for example, the University of Cambridge addressed Charles II in these terms: "It belongs not to subjects, either to create or censure but to honour and obey their sovereign, who comes to be so by a fundamental hereditary right of succession, which no religion, no law, no fault or forfeiture can alter or diminish."

Some sixteenth-century theorists, notably Jean Bodin, had maintained that the King's sovereignty, absolute in respect of other men, was limited by the laws of God and of nature, and by the fundamental constitutional laws of the State. Others held that a king was free from every restraint except that of his own sovereign will. The most favoured view, however, was that the King's power was limited by Christian principles. As the former Coadjutor of Paris had put it, when receiving the red hat of a Cardinal from Louis's hands: "Sire, your rule will be like that of God, because your power will have no limits but those which you yourself impose in accordance with justice and reason."

Thirdly, like the early Christian emperors, the King of France was responsible for the spiritual welfare of his subjects. He must be careful to maintain orthodoxy. One of his most important functions was to appoint all but a few archbishops, bishops and abbots. He considered himself proprietor of the Church's wealth, in virtue of the maxim that there is no other proprietor in the kingdom but the King. As King, he would never allow a papal Bull to be published in France until Parlement had decided whether it interfered with the liberties of the French Church or his own authority.

Fourthly, Louis was lord of a domain called France. But what was France? Originally, the Ile de France, and now a collection of provinces, many of which owed strong allegiance to local lords. Towns like Orléans and Bordeaux, when it came to a clash of loyalties, had lately chosen to favour their local lord rather than their lord's overlord. To be King of France in reality as well as in name, Louis must win or command the loyalty of all such nobles.

The word France was vague in another way. No Frenchman, not even Louis, could yet define her frontiers. The country was still expanding outwards, still being formed. Louis's official title, "King of France and Navarre," bore witness to this. Only under Henri IV had the two crowns been united. Again, Alsace had been annexed only six years ago; soon other independent prince-doms and duchies would doubtless also become part of France, if Charlemagne's frontiers were taken as the ideal. It followed that France's unity, within and without, depended on Louis's will and Louis's own conception of what France should be.

The fifth aspect of Louis's kingship followed from the fourth. Louis was now the personification of France. France—as opposed to this or that province—was still a comparatively new concept, a vague geographical abstraction, unreal to most because of poor communications; certainly not an economic unit, for the land was criss-crossed with customs barriers: for most Frenchmen France meant the King who gave unity. Indeed, the identification was so close that the King could be called simply France, as in Shake-speare's plays, and the King's children *"enfants de France."* For it was an age which thought in terms of persons rather than of things. Unmoved by the phrase, "A terrible battle has just been fought," people responded to "Bellona, with bloodshot eyes and tangled hair, breathed fire upon the battlefield," while a favourite book was Plutarch's *Lives*, which interprets Greek and Roman history in terms of statesmen and generals. If Louis were to prove himself a skilled horseman or a brave soldier, then all France would gain a reputation for horsemanship or courage.

Sixthly, Louis was considered "a demi-god." This concept resulted partly from his majesty, partly because he embodied France, but chiefly because he was a direct successor of the much-admired Roman emperors, who had claimed for themselves semi-divine honours. To mark the end of the Fronde Paris had erected the first public statue of Louis: no one was surprised to see him portrayed as a demi-god in Roman dress. For his cousin, Mademoiselle, "the King is like a god," while a trained lawyer, Omer Talon, could declare without hyperbole that "kings belong to the race of gods." This belief operated at two levels: among the people it was hero-worship—"The French are the only nation in Europe to idolise their sovereign," remarked Evelyn, watching Louis's state entry to Paris in 1652; among the educated it was linked to a genuine, fond but unthinking belief in the gods and goddesses of antiquity, who represented an intermediate level between ordinary mortals and the Christian God.

Lastly, and most important of all to the ordinary peasant or householder, the new King Louis was the one man who could protect them from oppression and injustice. Time and again the King is hailed as guardian of the people's rights. The phrase was sincere. During the Fronde and even for a short time afterwards in provinces like Auvergne where the King's power was still weak, noblemen robbed, tortured and murdered with impunity. They might turn out counterfeit money or stick a tax on bread. They demanded payment for settling disputes. A nobleman might kill a man for failing to salute him. Only a strong king could hold these tough lords in check. If the ordinary man in the street wanted Louis to be a great king, it was not least because he would then stand a better chance of a decent life.

A less easily defined aspect of Louis's kingship appeared two days after his coronation, when Louis drove out to the park of the Abbey of Saint-Remi. Here two thousand men, women and children stood awaiting his arrival, all suffering from a swelling of the glands of the neck called scrofula, or king's evil. One by one they passed in front of Louis, who touched them with his open right hand from the forehead to the chin and from one cheek to the other, thus making the sign of the cross on every face, repeating each time the words, "The King touches thee, God heals thee." After the velvet and gold, these

> strangely-visited people,
> All swoln and ulcerous, pitiful to the eye,
> The mere despair of surgery, he cures.

Despite its formula, this was a pagan not a Christian rite. From early times the people of temperate or cold countries had tended to identify their king with the sun, and to ascribe to him the sun's healing powers. It was this tendency which lay behind the medals and poems hailing the new-born Louis as the sun at dawn, and lately it had been growing in force. A year ago in a ballet to recall the end of the Fronde, announced by Monsieur as the Morning Star and preceded by Dawn, Louis had appeared in a dazzling costume as the Rising Sun: on his head a diadem with golden rays surmounted by plumes, flame-like beams of gold radiating from his neck, shoulders, cuffs, thighs, garters and shoes. This went beyond mere allegory, it was an expression of the cosmic powers believed inherent in kingship. Long before he officially adopted the name of Roi-soleil, Louis was widely regarded as the sun of France: as such the possessor of healing and possibly also of other magical virtues.

The coronation and its festivities drew to a close with an amnesty for six hundred prisoners. Anne and the Cardinal, Court and people alike had been pleased with Louis's grace and bearing during the long ceremonies. Only one jarring note had been heard: in one of the many sermons a certain Pierre de Bertier, Bishop of Montauban, had attacked the Protestants of Guyenne and Languedoc, and actually suggested the King take rigorous measures "towards those of the so-called Reformed religion." Not for many years had this distasteful formula been heard in public or used in official decrees; it was considered unfortunate to say the least at a time when all Louis's subjects, of whatever Church, were united in loyal homage.

Immediately after his coronation Louis joined his army. After the capture of Stenai in Lorraine and the relief of Arras, capital of Artois, he returned to Paris for the winter. His *valet de chambre*, Dubois, tells how the sixteen-year-old King spent his days at the Louvre.

When he woke, the Abbé de Péréfixe read aloud to Louis from the Bible or from his Life of Henri IV. The King washed and said his prayers in the presence of an almoner and a few courtiers, then, wearing a singlet and light trousers, he went to his improvised gymnasium. "He vaulted with admirable agility; winding up the wooden horse as high as it would go, he leapt on to it like a bird, landing in the saddle as silently as though on a pillow." Then came a fencing lesson from Vincent de Saint-Ange, pike and musketry drill under Jacques de Bretonville, and a dancing lesson from Beauchamp, a professional ballet dancer. After a brisk rubdown he changed into everyday clothes—long stockings, knee-length breeches, jerkin and jacket—and ate a big breakfast, which might include light broth, cutlets and sausages. Then, going up to Cardinal Mazarin's apartments, he entered another world, of art and luxury: Titians and Correggios on the walls, Greek and Roman statues, warm, velvety Persian carpets, the fragrance of rare perfumes. Here one or two Secretaries of State would be annotating documents. Mazarin had begun to introduce Louis to politics without boring him. He arranged special sessions of the Council at which only simple business was transacted and easy questions discussed; and every morning, from nine to eleven, he went through the latest dispatches with Louis, letting him ask questions, testing him, and finally explaining what course of action should be taken and why. Mazarin was well pleased with his pupil's progress and told Louis, "You have the stuff to make four great kings, and an honest man besides."

At eleven, when Anne woke, Louis went to his mother's bedroom and stayed with her during breakfast, though he no longer formally handed her her vest as he had done in his boyhood. Then he hurried down to the riding school, where Arnolfini taught him how to gallop at a suspended hoop and carry it off on the point of his lance.

Louis and the Queen heard Mass and lunched together. This, Louis mentions in his Memoirs, was a pleasure not a duty. Mother and son got on very well together. They were brought close by Anne's widowhood, shared danger and tastes in common, such as for flowers and gardens. Moreover, Louis had inherited not only his mother's robust health but some of her Spanish characteristics: a serious turn of mind and strong sense of dignity. During the meal Louis's own group of ten violinists played, performing so well "that courtiers would attend the lunch in order to hear the concert."

Already, then, Louis had formed the habit of taking his meals in public. For by nature he was extremely sociable. He was interested in people, whatever their rank, and usually liked them. Often he would go unannounced to lunch with the Maréchal de Villeroi, or the Duc de Danville, who lived near the Palais Royal —taking care to send ahead extra food from the royal kitchen.

In the afternoon he studied with his tutor, but only for an hour or two. War had disrupted his education and as a result he learned little from books. He never mastered Latin. On the other hand, he picked up fluent Spanish and Italian from his mother and Mazarin. The rest of the afternoon was spent in physical exercise, at which he was so proficient: a game of *jeu de paume* (tennis), hunting or shooting (in a single day at this period he bagged thirty hares and a hundred and fifty-six rabbits). In the early evening he might drive in his carriage up and down the Cours la Reine, the avenue of horse-chestnut trees beside the Seine designed by his grandmother, Marie de Médicis. As many as seven hundred carriages could be seen there on a spring evening.

After supper there might be parlour games with the Queen's ladies-in-waiting. A favourite was *Roman*: one player begins a story and goes on until inspiration fails; the next player continues it, and so on in turn. Another game was charades of proverbs: once Louis chose to act "All that glitters is not gold." Some evenings there might be gambling, either at cards or at *hoca*, a forerunner of roulette which Mazarin had introduced from Italy. Mazarin himself was a confirmed gambler, played for high stakes and did not hesitate to cheat, which he called "correcting chance."

This most reasonable of men believed in good and bad fortune: the first question he asked prospective employees was, "Are you lucky?"

As for Louis, he was usually lucky. One evening he won quite a large sum from the nineteen-year-old Chevalier de Rohan —the Rohans of Brittany were one of the oldest and proudest families in France. The Chevalier found himself short of gold louis, in which losses were usually paid, and wanted to settle in Spanish pistoles. Louis refused the enemy currency, whereupon the Chevalier, well known as a hot-head, threw the pistoles out the window, remarking "In that case, they're good for nothing." The incident cast a chill over the company. When Louis complained to Mazarin, the Cardinal, a man of peace rather than of principles, replied, "Sire, the Chevalier de Rohan acted like a king, and you like a Chevalier de Rohan."

On other evenings a play would be given. Like his father, Louis enjoyed comedy and knockabout farce. Among the comedians and clowns—mostly Italians—Louis's favourite was Scaramouche. His mother recalled how at the age of two Louis had been crying in Richelieu's palace, crying inconsolably. Scaramouche had come in, tossed aside his black cloak, taken the child in his arms and begun pulling funny faces: in a few moments Louis's tears had stopped and he was laughing delightedly. Scaramouche's most famous trick was to kick himself on the backside; he also ventriloquised seated between a dog and a parrot, strumming a guitar.

Louis's favourite evening diversion was the ballet. He loved dancing and was outstandingly good at it. Since his first public appearance at thirteen he had played a variety of roles: bacchante, man of ice (the libretti were incredibly naïve: "Already my coldness inspires deep fear; at my royal appearance all tremble and are chilled with respect"), King of the Titans, man of choler, Century of Gold, a fury and a dryad ("Although his branches are still tender, he belongs to the same wood as Caesar and Alexander"). As the Rising Sun, he danced to his own castanets, pointing his little fingers to suggest the sun's rays. This performance he gave five times in public at the Salle du Petit Bourbon. Since Catherine de

Médicis first imported the ballet, it had been customary for members of the royal family to dance on the stage. The dance was considered a very manly sport, an excellent expression of character, physical strength, stamina, poise, timing, grace and control. What more natural than that a king should follow David's example and dance before his subjects, just as he rode and tilted before them—giving of his best in a way that all classes could appreciate?

Games and diversions usually ended early and Louis would be in bed by midnight. For the atmosphere at Court was still far from carefree. War with Spain still dragged on and an army of 17,000 men had to be kept in the field for nine months of the year. Nicolas Fouquet, the clever young Superintendent of Finances, had devised new ways of raising money, including stamped paper for legal documents and a tax on baptisms and burials. Louis had signed the necessary edicts—seventeen in number—and on 20th March, 1655, went to Parlement to get them registered. Despite a plea from the Attorney-General that the King "should take pity on his people's distress" Parlement voted in favour of the edicts and duly registered them.

Next day, however, the younger members of the Chambre des Enquêtes—those who had most bitterly criticised absolutism during the Fronde—demanded a new meeting: "the presence of the King having deprived councillors of their right to vote freely, the edicts should be examined anew in his absence to see whether they conform with justice." A new meeting was held at the beginning of April during which the Chancellor admitted that he had had no advance knowledge of the edicts before the session of 20th March and that he had even affixed the great seal without having read them. Angered by what they considered the Chancellor's subservience to Mazarin, the members of the Enquêtes began to discuss the edicts in detail and to criticise them sharply. The Court grew alarmed: a precisely similar situation had touched off four years of civil war. For the moment, however, Mazarin applied his usual maxim: "Time and I."

On the morning of 13th April Louis rode out to Vincennes, which Cardinal Mazarin used as a stronghold and summer palace. It was heavily guarded by cannon, three hundred soldiers in Mazarin's green livery, and a dry moat in which roamed lions, bears and tigers. The Cardinal joined the King and together they went hunting. This was Louis's favourite sport, for it combined four things he loved: the open air, woods, horses and dogs. After his month's virtual imprisonment during the Fronde it was to Vincennes that he had hurried, to go hunting. The forest had been well stocked by Mazarin with stags, buck, does and wild boar, and the two men were enjoying a good morning's sport, the hounds in full cry, when an unexpected messenger arrived from Paris: without authorisation and without having informed the Prime Minister, all chambers of Parlement were at that moment assembling in the Palais de Justice for a new joint session.

The message came as a severe shock. Such a meeting of Parlement without the King's approval was not only illegal but a direct challenge to royal authority. Parlement's evident intention was to curtail the seventeen edicts, that is, to deny the King the money without which he could not rule—thus breaking the agreement concluded in the last months of the Fronde whereby the magistrates renounced all interference in financial matters.

It was obvious that if Parlement's action went unchecked, it might lead to a new civil war. But Mazarin was prudent by nature and at fifty-three averse from head-on clashes. Twice he had chosen exile rather than see out a dangerous crisis. Louis, on the other hand, had recently been crowned and was eager to prove himself King in fact as well as in name. Parlement's action was a personal challenge to him. It seems to have been Louis's decision alone immediately to leave the hunt and take the road for Paris. Riding most of the four miles at full gallop, he dismounted outside the Palais de Justice, ran up the steps and, unannounced, entered the vaulted Grand' Chambre, or Gilded Hall, which had once been the bedroom of St. Louis.

The two hundred and twenty presidents and councillors, clad in their scarlet robes, looked up in surprise and annoyance at this strange figure wearing a red jerkin, high boots, grey hunting hat, a riding crop in his hand, who had forced his way into their midst; then as they recognised the dark eyes, high-bridged nose and curly chestnut hair a murmur of astonishment ran through the hall.

Never before in the leather-bound records that went back four centuries had a king arrived in their presence alone, or unannounced, or in any dress but his formal robes.

Without so much as a nod to the Chancellor, Louis's habitual spokesman, the sixteen-year-old King sat down on the seat reserved for him, looked round the assembly "with a severe, haughty air" and in a tone "less sweet and gracious than usual" spoke these words:

"Everyone knows how much trouble your meetings have caused in my State and how many dangerous results they have had. I have learnt that you intend to continue them on the pretext of discussing the edicts which, not long since, were published and read in my presence. I have come here expressly to forbid you to do this"—here he pointed at the members of the Enquêtes—"which I do absolutely, and to forbid you, Monsieur le Premier Président" —again he pointed—"to permit or tolerate this, whatever pressure Messieurs des Enquêtes may bring on you to do so."

Louis then got up and before any of the lawyers—normally so fluent—could utter a word, walked out of the hall. He rode to the Louvre, and later in the day rejoined the Cardinal at Vincennes.

Legend, which likes to heighten momentous occasions, later attributed to Louis on this fateful spring morning a threatening manner, the cracking of his riding whip and the words, *"L'Etat, c'est moi."* Contemporary records are silent on all three scores. As King of France Louis had no need of threats, verbal or symbolic, towards his subjects; moreover he knew that if he was acting bravely he was also acting within his rights. As for *"L'Etat, c'est moi,"* a terse epigram like that would have been out of place in seventeenth-century court speech: legend probably lifted it from a phrase in Bossuet's *Politique tirée de l'écriture sainte*, written some years later: *"Tout l'Etat est en lui."* But the epigram has this of truth: it conveys the essence of the occasion—Louis's first use of his personal authority.

Louis's sudden and dramatic action had put Parlement in a quandary. The King, being of age, had clearly expressed his will: how could they do what no Parlement had ever done—openly resist the King's will? But next morning, to save face, the First

President, Pomponne de Bellièvre, accompanied by all the High Court presidents, went to Mazarin and told him of the unfortunate impression caused by yesterday's meeting "where everything had happened in such a strange way, so very different from the days of His Majesty's predecessors."

Mazarin listened politely and made vague promises about debating future edicts. Not in the least gulled, the First President went to Louis and asked permission to discuss the seventeen edicts at leisure. Louis stood firm and replied that he did not wish to infringe Parlement's privileges, but since the good of the State and the present situation made it impossible for him to permit deliberate assemblies, he forbade them unreservedly.

That might well have ended the matter. However, to ma¹ absolutely sure, Mazarin tactfully called on Maréchal de Tuɪ ɪne to explain the case for new taxes—the Spanish threat, Condé, the possibility of a new Fronde. The High Court presidents were only too glad to save face by bowing regretfully to the need for cannon and muskets. Among senior magistrates only Bellièvre, the First President, hesitated. Mazarin decided to "correct chance" and made Bellièvre a secret present of £100,000. With surprising speed Bellièvre persuaded the members of the Enquêtes to heed the gravity of Turenne's plea and cease all further protests. The seventeen edicts smoothly became law.

It was an important victory. Louis was now not only crowned King, he had been voted the money to govern. But it was an allied rather than a personal victory: Louis and Mazarin together rather than Louis alone.

CHAPTER 5

First Love

LOUIS had strengthened his own position but he had also strengthened the Cardinal's. The self-made son of a Sicilian major-domo now found himself the richest and most powerful man in Christendom. He was Prime Minister and head of the Council; superintendent of the Queen's household and the King's education, as well as that of the Duc d'Anjou; governor of Brisach and La Rochelle, captain of the castles of Fontainebleau and Vincennes, grand bailiff and master of the waters and forests of La Fère, Ham, the county of Marle and the forest of Saint-Gobain; though not ordained, he was prior of Chastenoy, abbot of St. Germain l'Auxerrois (parish church of the Louvre), of Notre Dame de Cercamp, Saint-Denis, Cluny and fourteen other churches. He held shares in a whaling company, owned cargo ships, and he had founded a business to trade in Algerian cork and coral. He bought and sold grain, spices, sugar, soap and amber.

Nothing was too small for him. Firewood and hay from the Fontainebleau forest were sold for Mazarin's account, bringing in £2,500 annually. He is even said to have made money out of Mazarinades. "One day he ordered all the copies of these atrocious libels that could possibly be found to be brought to him, saying that he was going to have them burnt. A great many were seized, but when he got them into his possession he sold them secretly and made ten thousand crowns out of the transaction, over which he had many a good laugh. 'The French,' he used to say, 'are nice people. I allow them to sing and to write, and they allow me to do whatever I like.' "

Mazarin hoarded away his profits in gold and diamonds which

he locked up in the castle of Vincennes, or in works of art for his own apartments. From the late King of England's collection he had bought Correggio's "St. Catherine," a "Venus" by Titian, a second Correggio and "The Deluge" by Annibale Carracci. He owned (and opened to the public) the best library in France—40,000 leather-bound volumes—including no less than twenty copies of the rare first printed Bible, known since then as the Mazarin Bible.

An expert numismatist, he had the royal mint cast for himself a medal showing waves breaking on a rock, inscribed *Quam frustra et murmure quanto*—"With what an uproar and all in vain!"—a motto which also figured on the standard of his own infantry regiment. From the capitals of Europe he ordered furniture, fans, fine silks. He blamed one of his agents, an abbé, for sending silver muslin from Naples without exempting it from duty—customs are "for people without friends," and also for sending two cases of relics: he must never again send such things, unless he receives special orders, "because it is a useless expense." He never forgot what it felt like to be penniless, to be educated on charity. As a young man, after gambling away a small sum—all he possessed—he had been heard to remark, "Oh, what an ass man is without money!" and as a vice-legate at Avignon to murmur in front of the monument to John XXII: "He was a great pope, he left eight millions!" Mazarin's own fortune now amounted to fifty millions—some £17 million.

If the French people reproached him with "living voluptuously." the nobles envied him his power. He never let anyone sit down in his presence, not even the Chancellor or Maréchal de Villeroi, and would hold Council meetings while his beard was being trimmed or he toyed with his warbler and pet long-tailed monkey. He possessed more power than he had ever dreamed of, and yet he dreamed of more. In April, 1657, the Emperor Ferdinand died, and Mazarin conceived the idea of trying to have Louis elected as his successor. Thus the Empire, which in 800 had been transferred from the Romans to Charlemagne, and in the eleventh century from the Franks to the Germans, would revert to France. And while his godson ruled the Empire from Paris, he himself—this was the dream—would rule Christendom from Rome. In December, 1655, a Jesuit friend had written of the Cardinal from that city: "In all the antechambers, at all the parties people are talking about Christendom's debt to him, and his praises are heard on all sides. The experts believe that he will be the arbiter of the conclaves and will be able to place the tiara on whatever head he pleases, even on his own, should he wish." Since his French ties might prove embarrassing to Rome, which had grown accustomed to elect Italian Popes, the Cardinal took care to sign all his letters and documents "Mazarini."

So much for the future. For the present, Mazarin was agreeably concerned with his own sisters' children. They had been brought up in a huge palace in Rome built with his money, and as they reached marriageable age he sent for them. The first batch had arrived in 1647—Paul Mancini, a brave boy whom Mazarin had hoped would be his heir, but killed during the Fronde; and three nieces, Anne, Laure and Olympe. Paris had called them the "Mazarinettes" or "the squadron," in reference to the fast young Italian girls who had spied for Catherine de Médicis and chosen their lovers at her command. Other Mazarinettes followed. In 1654 Mazarin's sister, Madame Mancini, arrived with two daughters, Hortense and Marie, to be joined the following year by Marie-Anne, a precocious six, who already wrote verses and made little *bons mots*.

The girls were clever, lively and attractive; they would bring their husbands huge dowries and, still more important, the Cardinal's favour. It pleased Mazarin to watch the proudest nobles of France, who had once vilified his low birth, throng round his nieces and beg him for their hands. Eventually he would give Laure Mancini to the Duc de Mercoeur, grandson of Henry IV; Anne Martinozzi to the Prince de Conti; and Olympe Mancini to Eugène de Savoie, Comte de Soissons. All three were princes of the blood royal.

Louis was very fond of the three elder Mazarinettes, who lived in the Louvre and whom during winter he saw almost daily. In fact the young King was growing up a true Bourbon in his taste for female society. Anne did what she could to guard her son's innocence, but without success. On a certain evening when he was sixteen, coming back from the bath he met his mother's personal maid, Catherine Henriette de Beauvais: not a noblewoman, but the daughter of a second-hand clothes dealer and widow of a ribbon-maker. |Madame de Beauvais was prized by Anne as a deft needle-woman and by several courtiers for quite different accomplishments. Despite a plain face she was attractive to men; and to Louis too, returning from his bath. Without fuss she initiated her King into the pleasures of *le doux scavoir*. It was an incident without sequel for Madame de Beauvais was past forty, but Louis always remained grateful to her. She was given a pension and a fine house in the Marais and henceforth enjoyed special prestige at Court.

Physically Louis had matured early. He was now in many ways a man, with a man's desires. On the other hand, he had no experience in love; he was shy with girls, and inhibited too by the tone of the Court, which was set by Anne and Mazarin—both, for different reasons, inclined to strictness in such matters. Before long a conflict was bound to arise.

At first Louis's favourite among the Mazarinettes was Olympe. She was dark and quick, hence her nickname, "the Snipe." Though not beautiful, she was high-spirited and had a gift for impersonation. Like all the family, she gave the impression of belonging to an older and more knowledgeable civilisation than that of France. But when he was seventeen Louis met her younger sister, Marie—fresh from the Val de Grâce convent school, where for two years she had been learning a vast amount of poetry—and Olympe was soon forgotten. Marie was sixteen, tall, with big dark eyes, beautiful teeth and glossy black hair parted in the centre and bulging at each side on a level with the brow. Her plump cheeks were prettily dimpled and she had a mischievous twinkle in her eye.

In 1656 Marie was a member of the Court which travelled to La Fère in Picardy to be near the King, who was much with his army in Flanders. When he returned from a skirmish and a courtier would tell how the King had spent fifteen hours continuously in the saddle or narrowly missed being hit, he would always be watching Marie's face for the tears in her eyes and her proud smile.

Once he whispered to her, "There's not much I wouldn't do to make your eyes shine like that!" She had a gift for declamation and, since heroism was in the air, would read Louis scenes from the latest tragedies and romances, her slight Italian accent enhancing their charm. In her own language she would recite Ariosto and Tasso.

Louis began to learn something about Marie's life. Her father, an amateur astrologer, had predicted that Marie would make trouble in the world. Her mother had taken this prediction so seriously that Marie, who had been a plain, sallow-faced little girl, became the Cinderella of the family. She was placed in a convent at the age of seven but became unwell and had to be taken home. She was not allowed to accompany her sisters to parties and plays, and when she protested to her uncle, all he did was scold her for lack of filial submission. "His words remained in my memory, but did not affect my spirit in the least." When Madame Mancini lay dying in her forty-second year (her husband had predicted this too) she begged Mazarin to force her headstrong daughter to become a nun, a plea which the Cardinal ignored, for he was enjoying making brilliant marriages for his nieces.

Marie was almost the exact opposite of Louis: impulsive, demonstrative, unsociable, making up for an unhappy childhood by a dream-world fed from poetry and novels. Of this world Louis had only had occasional glimpses in *Peau d'Ane*, in the ballets and plays at Court, but now he began to feel the attraction of knight errantry and lovers risking their lives to meet by moonlight, to sense the romance of this strange orphaned Cinderella from a strange land. He began to see more of Marie Mancini. Sometimes he accompanied her songs on the guitar. But he was shy with her, and did not yet dare to hold her hand.

"I knew already," writes Marie, "that the King did not altogether hate me, having the instinct to understand that eloquent language which is more persuasive than the most beautiful words in the world. It is also possible that having found in the King higher qualities and greater merit than in any other man I ever met, I naturally became wiser in that silent language than anyone else. . . . But the King himself was so assiduous in his attentions to me and so happy when he was with me that I could have no doubt at all in the matter."

The Court noticed Louis's attentions to Marie Mancini without attaching importance to them: after all, the King had found other young ladies attractive, such as Madame de Frontenac and Marie's sister, Olympe. Besides, in the summer of 1656 the Court was much more interested in another foreign young lady, Christina of Sweden, who was about to pay a state visit to Louis at Compiègne. Even Louis himself was probably more interested in this daughter of Gustavus Adolphus than in Marie: he was still learning how to play the King and here was someone whose ten years' reign had been the talk of Europe.

Like Louis, Christina had come to the throne as a child; unlike Louis, she was brilliantly clever and very studious. At eighteen she knew eleven languages, including Hebrew. Her favourite reading was *La Traité des Passions*, and she summoned its author, Descartes, to Stockholm to write verse for her ballets and to give her philosophy lessons at five in the morning, "when my mind is clearest." She loved France, Sweden's traditional ally, and things French, inviting to her Court a French doctor, savants like Huet and Rochart and the painter Sébastien Bourdon. She wrote verse and patronised poets, sending a gold chain to Mademoiselle de Scudéry, who dedicated her poem *Alaric* to Christina, and another gold chain to the burlesque poet Scarron. She was known as The Second Sun, the Sibyl of the North or the Tenth Muse.

At seventeen she sketched this self-portrait: "Distrustful, suspicious, I refuse to take second place. My ambition is to be first, and not to disappoint my teachers. I can't bear anyone to outclass me. . . . I like nettling and poking fun at people, but if they retaliate I fly into a fury. In fact, I'm very short-tempered." Christina's aim in life was to attain complete freedom. She announced that she would never marry, she flouted the law by distributing crown lands to her favourites, and finally she decided to free herself of her throne. In 1654 at the age of twenty-eight she abdicated in favour of her cousin, and set sail for Germany with ten ships to carry her furniture, paintings by Raphael, Titian, Veronese and Correggio, 8,000 Hebrew, Arabic and Greek manuscripts as well as thousands of books, bronzes and marbles. To mark her abdication she struck a medal: on the reverse Pegasus flies to Olympus: *Sedes haec potior solio!* "This seat is preferable to a throne!" It was Christina's way of saying she refused to accept the human condition.

She travelled dressed as a man under the name of Comte de Dohna. At Hamburg she became very friendly with a young Jewish girl, and shrugged off cries of scandal: "The more passions and desires one has, the more ways one has of being happy." At Brussels she gave Europe another shock by becoming a Catholic —at least in name. When a Jesuit at Louvain said she would one day join the saints and stand beside St. Bridget of Sweden, she replied that she would rather join the sages. One evening she left her book in her pew at Vespers: the priest who retrieved it discovered under the black binding a copy of Virgil.

In 1656 she landed at Marseille and was met at Lyon by the Duc de Guise, who wrote to the Court: "The Queen is not tall; she has a full figure and is rather wide in the beam. She has white, well-made manly hands, aquiline nose, rather big mouth, tolerable teeth, fine shining eyes. She wears a lot of powder and pomade, and almost never wears gloves. She wears man's shoes, has a man's voice and carries herself like a man. She likes to play the amazon. She is at least as proud as her father, the great King Gustavus. She wears a man's wig, very thick on the sides." He might have added that she looked like the great Condé—"the man I most admire in the world."

At Lyon Christina surprised the lovely Marquise de Ganges bathing in the Rhône. "What a masterpiece of nature!" she cried, kissing the marquise on the throat, the eyes and the brow. Unable to persuade her to share the royal bed, she wrote the marquise a long love letter: "While waiting for a pleasant metamorphosis to change my sex, I want to see and adore you, tell you every moment that I adore you."

Louis's cousin, Mademoiselle, still in disgrace and exile, was the next person to entertain the Queen. In some ways the two ladies were rather alike: both with a touch of the amazon, both admirers of daring deeds. During a firework display over the canal at Essonnes, Christina held Mademoiselle's hand. Suddenly a rocket fell nearby and the French princess shrank back.

"What!" cried Christina. "A lady who's performed such brave deeds—afraid?"

"I'm only brave occasionally," admitted Mademoiselle.

"My dearest wish is to take part in a battle," sighed Christina.

From Essonnes Christina travelled to Paris, where Louis's mother met her. After riding to the Louvre in an interminable State procession she startled Anne by calling for a stiff drink, and then hurrying off to the Place Royale to visit the courtesan Ninon de Lenclos, whose wit and independent life she admired.

Now in mid-September the Queen was travelling to Compiègne. Mazarin had gone to meet her half-way at the Condé family seat, Chantilly, where she would dine and spend the night. At the last moment Louis decided that instead of waiting for the stiff, impersonal meeting next day, he would go to Chantilly too and surprise Christina: already he had formed a taste for seeing people as they really were. He and Philippe dressed as mere gentlemen and rode the forty miles to Chantilly, arriving two hours after dinner. Louis, who knew the castle, led the way up a side staircase and entered Christina's apartment by a small door at the corner of the balustrade surrounding her bed. Unnoticed, they mingled with the crowd and looked around. That must be she—in a grey skirt with gold and silver lace and a tight-fitting angora jacket of flame colour. The odd thing was, she did not have a single lady-in-waiting: she was attended by three Italians who called themselves "counts."

Mazarin spotted the King and his brother, and presented them to Christina.

"Here, Your Majesty, are the two most outstanding gentlemen in France."

Louis and Christina looked at each other: he saw a lady of thirty with piercingly direct blue eyes, aquiline nose and white skin, she saw a sturdy, handsome, sun-tanned youth who reminded her of someone—of a portrait she had noticed only the other day at the Louvre. And his brother too. Whose? Then she remembered.

"Yes," she smiled. "I can well believe it. They seem destined to wear crowns."

Louis was delighted that the Swedish Queen had seen through his disguise: it was the beginning of a bond between the Rising and the Second Suns. He found he liked Christina very much—liked her perspicacity and intrepid honesty. For example, she said she had found only one book to interest her lately—Pascal's *Les Provinciales*—fully aware that these Jansenist letters, then appearing in instalments, were frowned on by the Court. She told Louis that his Italian comic actors were third-rate, though better than the Jesuits' pupils who performed a tragedy for her at Compiègne. Her behaviour during plays was extraordinary: she yawned, joked, repeated lines and hung her legs over the arms of her chair —"I've never seen such postures taken by anyone except clowns," said Mademoiselle. When Fr. Amat, Louis's Jesuit confessor, came to pay his compliments, Christina told him that for confession and tragedy she would never go to the Jesuits.

In the week she spent at Compiègne Christina saw what others missed: that Louis was very attracted indeed to Marie Mancini and was beginning to fall in love with her. Christina did not find Marie very pretty—she preferred blondes. Never mind: Louis thought her beautiful beyond words. Did he intend to marry her? But she was forgetting: kings were supposed to marry princesses, and Louis would doubtless do the same. Rulers were slaves. But they need not be—hadn't she proved that to the world? And so she told Louis, in Marie's presence, "If I were you I'd marry somebody I loved." Throw the rest overboard, she added, just as she had thrown overboard the business of ruling.

Louis had certainly given some thought to marriage, and there had doubtless already been times when he wanted to make Marie Mancini his wife. So he would have weighed Christina's words carefully. Christina's blue eyes were sometimes gentle, sometimes bold, just as she herself was sometimes honest, sometimes out to shock. "Marry somebody you love"—was this honest advice, or mere revolt for the sake of revolt? But marriage was not Christina's way of conceiving revolt: she had announced that she would rather die than marry, that the best of husbands was worth nothing; she told Mademoiselle never to marry and said she thought it was abominable to have children. So "Marry somebody you love" must be honest advice.

It was also very attractive advice to a young man of eighteen with strong desires. It was pleasant to think that he could be master not only of France's destiny but of his own. But what would his proud mother say? "I'll strangle that girl with my own hands"— something like that: she who believed in the unbridgeable gap between kings and commoners. And Mazarin? The Cardinal would doubtless consider his marriage in political, not human terms; the King must be played carefully, to win another court card.

Louis still felt unsure of the depth of his feelings for Marie and unsure of his chances of success if it came to a clash with Mazarin. That winter, after Christina's departure, he seems to have suffered from this double uncertainty, for he began to lead a wild life. He tried to forget Marie Mancini by joining a fast set called *Les Endormis*, the sleepyheads, led by Marsillac, the future Duc de La Rochefoucauld, and running after Mademoiselle de La Motte-Argencourt, a flirt who liked to get herself talked about. Soon all the Court was discussing Louis's gallantry towards a mere maid of honour. With Anne's consent Mazarin, who had been watching closely, suddenly struck at *Les Endormis*: one morning Louis woke to learn that Marsillac and Mademoiselle de La Motte-Argencourt had been asked to leave Paris. For an indefinite period they would have to content themselves with rustic pleasures.

This interference in his private life angered Louis. Who after all was Mazarin to direct the love affairs of the King of France? At every turn now he felt the irksome restraining hand of Mazarin. If he wanted to buy a horse or a gun-dog, he had to go cap in hand to Mazarin. Not only was Mazarin many times richer than Louis, he made the fact disagreeably plain. One evening in Lent, for instance, Louis had to be content with two soles for supper, while Mazarin had forty of the same fish on his table. Even adventure was rationed. In 1655 Louis had set his heart on accompanying French troops across the River Escant: "I have continual arguments with him," the Cardinal wrote to Anne, "for he wants to do something to which I absolutely cannot consent, for it is contrary to his dignity, his duty and his safety. I hope he will end by yielding to reason."And Louis did yield—that was the trouble with Mazarin, he always had reason on his side. But should he always yield? Would Christina, for instance, have yielded? Louis began to feel rebellious towards His Eminence, but for the moment his rebellion was only verbal. One day at Compiègne he pointed out Mazarin to a friend: "There goes the Great Turk!"

In the spring, when Louis rejoined his armies, the Court moved to Sedan, and Louis continued to see Marie Mancini. He was still feeling his way, not yet putting into practice his theories of independence. But Anne was aware of his mood, and aware too of Marie's growing influence. She saw danger ahead and took a step to try to forestall it. Quite suddenly she summoned Louis's first cousin, Mademoiselle, to Court. Mademoiselle was not the perfect match, but at least she was more suitable than Marie.

For four and a half years Mademoiselle had been living in exile, redecorating her country house, playing active games like battledore and shuttlecock, riding to English hounds—"they're too fast for most women, but I follow them everywhere"—studying Italian and writing her memoirs. When she arrived at Sedan on 1st August, 1656, Anne came out to meet her, kissing her and saying she was delighted to see her.

"I've always loved you," she said, "though there were times when you made me angry. I didn't hold your actions at Orléans against you; but as for the Porte Saint-Antoine . . . if I could have laid hands on you then, I would have strangled you."

Mademoiselle was suitably penitent. "By displeasing you I deserved strangling. And as a result I found myself with people who made me forget my duty."

"I wanted to talk to you about that and tell you what was on my mind, but now I've forgotten the whole affair. Let's not speak about it. And remember, in future I shall love you more than ever. . . . You haven't changed at all, though it must be six years since I saw you. You're prettier, though: less thin and with a better complexion."

She told Mademoiselle that she would find the King much

changed, that he had "grown tall and broad and was no longer just a pretty boy." Six days later he arrived. "The Queen was expecting him for dinner," writes Mademoiselle. "He arrived at the gallop, so wet and splashed with mud that the Queen, who was watching from the window, said to me, 'I'd prefer you not to see him until he's changed his clothes.' I replied that he mustn't trouble just for me. He came in in his travelling clothes and I thought he looked very well.

" 'Here is a young lady whom I present to you,' the Queen said. 'She's very sorry she was naughty. She'll be well-behaved in future.' "

Louis laughed and began to tell them about the siege of Mont-médy, which had just fallen. The courtiers around him informed the Queen that during a certain skirmish the King had been the first to enter a dangerous wood: "We did all we could to hold him back, but it was useless." Then there arrived the King's brother, who kissed Mademoiselle and told her that she had grown even more beautiful; and the Cardinal, who embraced her knees and told her that he had been looking forward to this reconciliation. It was a happy family gathering.

In six years Mademoiselle found that the Court had become more informal. It surprised her that when Louis came late to table he should take the last place, and it surprised her even more to see him offering food to fellow officers, insisting that they should eat with him.

On the second afternoon "the King came to see me and talked to me in the politest possible way. Afterwards I wanted to escort him to his lodgings; but he said no, he would escort *me*. At last he let me come as far as his coach. I said to him, 'Please will Your Majesty let me escort him in case people think I am not doing my duty.' 'I have a duty too,' he replied, 'a duty not to let you escort me.' As he stood by his coach, he said, 'Will you order me to get in; otherwise I shouldn't dare to go before you.' " Evidently Louis remembered what store Mademoiselle set by the niceties of precedence; delightedly she wrote that the King was "as courteous as could possibly be."

Every night after supper Louis danced with Mademoiselle. His talk was all of his army, which pleased her immensely: "above all others, I like warriors, and hearing them talk about their art." He spoke of his musketeers and his bodyguard, asking how she liked their surtouts—"there's nothing finer than the two blue squadrons; you'll see them soon, because they're going to be your escort"; of his life-guards and light cavalry; each regiment, he told her, had its trumpeters, the best trumpeters in the world—and very smartly turned out. A gleam came into his eyes. "Have you ever heard kettle-drums?"

Mademoiselle was delighted by the King's friendly attitude and martial bearing. "His ideas seemed admirable to me. I was completely satisfied with him." Mazarin, for his part, encouraged Mademoiselle's hopes. She would already be Queen of France, he told her, but for her father's part in the Fronde. However, memories of the Fronde were growing dim; once Condé was crushed and the kingdom quite secure . . .

Mademoiselle knew that if she were to marry, it must be soon, for she was thirty this year. At various times husbands had been proposed to her: Anne's brother Ferdinand, Cardinal-Infante of Spain; another Ferdinand, Holy Roman Emperor; the Archduke Leopold; Ferdinand-Maria, Elector of Bavaria; Philip William, the Count Palatine; and Charles Stuart, who had left France three years before when Mazarin officially recognised Cromwell's Government: at the last moment all these men, or the match-makers, had drawn back. Yet Mademoiselle was quite good-looking, enjoyed excellent health, talked well, had a sense of humour, was brave and loyal. What was it she lacked? The answer seems to be, a twinkle in her eye. She guessed it herself: the poetry she liked least was love poetry, "for romance doesn't appeal to me," and even the pleasures of the table seemed to her tiresome; in short, she was quite unsensual.

Louis seems to have felt this lack, as other prospective husbands had felt it. Mademoiselle admired him, she believed he was almost a god—but love affairs are not made of hero-worship. And so, when the young couple went riding around Sedan, instead of lingering in the woods at dusk, Louis showed her all his horses and talked earnestly of troop movements. At the end of her twelve days' stay it became clear that she would never become Queen of France. "I could take pride in many things," she says in her self-portrait, "but the one thing I am really proud of is being an excellent friend." In future that was to be her role in Louis's life.

During the same summer the "Queen of the Goths," as Mademoiselle called Christina, she who had set Louis's thoughts on a love-marriage and on freeing himself from convention, returned for a second visit to France. This time she lodged at Fontainebleau. Louis, who was taking an active part in the siege of Saint-Venant and later paid a two-month visit to Metz, was too occupied to see her. However, he got frequent news of the Swedish Queen. Her behaviour continued eccentric—she still put her feet up on the furniture—but there was now a new sharp edge to her eccentricity: as though, three years after abdication, she was still unsatisfied. Finally, in November, she made a drastic attempt to achieve her goal of total freedom.

She happened to discover a packet of letters vilifying her and revealing her recent intrigues in the Kingdom of Naples. The handwriting seemed to be that of Francis Santinelli, one of Christina's three Italian "counts," but in fact the letters had been forged by another of the trio, Monaldeschi, who was Santinelli's rival for the Queen's favour. Christina sent for Monaldeschi and made him read the letters.

"What punishment do you think the writer of these letters deserves?"

"Death," said Monaldeschi.

"Don't forget that word: I promise you I won't grant a reprieve."

Four days later, on 10th November, she summoned Monaldeschi to the Galerie des Cerfs at Fontainebleau, where the antlered heads of stags were hung as trophies. Here the third "count," Louis Santinelli, was waiting beside her with three of his guard, swords drawn. Also present was Fr. Le Bel, a local priest. The Queen confronted Monaldeschi with the originals of his letters and told Fr. Le Bel to prepare the traitor for death. The terrified priest begged her to be merciful: "Remember, you're a guest of the King of France." At this Christina flared up. "Justice belongs to me. . . . The King of France holds me neither captive nor subject: I'm my own mistress, answerable only to God."

Monaldeschi was down on his knees, begging for mercy, but Christina's blue eyes did not soften. After more pleas and delays he garbled his confession in a mixture of Latin, Italian and French, and received absolution. Santinelli lunged at the traitor's heart with a sword, but the blade was turned aside by chain mail under his shirt. One of the guards ran his sword through the wretched man's neck, then stabbed him to death. The walls and floor of the Gallery were drenched with blood. The body was taken to the church of Avon and buried that night. As a final irony, Christina calmly emptied her purse for requiem masses.

The news reached Court the same day. Anne was horrified—she who had spared many far worse traitors. "We are not used to such tragedies here," was Mazarin's comment. But the most shocked of all was Louis. He had liked Christina and admired her directness. She had opened up vistas of independence, of a life which satisfied the emotions as well as reason. And now a cold-blooded, remorseless killing. This was what came of making one's own rules.

The cautious Cardinal advised Christina to say the death resulted from a quarrel between the "counts"—it would be unwise to accept responsibility for killing a subject of the Pope in a residence of the Most Christian King. Christina retorted that Louis had no authority over her—they were equals. Besides, what about the assassination of the two Guises by Henri III, and of Maréchal d'Ancre by Louis XIII? She tried to get herself invited to London, but Cromwell showed no eagerness to receive this new convert to Catholicism. Then she announced that she intended to come to Paris, but was persuaded to wait a little, until the scandal had died down.

She arrived at the Louvre for carnival time, 1658, attending fancy-dress balls as a gipsy or as Queen of the Turks. Louis declined to take her to the Saint-Germain Fair and as soon as he heard her loud voice shut himself up in his room. Presently Mazarin hinted that she should leave for Italy and gave her money for travelling expenses. As a last amusement she had herself invited to a meeting of the Académie Française. After madrigals and odes, she was asked whether she would like to hear a reading from the dictionary the Academicians were compiling. The book was opened at the word *jeu*, and one of the members read the first illustrative quotation: *"Des jeux de princes qui ne plaisent qu'à ceux qui les font."* "When royalty plays, only royalty is amused." In the silence that followed the Academicians gazed stonily at their guest. The Sibyl of the North gave a hollow laugh, then stalked out of the room in her square-toed man's shoes.

CHAPTER 6

A Marriage is Arranged

BOTH MAZARIN and Philip, King of Spain, had for long been trying to secure England as an ally. Although England had only a small population of about five and a half million, it was believed that her fresh, well-disciplined troops could turn stalemate into victory. At first Cromwell had seemed to favour Philip, but in return for his help he demanded freedom for British ships to trade in the West Indies and for Englishmen resident in Spain to possess a bible without being troubled by the Inquisition. These demands were refused, whereupon English forces seized Jamaica and war broke out between England and Spain. Mazarin profited from the war to propose an alliance to Cromwell. British troops were to help the French to cut off the Spanish Netherlands (present-day Belgium) from Spain, its source of supplies and troops. They were to do this by capturing Gravelines, Mardyck and, above all, Dunkirk, chief supply port for the Netherlands. In return, England would be allowed to keep Mardyck and Dunkirk. A port in the Continent—that was a tempting prize—and in 1657 Cromwell signed the treaty of alliance.

In early summer, 1658, Turenne's army of 20,000 was joined by 6,000 Ironsides, "stout men and fit for action, each with a new red coat and a new pair of shoes." Louis had inspected three regiments of Ironsides the previous summer and been impressed by their turn-out and discipline. These English troops were tough and demanded larger rations of meat than the French received; when their pay was in arrears, they threatened to sail home; Turenne had to stay them by melting down his own personal plate and stamping silver pieces with a fleur de lys to the tune of £10,000.

At the end of May Turenne began to invest Dunkirk. Because the countryside was flooded the Spanish army, arriving from the east, took up positions on the dunes, its lines at right angles to the sea. On 14th June just before battle Condé said to the Duke of Gloucester, Charles II's brother, who was serving with the Spanish against Cromwell: "You say you have never seen a battle lost? Well, you'll see one now." Condé meant that the Spanish commander had not allowed for the fall of the tide; as the sea receded, his right wing would be exposed. That was just what happened. While the main French force and the Ironsides engaged the Spanish centre and left in the sand-hills above high-water mark, a body of French cavalry rode up along the hard sand and charged the Spanish line in flank. The Battle of the Dunes, as it was called, was an important Anglo-French victory. Thirteen hundred Spaniards fell, four thousand were taken prisoner and Dunkirk capitulated. On the 25th Louis made his formal entry into the town before handing it over to Lockhart, the English commander.

All this while, Louis was painfully eager for adventure and battle. He had a wild plan for deciding the war by a single-handed combat between himself and Philip of Spain. Even in Paris he was delighted when his coach outrode its escort for then, he thought, bandits might attack. He longed to make his mark as a soldier, like Henri IV, but still Mazarin held him back. He was not allowed to take part in the Battle of the Dunes: Mazarin argued that the person of the King was more valuable to France than all her armies combined.

Louis did, however, insist on sharing his troops' life as far as possible. After Dunkirk fell he hastened to Mardyck, the nearest town to his armies, although Mazarin had strongly advised him to return to Calais: at Mardyck the water was bad and the air unhealthy because the dead of the preceding year had often been only half buried. As usual, the Cardinal was right: Louis picked up a germ and on 30th June admitted that he felt tired and needed a rest. Next day he was examined in Calais by his doctors, who diagnosed a touch of the sun and over-exertion on horseback. In fact it seems to have been typhoid. He quickly developed a high fever, with periods of trembling and near-convulsion.

Louis was bled eight times and purged four times with cassia and senna. The fever grew so bad that the doctors despaired of his life. Louis called for Mazarin: old differences between them were now forgotten. "You are a man of decision and the best friend I have. Please tell me when I'm near the end—the Queen won't dare to, for fear of making me worse." He was given the Last Sacraments and in all the churches of Paris the Blessed Sacrament was exposed. Mademoiselle echoed the feelings of France: "To see a young King die is a terrible thing. I myself was terrified when I thought of the future, and the affliction of the Queen."

As a last resort a local doctor from Abbeville named du Sausoy was called in. He shocked the Court by seating himself on the royal bed and making the odd suggestion that instead of being bled and purged the patient should be given three ounces of emetic wine. The wine was administered and caused Louis to vomit twice. Next day he was out of danger.

Among those at Louis's bedside was Marie Mancini. French ladies were brought up to restrain their feelings, but Marie Mancini was not French. Day and night she had wept for the King, and now with tears in her eyes she told him of her anguish, how if he had died she would have died too. Louis was deeply moved by her obvious sincerity and pitch of feeling; moreover, as a result of his brush with death his own love seems to have increased. At any rate it now took on a new importance. For the moment soldiering was forgotten and only Marie Mancini mattered. When he went to convalesce at Compiègne and Fontainebleau he and Marie were inseparable. She lent him romances and poetry, which he actually read, something new for him. She mocked at her uncle Mazarin, and wanted Louis to act as master.

They knew they were courting danger and deliberately sought more danger. One evening in the forest of Fontainebleau they decided to picnic on a rocky pinnacle called the hermitage of Franchard. It was getting dark when Louis and Marie with another couple began climbing the steep sandstone precipice, "never attempted before by human beings," says Mademoiselle. When they reached the top, Louis called down for his violins, and the rest of the party was ordered to follow. Mademoiselle and the gentle Court ladies struggled up the rocks: "we ran a terrible risk of breaking arms and legs and even our necks." The evening ended with a flambeau-illuminated drive which accidentally set fire to part of the forest.

Meanwhile Mazarin watched. There could be no doubt now that the King was in love with his niece. A little encouragement and he would marry her. What glory that would be—to unite his nearest kin to the greatest monarch in the world! No higher honour existed save the papal tiara. It would be so easy to say yes; and according to Madame de Motteville Mazarin did actually suggest the marriage to Anne. The Queen quickly disillusioned him. "I do not believe that the King is capable of such baseness, but if he *were* to think of it, all France I warn you will revolt against you, and I will put myself at the head of the rebels to restrain my son." Mazarin immediately dropped the idea; and on reflection decided that Anne was right: Louis must marry as a King, for France.

Anne would have liked the Infanta of Spain as a daughter-in-law, but Philip seemed to have no wish either to sign peace or to give the Infanta's hand. Finally Mazarin said that they must be content with a second-best marriage. In October he proposed that Louis should travel to Lyon to meet his first cousin, Marguerite of Savoy. Savoy, though small, was the key to North Italy and her friendship would be valuable to France. Unless Louis positively disliked the princess, a marriage was to be arranged.

As usual Mazarin had reason on his side. Louis recognised this and made no protest. His attitude was that as long as he and Marie could be together he was content to live in the present. Preparations were made for the journey, and it is noteworthy that although Anne showed little desire for the marriage, Louis persuaded her to accompany him: he said that he wanted to be sure that *she* liked Marguerite.

On 26th October the Court set off for Lyon. Louis and Marie rode together beside the carriages: she in a velvet jacket of tragic black trimmed with fur and a velvet bonnet with immense black feathers. At Lyon both lodged in the Place de Bellecour, but in different houses. Marie's governess, Madame de Venelle, kept close watch on her ward's ground-floor room. One dark night, at Mazarin's orders, she groped her way to the bed to feel whether Marie was there. Accidentally she put her finger into the sleeping girl's mouth. In her fright Marie bit to the bone, and poor Madame de Venelle screamed.

Madame Royale—the Court title of the Duchess of Savoy—was a daughter of Henri IV: a showy, rather overwhelming widow who talked ceaselessly. With much fuss and fluttering she presented Marguerite to Louis.

"Well, my son?" Anne asked him afterwards.

"She is very small. But she has the prettiest figure in the world. Her complexion is rather . . ." he searched for the word, "rather olive. But that suits her. She has beautiful eyes. She's just the sort of girl I like."

Anne was pleased, but Marie drew Louis's attention to Marguerite's heavy Bourbon cheeks and not very pretty nose. "Aren't you ashamed that they should want you to have such a hideous wife?"

The days passed. Louis played games of hand-ball and spent the moonlit evenings with Marie. Mazarin began to discuss Marguerite's dowry with Madame Royale and let it be known throughout Europe that the marriage would soon take place. But all the time he was watching anxiously the road south-west to the Pyrenees.

Presently an envoy arrived along that road—a certain Don Antonio Pimentelli. Mazarin received him privately, then went straight to the Queen's bedroom.

"I have news for Your Majesty, unexpected news that will surprise her to the last degree."

"Does my brother the King offer the Infanta?"

"Yes, Madame, precisely that."

It was indeed a surprise—for all but Mazarin. He knew that recent losses had made Philip more inclined for such an alliance, but also that Philip was too proud and too conservative to take such an epoch-making step unless he received a shock. So Mazarin had announced and almost concluded a marriage he hoped would never take place. When he heard of the meeting in Lyon, Philip had cried, "That cannot and will not be": for if Savoy became a close ally of France the Hapsburgs in Italy would be isolated from

the Hapsburgs in Austria, and France could resume war against
Spain with a marked strategic advantage. He had sent Pimentelli
poste-haste to offer peace, and the Infanta.

Louis, in love with one girl, prepared to wed a second, was
now informed that politics demanded he should marry a third.
"He had the good sense to realise the infinite distance separating
the Infanta and the Princess Marguerite and did not hesitate a
moment to give his consent." Madame Royale wept, screamed
and even "beat her head against the wall." Mazarin gave her
diamond ear-rings and a casket of the jewels he knew so well how
to choose: these immediately stopped her tears. As for Marguerite,
she behaved with a self-control which was much admired. Her
brother the Duke proved more demonstrative: he did some stunt-
riding round the Place de Bellecour, jumped right over the fences
of the mall, and shouted as he galloped away: "Good-bye, France,
for ever; I leave you without regret."

Louis and his Court returned to Paris, where Mazarin began
the long business involved in uniting two traditional enemies.
Already hostilities had ceased, and in February, 1659 the Spanish
commander in the Netherlands, Anne's nephew, Don Juan of
Austria—a natural son of Philip IV and the actress Maria Calderon
—paid a courtesy visit to Louis. His suite included one of the
dwarfs so dear to the Spanish Court: a little woman with a squint
who dressed like a man, hair cut short and a sword at her belt. At
first Louis, who loved jesters and clowns, took a great fancy to
La Pitore. But she made so many pointed allusions to the Infanta's
charms and jokes at the Mazarinette's expense that Marie Mancini
protested. "I don't know how you can be amused by that fool.
She never stops insulting me." At once Louis took Marie's part,
began to dislike La Pitore and finally had her sent away.

From the summer of 1658 to the summer of 1659 Louis and
Marie were constantly together, and all that time their love was
growing. In little ways she had begun to influence him, for example
in her taste for drama. In the forest of Fontainebleau the hilt of his
sword happened to knock against Marie's hand. With a gesture
of anger Louis drew his sword from its scabbard and tossed it away
among the trees. And when she spoke of the future Louis declared:

"I will never marry the Infanta. You will be my Queen. If I want you, who can prevent it?"

He was forgetting Mazarin. In June the ever-watchful Cardinal decided to intervene. Too much was at stake—including the peace of Europe—to take any risks. Summoning his niece, he told her that she must leave Paris for Brouage, a sad little town on the salt flats three hundred miles away, and stay there until Louis had married the Infanta. She must leave at once, and she herself must tell Louis.

As soon as he heard the news Louis rushed to Mazarin. He found him with the Queen. A firm line was out of the question —Louis knew that reason was against him and that Marie, an orphan, had been given into Mazarin's sole charge—so he flung himself down in front of the Cardinal and begged for Marie's hand. "I would do anything to prevent her suffering. Monseigneur, I ask your permission to marry your niece."

Mazarin, now a complete convert to Anne's views, replied that he would rather kill Marie than allow such an indignity to the Crown, such a violation of the trust he held from Louis XIII to maintain the glory of France. Then Anne, moved by her son's grief, begged Mazarin to revoke Marie's exile. No, said Mazarin firmly, and while Louis fled in a fury of tears to the arms of Marie, the Cardinal reproached Anne for her weak suggestion.

"What do you expect?" replied the Queen. "In his place I would behave just as he is behaving."

It was clear now that Louis the King would have to go back on the promise given by Louis the young man in love. From the impoverished Henrietta Maria he bought a nine-strand necklace of perfectly matched pearls—he had to ask Mazarin for the money —and gave it to Marie to soften the bad news.

"I'll never have a chance to wear it," Marie said.

"You will wear it on your wedding day." He was still hoping for a reprieve.

They said good-bye in the Louvre courtyard, clinging to each other, while Marie sobbed weakly. It was a dramatic moment: Marie knew it and had her curtain line ready.

"You love me, you are King—you weep, and I must go."

Her words were overheard and remembered: eleven years

later they would inspire Racine to write the tragedy *Bérénice*. Then Marie threw herself into the waiting coach, sobbing, "Oh, I'm abandoned."

Louis was in despair. Every day he wrote by special messenger telling Marie how much he still loved her, while from the Spanish frontier Mazarin plied him with long eminently reasonable epistles, telling him to master his passion and be a great king, otherwise he—Mazarin—would be obliged to resign and retire with his family to some distant corner of Italy. Louis promised to comply but continued to write Marie passionate letters.

In July, while Mazarin and the Spanish Prime Minister negotiated the peace treaty and marriage contract, Louis, Anne and the Court began their journey south for the wedding. They stayed a night at Chambord with Gaston d'Orléans, now no longer a dangerous frondeur but a slightly ridiculous, old-fashioned figure. Louis had allowed his uncle to return to Court but treated him coolly. One evening, says Mademoiselle, Gaston went walking with Louis and Anne and "as the King almost never wears a hat, that embarrassed my father, who wasn't as young as the King, and was frightened of the evening dampness. The King and Queen let him go for a long time without telling him to put on his hat, even though he had put his gloves on his head as a hint of how worried he was lest he catch a chill." It was Louis's one small revenge for Monsieur's repeated acts of treason.

Marie, meanwhile, was studying astrology in Brouage with an Arab doctor, seeking to know her future, and with her sisters Marie-Anne and Hortense designing impossibly rich grey and silver uniforms for the family footmen. Mazarin had reduced her allowance and when in August she received a letter from Louis asking her to meet him on his way to Bayonne, all she could find to wear was a plain grey dress trimmed with lace.

On 13th August Louis and Marie met at the little cross-roads town of St. Jean d'Angély, while Mazarin wrote coldly: "You practise all imaginable expedients to heat your passion, whilst you are on the eve of marrying someone else: thus do you labour to make yourself the most miserable of men." They spent a last evening together, gazing into each other's eyes and letting their hands touch, still hoping against hope that they would be able to marry. As a parting present next morning Louis gave Marie a favourite puppy, Friponne, with a collar engraved "To Marie Mancini."

Marie returned to Brouage. Lonely, broken-hearted and in need of support, she looked about for someone who could be a real friend. Her choice fell on a lady she had known in Paris, one of the literary set with more common sense than most of the Précieuses: a certain Madame Scarron, later to take the name of Madame de Maintenon. But Madame Scarron replied that she was too poor to afford a move to Brouage; Marie had to face her grief alone—and worse still, when Louis's marriage agreement was signed, submit to the uncle on whom her future depended—"I have no other thought but to conform in everything to your ideas, and to follow absolutely everything that you command." The Cardinal wrote back recommending his niece to seek comfort, not as one might have supposed in St. François de Sales or one of the Italian saints—but in Seneca.

For five months, on a small island in the Bidassoa, Mazarin bargained with Don Luis de Haro, the Spanish Prime Minister. They conferred in a pavilion with two doors, two tables and two chairs, so arranged that the statesmen could carry on their business without either of them leaving his own country. Spain, after a hundred years' hegemony, was now "like a great old tree which has lost its branches and leaves and no longer affords shade." She still possessed a large Empire, the Spanish Netherlands, Naples and Sicily: was still closely linked with the powerful Hapsburgs of Austria—but these were like quarterings on a crumbling castle: her silver and gold squandered abroad on goods she could not manufacture herself, Spain was virtually bankrupt.

Mazarin knew this; Don Luis de Haro knew also, but refused to face up to the fact. Spain was great, somehow Spain would remain great. So that when Mazarin demanded that the Infanta should bring Louis the not unreasonable dowry of half a million gold écus ($£$500,000) the first instalment payable on the wedding day, Don Luis de Haro agreed, agreed also that France should be given some compensation if payment were not forthcoming. Now the Spanish Prime Minister had stipulated as a condition of the marriage that the Infanta, like Anne before her, should renounce all her rights over Spain and Spanish possessions. Mazarin therefore put forward this proposal: if the dowry were not paid, then the Infanta would retain these rights—he was thinking particularly of her rights over the Spanish Netherlands. But, Mazarin hurriedly added, of course the dowry would be paid. A precautionary clause to this effect was included in article two of the Treaty of the Pyrenees. When France signed the Treaty on 7th November, 1659, she found herself, after forty-one years, at peace with all her neighbours.

Philip IV, in the finest traditions of chivalry, had stipulated that Condé should be pardoned. Louis agreed and at Aix on 27th January, 1660, received his old enemy in audience. Condé knelt, head bowed, and declared that "he would like to buy back with the best part of his blood all the trouble he had caused inside and outside France."

Louis raised him up. "My cousin, after your former great services to the Crown, I intend to forget actions which have harmed only yourself"—"a pardon granted so proudly," said Condé later, "taught me that from now on I had a master."

Louis "talked with Condé about everything he had done in France and Flanders as agreeably as though it had all been done in his service." Then he reinstalled the Prince as Governor of Burgundy, while the office of Grand Master of France was allowed to pass to his heir, the Duc d'Enghien.

Far more difficult for his pride, Condé made his peace with the detested Mazarin, even calling himself "your servant"—"it was either that or withdrawing to one of my estates, and hunting hares." Then Louis visited and pacified the main towns of Provence, stamping out, particularly in Marseille, the last embers of the Fronde. In February news arrived of the death of Gaston d'Orléans, marking the end of the era of civil disturbances. At home as well as abroad France was now peaceful.

Louis's wedding was fixed for June, 1660. On the 6th he and his mother went to meet His Catholic Majesty Philip IV on the Island of Pheasants, neutral ground in the Bidassoa River. King

Philip had an oblong head, upturned moustaches and eyes that looked a foot above you. He was so stiff and pompous that he gave the impression of leaning backwards. He was a patron of the arts but a lazy ruler, oscillating between debauch and ostentatious piety. He was said to have laughed only three times in his life.

Anne, who had last seen her brother at the time of her own marriage forty-six years before, hurried to kiss him on the cheek, but Philip drew away and merely laid his hands on her arms. He and Louis then exchanged formal greetings, heard the articles of the Treaty read aloud and took an oath to observe them.

Anne's sisterly tenderness again broke through. Referring to the war, she said, "I believe Your Majesty will pardon me for having been so good a Frenchwoman; I owed it to the King my son, and to France."

"I esteem you for it," said Philip gravely. "The late Queen, my wife, did the same; for though she was French she had nothing in her soul but the interest of my kingdom and the desire to please me."

Louis seems to have found his uncle's pompous manner and Spanish etiquette in general very amusing. But he was now quite resigned to the marriage and impatient to glimpse his bride. So during a State reception he slipped into the hall incognito. From her seat on the dais the Infanta saw him, knew him at once, and blushed. Louis's brother, who sat beside her, stared at Louis in the entrance: "What does Your Highness think of that—door?"

Laughing, she replied, "That door seems to me extremely beautiful and very nice."

Louis stole a quick glance at the princess whom Velasquez has painted so memorably. He was put off by her old-fashioned clothes —a farthingale, narrow waist, and uncovered shoulders, as well as by her hair style—brow left bare, hair padded out at the sides and falling tassel-wise: all the same, Louis told the Prince de Conti, he thought he would be able to love her.

It was on the 9th in front of the altar of the little church of St. Jean de Luz that Louis had a first close look at his bride. She was the same age as he, twenty-one; she had a beautiful white skin and silver-blonde hair; she was a good deal less tall than he;

her eyes kind and rather shy. She wore "a royal mantle of purple velvet embroidered with fleurs de lys, under it a dress of white brocade covered with jewels, on her head a crown." And so the Bishop of Bayonne united in marriage Louis, the fourteenth of that name, King of France and Navarre, with his first cousin Maria Teresa, daughter of Philip IV, King of all the Spains.

As the day wore on and evening fell, Mazarin noted with satisfaction that not one penny of the half million écus had been paid. This meant that when Philip IV came to die France would be able to claim the Spanish Netherlands: a dowry worthy of his diplomatic skill!

After supper on the wedding day Louis rose early from the table and pointedly said good night to his mother and the courtiers. "It is too early," his bride said, turning with blushes to Anne. With tears in her eyes she was persuaded to go to her apartments, and there her mood changed. "Hurry, hurry," she told her maids, as they undressed her for the night. "The King is waiting for me."

Next morning Louis was seen to be unusually gay. "Never leave me for an instant," his bride begged him, and Louis gave orders to the controller of his household that they were not to be separated during the journey north.

The honeymoon began—with all the French Court in attendance. By slow stages they travelled across France and Marie Thérèse, as she was now called, came to know at the same time the King and his kingdom, at last enjoying the fruits of peace. By way of Bordeaux, Poitiers, Richelieu, Amboise, Chambord and Orléans they reached the castle of Vincennes, where they rested a month before their State entry to Paris on 26th August.

A monumental arch had been erected near the fateful Porte Saint-Antoine, and here Louis and his bride, enthroned, received the keys of their capital from the Provost of the merchants. Then the King mounted his Spanish bay, the Queen got into her golden coach and they began to make their way through the streets of Paris, lined with cheering crowds, the cobblestones spread with fresh flowers and herbs from which the passing wheels crushed out fragrance.

The Cardinal, suffering from gout and the stone, watched the colourful procession from a window of Madame de Beauvais's new house in the Rue François Miron. It was his hour of glory and even absent he dominated the scene. By far the most magnificent contingent, says the Venetian ambassador, was the Cardinal's suite, which headed the cavalcade; even the mules' harness was of solid silver and plated gold.

Two young poets in the crowd, La Fontaine and Racine, wrote verses to celebrate the arrival of Louis and his bride. Racine, only nineteen, had quite a lot of trouble with his ode, *La Nymphe de la Seine*. First Charles Perrault criticised the comparison of the new Queen to Venus, since that goddess, he observed, was nothing better than a prostitute. Then the ode was shown to Chapelain, a pedantic versifier of high reputation, who objected to "Tritons in the Seine"—Tritons being found only in salt water. Racine was obliged to re-write the entire stanza—"Several times I wished them all drowned for the trouble they gave me." But it was worth the revision: the ode was shown to the King, who made Racine a present of a hundred louis (£330).

The procession was also watched, from a balcony of the Hôtel de Beauvais, by Anne, now the Queen Mother, Henrietta Maria of England, her daughter Henriette, and other ladies of the Court and their friends, including that same Madame Scarron, later to become Madame de Maintenon, whom Marie Mancini had invited to share her exile. When the King's escort arrived opposite the balcony, Louis reined in his horse, took off his white plumed hat and bowed to Anne and the Cardinal. It was more than a gracious formality: he was saluting a mother whom he loved fondly, and thanking Mazarin for securing peace for France.

Madame Scarron watched and found herself captivated. Next day she wrote to a friend describing the King's graceful gesture—and the wording of her last phrase is highly revealing of Madame Scarron's character, considering how little choice Marie Thérèse had in her marriage—"I don't think anything more beautiful could be imagined, and the Queen must have gone to bed yesterday evening well pleased with the husband she has chosen."

CHAPTER 7

Annus Mirabilis

LOUIS WAS BROUGHT UP at a Court where the climate was one of extreme prudishness and affectation. In his grandfather's day the Court had been an exclusively man's world of oaths, duels and bawdy jokes. But about 1620 a reaction set in, when the half-Italian Marquise de Rambouillet decorated her salon in pale blue instead of the usual blood-red and gave parties at which ladies were present and treated as equals, bawdy jokes and army slang were banned, and points had to be made with epigrams, not with the sword. In the past forty years this reaction had grown to extravagant proportions. More and more perfectly decent words were banned as impolite, while the exquisites or Précieuses evolved a private, flowery, vague and virtually meaningless language full of historical allusions. Each exquisite took a special Greek or Roman name: Paris was called Athens, the Place Royale Place Dorique. By scented candlelight the exquisites read and discussed Mademoiselle de Scudéry's *Grand Cyrus*, in which Artamène (the Prince de Condé —but only initiates knew this) performed prodigious deeds through ten volumes for love of an intolerably prim and priggish princess. They became frightfully self-centred and, what was worse, very cold: loving their lovers without sex and pulling long faces if they had to sleep with their husbands.

To receive guests, the exquisite usually took to her bed, which was prepared in a ruelle or alcove. Each lady had at her disposal an admirer or "alcovist" who directed the conversation and was responsible for the instruction of neophytes. The exquisite, it was claimed, "is not born of a father or mother but secreted by the alcove as an oyster secretes the pearl."

All the best people were exquisites. On the death of a parrot belonging to Mélinthe (Madame du Plessis-Bellière) sonnets and elegies were composed by a score of important men and women, including Nicolas Fouquet, Superintendent of Finances. No one had ever thought such behaviour, or the exquisites themselves, ridiculous.

No one, that is, before Jean Poquelin, whose professional name was Molière. Louis had first watched and met Molière before his marriage, in 1658. The actor-playwright was then aged thirty-six: the son of a Parisian dealer in tapestries and house furnishings, after touring the provinces for thirteen years without much success, he had come to Paris where he and his troop performed Corneille's *Nicomède* in the guard-room of the Louvre before Louis and his Court. Molière played the leading part, speaking his lines with discretion, without much sound and fury. After the last curtain he did an unusual thing—walked on and made a short speech: "Since His Majesty had been so good as to suffer their country manners, he begged very humbly to be permitted to present one of the small diversions which had acquired him a certain reputation and with which he had been accustomed to amuse the provinces."

Molière then played *Le Docteur Amoureux*, a sketch composed by himself, which was pure farce, mostly grimace. Neither the sketch nor the actors pleased the Court, who reserved their applause for the actresses—among them Molière's red-haired mistress, Madeleine Béjart. At the end of the evening it was generally agreed that no more would be heard of Monsieur Jean Poquelin.

But the Court reckoned without their King. Louis knew a lot about the theatre: he had taken the lead in plays and ballets, not to say in every scene of the daily Court ceremonial. He had his own opinion about the evening's entertainment at the Louvre, different from the Court's, different also from Molière's. Molière prided himself on being a writer and actor of tragedies: in Avignon he had had himself painted by Mignard as Caesar in *La Mort de Pompée*, laurel-wreathed, wearing a toga, his full lips tight and solemn. But Louis realised, on the evidence of that one evening's performance in *Nicomède*, that Molière would never make an outstanding tragic actor—for one thing, he carried himself abominably.

On the other hand, Louis liked *Le Docteur Amoureux* and believed Molière had gifts as a comedian.

Louis backed up this opinion by immediately taking Molière and his troop under his protection, allowing them to share a theatre with Scaramouche and his Italian actors. Scaramouche would give plays on the three most profitable days of the week—Tuesdays, Fridays, Sundays—Molière on the other four. Their theatre, the Salle du Petit Bourbon, communicated with the Louvre and had once belonged to the Constable de Bourbon; Molière, entering his new quarters, could read the Constable's motto in big letters above the portal: "Espérance."

Four days after his state entry into Paris, Louis, his Queen and his Court went to see a comedy by his protégé, the still unknown Molière, entitled *Les Précieuses Ridicules*. Louis knew the play already, for after its first performance the previous winter a copy had been sent to him post-haste in the South of France: "an alcovist of quality had prohibited its further performance." Louis read the play, which was indeed a sensational work, but instead of banning it, as many people had expected him to do, he allowed its run to continue.

The plot of the play was simple: the two heroines reject with scorn the suitors who crudely propose marriage without the circumlocutions and preparatory adventures described in the Scudéry romances. The rejected suitors contrive that their valets, who are likewise inclined to ape their betters, shall visit the ladies in the guise of the Marquis de Mascarille and the Vicomte de Jodelet. The ladies are delighted by the extravagant language and exaggerated dress of their visitors, which they take for the height of fashion, and are correspondingly chagrined and humiliated when the impostors are exposed. But the sting lay chiefly in the language. The footman is called a "requisite," the looking-glass "a counsellor of the graces," the chairs "commodities of conversation," one of which extends its arms to the visitor who is begged to satisfy the longing it feels to embrace him.

Nothing like this had ever been seen on the stage; ordinary people, not types, in recognisable situations. It was scandalous, yes, but wonderfully funny. Outraged though they were, the

Court and exquisites found themselves applauding—like all Paris. Ménage, leaving the theatre, took his friend Chapelain by the arm. "Sir, yesterday we admired all the absurdities which have just been so delicately and sensibly criticised; but, in the words of St. Remi to Clovis, we must now burn what we have adored and adore what we have burned." This was no exaggeration. Esoteric allusions, pedantry, stilted speech began to give way to common sense; prudishness was no longer the highest virtue; elegant ladies shut up court and tried, for a change, to please their husbands. An era had ended. As for the tone of the new manners and literature, that would depend on the King. But already there were signs of a new realism, a new zest. Life in 1660, in the persons of the young King and Queen, was found to be good—surprisingly good—and worth enjoying.

Five days later *Les Précieuses Ridicules* was again performed in Mazarin's presence. The Cardinal's illness had now grown serious and as a mark of respect Louis stood throughout the performance behind his godfather's chair. Afterwards Louis made Molière a present of £1,000. The unusually high sum shows the King's satisfaction with his new comic playwright.

That winter Mazarin lived on milk, partridge, broth and opium pills. At St. Jean de Luz he had made secret arrangements for Spain to support his candidacy to the see of Rome when Alexander VII should die. But it was clear now that he would die before the Pope. Never mind, he had accomplished much: more of lasting value than any other French Prime Minister save Richelieu. He left to Louis a secure frontier on the south, to the east the frontier of the Rhine; only the north was still vulnerable. He had consolidated "the square enclosed field," as Richelieu had called France. One last agreeable irony: he had married Marie Mancini to Prince Colonna—head of the family his father had served as major-domo—and it was the Prince who considered himself honoured. The marriage, incidentally, was not to last; Marie became an addict of astrology and led a restless wandering life.

On 6th February, 1661, fire broke out in the Louvre and Mazarin had to be hurriedly moved to his castle of Vincennes. It was a foretaste of the end. Looking round his art treasures the

Cardinal was heard to sigh, "I must leave all this! I'll never see these things again." He toyed with his warblers and monkey, and he still gambled, weighing in his hand the louis he won, putting the lighter ones aside to stake again.

He began to worry about his fortune, some £20 million, much of it gained by dubious means. Would his enemies get the King to confiscate it? On the suggestion of one of his secretaries, Jean-Baptiste Colbert, he decided to make a gesture which, though risky, might well assure the undisputed succession of his heirs: he offered his entire fortune as a gift to Louis. For three days Louis hesitated whether or not to accept, while Mazarin murmured, "Ah, my family, my poor family, it will have no bread." But as Mazarin was aware, Louis liked to cap a magnanimous gesture with another no less magnanimous. Poor though he was, he declined his godfather's millions and with a new sense of security Mazarin drafted and signed a will in favour chiefly of his nieces.

Anne was constantly at the Cardinal's bedside, nursing, fussing, quietly bearing his impatient cry, "Woman, you'll be the death of me yet!" To Anne, to Condé, and to Turenne he gave a choice jewel from his famous collection. During his last days he repeated to Louis this advice: "Govern! Let the politician be a servant, never a master. . . . If you take the government into your own hands, you will do more in one day than a Minister cleverer than I in six months." In a whisper he commended Jean-Baptiste Colbert to the King and warned him against Nicolas Fouquet, the Super-intendent of Finances.

Mazarin died at the age of fifty-nine in the castle of Vincennes between 2 and 3 a.m. on 9th March, 1661. By strict tradition a King of France must never look on the face of death, and so before the end Louis was led from the room. When the news reached him, he broke into tears: he had lost his guide, a faithful Minister and his best friend. Perhaps the most important lesson he had learned from the Cardinal was one never mentioned openly: obedience. Right until the end he, the master, had submitted his will to Mazarin's, the humble servant. As he says in his Memoirs, despite their considerable differences of opinion, if he had gone against his Minister, he would have again aroused "the same storms which had been so difficult to calm." That is only part of the truth. Louis had been only too well aware how much he owed Mazarin, and of Mazarin's greater experience; they had been linked by a hundred shared dangers and secrets, as well as by a deep affection: according to the Venetian ambassador, Louis's "mind and soul were subordinated" to the Cardinal. Often he had hated Mazarin for making him do what was right, but the moments of hatred had passed. Only death or the passing of many years could have ended his "subordination."

But now release had come, "I felt my mind and courage soar," says Louis. "I felt quite another man. I discovered in myself qualities I had never suspected, and I joyfully rebuked myself for having been unaware of them so long. Like every reflective person I had suffered from timidity, especially when I had to speak at length in public, but this very soon disappeared. Only then did it seem to me that I was king, born to be king."

For two hours after Mazarin's death Louis shut himself up alone, then, while it was still dark, summoned his first Council in the silent castle. Only three Ministers were present: Michel Le Tellier, aged fifty-eight, Secretary for War, a prudent, simple-living administrator from a legal family; Hugues de Lionne, aged fifty, Acting Secretary for Foreign Affairs, a widely experienced diplomat and for twenty years Mazarin's right-hand man; Nicolas Fouquet, aged forty-six, Attorney-General and Superintendent of Finances, by birth a member of the high bourgeoisie, married in turn to two heiresses, a man of wealth and dazzling gifts. Fouquet in particular was known to expect that Louis would let his Council govern the country; in fact it was generally believed that while Louis had a taste for the theatre he had none at all for politics.

At this first Council urgent business only was transacted. Lionne drafted a letter to Louis's father-in-law reporting that Mazarin "died like a monk in his cell." "No," said Louis, "that phrase is too low. Write: 'He died full of religious feelings.'"

After the meeting, which lasted two hours, Louis returned to Paris and next morning called a second Council. In addition to Le Tellier, Lionne and Fouquet, it was attended by the seventy-two-year-old Chancellor, by the Comte de Brienne, the elderly Secretary for Foreign Affairs, by his son—Louis's boyhood friend—who had the right of succession to his father's post, and by two Secretaries of State.

Louis was heard to remark: *"La face du théâtre change."* And Brienne *fils* headed the minutes: *"Annus novus a regimine novo."* Turning to his Chancellor, Louis said, "I have summoned you with my Ministers and Secretaries of State to tell you that until now I have been quite willing to let my affairs be managed by the late Cardinal; in future I shall be my own Prime Minister." To everyone's astonishment he then forbade them to seal any agreement, to sign any dispatch or to pay any money without his knowledge and order.

The same day the Archbishop of Rouen had an audience. "Sire, I have the honour of presiding over the assembly of the clergy of your kingdom; Your Majesty ordered me to consult the Cardinal on all matters; he is now dead; to whom does Your Majesty wish that I should address myself in future?"

"To me."

Louis's personal reign had begun.

He found himself sole ruler of the largest people in Europe: eighteen million, against fourteen million in Russia, Austria's six and a half million, Spain's six million, England's five and a half million. His capital city, the largest in Europe, had 25,000 houses and a population of half a million. His frontiers were reasonably secure. Great nobles who had betrayed him—Condé, Turenne, Harcourt—were now among his most loyal courtiers. He himself was young, strong, happy and confident. At a glance all seemed well with France.

But Louis and his inner Council knew that nothing could be further from the truth. France was at one of its lowest points in history. Of those eighteen million French people the greater part could not speak or understand the French language: their talk was Breton, Languedoc, Flemish or one of a hundred dialects. On their wedding day only twenty-four per cent of the men and fourteen per cent of the women would be able to sign the contract. Although the vast majority were peasants, they did not have enough to eat. In 1660 it had been necessary to import corn and sell it cheap from royal granaries, even from the Louvre. Fields lay deep in thorn and bramble. During years of war houses had been damaged or destroyed, livestock requisitioned, vines cut down. More than eighty churches in Champagne and Picardy alone lay ruined. Civil war had bred countless disputes and law-suits: 70,000 men were reckoned to make a living from the courts. Theft and murder were rife, and in all Paris there were only sixty policemen. The army lacked discipline and cohesion; provincial governors treated their garrisons and strongholds as though these belonged to them, not to the King; judges and lawyers meddled in government, bishops were absentee and neglected their dioceses. For a generation practically no new buildings had been constructed, no new workshops, no new ships; industry stagnated, trade was at a standstill.

The Treasury was empty. The national debt in 1661 amounted to £143 million, while the King's revenues—the money for running the country—totalled only £71-2 million. But the revenues for 1661 and 1662 had been anticipated and spent, while even part of those for 1663 had gone the same way. In the first half of 1661 revenues from late 1663 were being used to cover ordinary expenses. France was virtually bankrupt.

Louis had seen for himself these figures translated into terms of human poverty and misery. For fourteen years he had been travelling in France and there were few regions he had not visited. But with Mazarin alive, clinging to every penny—he even sold the office of washerwoman in the Queen's household and pocketed the proceeds—he had been able to give no help to his impoverished people.

Now, however, he could act; he was in a position to help. One of Louis's first measures was to reduce the land tax for 1662 —the heaviest tax on the peasantry—by £1 million, and again in the autumn, after hail had damaged corn and grapes, by a further third of a million, making a total reduction of about ten per cent. To achieve this he disbanded 1,000 companies of infantry out of a total of 1,800, and 600 cornets of cavalry out of a total of 1,000. For Louis, who took such pride in his troops, these were cuts which hurt. Unnecessary expenses he kept to a minimum: for example, Christina of Sweden was dissuaded from paying yet another visit—the last had proved very costly—and payment was deferred on Mazarin's legacy to the Pope for a crusade against the Turk. The only supplementary expense Louis permitted himself this year was £1000 to buy gun-dogs in England.

The disorder in all departments of finance, compared in the previous reign to "a squid which ejects ink to hide its doings from those who seek to pry," had grown worse during years of war, when even the Crown jewels were in pawn to the unpaid Swiss Guard. The three things which most struck Louis when he took over personal control of his kingdom were France's poverty, its partial cause—financial disorder—and abuses in the administration of justice.

He at once decided that he would supervise these matters himself. So from nine to eleven each morning he worked with his inner Council—Fouquet, Le Tellier and Lionne; in the afternoon he dealt with finances for two or three hours. Every other day he consulted the Chancellor on judicial matters. No amusement whatsoever was allowed to interrupt this five to eight-hour working day.

1661 was Louis's *annus mirabilis*. In that year his personal life was no less rich in events than his public life. To start with, there was the problem of his brother. Two years younger than the King, Philippe had been a very pretty boy, gentle and dainty. He had liked dressing up as a girl and instead of rough sports such as fencing and hunting preferred to help the Court ladies sew new dresses. His mother had seen no harm in this, for a bold, self-assertive younger son might in time have attracted a new Fronde. However, as he grew older, Philippe's effeminacy became more pronounced. He was prettier than ever: not very tall, but with a long, well-formed face, dark complexion, small rosebud mouth and dark curly hair. He loved sweets, parties, gossip, jewels, fussy clothes and the tinkle of bells. At Dunkirk, while Louis lived with his troops, Philippe strolled along the sea-shore, splashing and being splashed by the maids-of-honour, and bought ribbons and cloth sent over from England. When Gaston d'Orléans died, Louis told Mademoiselle: "To-morrow you'll see my brother in a mourning-coat so long it trails on the ground. I think he's delighted by your father's death for that reason: his dignity would never have allowed him to wear such a garment for anybody else." Sure enough, next day Philippe appeared wearing an extravagantly long coat and, being a stickler for etiquette, even instructed Gaston's widow in the minutiae of mourning.

Louis accepted his chattering, effeminate brother for what he was—and loved him dearly. He and Mazarin had first thought of marrying Philippe to Mademoiselle, shortly after her return from exile and Louis's realisation that Mademoiselle was not the girl for him. For three months Philippe had courted her. Mademoiselle, with her usual clear-sightedness, recognised that Philippe would never "achieve distinction by great deeds." Since she could not love him as a hero, she tried to love him in another way, as a funny little fellow, gay and slightly mad, for she was attracted by men of this type. And so, when Philippe began wearing scent or returned from a masquerade dressed as a girl, she would tease and rile him. But Philippe, she discovered, did not like teasing: he was far too dignified to take a joke at his own expense. Poor Mademoiselle saw that they would never get on and sadly said good-bye to yet another royal marriage—her eighth.

Like an earlier Duc d'Anjou, the notorious Henri III, Philippe began to surround himself with coldly vicious *mignons* such as the Chevalier de Lorraine, "beautiful as an angel," and the Comte de Guiche. Louis and his mother, deeply concerned, again looked round for a suitable bride. Their choice fell on Queen Henrietta Maria's daughter, Henriette, whose second name, Anne, was a tribute to the Queen Mother.

Louis had always considered Henriette "a little girl": she was six years younger than he; very thin—he had once called her "the bones of the Holy Innocents"—and until recently very poor, living on the French Court's charity. Anne had already tried to marry her to the Duke of Savoy and to Monsieur de Florence (heir to the Grand Duchy of Tuscany), but both had refused this penniless sister of an exiled monarch. Then, in 1660, Charles regained his throne and Henriette was suddenly sought after and desired.

The marriage of Philippe, Duc d'Orléans, known at Court as

Monsieur, with Henriette-Anne took place on 1st April, 1661. La
Fontaine wrote:

> O couple aussi beau qu'heureux,
> Vous serez toujours aimables;
> Soyez toujours amoureux[1]

—but Philippe was amorous for exactly two weeks. When friends
began to pay more attention to his wife than to him, Philippe
pouted and shut himself up with his *mignons*.

That spring and summer the two young royal couples lived at
Fontainebleau. The Court had now taken the measure of their
new Queen. Very different from her adaptable mother-in-law,
Marie Thérèse remained Spanish through and through. She spoke
French awkwardly, with a heavy accent; she ate her own special
Spanish dishes: clove-scented chocolate from Mexico, brown soups
and gravies, garlic stews with nutmeg and capsicums, pale thick
pastries. She still bore the stamp of the dull, old-fashioned Spanish
Court, where the chief diversion was a drive in a dark, leather-
curtained carriage and the Queen went to bed at 8.30 after a thrilling
game of spillikins.

Marie Thérèse was judged definitely not pretty and—the Court
could be very cruel—so short as to be almost a dwarf. What a pity,
they whispered; Louis had always said he wanted to marry someone beautiful. Her simplicity was astonishing. One day she was
asked if she had ever thought of any young man at the Spanish
Court. "How could I possibly? There was no other king there
except the King my father." Lack of wit could be excused, but
Marie Thérèse brought to the Court a heavy Spanish piety: that
piety symbolised by the Escurial, a palace built in the form of St.
Laurence's gridiron. When not with her dogs and dwarfs she
would be found at Mass or Benediction or visiting the Spanish
Carmelite nuns in Rue de Bouloi. This piety jarred on the Court
and jarred on Louis. Already his mother's conversation, particularly
since the death of Mazarin, revolved round charitable works, the
dangers of Jansenism, the merits of this or that Court preacher,
the hollowness of worldly pleasures. Marie Thérèse, who came

---

[1] You are a good-looking, happy pair: we shall always love you; and may
you always love each other.

under Anne's influence, began to talk in the same vein. Louis, at twenty-two, decided he wanted more from life than that.

That summer Louis gave balls and ballets at Fontainebleau, and put on a new play by Molière, *L'Ecole des Maris.* The Queen was present, but could not really participate. She missed the allusions, the exchange of glances which marked the beginning of a new love-affair, the familiar tunes, each with memories—subtleties which Madame, for instance, Philippe's new, neglected wife, was quick to appreciate. Madame, in fact, was quite the most brilliant lady at Court—and the fact did not escape Louis. Without being beautiful, she was pretty—tall, "with a roses and jasmine complexion," blue eyes and chestnut hair. One shoulder was slightly higher than the other but with her graceful bearing she managed to carry off this little defect. What impressed people most was her charm—"you can't help loving her."

Louis began to pay his sister-in-law a great deal of attention. He found that she shared his love of the theatre and music—she sang well and played the spinet. She, too, found Molière funny. But she did not merely echo the King's thoughts: "rarest thing of all at Court, she had a mind of her own." Despite her poor health, she always seemed gay and sweet.

Anne noticed her son's interest in this other first cousin. He was still faithful to Marie Thérèse, but it was obvious to Anne that he was no longer in love with her. So, to distract him from Henriette, Anne decided to try to interest him in some other lady of the Court. Three were chosen: Mademoiselle de Pons, Mademoiselle de Chimerault and Mademoiselle de La Vallière. They wore specially fine heron plumes in their hair, were given seats near Louis at dinner and the theatre, and danced beside him in ballets.

It was June when Louis first became aware of Louise de La Vallière. She was seventeen, the daughter of a brave cavalry major belonging to the Touraine nobility, poor but ardently royalist: the mantel of their old manor was inscribed: "To the prince, like an altar fire, love undying." When Louise was eleven, her mother had re-married: her new husband, the Marquis de Saint Remi, was superintendent of Gaston d'Orléans's household in Blois, and there Louise had glimpsed the King on his way to his Spanish marriage. Later the family moved to Paris, and Louise had attracted the attention of Madame de Choisy, a witty society lady who corresponded with the Queens of Poland and Sweden and had once said to the young King: "Sire, if you want to become an interesting man, you must often come and talk with me"— advice which Louis duly followed. As Madame de Choisy wished to establish relations with the new Madame—now the rising star— she presented Louise, her protégée, and got her appointed maid-of-honour. Louise was so poor that her mother had to borrow in order to buy her Court dress.

She was fair, with blue eyes, very curly ash-blonde hair and a slight limp : a country girl, not a lady born to the Court, sincere, shy, "a violet." Her shyness appealed to Louis as something new: Marie Mancini had been bold, and Henriette too was sure of herself. He began to do just what Anne had hoped—to accompany Louise instead of Henriette to all the parties and outings. They went riding together. "No one can ride like her," wrote an Italian visitor to Paris. "I saw her once in the Tuileries Gardens bare-back upon an Arab horse; as it trotted she several times stood upright on the horse's back, with only a silk cord round its mouth as a bridle." They went for walks in the beautiful shaggy beech woods. During one of these walks it began to rain: the King sheltered Louise's blonde curls with his own hat and gave her his arm back to the château.

Very soon, within the first few days of meeting, they fell in love. But not all the Court guessed. One day Brienne *fils* told Louise that he would like to have her portrait done by Le Febvre, whom he had recently summoned from Venice. Le Febvre specialised in representing lords and ladies as gods and goddesses, or in the dress of their patron saints. Since her name was not a saint's name but a feminisation of Louis, Brienne went on to suggest that she be painted as Mary Magdalen. At this moment Louis happened to pass and Brienne began innocently to develop his plan by remarking to Louis on her beauty. "Isn't she the ideal Magdalen? She has something of a Greek statue." Louise blushed and Louis passed on without replying.

Brienne sensed he had made a gaffe and spent a sleepless night.

Next morning he was beckoned by the King into a room known as the Cabinet de Théagène et Chariclée. There Louis shut and bolted the door.

"Are you in love with her, Brienne?"

"With whom, Sire? Mademoiselle de La Vallière?"

"Yes, I'm speaking of her."

Brienne now made his second, even bigger gaffe. He declared righteously that he was a married man.

There was a long awkward silence. Then Louis fixed him with a look.

"Brienne, you're in love with her."

"Ah, Sire, she pleases you more than me," stammered Brienne. "It is you who loves her."

"No matter who it is I love or don't love," said Louis coldly, "let her portrait alone and I'll be pleased."

Brienne did as he was told. Not long afterwards Louise was painted as Diana, the artist adding an advancing figure of Acteon —he who had surprised Diana in her bath and was changed into a stag. "Poor Acteon, that was I," comments Brienne in his Memoirs.

Louis was determined that no one, not even intimate friends like Brienne should interfere in this love affair. "Of a more amorous disposition than anyone in his kingdom," he was filled with longing to love freely and fully. This would be the first time, for Marie Mancini had never been his mistress. There was no longer a Mazarin to direct his sentimental affairs. On the contrary, everything urged him to make a conquest of Louise. Most people at Court believed that a king had no obligation to remain faithful to a wife chosen merely for the good of the State. In fact it was held to be part of a king's glory to indulge in love affairs, and the stones of Fontainebleau were proudly carved with intertwined cyphers of royal lovers who had been happy there: Henri II and Diane de Poitiers, Henri IV and Gabrielle d'Estrées.

For two weeks Louis courted Louise. They rode in the beech woods or strolled in the Garden of Diana, listening to the fountain and feeding the carp in ponds surrounded by tall grass. Fontainebleau was the wildest and most romantic of the royal palaces, with old-fashioned gables and salons decorated with sensuous Italian paintings of pagan gods and goddesses. It was an ideal place for lovers.

More and more Louis appreciated his companion's sweet nature and sincerity. Her character is seen in her handwriting—tall, clear, flowing and upright. As everyone recognised, she loved the King for himself, not for self-advancement. In the evening they would picnic while the King's violins played sentimental tunes, glide on the lake, watch or dance Italian or Italian-style ballet. Most of the ballets were invitations to love and whenever possible topical allusions were added to the libretti.

In July, at the end of that fortnight, a gala ballet was given, translated from the Italian. It was called *Impatience*, and Louis took the leading role, dancing with his usual grace and verve. The theme was the King's impatience for glory: glory in battle ("Whoever takes the measure of the earth and me Will find the earth has far less majesty") and glory in love. As though to fan the flames of passion, the chorus sang:

> Courons ou tendent nos désirs;
> Il n'est pas toujours temps de gouter les plaisirs;
> On ne peut en avoir trop tôt la jouissance:
> Il faut presser pour estre heureux,
> Et l'amour est sans traits, et l'amour est sans feux
> Quand il est sans impatience.[1]

Next day in a room lent by the Comte de Saint-Aignan, First Gentleman of the Chamber, Louise de La Vallière became the King's mistress.

---

[1] Let us speed after our desires; there is only a short while for pleasure; enjoyment cannot come too soon; we must hurry if we are to be happy; love is tame, love is tepid when it lacks impatience.

CHAPTER 8

Fouquet's Challenge

LOUIS possessed the gift of being able to pass straight from pleasure to work and from work to pleasure "without difficulty or awkwardness." Throughout the spring and summer of 1661 he would break off a flirtation with Henriette and later with Louise and hurry away to hold a Council: his Ministers "could not realise that it was the same prince." They and the Court, however, believed that Louis's interest in politics would pall, that in three months he would appoint Nicolas Fouquet Prime Minister and leave the government to him, as he had left it to Mazarin. As for his present business, the Court supposed it was mere routine: directing ten ships against the pirates of Barbary, dismantling Nancy, fixing Turenne's salary as Maréchal-Général. They did not guess that Louis was locked in battle with the ablest and most ingenious man in France, that on the outcome of this battle the whole future of the country depended.

Nicolas Fouquet, at forty-five, had a lean, oval face, long black hair, a thin moustache, flashing dark eyes and attractive long eyelashes. Both his parents were remarkable—his father organised France's merchant marine and colonised the West Indies, while his mother had been one of Vincent de Paul's first helpers when he founded the Dames de la Charité. Despite indifferent health their second son had almost inexhaustible reserves of nervous energy. His interests were universal. He wrote Latin verses and argued philology with the Jesuits. He not only protected but suggested themes to La Fontaine, Pierre and Thomas Corneille and Pellisson. To his friend the invalid Scarron he sent pâté and cheeses. Through his brother he bought old masters in Rome, and himself sat to Sébastien Bourdon, Philippe de Champaigne and Le Brun. He collected prints, coins, statues and rare manuscripts. The Orientalists Vatier and Barthélemy d'Herbelot were in his pay. In Fouquet's laboratory at Saint-Mandé Pecquet studied the circulation of the lymph and blood. Fouquet himself was no mean historian and geographer, interested above all in what was curious and complicated. He took seriously his family motto: "*Quo non ascendet?*"—"To what heights will he not climb?" The brilliant devious Nicolas Fouquet wanted to know everything and to do everything.

At Richelieu's suggestion he had begun his career in Parlement, then held financial posts under Mazarin. In 1653 he became Super-intendent of Finances, ranking as a Minister. In 1656, when Mazarin had desperately needed money to pay a defeated and demoralised army at Valenciennes, Fouquet raised no less than £300,000 in four days from his family and friends, sending the silver in wagon loads to La Fère. Mazarin thanked him warmly: "I have spoken at length of your help to their Majesties, who are both agreed to set great store by a friend like you."

It was a period of grim inflation: royal dues, say from fishing rights, remained the same, but what the Crown had to buy— muskets, powder, rations—was steadily rising in price. Again and again in moments of crisis Mazarin turned to Fouquet for money, and always Fouquet found it. How? By charm, innumerable friendships and cunning. For example, it was illegal to borrow at interest of more than five and five-ninths per cent. Fouquet, however, would sometimes have to offer eight, twelve or even twenty per cent. To conceal the illegality, he would write down the capital as much larger than it really was, and to right the balance between receipts and expenses incorporate imaginary expenses in the Treasury registers: even this became unnecessary after 1654, when Treasury officials were no longer required to keep registers. Sometimes Fouquet himself made loans at high rates, thus adding to a fortune already considerable but never adequate to satisfy his ambitions, interests and taste for luxury.

Mazarin had suspected fraud and even thought of investigating. Through his spies Fouquet got wind of this and became alarmed:

by temperament he oscillated between boundless hope in his star and black despair. In 1657 and 1658 he drew up detailed plans for withdrawing to Belle Ile, off the Brittany coast, to escape imprisonment. Mazarin finally decided to let him off with a fright: an easy decision, for an official financial inquiry would have harmed the Cardinal no less than Fouquet. But on his death-bed he had warned the King.

On the day after Mazarin's death, Louis, heeding the warning, appointed Colbert as assistant to Fouquet. On the same day at a secret interview Colbert revealed to the King that Mazarin had concealed at Sedan, at Brissac, at La Fère and at Vincennes £5 million of ready money, that apparently his intention was not to leave it to heirs, and that therefore he intended it for the King. Something like £6 million was in fact found in all the places indicated. It was Mazarin's posthumous gift of help to his young pupil —for it meant that for a short while Louis could be independent, if necessary, of his Finance Minister. At the same time, the revealing of the hoard proved to Louis Colbert's honesty and loyalty. When Colbert said that he too was suspicious of Fouquet, Louis decided to set Colbert to watch the Superintendent.

Plainly it was vital that Fouquet should not guess that he was being watched. Fouquet's skill in foreign affairs was only equalled by that of Lionne, so during the first half of 1661 Louis honoured his Finance Minister by employing him in the two most important affairs of State: arranging a marriage between Charles II of England and the Infanta of Portugal, and supporting the Duc d'Enghien's candidature to the throne of Poland by the discreet use of over £1 million.

Every afternoon Fouquet gave Louis his account of expenses and income, and every evening Colbert and Louis tried to check them against the few figures which Colbert had been able to obtain with any degree of certainty. For in financial matters there was no order, everything was exceptional—a tip-off here, a commission there. "It was necessary," says Colbert, "to disentangle a system which the cleverest men in the kingdom, who had been elaborating it for forty years, had snarled up so as to make of finance a science that they alone knew and which would render them indispensable."

But Colbert, a patient, indefatigable worker, gradually collected sufficient figures to show conclusively that every afternoon Fouquet was handing the King falsified accounts.

Next day Louis spoke to Fouquet about the accounts in a general way, taking care to cite the figures given by Colbert. Surely the expense sheet was unusually large, and the income much smaller than Mazarin had anticipated? No, Sire, said Fouquet, looking the King in the eye; the accounts are in perfect order.

On several occasions Louis spoke to Fouquet about the accounts, giving him every chance to regularise them without having to admit downright dishonesty. Fouquet believed the King's perseverance in governing France would not last, and that even if it did the financial tangle was too complicated for anyone but himself to understand. Moreover, an admission now would remove his chief source of income for the future. So each time he persisted in lying. This duplicity on the part of one of the members of his inner Council was not only a glaring affront to the King, it amounted virtually to treason.

What did a king do in such circumstances? There were two main courses open. He could have Fouquet killed—as his father had had the Italian embezzler, Concini, run through with swords— or he could bow to the situation and comfort himself with the thought that practically no French king had ever been master of the coins that bore his image. But Louis was neither bloodthirsty nor easy-going; he rejected both courses and chose a third. Without giving any outward sign he decided about the beginning of May to try and bring Fouquet to justice before a court of law, as an example to all the Superintendent's many unidentifiable accomplices who believed in government by intrigue.

But was this course feasible? Was Fouquet too powerful to break? Was he already a younger, more daring, irreplaceable Mazarin? Most qualified people would have answered Yes. Writers, artists, Jesuits—all supported him. Book after book appeared dedicated to the munificent Fouquet, whom Corneille called a genius. He was backed by the many financiers whose fortunes he had helped to make. His sisters were all nuns, but his elder brother was Archbishop of Narbonne, another brother Chancellor of the King's Orders, another Grand Squire of the Petite Ecurie. His eldest daughter was married to the powerful Marquis de Charost, Armand de Béthune. Fouquet himself was a personal friend of the Queen Mother. He had recently fortified Belle Ile with fifty cannon, bought the title "Viceroy of America" from the Marquis de Feuguières for £30,000, acquired control of the whale-fishing Compagnie du Nord with its twenty-five armed vessels, had bought six warships from Holland and placed them under his flagship, *Le Grand Ecureuil*. Most important of all, Fouquet held the post of Attorney-General in the Paris Parlement: by attacking Fouquet Louis would be attacking Parlement and risked starting a new Fronde.

Everywhere Fouquet had allies and spies. Lionne, Acting Secretary for Foreign Affairs and, like Fouquet, fast-living, was practically in his pay. So was the friar who acted as Anne's confessor. Mademoiselle de Menneville, one of Anne's maids-of-honour, was Fouquet's mistress and supplied him with news in return for £50,000 which she used as a dowry to marry the Duc d'Amville. Madame de Beauvais also passed on palace secrets.

Despite Fouquet's power, wealth and friends, Louis decided to go through with his plan, try to bring his Minister to justice, and thereby make himself master in his own kingdom. He began by checking the rise of any more of Fouquet's friends. Although Fouquet tried hard to get the governorship of Touraine for his brother Gilles, the post was given to the Duc de Saint-Aignan. This was not the only straw in the wind. One of Colbert's clerks was heard to boast that his master would be the next Superintendent, while another clerk, drinking in a wine-shop, predicted that Fouquet's fall was imminent.

Fouquet disregarded the warnings. Perhaps he had a streak of perversity, perhaps he thought that now the King was in love with Louise de La Vallière he would soon devote himself wholly to pleasure and at once appoint a Prime Minister, perhaps he was carried away by the stupendous plans with which his brain teemed. Lying on his bed with the bed curtains tightly closed he would note them down by candlelight (he said that daylight always furnished matter for inattention): organising sardine fisheries at Belle Ile, his purchase of Sainte Lucie in the West Indies, schemes for exploiting Guadeloupe and Madagascar, endless plans for adding to his wealth. How could he fail or fall, he who saw the King daily, he who was known to his intimate friends as "The Future"?

Louis, on his side, was quietly drawing the net close. He and Colbert found an unexpected ally in the Duchesse de Chevreuse. This veteran intriguer, now aged sixty, had recently married a certain Monsieur de Laigne, who happened to be an enemy of Fouquet. Colbert profited from this to form a close friendship with his wife. The Duchesse, convinced that Colbert was a rising man —later she would marry a grandson to Colbert's daughter— promised to use her influence to help him.

On 27th June Anne the Queen Mother paid the Duchesse a visit in her lovely Renaissance château at Dampierre; there she met Colbert and Le Tellier, also one of the Intendant's allies. She heard from the Duchesse the extent of Fouquet's power and the scale on which he lived, far in excess of his private fortune; she also heard how he advanced his friends and relatives by means of public money. Colbert and Le Tellier added details. The Queen Mother's faith in Fouquet was seriously shaken—perhaps she remembered a quip by Christina of Sweden: observing that Anne could not afford to complete a certain building, Christina advised her to take over for a while the post of Superintendent.

Fouquet, warned of the Duchesse's intrigue by intimate friends, notably the writer Pellisson, hurried to Anne and made a scene. Hadn't he mortgaged all his possessions in 1656 and with wagon-loads of silver saved the Crown for her son? And now, on the word of Mazarin's inveterate enemy, would she turn against him? But Fouquet went too far. He remembered the Queen's sentimental attachment to dangerous days when the government had been in her hands, but he forgot her Spanish pride. Anne was outraged at being addressed in cutting language by one born a commoner. She dismissed Fouquet and refused to give him a second interview.

Fouquet was nothing if not versatile. Never mind: the Queen Mother had lost much of her former influence with the King; it was Louise de La Vallière who counted now. Fouquet knew that few women could resist his power, charm and good looks. A long list of gifted ladies, including a very pretty young widow called Madame de Sévigné, had felt the attraction of Fouquet's long dark lashes, and something mysterious in his over-bright eyes. No doubt this country lass from Touraine would join the list.

Already he had close relations with several of Louise's friends, notably Mademoiselle de Montalais. Despite warnings from a Court lady, Fouquet now approached one of these friends and made Louise an offer: let her speak well of Fouquet to the King and she shall have 20,000 pistoles (about £70,000). The offer was transmitted to Louise. With scorn in her voice she replied that not for quarter of a million pistoles would she commit such an indiscretion. Quickly Fouquet tried to calm Louise's suspicions by speaking to her in Madame's ante-chamber, extolling the King's merits, calling him the greatest prince in the world, the handsomest, the most lovable. But Fouquet saw with astonishment that Louise's pretty face did not soften. Far from it. Cutting him short, she left the room. That evening she complained to Louis that Fouquet had insulted her.

Fouquet had blundered but the blunder might have turned to his advantage, for no behaviour was more likely to infuriate Louis and make him act precipitately. A servant of the Crown daring to interfere in so intimate and delicate a relationship! Plotting to buy the girl the King loved with money embezzled from the King! But Mazarin's phrase "Time and I" was now part of Louis's inheritance: he managed to control his anger. It was he, the younger man—only half Fouquet's age—who coolly waited.

A few days later—some time during July—Fouquet tried to retrieve his blunders. He told Louis that he had a confession to make. In the time of Cardinal Mazarin, he said, certain irregularities had been allowed to creep into the finances. As a result, in order to pay off old debts, he had been obliged consistently to overspend. Unwilling to trouble the King with such details, he had made no mention of these expenses in his daily accounts. He realised now that this had been a mistake. It would not occur again and in future he promised to serve the King faithfully. Louis listened in silence, then replied with a few friendly words which Fouquet, on a wave of optimism, interpreted as a definitive pardon.

It was Louis who made the next move. It would be insufficient, he saw, to order Fouquet's immediate arrest; first he must get him to give up his post as Attorney-General, otherwise Fouquet could elect to stand trial before his friends in Parlement. At the beginning of August he told Fouquet that he intended to restrict the powers of Parlement still further, limiting them to certain clearly specified judicial matters. This would arouse protests, and he counted on Fouquet to help him. There was one little difficulty, however: Fouquet's post as Attorney-General: obviously as an official of Parlement he could not launch an attack on Parlement's privileges. Not a word more did Louis add.

Now it was known that Fouquet hoped to replace the ageing Séguier as Chancellor of France as a further step to becoming Prime Minister. So Louis caused hints to be dropped that Fouquet could not hold the posts of Chancellor and Attorney-General at the same time. Fouquet fell into the trap. On 12th August he sold his office to M. de Harlay for £450,000 and, hoping to consolidate the royal favour, made Louis a present of this sum. "All goes well," the King informed Colbert. "He is digging his own grave."

Fouquet rejoiced. Already he saw himself as both Chancellor and Superintendent: nothing done without his signature and seal, nothing paid for without the money which he alone knew how to raise. Believing himself at the point of supreme triumph, he decided to give a celebration to outdo all other celebrations. He would invite not only all his friends, but the Court, the Queen Mother and the King himself.

Fouquet possessed three houses, one in the Rue Croix des Petits Champs, one at Saint-Mandé, on the outskirts of Paris, and a country estate at Vaux-le-Vicomte, some thirty miles south-east of the capital. He had bought the land as a rich young man in 1641, partly for its view, partly because it carried ennoblement, and for fifteen years set aside large sums for a future palatial house. In 1656 he summoned the leading French architect, Louis Le Vau, and together they drew up plans (in all the arts Fouquet liked to understand and collaborate). The façade on the *cour d'honneur* was to be no less than seventy yards long; there would be a heavy central dome; there would be two wings at right angles to the main block. Le Vau wanted a mixture of stone and brick, but Fouquet decided on brick only. Building advanced quickly. Fouquet called in Le Brun to paint ceilings and wall-panels, and to design other decorations, including tapestries, for which a special factory was built nearby. He summoned Michel Anguier and Puget to make statuary, and Le Nôtre to design gardens and fountains. Hundreds of yards of lead piping was imported from England—at cut price, through Fouquet's friend Hervarth. Trees and bulbs were planted, and the house filled with cloth of gold, armchairs of Chinese plush, Persian carpets, vermilion and silver vases, porphyry and marble tables, crystal chandeliers and gold clocks.

Louis accepted the invitation to Vaux. On 17th August, 1661, he and his Court left Fontainebleau at 3 p.m. and towards six arrived at the wrought-iron fence in front of Vaux, its new gilt gleaming in the sun, its stone supports crowned by statues of Greek gods. Entering the gate, they drove between lawns flanked by stables and an orangery across a moat to the courtyard. Fouquet and his wife welcomed the royal family and accompanied them to their apartments.

When the King had taken a short rest, Fouquet invited him to the dining-room. Above the mantelpiece hung a graceful portrait, painted by Le Brun without the King's knowledge. Louis was shown seated on his *lit de justice* holding his regalia. At the bottom Love held back Rebellion; near the border was a small portrait of Henry IV: perhaps a gentle reminder to Louis that he would do well to continue to follow his grandfather's footsteps and make of his Superintendent-Chancellor a new Sully.

Louis made polite remarks about the portrait. It is yours, said Fouquet with a flourish, then led the King to the other side of the house, on to the terrace and down the main *allée*, between two hundred *jets d'eau* and fifty fountains, which seemed to form "two walls of water." Nothing like this had ever been seen before in France: it outdid even Tivoli and Frascati. When they reached the pool marking the end of the gardens Louis was invited to climb to the amphitheatre dominating the last cascade and admire a column twenty feet high, "as thick as a man's waist." Turning, he could see the palatial house, and brightly dressed Court ladies walking among the pools and flower-beds.

After a tour of the park—the Queen Mother rode in a light four-wheeled carriage, for she was growing stout and inclined to be short of breath—they returned to their apartments, where a light meal was served under the direction of Vatel, Fouquet's dazzlingly efficient *maitre d'hôtel*. The King ate off gold, the Court off silver—there were 500 dozen silver plates in Fouquet's cupboards—and all the while they marvelled at this country house which made the King's palaces seem like dim provincial manors. Their eyes turned to Le Brun's "Apotheosis of Hercules," crowned by the winged figure of Glory, to the mural in the Chambre des Muses, declaring in the veiled language of allegory that there was nothing so sublime but the merit of Fouquet would attain it. At every corner they noticed the speaking arms: a nimble squirrel on a field of silver, with the ambitious motto: *Quo non ascendet?*

Louis loved magnificent houses and graceful furniture. He appreciated better than most of his Court the astonishing beauty of Vaux, its sobriety of line, the clean straight perspectives of its garden, the vertical *jets d'eau* which added a new dimension. But he knew now beyond all doubt—Colbert had given him ample proof—that Vaux was a palace built on fraud, that the fortune it had cost was money stolen from an impoverished France and from him personally. He knew, for example, that one of Fouquet's favourite devices was to give, in payment for a contract, a paper promise, not cash; to negotiate that paper at a heavy discount; then to present the full bill for payment by the Treasury and to keep the difference. While he himself had had difficulty in raising a dowry of £13,000 for Madame, Fouquet and his accomplices would gamble away ten times that sum in one evening's play. Within his kingdom lay hidden another more powerful kingdom, in which Louis was an unimportant subject.

Several times that evening his anger flared up. "Madame," he said to his mother, "shall we make these people disgorge?" He felt like arresting Fouquet there and then, but Anne restrained him. "No, not in his own house, not at an entertainment he is giving for you."

An outdoor theatre, decorated with intertwined branches and lit with torches, stood at the end of an avenue of firs. Here Molière appeared in town clothes and with an apologetic air announced to the King that he was all alone, without his troop: there would have been no entertainment had not help arrived unexpectedly. At Molière's request, Louis then made a sign for the show to begin. Slowly a huge sea-shell opened and a naiad appeared: in the name of the King she ordered the statues to walk and the trees to speak, then withdrew, leaving the stage to fauns, satyrs and two deities, who danced a pastoral.

This was followed by Molière's new short farce, Les Fâcheux— The Bores, with ballet in the intermission. Anxious to keep an appointment with his lady, the hero of the farce is at every turn waylaid and interrupted by bores, including an amateur musician who insists on singing his tunes, a card-player who describes his latest game of piquet and a man determined to carry out a reform of Paris inn-signs. Despite his other preoccupations, Louis was delighted by the play and even drew Molière aside afterwards. "There is a real bore," he said, nodding towards one of the courtiers. "Why not add him to your play?" The courtier in question was Maximilien de Belleforière, Marquis de Soyecourt, a wealthy landowner from Picardy, a duellist, dancer, gallant lover, Epicurean and sceptic, who after a distinguished military career had been appointed Master of the King's Wardrobe. Soyecourt's passion was hunting—later Louis would appoint him Master of the Royal Hunt—and at every turn he would button-hole friends to talk about covers, hunting-horns, dogs and kennelmen. One of his sayings is famous. Sleeping one night with friends, Soyecourt went on and on telling hunting stories. Someone in the room said irritably: "Be quiet, you're preventing me from sleeping." Soyecourt turned mildly upon his censor: "I wasn't speaking to you."

Louis's suggestion fell on fertile ground. Molière decided to re-write The Bores and later actually asked Soyecourt for certain technical hunting terms. When Molière's revised version was performed and the hunting-bore Dorante came on, curiously enough Soyecourt did not recognise himself. Perhaps he was thinking up more stories.

After the performance of *The Bores* Vaux was lit by lanterns placed along the cornices, and fireworks were let off from the amphitheatre, some in the form of names and fleurs de lys. A boat shaped like a whale glided up the canal, releasing more fireworks, while trumpets and drums emphasised this battle of fire and water. A final extravaganza: as Louis made his way back to the house, thousands of rockets went off, so that he walked under a vault of fire. After a supper served to the music of twenty-four violins Louis and his Court thanked their host and hostess and said good-bye. On the drive back to Fontainebleau it was generally agreed that Fouquet's entertainment was one of the most splendid ever devised.

At the end of August Louis had to go to Nantes to preside over a meeting of the provincial assembly, the Estates of Brittany, and he decided that Nantes should be the scene of Fouquet's arrest. On 1st September he summoned to the Castle of Nantes a forty-year-old captain in the Company of Musketeers, Charles de Batz, Seigneur d'Artagnan, a younger son from Gascony known to be trustworthy and, furthermore, in debt to Colbert. D'Artagnan was ill in bed, but at once got up and took a sedan chair to the castle. Louis, seeing d'Artagnan trembling with fever, had to revise his plans: he said briefly that he had chosen the musketeer for a special mission, then sent him back to bed.

On Sunday, 4th September, Louis again summoned d'Artagnan and since there were other people in the room began asking him questions, rather loudly, about the musketeers. Presently he led d'Artagnan to a window and, dropping his voice to a whisper, told him to arrest Fouquet early next morning and escort him to the Castle of Angers. He must keep Fouquet in sight all the time and take care he did not destroy any papers. Le Tellier then led d'Artagnan into the next room and gave him the warrant with a thousand louis (£3,700) for expenses. After a glass of wine—for again he was shivering with fever—d'Artagnan hurried away to prepare his men.

If Fouquet were to learn that the musketeers had orders to be mounted early, he might grow suspicious and flee to his impregnable Belle Ile. To explain their presence, Louis announced that he would go hunting next morning, after holding his Council early. He sent Brienne with this information to Fouquet's lodgings, the Hôtel de Rougé. Brienne was received by Madame Fouquet, who with friends was watching scarlet-clad peasant girls from Belle Ile performing traditional dances. Her husband, she told Brienne, was ill and in bed. Brienne returned in the evening and found Fouquet somewhat better: he said he felt well enough to attend the Council and settled down to an evening's gambling. During the night he received a warning note from a friend, urging him to send his sedan-chair, curtains drawn, but empty, to the castle, and to leave Nantes by another route. Still buoyed up by his triumph at Vaux, Fouquet ignored the note.

At six next morning a detachment of mounted musketeers, in blue velvet surtout with silver cross, assembled near the Castle of Nantes, while two squadrons of twenty musketeers each patrolled the courtyard on foot. Presently the members of the Council began to arrive; Fouquet was one of the first. After a short meeting, Colbert, Lionne and Le Tellier left, but Louis detained Fouquet under various pretexts, pretending to look for papers, until he saw from the window that d'Artagnan was at his post.

Meanwhile Le Tellier approached Boucherat, who recorded Council Meetings for Parlement, and put in his hand a note, whispering, "Read quickly and obey." Boucherat hurried downstairs and opened the note: "The King orders you to go at once and affix seals at the house of M. le Surintendant." As Boucherat pocketed the paper, Fouquet passed, said good day to him and got into his sedan-chair.

D'Artagnan was pacing under the trees. His orders said that he must arrest Fouquet only when he had left the castle walls, not to infringe the rights of the captain of the bodyguard, whose job it was to police the royal residences. Catching sight of Le Tellier, he crossed to meet him and asked if his orders had been changed in any respect. No, said Le Tellier.

During d'Artagnan's moment of inattention, Fouquet's sedan

had disappeared. D'Artagnan ran to the courtyard in front of the castle; there he was told that Fouquet had already left the Council. Fearing he had missed him altogether, d'Artagnan sent his adjutant, Maupertuis, to tell the King, while he himself ran out of the castle with fifteen musketeers. To his relief he caught sight of the sedan in the Place de la Cathédrale; crowded round it were people soliciting favours from the powerful Minister. D'Artagnan pressed through, saying he had an urgent message. Fouquet got out and raised a hand to take off his hat. "Monsieur," said d'Artagnan, "I arrest you by the King's orders." Fouquet's hand fell. He asked to see the warrant and read it several times. "I thought I stood higher with the King than anyone in France," he murmured, then asked d'Artagnan to effect the arrest without any scandal.

When one of d'Artagnan's musketeers brought him the news, Louis entered the Salle des Gardiens, where all his courtiers were gathered, including Condé, Turenne and Villeroi. "I have had the Superintendent arrested," he announced. "It is time I looked after my own affairs. I decided on his arrest four months ago. I delayed until now so as to strike at the moment when he believed his fortune stood highest, and in the province where he prided himself on having most power and friends."

The news of Fouquet's arrest, less than a month after the reception at Vaux, took the Court by complete surprise. It was clear now to all that Louis had meant his words of six months ago: "I shall be my own Prime Minister"—words more revolutionary than they sound, because for fifty years, ever since Sully, favourites had ruled France. Noticing that Fouquet's close friend, Lionne, had turned pale, Louis reassured him: "You were among his friends, but I'm content with your services." Lionne then asked the King to allow Madame Fouquet to share her husband's arrest. No, said Louis, and ended with a warning against anyone who should aspire to Fouquet's place.

Some hours later Louis wrote to his mother, describing the scene: "As you can imagine, a good many people looked sheepish, but I'm glad they see I am not such a dupe as they thought, and that it's in their best interests to become attached to me."

Fouquet was tried in the Arsenal by a special court on charges of malversation and treason. Nine of the twenty-two judges voted for the death penalty, but Fouquet's innumerable friends used their influence to good effect, and the court's sentence was the relatively mild one of exile for life. To leave at large a man with Fouquet's character and record would have been an act of madness. Louis realised this and, exercising the royal prerogative, changed the sentence to life imprisonment in the Piedmontese fortress of Pignerol.

Fouquet's fall marked the end of government by a powerful Minister, of rule by intrigue and fraud, of the impulsive, unpredictable, partisan confusion which was the wreckage of years of civil war. Henceforward Louis himself would take all important decisions, financial as well as political. Instead of "groaning under the oppressive lash of a thousand tyrants," as he writes in his Memoirs, France would now thrive. For "nothing can so securely establish the happiness and tranquillity of country as the perfect combination of all authority in the single person of the Sovereign." And because there is a limit to the facts which any one man can master and hold in his mind, even with Louis's application and retentive memory, every feature of government, from raising taxes to raising armies, had to be simplified and organised according to a few clear rules. In this way, as a natural outgrowth of the monarchical system in a very large country, and not, as Louis supposed, by the deliberate application of certain principles, there began to be imposed on the government three qualities characteristic of the whole reign: order, regularity and unity.

CHAPTER 9

Louise de La Vallière

AS A YOUNG MAN Louis was strikingly handsome. He was above average height, broad-shouldered and muscular. At a masked ball he could be recognised by his legs, the shapeliest in the kingdom. His head was beautifully modelled. The powerful nose and cleft chin were softened by round cheeks and sensual lips. His brown eyes tapered at the sides, lending his expression just the slightest touch of mystery. His hair was abundant and from chestnut had become dark-brown. During his twenties he wore it long to his shoulders and also grew a light, slanting moustache. One evening when Anne lay ill and Louis, watching at her bedside, had fallen asleep, Madame de Motteville gazed at his face and found it so attractive "she hastily said her prayers."

His good looks helped to give Louis his air of authority and tremendous presence in public. He had only to enter a room and all the chattering courtiers fell instantly silent. There was a dignity and grace about all his movements, even the way he took off his hat to a lady. His usual expression was rather serious, but there was nothing solemn or pompous about him: indeed, he liked telling amusing stories, and told them neatly, with a light touch.

With the arrest of Fouquet Louis became master in his own kingdom, and in a new mood of carefree serenity returned to the arms of Louise de La Vallière. They made a well-matched couple, Louise with her blue eyes and ash-blonde hair, very slim, shy and inclined to blush; the King dark, tanned by outdoor sports and completely self-assured. During the autumn and winter of 1661 they seem to have been perfectly happy. Officially Louise was merely one of several maids-of-honour to Madame[1], unprotected,

[1] The Court name of Henriette, wife of Philippe d'Orléans.

a nobody; for the King to be alone with her without infringing Court etiquette was often hazardous and added excitement to their meetings. Only now and then did the Court glimpse the King's feelings. Once at a lottery party given by Anne he drew the main prize, a pair of bracelets set with diamonds. For a moment he sat still, looking round the company while a hundred titled beauties held their breath, then crossed the room and handed the bracelets to Louise. She admired their workmanship, then returned them with a deep curtsy, saying that they were very beautiful. "In that case, Mademoiselle, they are in hands too fair to resign them."

A little later Louise bought from her savings—she received £35 a year as maid-of-honour—a coat trimmed with fur, which she sent to Louis with a shy note. Was it for her to make presents to the King? Yes, he replied delightedly: "Because I possess your heart, all other possessions give me joy," and he wore the coat every day for a fortnight.

Their love affair was a pastoral. Whenever possible they went off riding or hunting in the green, wooded country of Ile de France. True daughter of an army officer, Louise was a crack pistol shot and extremely deft with the boar-spear. They were accompanied by a few close friends whom Louis allowed to wear a cloak of blue watered-silk, trimmed with gold and silver, like one which he himself often wore. Long plumes on their hats shaded the ladies' faces. "In their embroidered jackets," says Condé, "these Amazons are the most piquant in the world, particularly Mademoiselle de La Vallière."

Among the first to know that Louise was the King's mistress were two sophisticated intriguers. One was Anne-Constance de Montalais, a childhood friend of Louise's who had become a maid-of-honour to Madame; the other was Marie Mancini's elder sister, Olympe, "the Snipe," now Comtesse de Soissons. Both were envious of Louise, as well they might be: "Every single lady at Court has the ambition to become the King's mistress," writes Primi Visconti. "Many ladies, married or single, have told me that it is no offence either to husband, father or God to succeed in being loved by one's prince. So we must be indulgent for the King if

he succumbs, with so many devils around busy tempting him."
Anne-Constance and Olympe not only envied Louise; finding
that she would not wheedle favours for them from the King, they
began to lay plots against her. Their first plot aimed at dragging
her into a love affair between Madame and the Comte de
Guiche.

Armand de Gramont, Comte de Guiche, son of the Maréchal de
Gramont, was a cupid-faced, intelligent young Gascon, as insolent as
his father was suave. He had invented an involved kind of talk—
"if he leaves Memoirs it will be necessary to have them translated
into French," says Madame de Sévigné, who notes elsewhere that
she could converse with him only through an interpreter. He was
one of Monsieur's favourites, but publicly ridiculed his effeminate
protector and once kicked him on the backside at a Court ball.

During the winter of 1661-2 Madame was ill and confined to
her bed. De Guiche wrote her involved, affectionate letters three or
four times a day and once, disguised as a woman, paid her a visit
to the Tuileries. Their go-between was Anne-Constance de
Montalais. Madame enjoyed flirting and Anne for one had no
doubt that her friendship with de Guiche was quite innocent. But
de Guiche looked on it in a different way and his behaviour began
to cause scandal.

Louis, aware of what was happening in the Tuileries, forbade
his mistress to have anything to do with Anne-Constance de
Montalais: he knew she was a trouble-maker and had spied against
him for Fouquet. But for generations the La Vallières had been
known for loyalty, and Louise continued to see her childhood
friend, who now confided the secret of de Guiche's visit in disguise.
One day in the last week of February, the King questioned Louise
about her meeting with Anne-Constance. Louise would say nothing.
Louis grew angry, but still she refused to betray her secret. Unused
to being thwarted, Louis stormed furiously out of the room.

"They had often vowed that, whatever they might quarrel
about, they would never go to sleep without making it up, and
writing to one another." Yet the night came and passed with
never a word. Believing the King had not forgiven her and never
would, Louise fell into despair. At dawn she slipped out of the

Tuileries and hurried to the Visitandine convent at nearby Chaillot. There she sank down in the parlour, worn out with cold and misery.

Later the same morning Louis received the Spanish ambassador in a farewell audience at the Louvre. The stiff pattern of protocol —bowing, clicking of heels and kissing of hands—suddenly slackened as a name was whispered from group to group—the name of the King's mistress. What is it? the King demanded. Tell me. "La Vallière has taken the vows at Chaillot." Louis immediately left the Louvre, called for a horse and, hiding his face in a grey cloak, galloped to the convent. He found Louise still in the parlour, lying on the floor, sobbing. He lifted her up and comforted her, while she in a wave of tenderness and gratitude told him all that she had concealed. A carriage was called to take Louise back to Paris. There she and the King were seen to be more in love than ever.

The second plot was this. Olympe de Soissons persuaded the Marquis de Vardes to compose an anonymous letter to the Queen: "The King is throwing himself into a debauchery of which no one but Your Majesty is ignorant. Mademoiselle de La Vallière is the object of his love. It is for you to consider whether you can tolerate the thought of the King in the arms of another, or if you will put an end to a situation so humiliating to your dignity." This little piece of poison was translated into Spanish and slipped into a used envelope which Olympe had filched from the Queen's room. The letter arrived in the usual way with the post and was transmitted to the Queen's Spanish lady-in-waiting, Dona Molina. Fearing bad news of the King of Spain, who was ill, Dona Molina opened and read the letter. She was a sensible woman and devoted to the Queen; instead of shrieking or throwing the vapours she carried the letter to Anne, who ordered her to show it to the King as soon as he returned from the country. Louis read the letter and asked Dona Molina several times whether the Queen had seen it; then, reassured, he put it carefully into his pocket. He made inquiries and even, ironically enough, asked the advice of Vardes, but failed to discover who sent the letter.

It was the Queen Mother who took the next step against Louise.

During a visit to Metz she had been impressed by the sermons of a young abbé named Jacques-Bénigne Bossuet. A petit bourgeois from Dijon, Bossuet had already attracted attention at the age of sixteen by improvising a sermon one night at the Hôtel de Rambouillet on an unprepared subject, causing Voiture to remark: "I have never heard anyone preach so early or so late." Anne, recalling his sincerity and powerful arguments, summoned Bossuet, now aged thirty-four, to deliver the Lenten sermons in 1662. Anne chose his theme and in Ciceronian periods which hammered home the logic of his argument, Bossuet preached not like a tactful Court almoner but as he might have preached to the stolid bourgeois of Metz, urging an end to sin. One of his subjects was the Prodigal's return. While Louis sat fingering his rosary, Bossuet boomed from the pulpit: "Plunged by unlawful pleasure into an abyss of misery, it was through this misery itself that he found his way to the reality of happiness." It was all very galling. However, Louis recognised brilliant oratory when he heard it and after the first sermon was fair-minded enough to write in his own hand to Bossuet's magistrate father congratulating him on such a gifted son. But that year Louis did not perform his Easter duties. He was a man who knew what he wanted. For the moment he wanted Louise and no one, neither his mother nor Mother Church, was going to make him give her up.

By the end of 1662 the courtiers had come to accept the fact that Louise was the King's mistress and that it would be imprudent to try to dislodge her. There were, however, exceptions. One was the Duc de Mazarin, a brave soldier several times wounded, who carried prudishness to extraordinary lengths. For example, he forbade the women on his estates to milk cows lest they should get indecent thoughts and he mutilated many of the four hundred classical nude statues inherited from Cardinal Mazarin through his wife Hortense Mancini, explaining that the statues shocked his modesty.

One day the Duc de Mazarin stalked up to Louis, eyes burning with zeal. "Sire," he said, "the archangel Gabriel has commanded me to remonstrate with Your Majesty on the subject of his immoral relations with Mademoiselle de La Vallière."

In living memory no one had dared address a king of France in such terms, calling one of God's archangels to witness against God's representative on earth. There was a long painful silence; at last Louis managed to turn aside the affront.

"I always knew you were touched there," he replied dryly, fixing his eyes on the Marshal's battle-scarred brow and tapping his own.

More painful than the Marshal's prudishness were the Queen Mother's religious scruples. Louis knew how much his liaison hurt his mother, while her disapproval constantly clouded his happiness. For a long time they had avoided each other and if they met never spoke. The courtiers watched for some climax. On a certain morning Anne and Louis surprised each other in an otherwise empty salon. Would either begin a conversation? Louis strolled to the window, gazed out, returned, made a deep bow, and left. Anne could not hide her tears and ate no dinner that night. Later, as Dona Molina passed through her oratory, Anne looked up with red, swollen eyes and sighed. "Ah, Molina! These children!" Finally Anne's confessor stepped in with advice. She must humble her pride, he said, and speak first. When Anne did so, Louis answered that he often felt pain and shame—but, he added, in confessing his passion to God it became all the stronger; he could not resist it, and furthermore no longer had any desire to.

As for Marie Thérèse, Louis slept with her every night, took great pains to spare her feelings and saw that Louise treated her with scrupulous respect. When she bore him a son in 1661 he held her hand throughout her long and difficult labour. But Louis, who was so French in his admiration of subtle allusions and neat turns of phrase, felt more than ever distant from one who still said "servilliette" for "serviette," "Santa Bierga" for "Sainte Vierge," "eschevois" for "chevaux," who dressed in heavy, old-fashioned brocade and who believed naïvely whatever she was told. She had remained a child, an Infanta, unable to stimulate and hold a man's love.

In the autumn of 1664 Louis decided to take Louise with him to a house party given by Monsieur. Marie Thérèse was pregnant and had to stay behind at Vincennes. The night before he left

Louis found her bathed in tears in the oratory, where she spent half her waking hours. He took pity on her, tried to comfort her, saying he sympathised with her troubles, and finally gave a promise that he would settle down soon and be a model husband. How soon? Louis was twenty-six at the time. "When I am thirty," he said.

All this while Louis was steadily increasing his prestige as King. In June, 1662, to mark the birth of his heir he staged a carousel or tilting-match so lavish and memorable that it has given its name to the open space between the Louvre and Tuileries. Ten thousand spectators, including Louise, applauded a parade to music of five magnificently costumed groups of horsemen. There were Red Indians and Africans, turbaned Turks led by Condé and smooth Persians by Monsieur. Louis himself in orange-red, with matching plumes in his hat, headed the parade as King of the Romans.

King of the Romans was the title of the heir to the Empire. Mazarin's hope of getting Louis elected Emperor in 1657 had come to nothing, but the dream remained. Louis definitely saw himself as successor of the Roman Emperors. He also considered himself the ranking king in Europe. In a misguided moment more than a thousand years before, a Pope had said of the French crown, "that it is as much above other crowns as the King is above ordinary men." It was a remark that Frenchmen, Louis in particular, never forgot.

Already in one or two small ways Louis had managed to assert his authority abroad. For example, Monsieur d'Estrades, French ambassador to the Court of St. James, had recently driven out to meet the Swedish ambassador, who was making his official entry to London. On the way his coach was blocked by servants of the Spanish representative, the Baron de Vateville. D'Estrades, impatient at the delay, ordered his driver to go on, no matter how. At once the French and Spanish servants were fighting with fists, staves and swords. Vateville had the larger retinue and also gained the support of the French-hating mob; in a few minutes d'Estrades's forces were wounded or dispersed, his carriage horses killed and left lying in the traces.

All this was described in a letter to Louis and received the following week at Fontainebleau, just as the company was settling down to a game of ombre in Monsieur's firelit salon. Louis took the dispatches and withdrew to a nearby writing-table to look them over. In an instant he was up again, hitting the top so hard that the ink-well rattled, and striding to wave the papers at Saint-Aignan and Le Tellier.

"Here's news for you, gentlemen. Our ambassador in London has been publicly insulted by the Spanish envoy." He let them read. "What do you think of that, gentlemen? Should I wait to answer this insult from my father-in-law till my moustache is as long as his? No doubt he thinks we're still under Mazarin's thumb."

"I beg, Sire, that you consider the matter and do nothing in haste."

"M. Le Tellier, let my ambassador in Madrid leave the city at once and let the Spanish ambassador here leave Paris within twenty-four hours." Half-way down the room he wheeled and came back. "The conferences in Flanders are at an end, of course. And it should be made perfectly clear to Spain that unless the superiority of the French Crown is made known, publicly, she may hold herself prepared for war."

In due course Louis obliged the Spanish representative to apologise in the presence of thirty ambassadors or residents, while the French right to precedence over all save the Emperor's ambassador was assured. In case anyone should forget, Louis issued a medal to commemorate the event.

A somewhat similar incident took place in Rome in August, 1662, when servants of the French ambassador, the Duc de Créqui, exchanged insults and blows with some of the Pope's Corsican Guard. The entire Guard, encouraged it was later said by the Pope's own brother, surrounded Créqui's house and fired on the Duchesse as she got out of her carriage. A page was killed and several attendants wounded. Louis was furious. He demanded that the Pope disband his Corsican Guard, raise a pyramid in Rome bearing a full account of the crime and its expiation, surrender Avignon to the Crown of France, and send his nephew, Cardinal

Chigi, to Paris to read a full public apology. Such demands were unprecedented, but the Pope hastily met them.

These two successes were won not by empty threats or boastful names but by Louis as a person. Already the courts of Europe were beginning to form a picture of him: handsome, gifted, popular, self-assured, hard-working, majestic in all he did, and when they compared him with his two leading contemporaries, the pleasure-seeking Charles II of England and the Emperor Leopold of Austria, gaping-mouthed, mistrustful of himself and others, "whom his Ministers had to wind up every so often like a clock," there seemed some truth in Louis's claim to be the first king in Europe. Ambassadors were impressed by his strength of will and something commanding in his gaze which caused Racine to say that even if he had been born obscure people would have recognised him as a master. Here is an Italian traveller describing Louis at Mass in St. Germain l'Auxerrois: "My eyes met his only once. The moment I began to look at him I felt the secret power of the King's majesty and an insatiable curiosity to study it; but I found that I had to drop my eyes. Afterwards I dared to look at him only when I was sure he could not see me."

The sun image which had been intermittently applied to the King since childhood was found to be increasingly appropriate to Louis's personal majesty as a young man and to his growing prestige. Louis himself liked it. At the carousel his coat-of-arms depicted a sun piercing the clouds, with the motto *Ut vidi vici*, while other "kings" in the parade wore devices symbolising their dependence on the sun: a planet, for instance, and a sunflower. Many French kings had adopted a symbol—Louis XII a porcupine, François I a salamander, Henri II a crescent—and soon after the carousel Louis decided to follow their example. He took as his official symbol the sun. A certain Douvrier designed a medal showing the sun shining on the earth, with the motto *Nec Pluribus Impar*—"Not unequal to many." Louis liked the medal and made Douvrier a present of £1,000. Henceforth this was to be the official version of the sun image.

The motto was somewhat mysterious. As a savant pointed out, composed of two negatives, it possesses the beauty of antithesis and opposition, and while allowing many interpretations pinned all of them down to a particular image. Did the motto signify that Louis was powerful enough to govern several kingdoms, or merely to stand alone against several other kings? Or was there some other meaning? It was for Louis's life to make that plain.

In one minor respect the sun image was certainly appropriate, for Louis loved display. The first example was the carousel; the second, even more magnificent, was the outdoor fête which he gave in May, 1664, ostensibly in honour of his mother and the Queen, in reality for Louise, who six months before in utmost secrecy had given birth to a son by the King.

The fête, entitled *The Pleasures of the Enchanted Isle*, was held in the gardens of Louis XIII's brick hunting lodge at Versailles. It took as its theme Roger in the island and palace of the enchantress Alcina, from *Orlando Furioso*. It opened with a flourish of trumpets, and the appearance of the paladins of Charlemagne, led by Louis as Roger. The paladins were followed by a huge gilded chariot driven by Time, on which sat Apollo enthroned, having at his feet the Ages of Gold, Silver, Bronze and Iron. The chariot, drawn by four horses, was escorted by the Twelve Hours, the Signs of the Zodiac and a crowd of pages.

In the afternoon a running at the ring was held. Louise's brother, the Marquis de La Vallière, won first prize, a golden sword with a diamond-studded hilt. At dusk the six hundred guests watched a ballet danced to the music of violins. Then supper was announced by the seasons: Spring on a thoroughbred horse, Summer on an elephant, Autumn on a camel, Winter on a bear. Diana appeared, and Pan—played by Molière—each addressing a compliment in verse to the Queen. In the flickering light of four thousand torches supper was eaten under a clear sky.

On the second day Molière and his troupe gave a new play, *La Princesse d'Elide*, and on the third a spectacle was held on the Bassin d'Apollon. Alcina appeared in her barge on the enchanted lake, and addressed the two Queens in verse. When she waved her wand her enchanted palace stood glittering in lines of light. Alcina's subjects—demons, dwarfs and giants—danced a brilliant ballet, after which Roger (who on this occasion was not the King) appeared with other knights and prepared to storm the castle. Alcina rallied her subjects, but since Roger had the ring which destroyed enchantments, the palace vanished in a whirlwind of fire. In a final display of fireworks looping double L's lit up the night sky.

It was Louis himself who had chosen this extraordinary subject. Influenced partly by Mazarin and Marie Mancini, he still had a taste for romance, particularly Italianate romance. The libretto, music and décor of the fête, even the fireworks, were all by Italians. The allegorical figures—Diana, Pan and the rest—although believed to be classical, were in fact Italian. The fête was really a dream and a wish: a dream of a pagan world of gods and goddesses, and a wish that France, through her king and his link with Charlemagne, might somehow inherit the splendour of ancient Rome. A mainly classical education had given all at Court, including Louis, a distinct feeling of inferiority towards ancient Rome. Rome had produced so much, France so little, either in the way of art or beauty or grandeur. Go back only two hundred years and France was building Gothic cathedrals, atrocious and best forgotten. For Louis and all at Court classical Rome was at once a dream world and a powerful ideal. As such it lies at the root of much of Louis's behaviour.

In the fête Roger had triumphed and lived happily ever after. In real life Louis also lived happily, still deeply in love with Louise, still taking pains for the Queen's sake to preserve appearances. Like other young men in love he sometimes tried to express his feelings in verse. One morning he handed a madrigal to the Maréchal de Gramont. "Here is a poor piece of work. Now that people know I've taken a liking to poetry, they shower all kinds on me."

Gramont read the madrigal. "Your Majesty judges divinely well in everything. It is true that this is the most idiotic and ridiculous madrigal I have ever read."

Louis smiled. "Would you describe its author as a conceited ass?"

"Sire, there is no other word for him."

Louis began to laugh. "I wrote it."

Gramont looked horrified. "Sire . . . I've been guilty of treason. I read it hastily: if Your Majesty would let me see it again . . ."

"No, Monsieur le Maréchal," said Louis, laughing more than ever. "First impressions are always truest."

Under no illusions about his own talents as a poet, Louis was generous in recognising talent in others. The arts were to play a very important part in Louis's life, and these years of his love for Louise were particularly fruitful in ballets, operas, plays, verses and music which partly at least owed their inspiration to Louise: love seemed to foster the arts which in turn fostered love.

Although he seldom read books Louis had an intense admiration for good writing, and in 1662, soon after Mazarin's death allowed him to dispose of his revenues as he wished, he ordered Chapelain the poet to draw up a list of forty-five French and fifteen foreign writers and savants whose work merited financial reward. The first known list, dated 1664, includes Sainte-Marthe, Molière, the two Corneilles, Fléchier, Racine, Benserade, Quinault and Charles Perrault; Graziani, "well versed in letters and an excellent Italian poet," the historian Conrigius and Johannes Hevelius the astronomer. To each Louis sent an annual gift of gold coins in a silk purse, sometimes amounting to £1,000. French kings before Louis had patronised painters, architects and craftsmen: none had ever offered this consistent support to men of letters.

Louis, moreover, was continually on the look-out for new talent to reward, writing for instance in 1663 to Comminges, his agent in England, for a report on English authors (he was recommended "a Latin poet named Miltonius"): "My intention is to be informed of all that is best and exquisite in all countries and in all branches of knowledge." In the same year Louis founded the Petite Académie des Inscriptions et Médailles, to invent inscriptions and mottoes, to design commemorative medals, to describe and organise royal festivities, to superintend the composition of Court operas and ballets, to revise any prose and verse written in the King's honour. "I am sure you will achieve wonders," Louis told the four members, of whom Douvrier was one. "For my part I shall try to provide you with material worthy of your gifts."

This official patronage of the arts would have meant very little had not Louis personally helped and protected the artists with whom he came in touch. In his twenties Louis had three particular favourites: Molière, Jean-Baptiste Lully and Philippe Quinault. Louis was a good friend to Molière. In 1663 he did him the unprecedented honour of standing godfather to his first child, although gossips whispered that the child's mother, Armande Béjart, was the playwright's own step-daughter. Again when Molière ridiculed fainéant marquises in *La Critique de l'Ecole des Femmes*, Louis openly took his side against the Court. He allowed the first three acts of *Tartuffe* to be performed at the fête of the *Enchanted Isle*, though Church opposition obliged him to cancel the public performance in Paris because the play showed "so great a resemblance between those whom a sincere devotion put in the way of heaven and those whom a vain ostentation of good works did not prevent from achieving bad ones."

Jean-Baptiste Lully was the son of a Florentine miller, formerly in the service of Mademoiselle, and discovered by the Comte de Nogent, who hearing Lully play to the maids on the kitchen table with his violin, announced that Mademoiselle was harbouring Orpheus in her underworld. Young Lully was a passionate little fellow, with dark skin, full lips, short-sighted eyes and a broken nose—always up to pranks. Once in the Tuileries gardens Mademoiselle noticed an empty plinth and said she must think about putting a statue there. Next evening, walking in the garden with friends, she saw what seemed a statue of a naked shepherd playing the flute. She was asking who had granted her wish when "the statue" jumped to the ground and tootling on the flute ran down the avenue.

In 1655 Lully entered the King's service as a ballet dancer, and later became Master of the Music and composer of Court operas. He was dirty, untidy, coarse and a heavy drinker, later becoming totally debauched, but Louis, having once given his friendship, remained loyal to him, laughed at his jokes and overlooked the scandals. He exerted a considerable influence on the Florentine, developing in this "court jester" a sense of the grand, heroic and majestic.

Louis chose the libretti for Lully's operas from among the

works of Philippe Quinault, another artist from the working class —he was the son of a Paris baker—who owed his advancement to the King. The usual theme of Quinault's plays was one which specially appealed to Louis: the clash between love and duty. But love was expounded in long, eminently sensible speeches; passion was absent; as Boileau points out:

> Les héros chez Quinault parlent bien autrement,
> Et jusqu'à: Je vous hais, tout s'y dit tendrement.[1]

About 1661 Quinault bought the post of *valet de chambre du Roi*, which entitled him to make the top part of the King's bed, the bottom part being made by the *valet de chambre tapissier*, a post which Molière had inherited from his father. This sinecure brought a small steady income and allowed Quinault to be present for three months every year in the royal household. On one occasion Louis and a group of courtiers were playing a popular game, Love Questions, to which Louis invited Quinault to reply. Here are the questions, with Quinault's answers.

1. Does the presence of the beloved cause more joy than the marks of her indifference cause pain? Quinault thought yes.

2. Whether we should follow the dictates of the heart or the head? The heart.

3. Should one hate someone who pleases us too much when we cannot please her? Yes, but it would be difficult to do so.

4. Is it sweeter to love someone whose heart has already been pledged than one who is insensible? No.

5. Does the reward of being loved make up for the pain of not being loved? No.

The questions show the Court's interest in the psychology of love and, more generally, in passion—that passion which Louis told his mother "he could not resist"—for here was one aspect of man which eluded the Cartesian rules of order, regularity and reason.

Louis's interest in poetry, the theatre and opera during the years 1661-5 was equalled by his taste for building. A good king, he had been taught, must endow France with fine buildings, and it so

---

[1] Quinault's heroes speak quite differently,
   They even say "I hate you" in a kindly way.

happened that Louis had very definite ideas about what constituted beautiful architecture. His first important building was an addition to the Louvre. The square courtyard had been completed in 1659 and the architect, Louis Le Vau, had consciously worked in the now archaic style of Pierre Lescot, who had begun the courtyard under François I. What was needed now was a grand façade to the east. Informally, through the director of the French School in Rome, Louis invited Bernini to sketch plans. These were found to provide insufficient light to the apartments, while the proposed terraces and flat roofs would not have withstood the rain and snow of Paris. The plans were modified. Finally, in 1665, Louis invited Bernini to see the site for himself and discuss the building.

Bernini was sixty-six and the Piazza of St. Peter's had shown him to be the leading architect of his day. On the journey he was treated like a prince, with ice always ready to cool his drinks. He was a rather short man, with piercing eyes and ascetic features, and spoke in flowery baroque sentences. It soon became clear that he held very odd ideas. He would cut arguments short by appealing to what he considered an infallible authority, Michelangelo. "As Michelangelo Buonarroti used to say," was a phrase continually on his lips. Now leading French artists such as Chambray considered that Michelangelo had brought disorder into architecture by his startling innovations; his baroque contortions were disliked, "as though his only model had been a stevedore." Bernini soon had a violent quarrel with Charles Perrault, the poet, telling him that in artistic matters he was not worthy to wipe the dust from his shoes. This was true enough to hurt and the French Court grew rather cross.

Louis smoothed matters over by commissioning a bust from Bernini. On 21st June the Italian ordered three different blocks of marble and began work on all three simultaneously so that he could quickly decide which was most suitable. He was invited to visit Louis at Saint-Germain, where he spent a long time watching the King play tennis and made a number of sketches. Two days later he watched Louis at a Cabinet meeting. During a lull their eyes met and Bernini remarked:

"Sto rubando." ("I'm stealing from you.")

"Si, sua è per restituire" ("Yes, you must give it back"), Louis replied.

"Però per restituir meno del rubato" ("I'll give back less than I take"), laughed Bernini.

Louis got on well with Bernini, as he did with most artists. He sat thirteen times, generally for an hour in the early afternoon, so that the light was always the same. Bernini worked on one part of the face after another, directly on the marble—to the astonished admiration of French sculptors. On one occasion he remarked that Louis's eye-sockets were big, whereas the eyes themselves were small. From the very beginning Bernini compared Louis's head to that of Alexander the Great and was very pleased when a collector of coins, the Abbé of Saint-Germain, pointed out the close similarity between the bust of Louis and the head of Alexander on certain coins. Like others of his age, Bernini believed that antiquity had permanently and absolutely formulated certain ideals, to which modern artists had in the main to adhere. But the similarity may also have been dictated by Bernini's subject: the personal reign had only recently begun, Louis had achieved very little, and his chief title to fame was that he recalled Alexander.

Bernini noticed that one side of Louis's nose was slightly wider than the other. Louis, examining the bust, asked his brother in a whisper whether his nose was really misshapen. The Abbé Butti came to the rescue with the remark that it would of course be altered. Bernini said gruffly, "That's how *I* see the nose." However, he did make it less irregular at the last sitting.

All agreed that the bust had authority and movement. Bernini's allusion to Alexander was expressed by physical and psychological affinities, whereas French portraitists went in for more obvious allegories by means of external attributes. Louis himself had only one criticism—he would have liked to see his cravat polished—an accentuation of just that feature which Bernini wished to minimise.

Bernini the sculptor pleased Louis better than Bernini the architect, for the Italian had produced plans for a sweeping convex façade with columns. But even this called for Egyptian and Italian marble, and tall gesticulating statues above the line of the roof— a baroque Italianism which would jar with the rest of the Louvre and with the Gothic church of St Germain l'Auxerrois immediately opposite. Here was a dilemma. Bernini was too important to offend: on the other hand the Louvre was too important to spoil. Louis solved the problem like this. No promises had been made to the Italian, so Bernini was thanked, the foundation stone of a new façade laid with due pomp and a medal cast showing the façade exactly as planned by Bernini. While the Italian returned home with an annual pension of £2,000, a large gift of gold louis and a commission for a statue of the King on horseback, Louis quietly gave orders for the plans of the world's greatest architect to be replaced by those of a Frenchman. And what a Frenchman! A physician who spent his spare time dissecting camels. The established French architects threw up their hands in horror.

Claude Perrault was a brother of Charles Perrault the poet and assistant superintendent of royal buildings. He had spent ten years translating and annotating Vitruvius, had invented a catapult for throwing grenades and a system for stopping chimneys from smoking, but had never actually designed a building before Louis invited him to draw up plans for the east façade of the Louvre. He made a complete break with French architecture of the past century and a half, the keynote of which had been fantasy, several parts of varying height, bas-reliefs and steep roofs. Returning to the ideals of classical Rome, Perrault sought instead parallel lines, symmetry and above all unity. What he did at the Louvre was to frame a storied building with the façade of a Roman temple. His Colonnade set columns in pairs (an unusual feature in classical times—but Perrault was able to cite the Temple of Bacchus and the Arch of Pola), supporting heavy stone ceilings, so that the rather small columns had to be reinforced with iron. The Colonnade was no less different in style from the rest of the Louvre than Bernini's baroque, but it did not jar; it matched restraint with restraint. It was universally admired and marked the coming-of-age of French architecture. From now on Louis's architects would design their own buildings without calling on Italians or borrowing Italian ideas. They were now themselves in touch with classical sources.

The Louvre Colonnade still stands, while the ballets and fêtes,

Lully's music and Quinault's plays are hushed, and hushed too are the King's whispers and soft words to Louise: irretrievable as the looping double L's in the May sky. Yet it was the love affair which mattered most to Louis during these years 1661-5 and gave an impetus to the aesthetic achievements; the love affair belongs beside them, for with Louise as with the artists he helped, in the face of convention and sometimes of hostile intrigue, Louis chose and stood by the beauty he loved.

CHAPTER 10

The Rebuilding of France

WHILE THESE EVENTS WERE TAKING PLACE in his private life and in the arts, Louis was working an eight-hour day to rebuild his kingdom.

At the end of his life Mazarin is reputed to have said to Louis: "Sire, I owe you everything, but I believe I can repay some of my debt by giving you Colbert." The first words alone would be enough to prove the whole phrase a legend: as for Colbert, he was merely one of several able men in the department of finances. It was Louis who singled him out for his orderly mind, zest for work and incorruptible honesty.

Jean-Baptiste Colbert was forty-one when Louis in 1661 appointed him Intendant of Finances and assistant to Fouquet. The son of a Reims draper, he was stockily built with deep-set eyes and thick black eyebrows which made him seem fierce and scowling, though in fact he was just preoccupied and humourless. His temperament and manner were extremely cold. The witty Madame de Cornuel, after talking at Colbert for a time that seemed interminable, finally cried out in exasperation, "My lord, at least make me a sign that you are listening." He conserved all his energy for a ten- to fifteen-hour day. The only rest he took was to change from difficult to less difficult work, almost his only distraction collecting rare books. He never touched wine. He was known as "The North" or "man of marble."

Being a sound bourgeois from a traditionally royalist town, Colbert held that Louis was master of that part of his subjects' possessions necessary for the defence and aggrandisement of the State, that the dignity of France lay in the person of her King, and that her greatness should show itself in his house and style of living. He admired Louis tremendously and saw him as a rich, magnificent King, respected at home and abroad. He himself was cautious, conservative and self-effacing. He brought the administration of France clarity, exactitude, personal inspection, accounting techniques, orderliness, experimentation, and thoroughness in the formulation and presentation of information. From this information Louis, using "the common sense natural to kings", would formulate a programme first for rescuing France from bankruptcy, then for making her great.

The initial step was to find sufficient money for running the country. This was achieved not by increasing taxes—in fact, the chief tax on the poorer people, the *taille*, was reduced from £14 million in 1661 to an average of £12 million for the years 1662-72— but by reform: forcing financial officials to keep regular accounts, auctioning certain taxes instead of selling them privately to a favoured few, revising inventories and removing unauthorised exemptions (for example, in 1661 only a tenth of the income from the royal domain reached the King). Reform proved difficult, because the *taille* was levied by officers of the Crown who had purchased their post at a high price: punishment of abuses necessarily lowered the value of the post. Nevertheless, excellent results were achieved. In 1661 the receipts were £26 million, of which £10 million reached the Treasury. The expenditure was £18 million, leaving a deficit of £8 million. In 1667 the net receipts had risen to £20 million, while expenditure had fallen to £11 million, leaving a surplus of £9 million.

Why did expenditure fall? Because Louis himself kept a check on it. "His Majesty," writes Colbert, "sees or listens to every expense no less than six times: when he orders it verbally, when he signs the order, when he hears it read out in the monthly account, then again in the annual account; when he decrees payment from the royal treasury, and finally when he makes the payment law."

Part of the money saved Louis devoted to poor relief, notably at the Salpêtrière in Paris: his intention was that "everyone in my kingdom, even the most unfortunate, should have enough to eat, either by working for it or by regular State assistance." But most of the surplus was set aside in order, somehow, to make France prosperous.

The task was a formidable one. In 1661 the woollen industry, once thriving, had almost ceased to exist in Languedoc. The silk mills of Tours and Lyon were declining. Foundries, forges and tanneries had been almost abandoned. Nearly all luxury goods had to be imported. France's few exports—dairy products, wine and brandy—were virtually all carried in foreign ships. The result was an unfavourable balance of trade, the deficit running between £4 million and £2 million annually.

Both Louis and Colbert had been brought up to believe that prosperity meant the possession of large stocks of gold and silver. Their policy therefore was to prevent the outflow of these metals by making France self-supporting. France must manufacture everything she had hitherto imported. In short, she must become an industrial country—not in two or three generations, but now, at once, virtually overnight, for Louis was impatient for greatness.

At full speed Colbert, on Louis's orders, recruited cloth-makers and weavers from Flanders, metal workers from Germany, tar-makers from Scandinavia, lace-makers from Italy and Flanders, hatters, weavers and leather-workers from Spain, glass-workers from Italy, goldsmiths, steel-workers and stocking-makers from England, sugar refiners from Holland and Germany, master leather-workers from Russia, as well as innumerable other foreign artisans, and with the help of generous subsidies set them all to work in France. Louis took a personal interest in their welfare. "In order to establish the manufacture of tar in France," writes Colbert, "the King brought from Sweden a certain Elias Hal. This man, after three or four years' work, informed me of his desire to settle in France. His Majesty ordered me to take the trouble of arranging a marriage for him—he gave him 2,000 écus (£2,000) for use at his marriage and disposed 2,000 livres (£666) of appointments for him annually, which has always been regularly paid. I found a girl at Bordeaux who brought him a very honourable marriage."

Sometimes this recruitment ended badly: in 1666-7 two first-rate mirror-workers smuggled out of Venice by Colbert's orders to work in his new Paris mirror factory were poisoned by Italian agents. But generally the foreigners settled down, made money, expanded and engaged French apprentices. Their new products were carefully publicised: in 1666-8 Colbert had high-grade woollens brought from Carcassonne to Paris and distributed free to the Court. It is no exaggeration to say that during the first decade of Louis's personal reign an industrial revolution took place in France, not only in some cities and in a few trades, but across the whole country in virtually all known industries, as Colbert records with breathless pride in 1669:

London serge: 120 looms at Autun, Auxerre, Gournay: increasing and improving daily. Manufacture of English stockings established in more than thirty towns: 6000 looms. Needle-point lace: 6000 looms. Bouracans, at La Ferté-sous-Jouarre, 60 looms. Moquettes, *idem*, 12 looms. Damask at Meaux, 20 looms; Brussels camlets at Amiens. Dimities and fustians at Paris. Sheets, at Abbeville, 50 looms, Dieppe, Fécamp, Rouen, Sedan, Carcassonne. Brass at Bellencombre and Ferté-Alais. Cannon, weapons, tinplate and all kinds of iron manufactures, which came from Biscaye and Sweden, now established in Nivernais and Dauphiné. Saltpetre, gunpowder and matches everywhere. Holland cambrics at Moret, Laval, Louviers and le Bec. Sail-cloth at Vienne. Large anchors at Vienne and Rochefort. Jacks in Nivernais. Iron and brass, wire in Burgundy. Tar in Médoc, Provence and Dauphiné. Coarse cloth for ships in Auvergne. Masts in Provence, Vivarais, Dauphiné, Auvergne, Pyrénées. Glass for mirrors in Paris and Cherbourg, beginning to be exported. Looking for mines everywhere, in Languedoc, Rouergue, Foix, Roussillon, Auvergne, Normandy. Marble found in the Pyrénées, Provence, Languedoc, Boulonnais, Auvergne. Hemp bought in all the provinces, instead of being imported from Riga and Provence. Foundries established at Lyon, Toulon and Rochefort. Sugar-refineries established at Bordeaux, La Rochelle, Nantes, Rouen,

Dieppe and Dunkirk. Silk stockings at Lyon and the Château de Madrid. Crêpe at Lyon.

There follows a list of buildings under construction and then, no longer able to contain himself, at the bottom of the page this sober civil servant wrote with a flourish: Grandeur and Magnificence.

Just as he had freed himself from dependence on Fouquet or any other Minister, so in every field Louis determined to free France from dependence on foreign countries. In 1667 he doubled the tariff on all important foreign imports. To reduce the large sums spent on foreign, particularly English, horses, he established breeding studs in Normandy, Poitou, Berry and Languedoc. To conserve supplies of timber, he protected seventeen million acres of forest from indiscriminate felling. French Savonnerie carpets and Gobelins tapestries became so excellent that imports of these goods diminished to a trickle. In 1665 Frenchmen were encouraged to make new inventions by publication of the world's first scientific journal, the *Journal des Savants*, which specialised in new processes useful to industry. In the following year Louis founded the Academy of Sciences, to further the discoveries recently made by Bacon, Galileo, Kepler, and Newton. Louis paid such high salaries that foreigners like Huygens and Cassini joined the Academy and came to work in Paris. Particular progress was made in logarithms, the slide-rule and calculus, and as more and more natural phenomena were found to obey the laws of geometry and mechanics—that is, of regularity, measurable order and deduction from a few "obvious" axioms—so weight was added to the already strong opinion that human affairs should be regulated by just such laws.

While establishing industries and encouraging science, Louis made every effort to promote trade. One trouble was that French people considered trade demeaning: it was sufficient for one generation of a noble family to indulge in trade for the family to lose its title. A successful merchant would very rarely pass on his business to his sons, for his one desire was to buy land or an office carrying with it a title—and gracious living. For, says Molière's Bourgeois Gentilhomme, "when I mix with the nobility I am able to show off my taste and discernment." Colbert, true to his mercantile origins, combated this attitude by recommending Louis

to "receive with special marks of favour and protection all merchants who come to Court. Aid them in everything which con-
cerns their commerce. Permit them to appear in person before
Your Majesty's Council when they are involved in important
business." Louis did so and went still further: he decreed that
noblemen might engage in sea trade without forfeiting their titles.

Among Louis's other measures to facilitate trade were the
lowering of certain customs barriers between provinces, the construction of a 175-mile canal between the Atlantic and the Mediterranean (1662-82) and the improvement of roads by the establishment
of a commission for bridges and highways in 1669.

So much for the land of France. At sea the achievement was no
less striking. When Louis began his personal reign, out of a world
total of 20,000 ships, only 600 were French. The King at once
encouraged shipbuilding with a subsidy of almost £2 for every ton
of carrying capacity. As for the French navy, "For ten years not
more than two or three French war vessels had been seen on the
sea; all the naval arsenals empty; all the vessels reduced to twenty
or twenty-two; a number not even fit for action having almost
fallen to pieces, in part without seeing service; from such long lack
of employment the best sailors and an infinity of others gone into
foreign service." In 1661 in all the naval arsenals of France Duquesne
could not find a single mast to repay those given to a French ship
in distress by the Duke of York.

As though they did not already have enough to do, Louis and
Colbert determined to build a navy. They set aside £3 million
annually for this, buying masts in Savoy, copper for cannon in
Sweden, tar in Prussia and naval stores in Holland, while making
arrangements to produce these goods at home. Through his
brother, Colbert sought to secure one of the best English master
carpenters, and in 1669 he wrote to his cousin, Intendant of the
Marine at Rochefort, saying he hoped to engage a Dutch master
carpenter and forty assistants. It is typical of Colbert's thrift that
despite the large budget at his disposal he ordered the number of
naval salutes to be reduced to save powder.

Colbert gave orders that the lines and construction of the best
of each class of ship were to be studied and all defects noted; thereby

he sought to establish a general theory of ship construction, "so that by building a vessel according to set measurements, one might be certain that it would surpass in quality and in beauty all foreign ships." This ideal, so characteristic of the man and the reign in its trust of reason, remained unfulfilled; nonetheless the French flag-ship, *Le Royal Louis*, was a most palatial vessel, adorned with carved tritons, nymphs, sirens and sea-horses; paintings and designs by Le Brun, sculpture by Girardon, marquetry work in ivory, ebony and olive wood, ceilings in azure blue thickly strewn with gold stars, crowns and fleurs de lys, and murals of Apollo in pursuit of Daphne, landscapes and naval battles.

By 1667 France had fifty men-of-war; by 1671 more than a hundred. In the latter year Colbert wanted to devote more money to the navy than Louis was willing to spend. This led to a scene, and the resulting letter which Louis wrote to Colbert shows that although the Superintendent worked with Louis for twenty-two years and became important enough to marry three daughters to dukes, there was never any doubt about who took the decisions:

I was master enough of myself, the day before yesterday, to conceal from you the sorrow I felt at hearing a man whom I have overwhelmed with benefits talk to me in the fashion you did.

I have had a very friendly feeling toward you; it has appeared in what I have done. I still have such a feeling now, and I believe I am giving you real proof of it by telling you that I restrained myself for your sake, and that I did not wish to say to you myself what I am writing to you, so as not to give you an opportunity to displease me further.

It is the memory of the services that you have rendered me, and my friendship for you, which made me act as I did. Profit thereby, and do not risk vexing me again, because after I have heard your arguments and those of your colleagues, and have given my opinion on all your claims, I do not ever wish to hear further talk about it.

Now, if the Navy does not suit you, if it is not to your taste, if you would prefer something else, speak freely; but after a decision that I give you I wish no word of reply.

I am telling you my thoughts so that you may work on an assured basis, and so that you may not take false steps.

This is the only such letter from Louis to Colbert—one warning proved sufficient. It is interesting that Louis wrote his displeasure: he disliked criticising people to their faces. The "assured basis" is typical of the King: everything must be open and above-board, nothing left to chance or mood. As a result, Louis's relations with Colbert, as with his other ministers, were almost invariably cordial and harmonious.

Louis, King of France and Navarre, was also King of France's possessions overseas. In 1661 these included New France (Canada along the St. Lawrence), fourteen islands in the West Indies, and bases in France Orientale (Madagascar). This was a small empire compared with those of Spain, Portugal, England and Holland; moreover, England and Holland were expanding, as the Spanish Empire disintegrated. Louis decided to compete with these powers in the race for overseas bases and factories. Largely with his private money he set up a series of Companies, each having exclusive trading rights in a given area. The first was the Company of the East, established in 1663 to trade with Madagascar, Ceylon and India. Its efforts in Madagascar came to nothing, but it founded Surat and Masulipatam and acquired the land on which Pondicherry and Chandernagore were later built. The West India Company followed in 1664, the Company of Albouzême for trade with Morocco in 1665, the Company of the North in 1669, the Company of Levant in 1670, the Senegal Company in 1673. They were very much the King's own creations, and it was his will and exertions which kept them in being: overseas trade struck no chord in the French temperament and it proved difficult to attract shareholders. At a meeting of the East India Company held in the Tuileries in 1668 Louis remarked that he had examined the list of names of those who had given up their stock because they were unwilling "to risk some little sum" on an affair so important to the kingdom and so dear to its King. He would prefer, he said, not to remember these names, but "his memory was too good to forget them." Whereupon he himself subscribed a further £500,000.

Of all overseas enterprises, the West India Company was the most important. Its aim was to wrest industrial and commercial control of the French Indies from the Dutch and to a lesser degree from the English: in 1662 Colbert estimated that out of a total of 150 vessels which traded in the French Indies, three or four at most sailed from French ports, while the merchants of Flushing called the French planters "our planters." Louis began by forbidding the French islands to trade with any but French merchants. This rule proved difficult to enforce in one of the key islands, St. Christophe, where the French occupied the two extremities and the English the centre: it was only a matter of "one kick of the foot to roll a barrel of beef or a bale of cotton to the French, and another to roll a barrel of sugar in payment to the English." Despite such difficulties and the loss of five ships to English corsairs, as well as nine more in the war of 1666-7, the French Company, protected by French warships, gradually got its share of the Indies trade. In 1664 the Dutch had furnished France with almost all her sugar; by 1670 Colbert could write, "Foreigners no longer bring us sugar. We have begun in the last six weeks or two months to export it to them." The cycle of trade was this: French ships sailed to West Africa and bought slaves with French goods (the price of a male slave in 1670 was eighteen bars of iron). The slaves were carried to the Indies, where, fed on pea soup, cassava bread and Irish salt beef (subsidies were offered for the exportation of French beef, but supplies proved insufficient), they cultivated cane sugar, which was shipped to refineries in France.

The strictness of the French monopoly is apparent in the following decision. A group of refiners offered to take the rum and molasses of the French West Indies to Canada, provided they were allowed to dispose of the surplus in the English colonies of North America and bring back meat, live-stock and provisions, and that their goods be exempted from duty. The intendant recommended the plan to Colbert; he believed the English King would refuse to allow it, but the refiners assured him that "the English who dwell near Boston will not worry themselves about the prohibitions which the King of England may issue, because they hardly recognise his authority." Though the "proposal would have benefited the

Indies," Colbert rejected it. He believed, with Louis, that France and overseas France must live on their own resources.

The population of Canada in 1661, when Louis began to rule personally, was that of a large French village, stretched three hundred miles along the St. Lawrence, very poor but strong in religious zeal. It had three fortified settlements: Quebec, Three Rivers and Montreal; elsewhere Indian tribes such as the Iroquois swooped down in birch-bark canoes, burning log cabins and scalping missionaries. Economically, this first and largest of French colonies contributed almost nothing to France.

In 1663 Louis took the colony in hand, winding up the Company of New France and replacing it the following year by the Company of the West, with privileged rights of trade in West Africa, the West Indies, South America and—magnificent boast— "all New France, from Hudson's Bay to Virginia and Florida." The company's chief object was "the glory of God": it undertook to supply priests and "diligently to exclude all teachers of false doctrine." But Canada being deemed a country of "savages," the spiritual welfare of its people came under the direct care not of Louis but of the Pope, and the bishop in Canada remained until 1674 a vicar apostolic, directly responsible to Rome.

The first step was to increase Canada's population. Louis took immense pains over this, issuing many directives and writing innumerable letters. He sent out three hundred men annually to enter the services of colonists for three years at a fair wage and thereafter to become settlers themselves, and between 100 and 150 girls, called "the King's girls," chiefly from Normandy. They were shipped in charge of a matron paid by the King, and on arrival "these vestals were, so to speak, piled one on the other in three different halls, where the bridegrooms chose their brides as a butcher chooses his sheep out of the midst of the flock. There was wherewith to content the most fantastical in these three harems; for here were to be seen the tall and the short, the blonde and the brunette, the plump and the lean; everybody, in short, found a shoe to fit him. At the end of a fortnight not one was left. I am told that the plumpest were taken first, because it was thought they could resist the winter cold better. Those who wanted a wife applied to the directresses, to whom they were obliged to make known their possessions and means of livelihood before taking from one of the three classes the girl whom they found most to their liking. The marriage was concluded forthwith, with the help of a priest and a notary, and the next day the governor-general caused the couple to be presented with an ox, a cow, a pair of swine, a pair of fowls, two barrels of salted meat, and eleven crowns in money"—this dowry being paid for by the King. A girl was free to reject any applicant and her first question usually was, Did the suitor have a house and a farm? Later it was found that some of the girls had husbands in France, so Colbert ordered that each girl should obtain a certificate declaring her free to marry.

To stimulate the birth rate in Canada, a "King's gift" of £7 was given to each youth who married before twenty, and to each girl who married before sixteen. Families with ten living children, excluding those in religion, were given an annual pension of £100. Louis's conscientious intendant, Jean Talon, reported that Indian women impaired their fertility by nursing babies longer than necessary, "but," he added, "this obstacle to the speedy expansion of the colony can be overcome by a police regulation."

That Louis's efforts met with success is shown by the population figures: in 1666, 3,418; in 1667, 4,312; in 1668, 5,870. As a further step, Talon recommended that the regiment of Carignan-Salières, veterans of the Austrian war against the Turk, which had been sent out to curb the Mohawks, should be disbanded and encouraged to settle, on the Roman model: "The practice of that politic and martial people may, in my opinion, be wisely adopted in a country a thousand leagues distant from its monarch . . . [their purpose being] at once to hold the inhabitants to their duty within, and repel the enemy from without." Talon's plan was adopted but proved a mistake. The ex-soldiers "took to the woods," lived with Indian girls and eked out an often lawless existence as trappers.

Having increased the number of colonists, Louis set about encouraging them to work. A certain Hazeur constructs a saw-mill at Mal Bay. Finding a large stock of planks and timber on his hands, he begs the King to send two ships to carry them to France: and Louis obliges. One Riverin wishes to start a whale and cod fishery: Louis enters in considerable detail into his plans, ordering boats, harpooners and cordage to be sent to him, for which Riverin is to pay at his convenience. The Sieur Vitry wishes to begin a fishery of white porpoises, and begs the King to give him 2,000 lb. of cod-line and 2,000 lb. of one- and two-inch rope. Louis again obliges and later makes Vitry two gifts of £170. Subsidies are accorded shipbuilders, prospectors and tanners. The Sieur Follin is induced by the grant of a monopoly to begin making soap and potash. People are encouraged to grow hemp and to gather nettles for cordage, while in order to teach girls to weave and spin the Ursulines are supplied with free flax and wool.

Canada's chief wealth was the beaver. She supplied most of the skins used to make the smart beaver-skin hats worn by French gentlemen. Unfortunately until 1687 there was a glut of beaver-skins, partly because of a fashion for small hats, partly because of the hatters' practice of mixing rabbit fur with the beaver. Nevertheless, high profits could be made in this trade, with the result that the most energetic colonists led the wandering life of trappers.

Many trappers bought skins from the Indians in exchange for brandy. Canada spent no less than £33,000 annually on brandy and wine. When Talon in 1668 proposed to build a brewery, the abstemious Colbert approved the plan, not only on economic grounds, but because "the vice of drunkenness would thereafter cause no further scandal by reason of the cold nature of beer, the vapours whereof rarely deprive men of the use of their judgment." But brandy continued to be distilled and even imported. The Indians got drunk on it, and if refused it by the French, obtained it from the Dutch and English of New York—in return for beaver skins. This, ran one argument, lost the French money and turned the Indians' souls to heresy. The problem was referred to the King. Now Louis at heart was never a prohibitionist. Despite the Sorbonne, which pronounced the selling of brandy to Indians a mortal sin, and the Archbishop of Paris, whom he also consulted, Louis wrote to Saint-Vallier, Laval's successor in the bishopric: that the brandy trade was very useful to France, that it should be regulated but not prevented, that the consciences of his subjects must not be disturbed by denunciations of it as a sin, and that "it is well that you—the bishop—should take care that the zeal of the ecclesiastics is not excited by personal interests and passions."

Chiefly as a result of Louis's subsidies and supervision, Canada grew in numbers, prosperity and extent. Albanel penetrated to Hudson's Bay, and Saint-Lusson took possession in the King's name of the country of the Upper Lakes. The Iroquois and Mohawks were held in check. Important discoveries of iron were made, fisheries developed, and a useful trade established in beaver and moose-skins. All this was achieved with colonists naturally averse to leaving their mother country. The work involved for the King in Canada, as in his other colonial and commercial ventures, was simply enormous, and lends point to Louis's advice to his son: "Never forget that it is by work that a King rules."

By the end of his first decade of personal rule Louis, with Colbert's able assistance, had set his nearly bankrupt kingdom on a prosperous course. Mines, looms, foundries, mills and refineries were busy producing first-class goods. Toulon, Rochefort, Brest, Le Havre and Dunkirk, formerly deserted and in ruins, were now thriving ports, with new naval dockyards, from which colonists under the protection of the French flag departed for Canada, the West Indies, India and the coasts of Africa. Both at home and overseas had Louis put his kingdom to work, and laid the economic foundations for France's greatness.

CHAPTER II

Athénaïs de Montespan

THE KING as well as his kingdom changed during these first years of personal rule. By 1665, in his twenty-seventh year, Louis was a mature man. Politics, new challenges and a better knowledge of people had toughened him, strengthened his will and also added to his assurance. Like his subjects, he shared in France's prosperity; he had money to spend and was able to indulge a taste for finery starved in boyhood and early youth. Here he is reviewing a military parade:

His hair was tied with two wide flame-red ribbons to match his flame-red high-plumed hat. He wore a Venetian lace collar over a gorget of gold. His jerkin was of pale blue moire, the blue being almost completely hidden by gold and silver embroidery. Under the jerkin could be seen a knee-length coat of gold brocade fastened with gold braid inlaid with diamonds. His swordbelt was secured by two gold lilies each set with a large diamond. He wore fine woollen knee breeches, garters of flame-red ribbon embroidered with gold, snuff-coloured stockings, matching calfskin shoes and violet-enamelled spurs attached with gold buckles encrusted with diamonds.

Louis's courtiers, too, had more money and, since conditions were stable, felt more inclined to spend it. They wore satins and brocades, bought jewels and new carriages, they gave parties, they gambled for high stakes. Pleasure became the order of the day and Louis, who was responsible for the change, was eager to share in it.

The one important influence in the opposite direction was Anne the Queen Mother. She kept up her strict tone and could never resign herself to her son's affair with Louise. But Anne was now in her sixties, grey-haired, stout and short of breath. In the autumn of 1665 she fell seriously ill and was found to have cancer of the breast. Every possible remedy was tried, including poultices of hemlock water and relics of even the obscurest saints, but nothing could save her. Louis slept by her bedside until the last night; as she grew weaker he fainted and had to be carried from the room. Anne died on 20th January, 1666, and was buried in her third-Order habit, while her heart was placed in the church of Val de Grâce, which she had built to celebrate Louis's birth.

Louis had loved his mother deeply; they had been exceptionally close and united. He suffered from her death, but there is no doubt that as the weeks passed it appeared to him something of a release, for lately he had been finding her strict religious principles oppressive. She had cast a gloom on the Court's new pleasures, and on his own too. For Louis was now less inclined to dream, less naïve, more interested in Court life, in its witty conversation and sophisticated amusements.

In October, 1666, Louise de La Vallière gave birth to a third child, a daughter, in the Hôtel Brion, a little house bought for her by the King in the grounds of Madame's Palais Royal. As usual, in order to save the Queen's feelings and preserve Court decorum, a masked confidant hurried the child away to its foster-mother. While Louise was recovering, the King often visited her. Louise was a good needlewoman and sang well but she had no small talk. She could never think up those witty remarks which were beginning to amuse her royal lover, and so she arranged for the most sophisticated of her friends to be present, a young lady who could make the dullest subject piquant.

Athénaïs de Montespan was dark, with big blue eyes, aquiline nose, small red mouth, good teeth, lovely arms and a full but beautiful figure. She had been born twenty-six years before in the château de Lussac, in Poitou, the second daughter of Gabriel de Rochechouart, Duc de Mortemart, Prince de Tonnay-Charente, and of Diane de Granseigne, lady-in-waiting to Anne of Austria. She belonged to one of the two or three oldest families in France. Her high birth showed itself in her proud bearing, so different from the shy self-effacement of both Louise and Marie Thérèse. She had been married for three years now to a wild Gascon—Louis, Marquis de Montespan—and had two children. She was extravagant but not very well off—the Montespans' combined income amounted to a mere £7,500—and for the carnival of 1664 she had had to borrow in order to buy a costume: happily her role as sea-nymph required only the flimsiest dress. Shortly after becoming lady-in-waiting to the Queen she had said of La Vallière: "If something like that were to happen to me, I should hide for the rest of my life." Playing up to the Queen's piety soon became a habit. Since her husband was seldom at Court, she had a number of suitors, including the Marquis de La Fare and the seventeen-year-old Duc de Longueville, and every day at the *coucher* of the Queen (which Louis also attended) she would joke about them and repeat what they had said to her, to show the Queen her good behaviour and to make the King realise she thought only of him. But at first she had not pleased Louis. A few months earlier he had joked to his brother about her flirting: "She does what she can, but I don't want her."

"Don't want to want her," would probably be nearer the truth. To start with, Athénaïs was a new sort of woman for Louis: sophisticated, witty, sure of herself, voluptuous, experienced, one of those women who knew that the best shop for beauty spots was "A la Perle des Mouches" in Rue St. Denis and knew exactly how to place them: a *passionée* near the eye, a *baiseuse* at the corner of the mouth; knew the smart names for a lady's three petticoats: the *fripon*, the *modeste* and the *secret*; knew that for a perfect glove the skin must be prepared in Spain, cut in France and sewn in England, while its scent should be ambergris or musk. Then, again, she was ambitious, reckless and a heavy gambler; at the moment her ear-rings, each set with nine diamonds, were in pawn with a bourgeois of Place Maubert for £500. But what chiefly deterred Louis was the tiresome fact that Athénaïs was a married woman. The memory of his mother was still fresh, and fresh, too, the memory of the principles she had inculcated.

Athénaïs de Montespan was not in a hurry. Unlike Louise, she knew how to hide her feelings. Throughout October, 1666, she continued to see the King at the Hôtel Brion; to be gay and amusing. She had an imaginative turn of phrase peculiar to all the Mortemarts: an example has been preserved in a remark made by her brother, who was fat and ruddy complexioned, during a literary discussion with the King: "Reading affects the mind the way partridges affect my cheeks." Saint-Simon says that Madame de Montespan had such a genius for the *mot juste* that she seemed to speak a language all her own. This and her vivacious beauty Louis soon found to his taste. On 5th November a rumour circulated at Court that at last the King had "noticed" Louise's friend.

In May, 1667, Louis left Saint-Germain to spend the summer with his army. With him went the Queen and her ladies-in-waiting, including Madame de Montespan. Louise, who was expecting a third child in the autumn, the King persuaded to stay behind. As a parting present he created her a duchess. This gave Louise the right to cover the interior of her coach with scarlet cloth—though it could not be nailed in position, a favour reserved for children and grandchildren of the King—to wear a train three yards long and to sit in the presence of the Queen on a tabouret, a folding stool on an X-shaped support of gilded wood, covered with a flowered, tasselled tapestry. In a society regulated by precedence the rank of duchess was a distinct honour, but to Louise, who set small store by appearances, her new title gave little pleasure. She believed that she was losing her good looks and that the King was tiring of her. The title, she remarked, was like one of those presents given to a servant on retirement.

Part of that summer the King and Court spent at Avesnes, near the Netherlands border. Madame de Montespan lodged with Julie de Montausier, chief lady-in-waiting to the Queen, once the idol of the Précieuses in her beautiful house, the Hôtel de Rambouillet, and now, at sixty, still romantic and eager to help young lovers. Their room was on the first floor, near the King's apartment, which was guarded by a sentry. Soon, Mademoiselle noticed, this sentry was removed to the ground floor, while the King was seen to be "wonderfully gay." Marie Thérèse complained to Mademoiselle: "Last night it was four o'clock and almost daylight before the King came to bed. I don't know what he can have been doing." Louis overheard. "I was reading dispatches and writing replies."

He had fallen in love with Athénaïs de Montespan. His love for Louise had been idyllic, a pastoral; this was much more sensual. For Louis had a strongly sensual side to his nature: he loved gamey food, luxurious materials—Chinese filigree was a favourite—and heady flowers—he would crowd pots of jasmine into his room, so that he could enjoy their scent while lying in bed. It was to this side that Athénaïs de Montespan chiefly appealed. She for her part loved the King, but instead of throwing herself into his arms as Louise had done, she held back month after month for a year, knowing that she had everything to gain by making the King wait.

It was probably during the following summer of 1668 that Louis made Madame de Montespan his mistress, and love carnal replaced love idyllic. In July of that year, when Louis gave a fête for Madame de Montespan at Versailles, the ballet was entitled *Triumph of Bacchus*. This time romance and gentle allusion were absent; his new mistress preferred tangible things, objects that had money value: and so a new note crept in. The flowers and fruit were served in massive baskets of silver between silver candelabra, and even the orange trees stood in silver tubs.

In September the Court moved to Chambord, where Louise de La Vallière had lived as a young girl. On the glass of one of the windows François I had scratched a famous couplet—*Souvent femme varie, Mal habil qui s'y fie*.[1] It is said that Louise pointed it out to the King—a silent reproach—whereupon he had the pane removed. Whether the tradition is true ir not, it is certain that Louise did gently protest. Louis admitted that he loved Madame de Montespan, but said that he still felt a real affection for herself. Louise, on her side, was more than ever in love with the King and could not bear to be apart from him. This suited Louis well, for while his affair with Louise was now common knowledge, only the Court suspected his passion for the Montespan, and it would not do for the King of France to be judged guilty at home and abroad of a double adultery. So Louise and Madame de Montespan were

[1] Woman is often fickle, Foolish the man who trusts her.

given adjoining rooms, and a courtly euphemism was coined: "His Majesty has gone to join the ladies."

At the end of July, much to Louis's annoyance, Madame de Montespan's husband arrived in Paris. Though he did not get on with his wife, this wild young Gascon army officer had decided to make a fuss about her relations with Louis. One evening he showed Mademoiselle "a harangue to the King in which he quoted countless passages from Scripture, including the example of David and Bathsheba, finally exhorting His Majesty to give him back his wife and to fear God's judgment."

"You are mad," said Mademoiselle. "You mustn't spread stories like that. No one will believe you wrote the harangue. People will think it's your uncle, the Archbishop of Sens, who's on bad terms with Madame de Montespan."

Monsieur de Montespan agreed not to send the harangue but soon afterwards he burst into Julie de Montausier's apartment. "Procuress!" he cried, then stormed out, slamming the doors, while the poor woman took to her bed with the vapours. Next he arrived unannounced in his wife's bedroom at Saint-Germain, boxed her ears and again disappeared. A third time he burst in on his wife and Julie de Montausier together, making a terrible scene and reducing them both to tears. Rumours began to circulate that Monsieur de Montespan with the help of another eccentric Gascon, the Comte de Lauzun, was plotting to carry his wife off to Spain. Louis believed him quite capable of such recklessness or worse. Only last autumn Montespan had seduced a working-class girl in Perpignan, dressed her up as a man and given her a place in his company of light cavalry. At her family's request a bailiff rescued the girl and for safety lodged her in prison. Furious, Montespan had sent his cavalry at midnight to storm the bailiff's house, seized the bailiff and beat him up. So now at Louis's orders Montespan was arrested, imprisoned for a few weeks in For-l'Evêque, then banished to his estates. Only one of his misdemeanours was made public: "having disapproved His Majesty's choice of Monsieur de Montausier as governor of the Dauphin." When Montespan arrived at his castle of Bonnefont, he insisted on passing through the great doorway "because my horns are too high to pass through the small one," and in March, 1669, hearing that his wife had given birth to a child by Louis, he informed his friends of "the death of my wife from coquetry and ambition," invited them to a sham funeral and went into ostentatious mourning, draping his carriage with black. A few months later he and his cavalry were storming a convent to carry off a new sweetheart.

Rid of her tiresome husband, Athénaïs de Montespan settled down to enjoy the various pleasures of her new position. While Louise had loved the King for himself alone, Athénaïs loved him also for his power and wealth. She wheedled from him gifts of jewellery and money, with which she paid her debts and bought a fine house near the Louvre. She arranged for her father, the Duc de Mortemart, to be named governor of Paris, and her sister Gabrielle Abbess of Fontevrault, a very rich convent. She married her niece to the Duc de Nevers, and their Majesties attended the wedding. She had become the most envied woman at Court, a position she intended to retain. Continually she devised new ways of holding the King's love. Because Louis liked blonde hair better than brunette, she dyed her hair blonde. She even invented a new hair style: curls on each side to just below the ear, small curls on the brow, and a braid of hair around the head, entwined with ribbons and pearls. When it became the fashion, the Queen adopted it, explaining in her simple way without the least trace of irony: "I've cut my hair like this because the King likes it, not to steal your hair style."

It was Louise who curled her rival's hair, Louise who tied her ribbons: "Only her fingers were nimble enough." Everyone was very surprised by their friendship. When the King went to the Netherlands in 1670 to inspect fortifications, he drove in a coach with what the Flemings called "the three queens," while with deeper insight Madame de Sévigné wrote: "The Dew and the Torrent (La Vallière and Montespan) are linked by mutual confidence and every day they see the Fire and the Snow (the King and the Queen). This cannot last long without causing great disorder." But strange to say it did—for six years. At first Louise seems to have accepted her embarrassing position because she loved the King unselfishly: it was his happiness she wanted above all, even if another woman provided it. Perhaps, too, she hoped against hope that she would learn enough from her rival to regain his love. Then, in 1670, Louise fell seriously ill. Her mind turned to religion and a second time she fled to the convent of Chaillot, only to come back at the King's request. Thereafter for a long time she was torn between her love for the King and a call to the religious life. With Bossuet's help she began to strengthen her will, eating sparingly, wearing a hair-shirt and sleeping on the bare floor. By the spring of 1674 she felt strong enough to "tear herself away." She went to ask the King's permission.

Louis was no longer the romantic youth who had fallen in love with Louise thirteen years before. Even his appearance was different, for in 1673 he had started wearing a wig. He did not need one, for his dark brown hair was still abundant, but a wig, with its sweep of curls, was one more sign of gaiety and panache, the equivalent of a flourishing signature. As for Louise, she had lost her good looks, and her piety did not fit in with the King's present taste for the theatre, balls, fêtes and sumptuous outdoor suppers. The King said yes, she might leave.

In the first weeks of their love Louise had posed as Diana; now in a very different mood she had her portrait painted by Mignard with her son and daughter—Louis's children—to leave them as a souvenir. Her hand is shown pointing to the ground where lie a purse full of gold, some cards—with an ace of hearts turned up— some jewels in an open casket, a mask and a guitar: thus symbolising her rejection of play, frauds and disguises. She holds between her fingers a rose, whence the petals are falling. Two books are visible, the *Imitation* and the *Rule of St. Teresa*. At the base of a column is the inscription: *Sic transit gloria mundi*. All rather heavy, but Louise's vocation was genuine.

On 18th April Louise said good-bye to her friends at Court. She threw herself at the Queen's feet to ask forgiveness, saying, "My crimes were public, my repentance must be public too." That night she dined with Louis and Madame de Montespan. Next day after Mass she left in her duchess's coach with her children, and Louis's eyes were seen to fill with tears. She drove to the strictest and holiest convent in Paris, the Carmel in Rue Saint

Jacques, kissed her children good-bye and passed through a stone doorway, the door being locked after her. Again she knelt. "My mother, all my life I have misused my will; now I resign it into your hands for ever." Her lovely ash-blonde hair was cut off and a brown serge habit replaced her embroidered silk. For the rest of her long life she was to be Sister Louise de la Miséricorde.

Next day the Court left for Franche Comté. For the first stage they talked of the favourite's retirement; ten miles farther on, Louise was forgotten by everyone, probably even by the King. "After all," shrugged Mademoiselle, "she is not the first converted sinner."

With the departure of Louise, the King became more generous than ever to Madame de Montespan. In 1674 he wrote to Colbert from army headquarters: "Madame de Montespan is absolutely opposed to my giving her jewels; but so that she will not lack for them, I want you to have a nice little case made to hold what I am going to describe [sets of jewellery of every available precious stone], so that I can lend her when necessary whatever she wants. You will think this extraordinary, but she won't listen to reason on the subject of presents. . . ." The truth was that the Montespan declined small presents in order to obtain large ones. She wanted her own château, but when Mansart, at Louis's orders, drew up plans for a country house on the road to Saint-Germain, she dismissed them as too small: "good only for a chorus girl." Whereupon Louis gave her Clagny, which took ten years to build (1,200 workmen were at one time employed) and cost almost a million pounds. The Montespan's taste for luxury appears in the garden, planted with eight thousand jonquils, and in the farm, which was stocked, according to Madame de Sévigné, with "the most passionate turtle doves to be found, the fattest sows, the cows giving the highest yield of milk, sheep with the curliest wool, and the goosiest possible geese."

Everyone sought to please the King's beautiful mistress. One day her couturier arrived with a dress she had ordered. When she tried it on, it did not fit. She went into a towering rage, while the couturier made a show of being frightened. "Madame, as time is short, see if this other dress won't do." Out came "a dress of gold thread, embroidered with gold, edged with gold and on top brocaded in gold mingled with yet another thread of gold . . . the fairies must have made it in secret: no living soul ever saw such a dress." She called the King to see it. "Who could have had it made?" she wondered. "It must be Langlée," said Louis, naming a rich marquis who sometimes entertained the Montespan to supper. And so it was: Langlée had devised this surprise to get into her good graces.

As she entered her ninth year as *maîtresse en titre*, how, the Court wondered, did Athénaïs manage to keep the King so enslaved to her body? For, as the royal physicians noted, Louis tended to over-tire himself at night and often complained of dizziness and head-aches. True, she took lots of trouble, spending a fortune on clothes and cosmetics and overcoming a tendency to plumpness by being frictioned with perfume, naked on her bed, for two or three hours several times a week. Even so, she seemed to have some uncanny power of arousing the King's passion.

While Louis was with his armies in 1676, the Montespan and the Queen paid a visit to Sister Louise, now the convent sacristan. The Montespan tried to draw her out on the subject of the King, but Louise said she had no special message for him. To brighten things up a little, the Montespan held a lottery for the nuns—she had brought some small prizes with her. This naturally caused a sensation. After the lottery the Montespan announced that she was famished, and asked what there was for dinner. The nuns' menu did not appeal to her. She sent one of her suite to buy, for four pistoles, such things as butter and spices and cream: then with her white hands in the convent of the Grandes Carmélites she cooked herself a rich sauce, which she ate with a hearty appetite.

Grasping and even greedy the Montespan might be, but no one could deny her courage. She appeared at her best gambling for high stakes: boldness went well with her proud profile and flashing eyes. One Christmas Day she lost no less than £230,000 and won it all straight back by staking 150,000 pistoles (£500,000) on three cards. In February, 1678, when Louis went to tour his frontiers, she insisted on accompanying him, although five months pregnant. Despite four bouts of fever in a fortnight, she continued the journey, over bad roads, sometimes lodging in farms, and always managed to be gay. It was this kind of behaviour which won Louis's admiration. She also shared his interest in the navy, fitting out three vessels at her own expense, *L'Adroit*, *Le Hardi* and *Le Soleil d'Afrique*, the crews recruited from her own part of France, Poitou.

Her fame became world-wide. When an ambassador arrived from the African state of Ardres to propose an alliance, he gave a tiger, a panther and two lions to Louis, a golden pheasant and a Moorish dwarf to the Queen and a string of pearls, bracelets and a large sapphire to "the second wife of the King." The good African himself had three wives. Years later, "the Elector Frederick III of Brandenburg, a prince of marked conjugal fidelity, wishing to model himself on Louis, added to his establishment a lady who had the title and court functions, though not the pleasures of being his mistress."

Fame and the King's continuing love increased Madame de Montespan's natural haughtiness. "Courtiers took care not to pass under her windows, especially when the King was with her; they called it 'passing through heavy fire', and this expresssion became a proverb at Court. She spared no one, very often merely to amuse the King, and as she was exceedingly witty and amusing in a subtle way no ridicule was more effective or more damaging than hers. The Queen found it difficult to support her arrogance, so different from the tact and respect she had received from the Duchesse de La Vallière, whom she always liked, whereas of Madame de Montespan she was often heard to mutter: 'That slut will kill me yet.' "

Madame de Montespan was a healthy creature and bore Louis seven children: handsome children who usually flourished, whereas of the Queen's children all but one died. The Montespan's children were cared for by a young widow, Madame Scarron—known since 1675 as Madame de Maintenon—the same who had been too poor to join Marie Mancini in her days of sorrow, and who had so admired the King on his parade through Paris with Marie Thérèse. Louis would pay visits to the nursery incognito. When the wet-nurse brought in the youngest babies, Louis, making a joke out of the mystery, would say to one of the nurses, "But whose child is this?" and the simple countrywoman would reply, "I don't know, but by the care that is taken of them they must surely be the children of some great person, perhaps a Judge of the High Courts." This sent Louis and the Montespan into fits of laughter.

Louis was happy with his sophisticated, sensuous mistress, who was nearly always gay and witty. But when she was bearing children and, increasingly, at other times too, the King found himself attracted by other pretty faces at Court. More than most of his line he possessed the Bourbon temperament: only his grandfather, Henry IV, could be compared with him in indefatigible zest as a lover. And during his thirties Louis drove that temperament to the very limit. While continuing to sleep with the Queen and to give Madame de Montespan proof of his love, Louis had an affair with Mademoiselle des Oeillets, the daughter of an actress. Another of his passing mistresses was Anne de Rohan, Princesse de Soubise, a red-haired beauty with a delicate milky complexion (she lived on veal, chicken, salad and fruit), whose presents from Louis enabled her to build one of the loveliest houses in Paris, the Hôtel de Soubise. In 1677 Louis became infatuated with Mademoiselle de Ludres; after a while she fell from favour because of her airs (she made princesses and duchesses rise when she entered the room, allowing them to be seated only at a sign from her) and because of the Montespan's cattishness: "She has scurf all over her body," she told Louis, "the after-effects of poison given to her when she was a young girl." Quinault made an opera libretto of the two women's rivalry, based on the legend of Jupiter changing the nymph Isis into a cow to protect her from Juno's jealousy.

Having triumphed over Mademoiselle de Ludres, in 1679 the Montespan found she had a new rival in a certain Marie-Angélique de Fontanges. She was a blonde, aged eighteen, "beautiful as an angel and stupid as a basket." She too immediately gave herself airs, having her pearl-grey carriage drawn by eight horses and attending Mass on New Year's Day dressed in the same material as Louis, with the same pale blue ribbon as his grand Order of the Holy Spirit, which was considered very daring. She originated a hair style, as the Montespan had once done: when she was riding with the King, her hair became windswept; she quickly piled it on top of her head and knotted it with a ribbon, thus setting a fashion that was to last for twenty years. The Montespan again became jealous to the point of frenzy and made furious scenes, once "like a new Medea" threatening to tear Louis's children limb from limb before his very eyes. She also reproached Madame de Maintenon for planning her downfall. Louis tried to heal the breach between his mistress and the governess; he would say laughingly, "It is easier to make peace in Europe than between two women."

In the end, as usual, Madame de Montespan triumphed. After Mademoiselle de Fontanges had given birth to a still-born child, she was packed off to the convent of Port-Royal, where she soon fell fatally ill of pneumonia. When Louis went to see her, she thanked him with a curtain line: "I die happy, because my eyes have seen my King weep."

While Mademoiselle de Fontanges was still enjoying her short flight of glory, the Paris police arrested a number of people accused of poisoning. It looked a routine affair, but because certain aspects were rather unsavoury a special Commission was appointed to take evidence in secret at the Arsenal. No one at Court thought any more about the matter; they were busy discussing Thomas Corneille's amusing new comedy, *The Fortune-Teller*, when suddenly on 25th January, 1680, the Commission ordered the arrest of six leading lights at Court, including Olympe de Soissons—Mazarin's niece, who had been one of the first women to attract Louis as a young man—her friend the Marquise d'Alluye, a former mistress of Fouquet, Madame de Polignac and the Maréchal de Luxembourg. This bombshell was immediately followed by a second. Mesdames de Soissons and d'Alluye disappeared to the Low Countries, and Madame de Polignac to Auvergne. Madame de Soissons was suspected of having poisoned her husband in 1673; her flight was taken as an admission of guilt.

Chief among the accused was a middle-aged Paris woman known as La Voisin: her real name was Catherine Monvoisin. Clad in a robe of crimson velvet embroidered with golden two-

headed eagles, she told fortunes and promised success in love, providing clients with charms and love philtres, and even occasionally
with poisons to rid them of tiresome husbands. Although of low
birth she counted among her lovers a comte, a vicomte and an
architect, as well as the headsman of Paris, whose function it was
to burn women convicted of crimes such as hers. La Voisin herself
did not implicate anyone high-placed, but she was found guilty
and executed. After her execution her daughter gave evidence. In
July, 1680, she claimed that her mother's clients had included
Madame de Montespan.

Now this in itself was not compromising. Many people still
thought of God and the Devil as two complementary powers; if
novenas to St Antony of Padua and St Denis failed to "improve"
one's husband, then one had recourse to black magic. According
to Visconti, the Duchesse de Foix was believed to have petitioned
the Devil for bigger breasts, Madame de Vassé for more attractive
thighs, and other Court ladies for the position of mistress to the
King. However, La Voisin's daughter soon began to make very
serious charges against Madame de Montespan. The verbatim
transcript of her evidence no longer exists, but here is the summary made by La Reynie, the honest, painstaking Lieutenant of
Police:

From 1667 Madame de Montespan was in the hands of La
Voisin, who had already collaborated with Mariette [a priest
of St. Séverin, then aged twenty-eight] in making spells for
her, to win the King's good graces and to harm Mademoiselle de La Vallière. She had Mariette and other priests pass
certain love-powders under the chalice. Lesage [a fortune-
teller who specialised in answering messages addressed to the
Devil] came to Paris and stayed with Voisin. Believing him
capable of black magic she introduced him to Madame de
Montespan, and he promised to achieve what she wanted. La
Voisin, Lesage and Mariette, with others in the same business,
paid several visits to several different places for this purpose.
Lesage and Mariette quarrelled with La Voisin and left her
house; after that Montespan saw them elsewhere. Mariette
and Lesage went to Saint-Germain at the beginning of 1668

and among other things they did was to go to the room of
Madame de Thianges [the sister of Madame de Montespan]
where Mariette, wearing his surplice and stole, sprinkled
holy water and said the gospel of the Kings on Montespan's
head while Lesage burned incense and Montespan recited a
spell written for her by Lesage and Mariette; the King's
name was in the spell, also that of Madame de Montespan
and Mademoiselle de La Vallière. [This spell has not been
preserved but another spell cited in the trial invokes Astaroth
and Asmodeus, Princes of Friendship.] The purpose of the
spell was to obtain the good graces of the King and to make
Mademoiselle de La Vallière die, though Mariette says it
was only to make her go away. Montespan then gave them,
at Saint-Germain, two pigeons' hearts for which they had
asked; these two hearts were given to Mariette so that he
could say Mass over them and pass them under the chalice.
This Mass on the two hearts was said by Mariette in a
chapel of the church of St. Séverin, and Madame de Montespan was present. Lesage said that the pigeons' hearts were
put under the chalice, while Mariette denied this and
claimed that he had merely put them in his pocket while
saying Mass.

After the Mass, Madame de Montespan went to Mariette's
room, where he repeated the ceremonies and spells performed at Saint-Germain. The same ceremonies and spells
were repeated two or three times in the same place. Lesage
says that he added other ceremonies with human bones, to
procure Mademoiselle de La Vallière's death, while Mariette
denies that and says that Montespan did not ask him to procure Vallière's death, only to make her go away. After all
these ceremonies, on Montespan's last visit to Mariette's
room, he and Lesage, in Montespan's presence, placed in a
little gilt vermilion box specially brought by her the two
pigeons' hearts given them at Saint-Germain for the Mass
said in St. Séverin, the written spell, the gospel of the Kings,
some words of a Church hymn, a star made by Lesage and
a small consecrated host. Mariette says that if Lesage put in

a host, he, Mariette, knew nothing about it. Lesage, on the other hand, says that Mariette provided the host and put it in the box, and that he carried it on his person and made the spell on his own account. After that Madame de Montespan once again went to find Lesage at the house of the woman named Duverger where he lodged and there, with an altar and lighted candles, Mariette and Lesage said the *Veni Creator* on Montespan's head.

Even more serious charges followed. For several years, it appeared, Madame de Montespan had added aphrodisiacs, without his knowledge, to the King's food and drink. She had also tried to kill her rival, the young Mademoiselle de Fontanges, either by impregnating her clothes with such poisons as arsenic, red sulphur, yellow sulphur and orpiment, or her gloves with a decoction of peach blossom.

The third charge was made by a friend and accomplice of La Voisin, a seventy-year-old abbé named Guibourg, ugly, blind in one eye and totally depraved. It was Guibourg's horrible practice to say Black Mass on the body of a naked woman. In the early 1670's, when the Montespan was still struggling against La Vallière, he confessed that he had bought a still-born child for the price of one *écu* (£1) in order to celebrate a Black Mass in the presence of Madame de Montespan—perhaps, though he did not specify this —actually on her naked body. He pierced the baby's throat with a knife and caught the blood in the chalice. A first Mass was celebrated with the baby's blood; during a second Mass the baby's heart and entrails were consecrated, in order to make "powders" for Madame de Montespan.

The fourth charge was that Madame de Montespan had impregnated with arsenic or some other poison a petition to the King asking him to pardon a friend of La Voisin who was serving a prison sentence. Madame de Montespan had lent her carriage to take the petition to Saint-Germain. In short, driven by frenzied jealousy, she had gone as far as to try to kill the King.

Such were the accusations made before the secret Commission, the verbatim proceedings of which were at once conveyed to the King. From the nature of the witnesses a certain amount of lying was to be expected, and the chief witness, La Voisin's daughter, had never actually set eyes on the Montespan; nevertheless the judges were convinced that the bulk of the events and actions described in its proceedings had really taken place—this is clear from the fact that of 218 persons arrested thirty-six were found guilty of capital offences and many others imprisoned. Nor were these sentences merely a burst of hatred against "witches"; few intelligent people believed in witches any longer, and in 1672 Colbert had directed that in future no charges of sorcery should be accepted.

The evidence fitted in with certain aspects of Madame de Montespan's character—her recklessness, her love of gambling, her haughtiness even towards the King, her cruel tongue, her jealousy—and with little incidents in her life: frequent references to poison and the Devil, and her superstitious remark when fire broke out in the house where her children lived: "Good! Fire brings luck." Moreover, aphrodisiacs would explain those curious headaches of Louis and the tiredness which made his doctors advise him "to take more sleep." True, the Montespan always made a show of piety, but this could have stemmed from superstition or been merely a device for keeping in with the Queen.

It seems certain that the evidence was sufficient to convince Louis, for a change now took place in his life, and later, in his old age, he burned the verbatim proceedings of the trial. He was now, suddenly, almost overnight, brought face to face with the fact that for twelve years he had given his love to a woman who practised impieties, profanations and black magic, perhaps even lent her naked body as an altar for Black Masses. Not for nothing did she bear a pagan name. The passionate embraces, the wit and perpetual good humour—all had been secretly tainted.

Despite his many love affairs, Louis was a God-fearing man and there is little doubt that these revelations profoundly shocked him. But there was a second aspect to the "affair of the poisons." Madame de Montespan had repeatedly tried to kill her rivals and even perhaps had tried to kill him. She was a dangerous woman who threatened the welfare of France and his own position as King. On assuming personal power, Louis had made a solemn request to his closest advisers: "I am young and women usually exert a lot of influence over men of my age. If you notice any woman, whoever she may be, acquiring an influence over me or controlling me in the slightest way, I order you to let me know. In twenty-four hours I will get rid of her."

Louis acted now on his own advice. Given the Montespan's position in the State, it was of course unthinkable that she should be brought to trial or even questioned. Louis was not a vengeful man, and anyway he could hardly disgrace the mother of his legitimised children. And so he continued to see her, continued to be generous—on 19th November, 1680, he made her a present of £17,000—continued for a few years to let her live at Court. But their love affair was at an end. Louis himself was a changed man. Henceforward sexual passion would be kept in check. He had learned that it could endanger everything he held most dear.

CHAPTER 12

In Search of Glory

"MY DOMINANT PASSION IS CERTAINLY LOVE OF GLORY"—
so wrote Louis at the age of thirty. In this he was not alone; love
of glory was perhaps the strongest emotion at work in seventeenth-
century France. Only recently had the word acquired a favourable
meaning. For Montaigne, glory had meant vanity and been
denounced as a vice, but in Louis's day, under the influence of
classical learning, the word meant what it had meant to the Romans:
great and honourable fame. It was of two kinds, amorous and
martial. A man acquired glory by winning the love of beautiful
women, by pleasing them with a courteous manner, wit, service
and carefully chosen presents; or by winning victories on the
battlefield and extending the frontiers of France. It was the second
kind which Louis desired so much.

Ever since childhood, in his history books, in poems, in the
plays of Corneille, in ballets, in opera, he had heard the word
"gloire" ring like an exclamation of awe: it was the ace, the high C
of words. The great Kings, Charlemagne and Henri IV, were
remembered for their glorious military exploits: so too the Roman
Emperors, always hovering in the background of the seventeenth-
century imagination: Julius Caesar, Augustus, Trajan. When
campaigning at the age of eighteen Louis was told, "The King,
your grandfather, wasn't as young as you when he first went to
war." "But he achieved more than me," Louis replied. "So far
I haven't been able to get to the front as often as I'd like, but in
future I hope to win a great name for myself."

The first step had been to render France prosperous and
financially independent. The next step came with the death of King
Philip of Spain in 1665. Two years later almost without a fight

Louis annexed part of the Spanish Netherlands as compensation for Marie Thérèse's unpaid dowry. But his seizure of another Spanish possession, Franche Comté, on France's eastern frontier, alarmed Europe.[1] England, Holland and Sweden formed the Triple Alliance against him, and Louis was obliged by the Treaty of Aix-la-Chapelle (1668) to give up Franche Comté, though he kept part of the Spanish Netherlands. In the late 'sixties, therefore, Louis was still looking for glory, and in particular for a suitable antagonist against which to win his laurels.

Among France's near neighbours was the United Provinces of Holland. It was the newest state in Europe, having proclaimed its independence from Spain in 1648 after a long war. Each of the provinces enjoyed a large measure of autonomy, so that jurists disputed whether there were seven states or one. Almost half its territory lay below sea-level: Holland had been born from the sea and from the sea drew its riches. The people had a reputation for thrift and prudence: "They are the great masters of the Indian spices, and of the Persian silks, but wear plain woollen, and feed upon their own fish and roots"; while Saint-Évremond says of their women: "It is not that there are not some very charming ones amongst them, but there is nothing to hope from them, be it from prudence or from a coldness which serves them as a safe-guard. . . . There is a certain habitual prudence universally established here." Their chief of State, the Grand Pensionary John de Witt, dressed in a plain coat and went "on foot like one of the townspeople, followed by a servant dressed in grey, who carried a red velvet bag in which were the most important papers in Europe." He and his fellow-burghers distrusted what the French nobility prized: pleasure, wit, splendour, panache and glory.

For a number of reasons Louis heartily disliked Holland. First, the republic, founded upon a revolt from the King of Spain and from the Church of Rome, was staunchly Protestant and forbade Catholics to worship publicly or to hold high office. Secondly, Louis resented Holland's political pretensions: not only had she checked his complete annexation of the Spanish Netherlands by forming the Triple Alliance, but to celebrate the Treaty of Aix-la-

[1] See map on pp. 200-1.

Chapelle had struck a medal whose inscription boasted that the United Provinces had "reconciled kings, re-established liberty on the sea, brought peace upon the earth by force of arms and pacified Europe." That was to usurp the leading role Louis wanted.

Thirdly, Holland was a centre of political opposition and anti-monarchism. Many French Calvinists had fled to Holland, advanced republican opinions were freely voiced there and banned authors harboured. It was a Dutch jurist, Isaac Dorislaus, who had drafted the death sentence on Charles I of England. Then again, Dutch newspapers and gazettes published personal attacks on the French King and his mistresses. "Make inquiries privately," Louis wrote to Godefroy d'Estrades, "as to who is a certain Italian, a Genoese by birth, living at Amsterdam, who busies himself distributing news-letters in manuscript, most impudently concocted, concerning the state of my affairs and my future projects, and if you discover anything about him, let me know before you do anything to hold in check this worthy man's insolence." But d'Estrades could not check the libels: "They would forgo anything here rather than newspapers, which form the principal freight of their boats and wagons."

A fifth and the most important reason of Louis's hostility was Holland's dominant role in world commerce and finance. For Louis, the Dutch were "the people who absorb nearly all the profits of trade in all parts of the world and leave only a very small portion to the other nations." The Dutch per head were richer than the French and becoming steadily richer. The gold and silver which in the space of sixty years had raised Spain to the leading position in Europe were now flowing into Holland and likely to do as much for her.

While France possessed no banks at all and many influential Frenchmen considered lending at interest a mortal sin—"The nature of money is that it produces nothing; it is a metal rich, but sterile, and everything derived from it is usury"—Holland had inherited from Genoa and Venice the traditional republican business of banking and speculation. An Exchange at Amsterdam dealt in stocks and shares of the leading trading companies, while the Bank of the same city, founded in 1609, was the largest in the world and attracted capital from every European country. In 1670 the Bank had cash in hand of no less than 4,841,334 florins, mostly in bars of gold and silver.

This bank, the heart of Holland, permitted the Dutch to keep their florin at an excessively high rate and depreciate rival currencies at will. Louis was rebuilding France, pensioning foreign savants, subsidising the King of England and a host of German princes all with an écu for which he received on the average fifty-six pence instead of the seventy-two it was really worth.

Ever since assuming personal power Louis had tried by means of tariffs to prevent the draining away of bullion and thus strengthen French currency. His latest move, in 1667, had been to double the import duty on nearly all foreign articles. But in 1671 Holland retaliated by putting an embargo on her most valuable import from France—wine and brandy, thus making clear her determination to retain and even enlarge her share of the world's bullion and foreign trade.

These then were the reasons why Holland incurred Louis's displeasure. No one in itself nor all together constituted a mortal threat nor sufficient justification for making war. Yet in the late 'sixties Louis began to plan precisely that. He did so first and foremost in order to cover himself with glory. His action cannot be excused by muddle-headedness about the meaning of the word "glory": it was a piece of coldly calculated aggression; in the pattern of Louis's life the act of hubris which was later to call forth retribution.

The war was carefully planned. First, Holland was detached from her two allies, England and Sweden; the Emperor Leopold was persuaded to remain neutral, while Cologne and Münster made offensive treaties with France. Meanwhile the army, one of the great loves of Louis's life, was built up until in 1672 it was like no other army in the world: 119,000 officers and men, four times the size of any standing army in Europe since Roman days; the majority no longer cavalry but infantry, and this infantry not a raggle-taggle of down and outs but trained soldiers who marched and even charged in straight ranks, capable of presenting arms and drilling in unison. Each regiment still dressed in its colonel's

Louis XIII   *Anne of Austria*

Jean-Baptiste Colbert   *Cardinal Mazarin*

The interview between Louis XIV and Philip IV, 6th June 1660. To the immediate left of Louis are Mazarin, Anne of Austria and his brother Philippe

Mademoiselle   Marie Mancini

Marie Thérèse   Louise de La Vallière

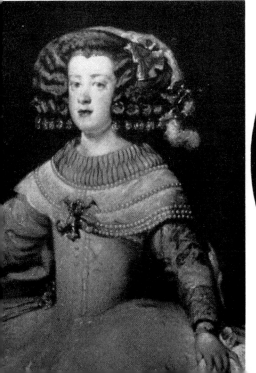

Louis XIV:
as 'The Sun';
aged twenty-six;
the bust by Bernini

Athénaïs de Montespan

Louis at the crossing of the Rhine

The Parterre d'Eau in the Gardens of Versailles

Louis receives the Doge of Genoa

Madame de Maintenon and her niece

Louis visiting the Gobelins

Louis, his son the Grand Dauphin, his grandson the Duc de Bourgogne, his great-grandson the Duc de Bretagne, with the latter's governess

Marie Adélaide, Duchesse de Bourgogne

Marly

Louis in 1706

colours—chiefly grey, red or blue; only in 1685 did Louis introduce a standard uniform. The main arms were still the fourteen-foot pike and wheel musket, fired from a forked stock, but an officer named Martinet, destined to become famous as a disciplinarian, had recently introduced the bayonet into some regiments. Formerly cannon had been hired from civilian contractors at so much the piece; now the army had its own train of artillery, ninety-seven four- and six-pounders.

Despite or perhaps because of this new discipline, the French soldier was a gay fellow, known as Jolicoeur, Sans-Souci or La Fleur; he marched to stirring tunes specially composed by Jean-Baptiste Lully and played by a band of pipe, hautbois and drum; he was physically fit—Louis himself often supervised musket drill and musket exercises—regularly paid and well treated; he could rise from the ranks, and he knew that his commander-in-chief took a personal interest in his welfare; Louis to Beaufort in Algeria: "I want to know whether Captain Laurier leaves a wife and children, so that I may do something for them, being anxious that people shall see that those who die in my service continue to live in my memory." The traditional rations had been hard biscuits, with a hole in the middle, carried on the bandolier: these biscuits were unpopular and it was Louis who introduced the portable oven, which in one day's halt could bake enough bread for the next six days.

This was the army which on 6th April, 1672, Louis ordered to invade the United Provinces. Three weeks later Louis joined it at Rocroi. He dispensed with armour, even the steel breastplate worn by some cavalry officers. He rode to war wearing jack-boots, long leather gloves and a red plume in his hat. He led the same life as his officers, sharing their rations and living under canvas. Because he believed that history was in the making, he took with him a historian, Paul Pellisson, and a Flemish painter, Antoine Van der Meulen, to depict the campaign with scrupulous exactitude as regards person and place, but not as regards violence—any kill must take place off stage.

"I have decided," Louis announced, "that it is more advantageous and more to my glory to attack four places on the Rhine simultaneously and to command in person at all four. I have chosen Rheinberg, Wesel, Burick and Orsoy." That was his mood as the French army marched down the Sambre and Meuse rivers to reach the Rhine at Neuss. Louis then captured all four of the towns he had named, continuing along the Rhine as far as Tolhuis, on the eastern frontier of Holland, which was reached on 12th June. The chief enemy towns, such as Amsterdam and Utrecht, lay on the other side of the Rhine. It was doubtless with extreme excitement that Louis ordered the river to be crossed—the Rhine of Caesar's Commentaries, the frontier of Roman Gaul! At this point it was some fifty yards wide, but because of a rainless summer comparatively shallow. The Comte de Guiche found a ford where the water was only four feet deep and despite the veteran Condé's scepticism—"This is a job for Polish or Tartar cavalry, not for infantry"—swam his horse across and established a bridgehead.

> We were still swimming the river [writes Guiche], when the enemy saw us, waded into the water and attacked us with their swords. The enemy right were so successful they reached me as I was still swimming. Pilois's horse panicked at the gunfire, and fell backwards on mine, almost drowning me; but my horse was extremely brave; I jerked the reins to the left and at one bound he got over the crupper of Pilois's horse and brought me safely ashore. The battle hung in the balance when just in time the King ordered our cannon to fire, and that forced back the enemy left. . . . I saw the most piteous sight in the world, more than thirty officers or horsemen drowned or drowning, with Revel at their head; the Rhine full of men, horses, flags, helmets and so on, for gunfire from the enemy right had frightened our horses into a strong current. I saw Brassalay, a cornet in the cuirassiers, thrown from his horse and start to swim with one arm, holding the regimental colours aloft with the other.

By seven that evening a bridge of light boats had been paddled into position, and Louis crossed the Rhine. He at once embraced Guiche publicly and promised him promotion. Sidney Godolphin, an English observer, noted that the French King "very seldom fails to reward those that deserve it before they expect it."

Map to illustrate the campaigns of 1672 and 1712
French frontier as in 1648

The crossing of the Rhine, though not a difficult military operation, had symbolic value of the first importance. "The King's life will seem incredible to future centuries," wrote Mademoiselle in enthusiasm, "never was a prince so successful." The crossing was depicted on the main bas-relief of the triumphal arch—the Porte Saint-Denis—erected by Paris, while Quinault wrote:

Et le Rhin qui borna les progrès de César
N'oppose â vos exploits qu'un murmure inutile,[1]

Bluff Boileau added his praises, though he could not resist a note of humour:

Des villes que tu prends les noms durs et barbares
N'offrent de toutes parts que syllables bizarres,
Et, l'oreille effrayée, il faut depuis l'Issel,
Pour trouver un beau mot courir jusqu' au Tessel . . .
Comment en vers heureux assiéger Doësbourg,
Zutphen, Wageninghen, Harderwic, Knotzembourg?[2]

So far all had gone well for Louis. He pushed on without delay to reduce the forts on the Ijssel, and Utrecht, abandoned by the Dutch army, was occupied on 23rd June, thus sealing the conquest of three of the seven provinces: Utrecht, Gelderland and Overijssel. Amsterdam and total victory lay only twenty miles and two days away.

The country through which the French were advancing was extremely flat, a green, hedgeless plain below the level of the medium height of the North Sea tides, from which it was protected by a chain of sand-dunes and dykes, and drained by a network of rivers, streams, artificial canals and ditches, the water in these ditches being pumped by little windmills into storage waters, which in turn were passed on to the tidal rivers at low tide.

Long before Louis approached their frontier, the Dutch had

---

[1] And the Rhine which barred the advance of Caesar
   Opposes you with merely a futile murmur.
[2] The names of the towns you capture are barbarous and queer.
   Each syllable bizarre and shocking to the ear.
   I have to travel miles from the Ijssel
   To find another pleasant name like Tessel . . .
   How in pleasing verse lay siege to Doesbourg,
   Zutfen, Wageningen, Harderwijk, Knotzembourg?

made plans for saving themselves by flooding. The procedure would be to pierce the walls and dykes along a particular set of storage waters and cover the adjoining land with water. The water-courses thus emptied would be filled again by opening the sluices into one of the tidal rivers at high tide, and in certain districts by opening a sea sluice or even breaching a dyke.

The Dutch began piercing the walls and dykes in the second half of June. Within five days an area of two hundred square miles around Amsterdam was flooded to a depth of about four feet, and a slightly larger area south of the Ijssel. All but a few higher roads along the deep rivers, made impassable by forts, were completely covered. A country born from the water had now in its death struggle reverted to water. This was the situation which suddenly faced Louis as he regrouped his army after the fall of Utrecht. Before him lay a lake, almost a sea: not since the Deluge perhaps had there been such a sight. With victory almost within its grasp, his army could advance no farther. To some it must have seemed that the elements for once had joined forces to cheat the King of his glory.

The fact remained, however, that Louis was deep in Dutch territory and a stalemate soon developed, to the disadvantage of the Dutch, who on 26th June unanimously voted in the States General for peace. Louis's terms were so humiliating—he wanted the frontier of the United Provinces withdrawn to the River Waal and a huge war indemnity—as to arouse public fury against the peace party. Holland then followed up her inundation with a revolution. John de Witt and his brother were massacred and dis-membered, while the twenty-two-year-old William, Prince of Orange, was proclaimed Stadtholder, Captain and Admiral-General. William rejected Louis's terms and the war continued.

During the winter of 1672-3 French troops advanced on Amsterdam across the frozen waters, only to be halted by a sudden thaw. Progress northwards was plainly impossible and in 1673 Louis decided to switch his attack to the Limburg area. He chose as his objective the large heavily fortified town of Maastricht. It was both defensively and offensively important: it stood on the Meuse, a traditional route into France, and commanded communications between Holland and the Empire, which William had persuaded to join in the war against France.

Louis arrived at Maastricht in June with 26,000 infantry, 19,000 cavalry and fifty-eight cannon—a large figure for the day. He at once surrounded the town and dug in his troops. Maastricht's defences consisted of four concentric walls, bastions, outworks, ditches and demi-lunes.[1] The traditional method of conducting a siege was to dig a narrow trench up towards one of the bastions, and from there mine the outer wall or launch an assault. The method was hazardous because the trench did not allow the troops protecting the diggers sufficient room to manœuvre: often they were overwhelmed by a quick enemy sortie.

Louis planned the siege of Maastricht with a young engineer named Sébastien de Vauban, whom he had singled out for his cautious, scientific siege-operations, "drawn from the heart of mathematics." Vauban proposed an entirely new method of attack which the Turks had recently used in Candia, and Louis gave it his approval. Instead of the old narrow trench running perpendicularly towards the town wall, they would dig a trench *parallel* to the wall, from there push forward a short but wide perpendicular trench, then dig another parallel about 250 yards nearer the town, and so on, up to within thirty yards of the town's outer defences. These "parallels" would be bigger than any trenches in the past: twelve to fifteen feet wide and three deep, with a high parapet. They would serve to hold troops who could protect those digging the advance trench without impeding their movements.

The digging of the parallels began. It was long, slow, arduous work, and it did not come naturally to French troops, whose strength in the past had lain in sudden bursts of impetuous courage. Louis got up at three in the morning and by dawn was touring the lines. By his example he inculcated a new discipline and steadiness. The work advanced.

After thirteen days' digging the third parallel was completed and manned. On the night of 17th-18th June the trench was opened: that is, the parapets and protective covering were removed and the troops assaulted the outer wall. Their numbers and impact

[1] For fortifications in Louis's reign, see p. 375

were greater than the old method would have allowed: they immediately destroyed a covered way and seized one of the horn-works protecting the main gate. Between the covered way and the hornwork stood a strong demi-lune and this they could not capture. Moreover, the Dutch in the demi-lune prevented further troops from reaching the hornwork and from seizing other parts of the defences.

For a week French troops assaulted the demi-lune, among them two young officers later to become famous: John Churchill, com-mended by Louis himself for bravery, and Villars, who left his idle cavalry troop "to learn how to fight as an infantryman." Finally it was d'Artagnan who led a successful night attack, though he lost his life together with 120 musketeers. The defences were inter-connected in such a way that, having occupied this one demi-lune, and the hornwork opposite, the French were able to secure the whole bastion and eventually all the out-works. In mid-August, in order to avoid bloodshed among the civilians, the governor surrendered. Louis then entrusted the fortification of the town to Vauban, who strengthened the outer wall with a series of jagged, angular strong-points, each flanking the other and giving mutual support. So well did he succeed that two years later, when the Dutch and their allies tried to re-take Maastricht they gave up the attempt after forty-one days.

The capture of Maastricht was very important: it put Louis in possession of a key Dutch town and it marked the first success of a new type of siege warfare, to be used and perfected throughout the reign; but also by displaying French military power it again alarmed all Europe.

In 1673 Spain entered the war on the side of Holland, together with Denmark, Lorraine, Trier and Mainz. As a result operations shifted from Holland to Flanders and France's eastern frontier. In 1674 Louis again invaded and conquered Franche Comté; a medal was struck: "Caesar once, Louis twice." The new French navy made itself mistress of the Mediterranean and helped the Sicilians to throw off Spanish rule, while Turenne won a string of notable victories in the Palatinate and Alsace —"You have restored a lily to my crown," Louis told him.

EUROPE IN 1667
Scale of Miles

| 0 | 100 | 200 | | 400 |

ITALIAN STATES
1 Genoa   3 Mantua
2 Parma   4 Modena

‿‿ Frontier of the Empire

Unfortunately for France the number of her enemies was steadily increasing, for Brandenburg had re-entered the war by attacking Sweden, while France's only other allies, England, Cologne and Münster all made peace during 1674. Louis now found himself virtually alone against Holland, Spain, the Empire and the leading German States. The war was costing France £30 million a year and becoming unpopular. There had been risings in Brittany, while Bordeaux, starved of its wine trade, had sent secret emissaries to Holland. Worse still, in the summer of 1675 at the battle of Sasbach a bullet "struck Monsieur Turenne upon the breast, and without any apparent wound more than the contusion, laid him dead upon the place, and by such a death as Caesar used to wish for, unexpected, sudden and without pain." It was not only a personal loss to Louis—he ordered Turenne to be buried at Saint-Denis in the very chapel of the Bourbons—but also a military disaster. The King immediately created eight new marshals, but these, as the people dubbed them, were merely "small-change for Turenne."

Louis decided that the time had come to try and negotiate a favourable peace. But was peace of any kind possible? It did not seem so. For one thing, the new Stadtholder of the United Provinces did not want peace. Stoop-shouldered, barely five foot tall, suffering from anaemia and asthma, William of Orange was nevertheless tenacious and coldly fanatical: for temperamental, political and religious reasons he loathed Louis and was determined to curb his power. Furthermore, all the Allies were committed by treaty to continue the war until Louis ceded all his gains since 1672. This Louis had no intention of doing. The next three years show how by clever diplomacy he succeeded in making peace despite the Stadtholder, and on his own terms, not on the Allies'.

His first move was very roundabout. He persuaded the new King of Poland's French wife to use her influence in favour of a Franco-Polish alliance, as a result of which 3,000 Polish volunteers under a French gentleman named Colonel Boham marched south to support a Hungarian rebellion which had broken out against the Emperor. The joint forces, calling themselves "soldiers of France," the.r coins inscribed "Ludovicus XIV, Galliae Rex, Defensor Hungariae," advanced to the gates of Vienna and caused the Emperor to withdraw the bulk of his troops from the Rhine area.

Louis next turned his attention to the Dutch. He fanned Dutch irritation against the Spaniards, who had let their allies down badly at the battle of Seneffe and were too poor to pay their promised war contributions. He then sent plenipotentiaries to the States General to sketch the advantages of peace: "Hold out hope of commercial advantages," Louis told them, "but only in general terms; refrain from using words which can be construed as a definite commitment." France, they were to suggest, was in no hurry for peace, but why, since Dutch soil was no longer threatened, did the United Provinces continue the war? Louis would restore Maastricht and give a promise not to attack the Netherlands again "on condition that the States General prevent Spain and her allies from making war on France from that direction"—gradually, imperceptibly, Louis's phrases aligned France and the United Provinces against Spain. While driving this wedge between the Dutch and Spaniards, Louis drove a second wedge between the Dutch republicans and the Stadtholder: he played on republican fears that William intended to make himself a dynastic monarch and that he was continuing the war in order to strengthen his military power while ruining the burghers.

This policy succeeded. By the autumn of 1676 Louis had persuaded the States General to hold a peace conference at Nijmegen. Denmark and Brandenburg were violently opposed to any peace talks, the Empire and Spain lukewarm. Interminable delays developed regarding protocol and precedence and prior consultation with this or that ally. Finally at the end of September Louis announced that he would recall his ambassadors unless those of the chief allies arrived in Nijmegen within one month. His bluff worked. The Allies were afraid the Dutch would conclude a separate treaty and hurriedly sent their delegates. Sensing his new strength, Louis next desired that all documents at Nijmegen should be drawn up in French instead of the usual Latin. Despite a feeble protest from the Danes, this wish, too, was obeyed like an order.

Difficult though Louis's task was in the United Provinces, it was even more difficult in England. Parliament and popular feeling were strongly anti-French and it looked as though England would enter the war on the Dutch side, which would have been disastrous for Louis. In the whole country he had only two friends: Charles, and Charles's beautiful, baby-faced Breton mistress, Louise de Kéroualle, Duchess of Portsmouth. Even Charles's friendship was uncertain and depended on regular gifts of money.

At first Louis decided to stake everything on Charles's friendship. Like the King of Poland's French wife, Louise de Kéroualle was persuaded to use her influence on Louis's behalf as a counterpoise to Danby, Charles's lord treasurer since 1673, who was hostile to France. Instead of reproaching Charles for making peace in 1674, Louis was kind and tactful to him, pretending that Parliament alone was to blame. To avert a declaration of war he then persuaded Charles to prorogue Parliament from November, 1675, to February, 1677, in return for continued financial help.

Louis suffered an apparent reverse in November, 1677, when, at Danby's instigation, William of Orange came to London to marry Charles's niece Mary. But the marriage did not bring England into the war, and even so Louis turned it to his advantage. He made the States General believe that William had sold himself to the English, that the liberties of Holland were endangered, and that their commerce would pass into the hands of London bankers.

After the marriage Louis decided to stop his payments to Charles since they were proving fruitless. Before long the English King was again short of money. Virginia had just revolted, he complained to the French ambassador, and that was costing him £80,000 in tobacco revenue, while quelling the rebellion would cost him a further £120,000. Unless help came soon he would have to call Parliament, if only in order to renew a tax on beer. Louis did not take the hint. Instead, he did what seemed an odd thing. To appease Parliament's growing fear about French maritime power, he signed a commercial and shipping treaty satisfactory to England, and what is more, signed it on 24th February, the day before Parliament was due to assemble.

In his desperation for money Charles now turned against the French King. He went to Parliament and asked for funds to provide 30,000 troops and ninety warships, these to be used, as he said, "to save the Spanish Netherlands." War against France—this was what Parliament had been urging for years, but to Charles's astonishment his request was received with extreme coldness, and Parliament declined to vote the money. What had happened was this. Unknown to Charles Louis had sent a secret agent, Ruvigny *fils*, to persuade the opposition that Charles could not be trusted to employ public money against France. Ruvigny made his point with gold. Buckingham and Algernon Sidney were among those who accepted it—and so prevented the war that would have dashed Louis's hopes. When Charles in dismay veered round and offered to support French terms at Nijmegen for a further subsidy, Louis could afford to say no. He had already—and more cheaply —attained his purpose.

In the spring of 1678 Louis had the Allies almost where he wanted them. He now decided on a show of strength. In a brilliant campaign he captured two fortress towns, Ghent and Ypres, then made a public declaration of his terms for peace. He would keep Franche Comté and the towns around Cambrai, but would hand back Maastricht and six other towns in Flanders. The Allies might take these terms or leave them, but in any case must decide before 10th May: after that date the terms, Louis hinted, might be stiffer.

This was bold language from a King who stood alone surrounded by enemies, but it corresponded with the facts. Psychologically Louis now had the advantage, for he had separated the Dutch from their allies and knew that as a trading nation they needed peace. The Dutch did in fact immediately accept Louis's terms. However, when the treaty was on the point of being signed they inquired on what date the six Flemish towns would be restored to Spain. When the Allies restored to Sweden all she had lost in the war, Louis coolly replied.

This unexpected demand alarmed both the Dutch and the anti-French party in England, who at once signed a treaty with Holland whereby unless France evacuated the Flemish towns within fourteen days, England would join in the war against France.

Louis realised that he had gone too far and would now have to act fast. He made it known publicly that he would not yield on the question of the six Flemish towns: he did so in order to lull the suspicions of William and some of the Allies, who were confident that peace had been thwarted. He then sent secret instructions to his ambassador Barrillon in London. Barrillon got in touch with a Monsieur de Cros, a Frenchman in the service of the Duke of Holstein. Cros, who according to Temple was an unfrocked monk, had lived in Sweden and had many friends at the Swedish Court. Barrillon and Cros managed to persuade the Swedish ambassador that it was desirable for Louis to sign the peace treaty without guaranteeing Swedish interests, on the understanding that when the time came Louis would ensure a return of all Swedish losses. Barrillon and Cros then met King Charles in Louise de Kéroualle's room. Without mentioning what had passed with the Swedish ambassador, Cros posed as a Swedish plenipotentiary and told the English King that if England would guarantee that no help would be given by Spain or Holland to the enemies of Sweden, then Sweden would ask France to hand over the six Flemish towns. To this plan Charles agreed.

Cros hurried as fast as he could to Nijmegen, where he spread the good news: not only had Sweden consented to the handing over of the Flemish towns, but England would guarantee the peace. The implication was that France and England were in closer agreement than ever—which was far from being the truth. The Dutch and the Allies were suitably impressed. On the last day for signing the treaty the French ambassadors declared to the Dutch that they had now received orders to consent to the handing-over of the six towns, and thereupon to sign the peace, but that it must be done that very day (they knew that William of Orange planned a last-minute objection). And so the Treaty of Nijmegen was signed shortly before midnight on 10th August, 1678, on the terms Louis had publicly announced in April.

Charles declared "that the rogue de Cros had outwitted them all," but the English King did not know that it was Louis who had given the rogue his instructions. "I never observed," says William Temple, "either in what I had seen or read, any negotiations managed with greater address and skill than this had been by the French in the whole course of this affair."

A special commercial treaty was negotiated between France and Holland, whereby the more liberal 1664 tariff replaced that of 1667. Louis then signed separate treaties with the other allies, thus obtaining what would have been denied him at a general settlement. He insisted that Denmark should give up all it had taken from Sweden, lower the toll duties in the Baltic Sea, and that the Elector of Brandenburg should give up Pomerania, which he had lately conquered. In vain did the Elector write a letter to him in the most submissive terms, in which he styled him "Lord and Master," humbly entreating that he might be permitted to keep what he had conquered, with many assurances of his zeal and future service, but the conqueror of the Swedes was obliged to restore all he had taken from them.

From the Dutch War Louis gained what he wanted most: military glory. The crossing of the Rhine, the capture of Maastricht and Ghent and Ypres were notable victories; moreover, he had added to his kingdom Franche Comté and half of Flanders. That this had been achieved against a formidable coalition added to the glory. At the peace conference he had spoken to Europe not as an equal but as a master—though the latter role owed less to overwhelming power, economic or military, than to clever diplomacy.

Louis had a great liking for diplomacy—"it is preferable to any other activity in the world"—and diplomacy was to play an important part in his foreign policy throughout the reign. Louis considered it to be first and foremost psychology. He writes to Béthune in 1680: "Give me an exact account of your audiences with the King and Queen of Poland, and note the exact words of their reply ... describe their public and private life as fully as possible, because often these little details can help me to understand more important matters." At the King's demand instructions, reports and memoranda became detailed and complete as never before, while the dispatches of one of his ambassadors, the Comte d'Avaux, were to serve as a text-book for the next century. Louis's own instructions are remarkable for exactitude. To Verjus in 1675 during negotiations with the Elector of Cologne: "Take care to insinuate my thoughts to the Ministers so adroitly that, although I see they are not disposed to conclude any agreement for the time being, the talks may serve to show the Elector and his Ministers that I trust them, and to arouse hopes that an eventual agreement may win them advantages from me." Secrecy was another characteristic of Louis's diplomacy. These and other instructions were conveyed in codes so ingenious that they were cracked only 150 years later.

Diamond necklaces and gold also played an important part in Louis's foreign policy. In his Memoirs Louis lists some of his gifts and subsidies: the Queen of Denmark receives a necklace, the King £100,000; the Electress of Brandenburg a necklace, the Elector £300,000. Dutch deputies, Polish lords, Irish Catholics, English refugees, Swedish senators, Swiss dignitaries, the Elector of Mainz—the list of beneficiaries is long, for in Louis's mind Portugal and Norway, the Sublime Porte and the Danish Sound all became part of a single grand design for furthering the interests of France.

After the Treaty of Nijmegen Europe expected Louis to rest content with his important gains in territory and prestige, such as had been equalled by few other French kings. But Louis's passion for glory was not yet satisfied. Peace, too, he decided, could be a time of conquest. The guiding principle of his foreign policy now as later was to make particular gains wherever and whenever occasion arose, and the first occasion after the Treaty of Nijmegen related to ten cities in Alsace.

By the Peace of Westphalia (1648) France had received the land-graviate of Upper and Lower Alsace in full sovereignty, and the "provincial prefecture" of ten Alsatian cities, the most important of which were Colmar, Landau and Münster, together with all rights depending on that prefecture; these ten cities and all the nobility of Lower Alsace were to be left in possession of those privileges which they enjoyed in relation to the Empire, provided, however, that nothing in this should detract from the "full sovereignty" already conceded. During the recent war these cities had proved a thorn deep in the side of France. Louis decided to take advantage of the highly ambiguous wording of the Peace of Westphalia to claim all ten cities, which from time immemorial had been in the hands of other masters, and to integrate them into France.

First he sent a historian named Denis Godefroy to examine

chest-loads of old title deeds, some water-stained, others partly eaten by rats, and to gather those which could justify France's claims. Then courts were set up at Douai, Besançon, Brisach and Metz to examine the deeds. Several sovereign princes of the Empire, the Elector Palatine, the King of Spain himself, who had several bailiwicks in this region, and the King of Sweden, as Duc des Deux Ponts, were summoned to do homage to the King of France under pain of having their possessions forfeited. It was an extraordinary situation. Not since Charlemagne had a King acted thus as the lord and judge of crowned heads, and conquered territory by judicial decrees. The Elector Palatine and the Elector of Trier were dispossessed of the lordships of Falkenburg, Germersheim and Velden. They carried their complaints before the Diet of the Empire assembled at Ratisbon, but in vain, for the Diet merely entered protests, while Louis made himself master of the ten cities.

Even this success did not satisfy Louis. Wherever there was weakness, he turned it to France's advantage. In 1681 he bought Casale from the frivolous Duke of Mantua, which gave France a key fortress in North Italy. Louis's next objective was the free city of Strasbourg, which had helped the Empire during the war. It was powerfully fortified with 900 cannon and outworks along the Rhine. The way was prepared by diplomatic intrigues and bribery, then an army of 20,000 men was secretly sent to blockade the city. One September morning the people of Strasbourg woke to find their outer defences in French hands and their burgomasters talking of surrender. On 30th September, 1681, France took possession of the city, Vauban began to fortify it, and a medal was struck: *Clausa Germanis Gallia*—"France Closed to the Germans."

More of those medals, each marking a solid, particular glory, were struck in the same year, when Louis's navy under Duquesne cleared the seas of Algerian and Tripoline pirates and punished Algiers. A certain Bernard Renau, "little Renau," an excellent mariner without ever having served on board a ship, proposed in council to bombard Algiers from the sea. Everyone present started at the idea, not having the least conception that a mortar could be fired anywhere but on solid ground. However, little Renau persuaded Louis to permit a trial. He then had five ships built, smaller but stronger than usual, without upper decks and only a platform on the keel, in which grooves were cut to receive the mortars. Thus equipped he set sail under Duquesne, who expected little success, but the effect of the mortar bombs filled both the admiral and Algerians with surprise. Half the city was destroyed on 28th October, 1681, and the Algerians hurriedly sent envoys to make peace. They delivered all the Christian captives in their possession and paid a large indemnity.

Louis next turned his attention to Genoa, which had been selling gunpowder to the Algerians and was now building four galleys for the King of Spain. Louis sent an envoy, Saint-Olon, to forbid the launching of the galleys, threatening instant punishment if they did not obey. The Genoese, who were staunch republicans, resented the threat and, counting on Spanish help, refused. At once fourteen men-of-war, twelve galleys, six bomb-vessels and several frigates set sail from Toulon having on board the new Secretary of the Navy, Seignelay, Colbert's fearless, ambitious son. On 17th March, 1684, the bomb-vessels threw 14,000 shells into the town of Genoa, reducing much of it to ashes; 4,000 marines were landed and quickly captured the city heights. Louis insisted that the doge and four of the principal senators should come to Versailles, renounce the Spanish alliance and implore his clemency. They arrived on 22nd February, 1685, and used words and gestures dictated by Seignelay. Louis gave them audience seated and with his hat on, but behaved towards them with courtesy as well as pomp. Louvois, Croissy and Seignelay treated them more haughtily, which made the doge say, "The King deprives our hearts of liberty by the manner in which he receives us; but his Ministers restore it to us again."

To sum up: in 1672 Louis had launched an aggressive war on Holland in order to cover himself in glory. In 1678 he signed a treaty which substantially increased France's political and military strength. But desire to play the master had by now become a habit and was continued into the years of peace. Diplomatic and military successes followed one another until all his neighbours stood in awe of the French King's energy, ambition and cleverness.

These successes played an important part in the development of Louis's character. They added immensely to his self-assurance and to the belief that whatever he willed he could obtain, by force if necessary. As in his affair with Madame de Montespan, which coincided with the Dutch War, he found that he could break society's sanctions and get away with it. His successes hardened him and increased his pride. They seemed to confirm Pope Gregory the Great's assertion that the French crown "is as much above other crowns as the King is above ordinary men." As a result Louis increasingly saw himself as the master of Europe, giver of peace and war, arbitrator of the nations, undisputed successor to the Roman Emperors. A swagger creeps into his pronouncements, the swagger of one who knows himself to be the most powerful and influential man in Europe.

CHAPTER 13

Versailles

VERSAILLES began with a love affair. Louis first became fond of the countryside in that part of the Ile de France on his hunting trips with Louise de La Vallière. Because Louise was with him, he saw the soft light, trees, ponds and distant views with the eye of love. Soon this countryside became almost as dear to the King as his mistress.

In the summer of 1661 Louis dreamed of living part of the year at Versailles. The brick hunting lodge with black slate roof was too small to house Louise and himself and the sixty chosen courtiers in blue cloaks who accompanied them, so he would have to build. So much the better: by making something lasting at Versailles, perhaps that summer's love and happiness would last a lifetime. He drew up plans with Le Vau, who had designed Fouquet's house, but shortage of money delayed the work.

About 1670 the dream of a country house for himself and Louise grew into something bigger. Louis had always preferred the country to the town—in 1650, as soon as his virtual imprisonment by the frondeurs was over, he had hurried out of Paris to ride and hunt—and now he decided to make Versailles his permanent residence. With Jules Hardouin-Mansart, who succeeded Le Vau in 1670, he planned a palace different from other palaces, such as Saint-Germain and the Louvre, which were tight and gloomy, skulking behind high walls, crenellated towers and deep moats, for fear of attack by powerful noblemen; it would be a palace of peace, with large windows and extensive gardens. It would be both a house for the royal family and all the Court, and the centre of government, where he and his Ministers would rule the kingdom. It would stand also as a visible symbol of France's unity and glory, and therefore it must be large and impressive. Its style would be sober without, luxurious within. If he were given time, it might be the greatest building ever achieved by man.

Throughout the 'seventies and early 'eighties several thousand masons, marble-workers, smiths, plumbers, carpenters, joiners and glaziers laboured at Versailles. Louis himself had the final word in the plans. It was he who decided to retain most of Louis XIII's hunting lodge, including its marble court; he who put beauty before comfort. When Mansart pointed out that unless certain chimneys were raised, the fires would smoke, Louis replied that he did not mind whether they smoked or not, provided the chimneys were not visible from the gardens.

It was Louis also who found the money. Colbert, staunchly conservative, kept pressing him to finish the Louvre; the Louvre would bring him glory, whereas Versailles was only a place of "pleasure and diversion," and he shuddered to think that Louis might go down to posterity as the creator of Versailles. But Louis was not to be dissuaded: regularly he set aside funds, inspected work in progress and even on campaign wrote to Colbert, listing details to be carried out.

On 6th May, 1682, Louis went to take possession of his new palace. Thirty-six thousand men and 6,000 horses were still at work, mainly in the gardens; off and on throughout the reign building and improvements would continue. But the huge palace —the garden front alone had 375 windows—was now substantially complete.

On that early summer morning when Louis and his Court approached Versailles, they came first to a blue and gold railing pierced by three gateways. Through those to the right and left passed the courtiers, while through the central gate, surmounted by fleurs de lys, horns of plenty and a crown, only the King might pass, with his Queen and princes of the blood. Beyond rose the palace, very extensive but giving an impression of harmony: a marble court in the shape of an inverted U between two long wings, the middle story of which was lined with columns and pilasters. In front of the marble court stood a second railing with a central gate through which only the carriages of specially privileged persons might pass. Everyone else must alight outside the railing in the Court of the Ministers—so called from low red-brick Ministry buildings on either side—and there hire blue sedan-chairs to take them to their rooms.

The marble court had brick walls and marble busts on stone brackets between all the windows. The three windows with a balcony on the first floor, facing the rising sun, were the windows of Louis's private apartments. To the left lay his grand ante-chamber, to the right his study, upholstered in green velvet, where he conducted affairs of state, took decisions and signed decrees. The ceilings of these private rooms were white, with friezes in bas-reliefs of gilded stucco; the walls decorated with large mirrors in gilded frames, the floor parquet, the doors richly carved and gilded. The King's bed stood under a canopy adorned with white plumes, behind a balustrade of carved and gilded wood. Nearby were the King's bathroom, his billiard-room and a small room for wigs.

Also in the central part of the palace were the Queen's private apartments, the rooms of the King's children, the State apartments of the King and of the Queen, the marble staircase and the grand staircase, on the first landing of which Louis received ambassadors when they came to present their credentials. The two long wings on either side were for the Court: the north wing for the nobles, the south for princes of the blood.

The general style of the palace showed Louis's taste for archi-tectural composition, precious materials, inlaid coloured marble, the contrast of dark tones and gilded brass, sculpture, medallions and reminiscences of Rome. In the King's five state apartments the walls were of marble, inlaid in geometrical patterns; marble, too, were the walls of the grand gallery, or Galerie des Glaces, eighty yards long and occupying almost the entire façade of the central section on the west side. Seventeen high windows cur-tained with white damask looked out on the gardens and were reflected in seventeen arched mirrors lining the opposite wall. The floor was covered with two Savonnerie carpets, big as meadows. The ornaments, here as throughout Versailles, were decorated with laurels, lyres, sunflowers, radiant crowns and all the classical attributes of the sun. The ceiling, the work of Le Brun from 1679 to 1682, comprised thirty paintings of events, chiefly victories, in Louis's reign. "The Marvellous Capture of Valenciennes," and "The Unbelievable Passage of the Rhine," Le Brun had captioned two of them, but Louis ordered the adjectives removed.

Furniture at the beginning of the century had still lived up to its original name, *mobilier*—something which could be easily transported from house to house. But the furniture of Versailles was all designed to remain in particular rooms in a particular palace. Its lines were stately and majestic. Lately the backs of chairs had been growing higher, and the pieces of iron which had protected furniture on journeys were now replaced by gilded bronze or gilded wood. By 1680 the arms of most chairs were slightly curved, the legs and cross-pieces decorated with scrolls. The furniture in the Galerie des Glaces was of silver; at night it reflected the glimmer of four thousand wax candles in silver chandeliers.

In the eighties courtiers at Versailles wore long brocade coats, parted to show an embroidered waistcoat. Knots of ribbon were often tied on the shoulders, and round the neck was swathed a silk band (scarlet was a favourite colour) knotted in a wide bow. Silk stockings led down to square-toed shoes with high red heels and decorated with very big silk bows. Long wigs covered the ears and fell to the small of the back. The round beaver hat was crowned with ostrich plumes. Ladies wore gaily-coloured embroidered dresses usually of silk or brocade with billowing skirts down to the ground, narrow-waisted and leaving part of the shoulders bare. They carried fans and, in winter, muffs.

Such was the setting for the drama of the King's day.

The King usually awoke at the time he had named the evening before, but if not, when the palace clock began to chime eight, the first *valet de chambre* approached the King's bed. "Sire, it is striking eight." As soon as the King was fully awake, his brother and his sons were allowed to enter and speak to him. At quarter past eight the wet-nurse who had suckled the King in his infancy came in and kissed him. After being rubbed down by his doctors and surgeon, the King washed his hands in spirits of wine and chose his wig for the day. He put on his slippers and a dressing-gown, passed outside the balustrade and seated himself in an elbow-chair. Every other morning he shaved. "He often spoke of hunting, and sometimes said a word to somebody. No toilet table was near him; he simply had a mirror held before him." He then put on his wig and signified that the *grand lever* might begin.

The hundred or so courtiers who had the privilege of attending the *grand lever* were now admitted to watch the King dress. First he put on his under-stockings, his knee-breeches, which had silk stockings attached, his shoes, ornamented with diamond buckles (one pair had battle scenes painted on their high heels), and his garters, which the King fastened himself. Still in his dressing-gown, the King then ate breakfast from a service of porcelain and gold. It was a very light meal of white bread, wine and water—Louis never touched tea, coffee or chocolate. After breakfast the King removed from a pocket of his nightdress the relics he wore day and night and gave them to the first *valet de chambre*, who carried them into the King's study, placed them in a light sack on a table with the King's watch, and stood guard over both. Meanwhile the King removed his nightdress and put on his shirt, which had been warmed if the weather was cold. As he did so, two *valets* held up his dressing-gown to shield him from the crowd. He put on his sword and the *cordon bleu*, on which hung the crosses of the Order of the Holy Spirit and the Order of St. Louis. He made his own choice of cravat and lace handkerchief. He put on his coat and was handed his hat, gloves and cane. These, like every other article of clothing, were presented to the King by a particular gentleman or servant. The highest privilege—handing the King his shirt—was usually reserved for the Dauphin and princes of the blood. The etiquette was very precise. For example, the Master of the Wardrobe had to draw off the King's nightdress holding it by the right sleeve, while the first *valet* of the Wardrobe held it by the left.

The *lever* ended when the King passed into his study. Here he issued orders for the day and gave audiences, before attending Mass in the palace chapel. During Mass he said his rosary: he had inherited it from Henri IV, and each small ivory bead was carved in the shape of a skull. After Mass he held a Council in his study, except on Thursday, when he gave audiences, and on Friday when he talked to his confessor.

Dinner was served at one o'clock. Like all the King's meals it was prepared in the kitchens of the Grand Commun, a large square building opposite the south wing, where 1,500 servants and gentle-men servants lodged. To reach the royal table the King's dinner had to cross the Rue de la Surintendance, enter the south wing, mount a staircase, pass through several corridors, cross the upper vestibule of the staircase of the princes, the salon of the shopkeepers (Versailles had its own shopping centre), the Grand Hall of the Guards, the upper vestibule of the marble staircase, and finally the Hall of the King's Guards. It was carried or guarded by a suite of ten, including three soldiers with carbines. If a courtier happened to meet the procession, he must doff his hat, bow and say in a low voice, "The King's meat." All food and wine were tasted first by gentlemen servants: a traditional safeguard against poison.

The King dined alone. His dinner was usually of three courses, with dessert. He was particularly fond of boiled eggs. He would cut the top of his egg clean off with a single stroke of his knife, and this little accomplishment was much admired by the populace, who were free to enter and watch the King dining. He was also fond of vegetables for dinner. The excellent kitchen garden supplied his table with asparagus and fresh sorrel in December, radishes, lettuce and mushrooms in January, cauliflower in March, straw-berries and peas in April, melons and figs (Louis's favourite fruit) in June. Potatoes were still virtually unknown in France and never eaten at Versailles: the staple vegetable was the globe artichoke. The King drank wine from Champagne, invariably mixed with water: only in later life did he change to Burgundy. In 1670 a Benedictine named Pérignon, cellarer of the abbey of Hautvilliers, had invented fizzy champagne, and substituted the cork for the hemp stopper, but this drink was little known, and it was a still champagne that Louis drank. All food at the King's table which remained untouched belonged to the plate-changer, and reappeared at the dinners of the gentlemen servants or *valets*; sometimes delicacies were sold to bourgeois families in the town.

After lunch the King spent a little time giving biscuits to his setters and pointers, of which he was very fond. Some of the bitches' names are known: Diane, Blonde, Bonne, Nonne, Ponne, Folle and Mitte. The afternoon was spent either stag-hunting, shooting on foot or walking in his gardens for exercise and in order to see his workmen. During his walks all the courtiers might follow the King. On his return he worked for an hour or more in his study.

The main meal of the day was served at ten o'clock in the first ante-room. It was always on a grand scale: the royal family at table, and many courtiers and ladies present, seated or standing. Louis was usually very hungry for it, since he never took snacks between meals, though sometimes he would suck a cinnamon lozenge. Supper began with several kinds of soup, which were very rich and thick—Soupe Colbert, for instance, named after the Minister, had poached eggs in it. It was not unusual for the King to eat four platefuls of different soups, a whole pheasant, a partridge, a plateful of salad, mutton hashed with garlic (he was very fond of spiced dishes), two good-sized slices of ham, a dish of pastry, followed by fruit and sweets.

After supper there was usually some amusement such as a ball, a concert, card-games or, if the weather was fine, a fête in the gardens. Otherwise the King spent about an hour talking with the royal family in one of his smaller private rooms. At the end of the day he passed into his bedroom for the ceremony of the *coucher*. The King undressed in public and with the same formalities as he had dressed in the morning. Then the Court filed out and the King was left with only servants and a dozen courtiers, privileged to be present while the King washed and his hair was brushed and combed. As a particular honour, the King would single one of them out to hold the candle. The King named the hour at which he wished to be awakened and told the Grand Master of the Wardrobe what dress he would wear on the following day. Then all withdrew except the first *valet de chambre* and *garçons*. After feeding and playing with his dogs, the King went to bed. The *valet de chambre* closed the bed-curtains, while the *garçons* put out all the lights and lit a night-lamp. After the *garçons* had left, the *valet* closed the doors. Then, lighting his own candle, the *valet* undressed and got into his camp-bed in front of the gilded balustrade. The Sun King slept; darkness fell on Versailles.

Louis had always lived in public and does not seem to have minded it. He was sociable and enjoyed having people around him. He had tremendous presence, and it was this that sometimes made etiquette at Versailles as formal and daunting as a religious rite. Yet the fact is that in comparison with other Courts of Europe Versailles was remarkable for its *lack* of ceremonial. In Spain, for instance, the King was seen in public only three or four times a year, his daughters had to beg audience, and when betaking himself to the Queen's bed, he was preceded by an officer with sword drawn. Another noteworthy point is this: it was not Louis who introduced ceremonial to France: details of the *lever*, for instance, had been fixed between 1578 and 1585.

Versailles was theocentric. That was why when the King entered the chapel, courtiers bowed to him, and he bowed to the Blessed Sacrament. But the Sun King was the visible head and centre of the palace. Around him circulated a whole solar system, each planet at a fixed distance and receiving a set amount of light. Rank was linked with the order established by God in France, and therefore to refuse a duke his honours or to permit any lady to sit in an elbow-chair in the Queen's presence was not only to lack respect for royalty but also to infringe an absolute set of values. Once when the Marquise de Torcy took the seat of the Duchesse de Duras, Louis sat speechless with anger all through the meal, and later complained that he had witnessed an intolerable, unheard-of incident, inadmissible in a woman of quality, let alone in a *petite bourgeoise*, daughter of a Pomponne, with the family name "Arnauld," married to a Colbert. Ten times, he said, he had been on the point of getting up and leaving. He remained angry for several days until Torcy apologised for his wife.

Distinctions of rank were reflected in niceties of politeness. The King, for instance, would be walking in the gardens. "For ladies he took off his hat completely, but to a greater or less extent; for princes and dukes half off, holding it in his hand or against his ear some instants, more or less marked; for the nobility he contented himself by putting his hand to his hat." "Never was man so naturally polite, or of a politeness so measured, so graduated, so adapted to person, time and place."

In the palace and town of Versailles lived several thousand courtiers and their families: nearly all the nobility who could afford to leave their estates. Exclusion from Versailles was considered the worst misfortune in this life. The Marquis de Vardes, exiled from Court for twenty years for interfering in the King's love affairs, had the wit to return wearing the same costume, now absurdly outmoded, in which he had departed. "When one displeases your Majesty," he informed Louis, "one is not only wretched but ridiculous." On another occasion Louis learned that a soldier had killed his lord, the Marquis de Châteaumorand, who lived on his estates. "I know the house of Châteaumorand," said Louis, "but not the marquis; he was certainly not much of a man; he did not come to Court or go to war."

The remark is revealing. Louis kept the nobility around him not to render them powerless—he detested uselessness in any shape or form—but so that they would give of their best in peace and war, so that by serving him they might serve France. Louis knew from experience, particularly with his armies, that with a smile or a small privilege he could win lifelong devotion, all the more so in a great palace where everyone talked prestige and status day in, day out. The courtier permitted to hold the candle during the royal *coucher* would henceforth seek in every way to do his will, that will continually directed to a single goal: the greatness of France.

The chief function of the courtiers was to defend the kingdom. As noblemen they were exempt from the *taille* and other taxes precisely because they were held to do more for France than men without rank. In war they were the first to shed their blood, and in peace they maintained a company or even a regiment of soldiers out of their own money. Versailles bred not idlers but brave army officers who also patronised artists, put up fine buildings (many of the hospitals and hostels of France were privately endowed) and generally lived with panache. Louis, for instance, blamed Mademoiselle for not ornamenting the façade of her new house at Choisy. "We have no right to be careless. . . . We must know how to carry our burden, and we must lay it down at no time and in no place." A similar standard was asked of courtiers.

Courtiers were expected to see the King every day as often as possible. "His Majesty looked to right and left not only at his *lever* and *coucher*, but at his meals, in passing through his apartments, or his gardens of Versailles. He saw and noticed everybody; not one escaped him, not even those who hoped to remain unnoticed." At the birth of the Duc de Bourgogne, "although the room was filled with the princes and princesses of the blood, and a large number of other people whose presence was necessary, the King, judging that the moment of the delivery was near, and with that presence of mind which never fails him, saw at a glance, despite the number of persons crowded in the room, that M. le Prince de Conti was not there. He gave orders that he should be summoned immediately."

A courtier was expected to conduct himself not only with regularity but with grace. To escort a lady, holding her hand by the tips of the fingers, to dance the majestic and complicated coyrante, to ride hard to hounds, to make the three reverences in approaching royalty, to scratch at a door with a pocket-comb or with the nail of the little finger, grown specially long for the purpose (one never knocked at Versailles)—in doing such things he would show that "court air" which La Bruyère claimed was as unmistakable as the Norman accent.

At Versailles Louis was surrounded by courtiers, but he was not thereby cut off from the people of France. On the contrary, what impressed foreign visitors was the King's accessibility to ordinary Frenchmen. Anyone was free to enter the palace (in 1682 a medal was struck showing Versailles, inscribed "The apartments opened to the public. Kindness and Magnificence of the Prince"). Anyone who had a valid reason for seeing the King was received in audience. When the Dauphin lay ill, Paris fishwives trooped in to kiss him on the cheek. Crates of fruit and vegetables from the kitchen garden were distributed to the poor. And Louis invariably touched his hat to women of the people, even to a palace washerwoman. The people sensed that he was fond of them and cared about their welfare: all his life he was immensely popular.

Two incidents among many show this concern for the feelings of his subjects. There was a hitch during the royal *lever*, and courtiers rounded on the *valet* who had made the mistake. "Let us remember," said Louis, "that he is much more upset about it than I am." During a review a soldier who passed in front of the four-year-old Dauphin lowered his halberd. "Hola!" cried the boy. "Beat that man for daring to pass me without taking off his hat." It was explained that the soldier had done right only to lower his halberd, and Louis made the Dauphin say sorry. The little boy promised to do so. "Why?" "Because Daddy and Mummy want me to." "And also because it's your duty."

As will appear later, Louis built on as lavish a scale for his people, particularly for Parisians, as he did for the Kings of France. Versailles, then, was not as some critics have claimed a monumental piece of selfishness nor did it confront in a mood of rivalry or enmity Paris and the people of France. It had come into being because Louis loved space and open air; hence the gardens and park of Versailles were quite as important as the palace itself.

The gardens had been begun in 1662, long before the palace. The original hunting lodge already had a garden in Renaissance style: a cluster of variegated parts separated by hedges or bushes. At Vaux Louis had seen quite another, much larger type of garden, with long straight *allées* radiating from pools of water or groups of statuary, set off by trees and *jets d'eau*. Its designer was André Le Nôtre, a kind, unambitious man of forty-nine with creases of laughter at the corner of his eyes and charmingly spontaneous, not a bit like his formal gardens: once he entered the Pope's study and instead of falling on his knees went up and kissed the Pontiff on both cheeks, saying, "Good morning, Reverend Father, how well you look. I am delighted to see you in such good health!"

When Louis summoned him to Versailles, Le Nôtre had just returned from England. He soon realised that this new garden would prove far more difficult than the one he had just designed for King Charles at Greenwich. The land was marshy and hemmed in with woods, there was a lack of large trees, while the nearest important source of water lay four miles away. However, he drew up plans and explained them to Louis on the spot. He began with two great pools of water to decorate the terrace in front of the château. He next explained his idea of a double flight of steps, adorned with yew-trees and statues. He passed then to the Allée du Tapis Vert, a pool to be called the Bassin d'Apollon, and a great canal. At each of the features whose position Le Nôtre marked and whose future beauties he described, Louis interrupted, saying, "Le Nôtre, I give you five thousand livres" (£1,700). At the fourth interruption, Le Nôtre stopped. "Sire, Your Majesty shall hear no more. I should ruin you."

Work was started at once and in the following year, in order to extend the park to the north-west, Louis bought the land and hamlet of nearby Trianon. Fields were ploughed up, earth shifted, trees felled, and when the lines of the gardens had been traced, new trees planted. Louis wanted to see the trees in his own life-time and so quite large oaks, elms, beeches, limes and ashes were hauled from Compiègne, Flanders, the mountains of Dauphiné and the forests of Normandy; in one year alone 25,000 trees were transplanted from Artois. In the 230 acres of garden 1,400 fountains were installed. It was Louis who ordered the then prodigious feat of raising the waters of the Seine by means of the "machine of Marly," fourteen hydraulic wheels and 223 pumps, to supply the fountains.

Immediately in front of the Galerie des Glaces lay a vast terrace ornamented with two fountains and two large pools, their marble borders supporting bronze groups of the rivers of France. Steps led down to the parterre of Latona, where fountains played among flower-beds and statues. Beyond stretched a straight narrow lawn three hundred yards long, lined with statues and the foliage of adjoining groves, sloping to a wide pool where Apollo sat en-throned on his chariot; behind gleamed the waters of the grand canal.

On either side of this central line lay groves, bosquets, fountains, flower-beds and lawns, all arranged in strict geometrical patterns, usually a number of straight paths converging on a circular pool, grotto or group of statuary. These straight paths and avenues were the chief feature. They divided up and regulated an otherwise unwieldly mass. They were a visible equivalent of the mind's method in dealing with brute experience. They were also applied geometry: they not only related magnitudes in space but literally measured the ground. Thus the two sides of the royal allée, which gave the impression of gradually converging, provided a demonstration in perspective, while the statues and vases placed at set intervals allowed one to count off the distance to the parterre of Latona.

According to Dézallier d'Argenville, a gardener must not only know the principles of architecture but also be "something of a geometer." Le Nôtre used to say that the flower-beds at Versailles were only for the children's nurses, who could admire them from the second story. A garden was primarily an arrangement of masses, space and light, in which colour played almost no part. This was a general artistic theory of the age. Speaking of painting, Fréart de Chambray stresses "proportion, symmetry and agreement of the whole with its parts, taught above all by geometry, the source and guide of all the arts," adding that colour was a matter of light and shade, "in a sense a branch of perspective."

This curious theory seems to have stemmed from Copernicus's discovery that the earth revolves round the sun, which showed that things are not what they seem and created a profound distrust of sense experience. Since we cannot trust sense experience, argued Descartes, we must make reason our supreme tribunal. Thus the existence of God was proved no longer from our experience of the world, which might be misleading, but from "reason," from man's ideas of God. This line of argument resulted in a belief that secondary qualities—colour, taste, texture, smell—were somehow less "real" than primary qualities—what can be weighed, measured and expressed mathematically, for the latter, it was argued, could be grasped by man's reason, independently of sense experience.

A subconscious acceptance of these principles underlay the lives of Louis and his contemporaries. Thus, Louis's language for all its strength lacks colour: its words are largely abstract and its beauty formal. Versailles, with its silver furniture and gilt mouldings, its tall windows and many mirrors, is a palace of light, not of colour; its surfaces are smooth and polished, like a model in solid geometry. Again the regularity of life in Versailles was the expression of mathematical order, in contrast to the disorder say of cloud formations, or of the branches of a tree.

Descartes prided himself on being able to define the properties of curved lines and even to analyse man's passions. The *grand siècle* believed that it could push still further the reduction of the unknown and seemingly arbitrary to mathematical formulae. Louis's love of order was a belief in the importance of geometry: of setting things out in rows or lines, and establishing a relation between them which would satisfy the mind. But what satisfied Louis's mind? Long vistas linked to a central feature, symmetry, and unity.

Louis considered it very important to visit each feature of the gardens in a certain order. That is why he wrote a short *Guide to the Gardens of Versailles*, in which each step is foreseen, as in a choreography or ritual. "Next we go to the Pyramid, where we pause a moment, then return to the château by the marble stairway between the *Ecorcheur* and the *Vénus honteuse*. At the top of the steps we turn to look at the flower-beds to the north, the statues, vases, crowns, the Pyramid and what can be seen of Neptune. . . ."

On the mile-long cross-shaped grand canal glided a hundred swans from Denmark, two little yachts from England, carved and gilded galleys decked with red-and-white streamers and hangings fringed with gold, a small warship and a fleet of gondolas, manned by fourteen Venetian gondoliers. Most of the fêtes and ceremonies at Versailles ended on the calm waters of the canal, whether balls, masquerades, operas or plays, the reception of ambassadors or of flags captured from the enemy, marriage feasts or tournaments. There, reclining in boats under the stars, Louis and his friends would listen to string music. For music was as much a part of Versailles as bird-song of the groves in spring. During Louis's *lever* and dinner the violins played. The hautbois, flutes and sackbuts of the Ecurie accompanied him during his walks in the gardens. At chapel he heard motets by Lully: he loved them and would often have them repeated. At supper the Petits Violons played extracts from the King's favourite operas; while after dinner there would often be a concert or ball. Even at his *coucher* someone would sing him a new tune or a cantata. And during his moments of leisure throughout the day Louis would hum one of Lully's gay, haunting songs, such as "Au Clair de la Lune."

In the gardens of Versailles Louis had imposed on nature a strong will and a mind which delighted in order and formal relationships. By their extent, the work involved and their geometrical pattern they were modern: they could never have been achieved in any previous century. Yet this is only part of what the gardens were. The paradox is that strict geometry was the framework of a dream, a dream of the past.

The groves and *allées* of Versailles were peopled with statues of the gods and goddesses of classical antiquity, with statues of Venus, Diana, Ceres, Galatea, Proserpine, Latona, Aurora and Amphitrite, of Jupiter, Apollo, Neptune, Bacchus, Saturn, Proteus and Zephyr, of nymphs and Tritons, Vestals, cupids and fauns. There were no statues of mortals: the least figure here was the demi-god Achilles. Nor were the deities confined to a single part of the gardens: whether near the open-air theatre or in the shady chestnut grove, among the vases and cressets of gilded lead, among the orange trees (some always in bloom), beside the marble steps and leaping waters or the obelisk formed by a hundred jets of gurgling foam gods and goddesses were to be found, not mere bystanders, but with gestures of play and innocent amusement, as though having been brought to life in the operas, ballets and fêtes of the 'sixties, when Louis was in love with Louise de La Vallière, they themselves had fallen in love with so beautiful a garden and decided to make it their home.

Versailles was not merely an actual garden in the Ile de France. La Fontaine, walking there, believed he met the divinities of Fable. Of the water in the Grand Canal he wrote:

> Qu'il soit pur, transparent; que cette onde argentée
> Loge en son moite sein la blanche Galatée.
> Jamais on n'a trouvé ses rives sans zephyrs:
> *Flore* s'y rafraîchit au vent de leurs soupirs;
> Les nymphes d'alentour souvent, dans les nuits sombres,
> S'y vont baigner en troupe à la faveur des ombres.[1]

---

[1] Let it be pure, transparent; let this silvery wave receive white Galatea on its moist breast. Its banks are never without balmy breezes: *Flora* cools herself

And the young Duc de Bourgogne, on his first visit, is said to have hailed the gardens like this: "Am I in lovely Paphos, or walking in the happy woods beside Tibur, in the country of Baiae, divided by streams, or in Tempe, with its well-watered woods?" The world of geometry, with its straight lines, regular curves and balance of masses, was real, but the world of the gods and goddesses of Rome was real also: that is to say, it was believed to have existed once and therefore might be made to exist again. Both mattered very much to Louis and his Court: both had to have their place in any masterpiece.

The gardens of Versailles might one day go the way of the hanging gardens of Babylon, and so it became important to immortalise them in works of art. When he commissioned Jean Cotelle to paint the gardens, Louis, as always, gave detailed instructions about what he wanted depicted. Cotelle's series of paintings show Louis's vision of Versailles, what it meant to the King. We find in the paintings the familiar groves and arbours, the fountains and marble columns, but who are these people in the foreground, these groups of figures in the sky? They wear Roman dress; they clasp bows and amphorae; they are attended by nymphs and cupids. They are, in fact, classical goddesses, and a few are gods. They are no longer statues, but actual beings, living, breathing, moving, taking part in the pleasures. The beauty of Versailles has given them life, or if they are still alive, attracted them from Olympus.

Versailles, then, was a house for the King and his Court and a place of government, but its gardens were part of the early dream with Louise de La Vallière. They were Louis's attempt to create a pagan paradise: finally to realise, in imagination, that world of beauty, harmony and innocence which was the subject of his education and so many of his favourite arts, a world where one did not have to marry for political reasons, and a man might love the most beautiful among the water nymphs without being touched by remorse or scruples, a world untouched by the passing of time.

---

there as they softly sigh; often on dark nights the nymphs from nearby go and bathe in groups in the shadowy waters.

CHAPTER 14

Madame de Maintenon

DURING THE LAST YEARS of Madame de Montespan's reign, while she was using poison, spells and intrigue against pretty young rivals like Marie-Angélique de Fontanges, unknown to her an older woman was beginning to interest the King. Madame de Maintenon was considered an oddity, because she always dressed in black, with gold or silver trimmings only because etiquette demanded them. But she was an admirable nurse, and later governess, to Louis's children by Madame de Montespan. Whereas the Montespan let them eat between meals and stay up very late for supper, Madame de Maintenon insisted on regularity and early hours. When they fell ill, it was she who nursed them, sometimes all night, while their mother gambled at cards. In 1680, the year of the Montespan's fall, when Louis was forty-two, Madame de Maintenon was forty-five: still very attractive, with dark hair, brown intelligent eyes and a good figure. Whenever Louis went to see his children, he found himself talking as much to her as to them. Soon he became curious about Madame de Maintenon as a person, not merely as his children's governess. He asked her questions, he listened to her childhood memories. Gradually he learned the story of her very unusual life.

She was born Françoise d'Aubigné, grand-daughter of Théodore Agrippa d'Aubigné—brave soldier, poet and historian, a staunch Huguenot and one of Henri IV's closest friends, though he could not forgive the King for becoming a Catholic. Always outspoken, it was he who had prophesied, pointing to the scar on the King's lip made by a would-be assassin: "Sire, you have only renounced God with your lips and He has been content to pierce them, but if you should renounce him with your heart, then He will pierce your heart." Agrippa d'Aubigné resembled some Old Testament leader, and felt himself guided by God. In later life he retired to Geneva, where he made occasional pronouncements of high moral rectitude and brooded on the fact that once, in a moment of temptation, he had fathered an illegitimate child.

Agrippa's son, Madame de Maintenon's father, had been a very different type of man. After a brief appearance at Court wearing rose-coloured stockings and roses on his shoes, he turned from playing the viola to counterfeiting money, betraying his political friends and repeatedly changing his religion. Having caught his wife sleeping with a lover, he coolly killed her. Imprisoned in Bordeaux's Château Trompette for having joined one of Gaston d'Orléans's conspiracies, he courted and eventually married the daughter of the prison governor, Jeanne de Cardilhac. Their third child, a girl named Françoise after her godfather, François de La Rochefoucauld, was born in the prison precincts.

"My mother never kissed me," Françoise once confessed: as the wife of a prisoner, she was too busy trying to support her poverty-stricken family. Françoise had no close or warm relationship either with her mother or with her father, and very early she had to fend for herself. Yet her childhood was fairly happy. She was sent to live with a dear great-aunt, Agrippa's sister, Madame de Villette, and brought up a Calvinist until the age of ten, when the whole family sailed for the West Indies. For eighteen months her father held a post in Martinique and Françoise was free to enjoy an exotic world of palm trees, hot golden sands and strange meals: sea-cow instead of beef, lizards instead of chicken, bread made from the cassava plant. When the family returned to France, poor as ever, Françoise again went to live with her Calvinist aunt, where she was known as "the young Indian girl."

The family of Françoise's mother, staunch Catholics, were highly indignant that this young girl was being raised as a Calvinist. Madame de Neuillan, Françoise's maternal aunt, obtained a formal order from Anne of Austria giving her control of Françoise's education. Presently she was taken into the Neuillan family, who treated her much less well than the Villettes had done. Her aunt had a coach and six, but Françoise was given clogs to wear and told to mind the turkeys, while memorising whole pages of Pibrac's *Moral Quatrains*.   One Sunday she was forced to attend Mass, but the little Calvinist bravely turned her back to the altar, for which she received a sound spanking.

At the age of fifteen she was taken to Paris and entrusted to the Ursuline nuns. After listening to a long debate between a learned Calvinist and a Catholic theologian, she was converted to Catholicism, but only after she had been assured that her dear aunt, Madame de Villette, would not suffer eternal damnation. Another important event occurred on this visit to Paris: Françoise was taken by a mutual friend to call on Paul Scarron.

Scarron was then aged forty-one. He came of a family of well-to-do magistrates. As a young man he had been wild and eccentric: once during carnival he had stripped to the skin, smeared his body with honey, rolled himself in feathers, and danced through the streets. When other revellers began to pick off his feathers, Scarron dived into the river and remained immersed until the crowd scattered. As a result he developed rheumatoid arthritis, and his body became terribly deformed, like a gnarled and twisted grapevine. But he remained a gay fellow and took his misfortune in good part. Going to Anne of Austria, he asked her to create for him a new post—"the Queen's Invalid," with a pension which would allow him to continue writing his witty verses. "If I live in the Louvre, Your Majesty will be protected from every dangerous disease, since I will be sure to catch them first. Also, Your Majesty will be founding a hospital, for in my body I have assembled practically every known illness." Anne made him a gift of 250 écus (£250), and a year or two later did indeed install him as "the Queen's Invalid," with a small pension. However, Scarron still remained short of money: he grew so tired of dedicating books to nobles who did not help him that he inscribed the third edition of his collected verses to Dame Guillemette, his sister's lapdog. In the year that Françoise d'Aubigné visited him Part I of his *Roman Comique*, a witty satire about strolling players, was making all France laugh.

Scarron was paralysed, except for his tongue and slight use of his fingers. He sat in a grey chair, with a small stick to scratch himself when necessary. Some even claimed that his hat was held by a cord which passed through a pulley, by which he raised and lowered it to greet visitors. As soon as she saw poor Scarron's Z-shaped body, Françoise burst into tears of pity. Presently she recovered herself and began to talk to the famous man, perhaps about the West Indies, for Scarron hoped to emigrate there in the hope that the sun would cure his arthritis. Françoise made a very favourable impression and when she left Paris, Scarron wrote:

Mademoiselle,

I always suspected that the little girl whom I saw enter my room six months ago with a gown too short, and who began to weep, I do not know why, was as witty as she looked. The letter which you have written to Mademoiselle de Saint-Hermant [a relative in Paris] is so full of wit that I am ill satisfied with mine for not having immediately recognised your merit. To tell you the truth, I had never believed that in the Islands of America, or with the nuns at Niort, one could learn how to turn a graceful phrase: and I cannot well imagine for what reason you have taken as much care to hide your wit as another takes to show his. Now that you are discovered, you ought not to make any stronger objection to writing to me than to Mademoiselle de Saint-Hermant. I shall do all I can to reply with as good a letter as yours, and you will have the pleasure of seeing that I am very far from having as much wit as you: such as I am, I shall be all my life.

Scarron felt sorry for Françoise, so rich in "wit" yet without a penny, and at the mercy of an ambitious aunt. She was a Cinderella figure who did not pity herself. Scarron generously offered to give her a dowry, with which she could either marry or enter a convent. With dignity she declined the dowry. Then he proposed marriage himself. Though she cannot have been physically attracted, Françoise said yes. And in 1652, at the age of sixteen, she was married to the burlesque poet Paul Scarron. She was his wife in name only. As Anne of Austria put it: "A wife was the least useful furniture in his house."

That house, in the Marais, Scarron called the "Hôtel d'Impécuniosité," for though there were fine carpets and hangings of yellow damask, few were paid for. Paul Scarron taught his wife Latin, Spanish and Italian, the pure language of the Précieuses and how to write verse. Madame Scarron began to hold a salon, where she received the wittiest and most famous men of France. According to Mademoiselle de Scudéry, "she had the most beautiful eyes in the world; they were black, brilliant, sweet, passionate and full of spirit." Scarron adored her but even for her sake would not stop spending large sums in the hope of a cure. He obtained the King's permission to install a private laboratory, "to study the secret of metals, minerals, semi-minerals and vegetables . . . to extract the essences and salts, and to compose balms and medicines," also to render gold into a potable fluid. His wife had no faith in these devices.

During her eight years of marriage Françoise showed a strong sense of duty, pleasure in a quiet, serious manner of living, a fund of prudent wisdom (Scarron spoke of it more than once) and an ability to make and keep friends. She showed little interest in material possessions, and refused to accept as lovers the rich men who courted her.

Two months after she had witnessed with such excitement the entrance of Louis and his bride into Paris, Françoise was left a widow. In his will Scarron bequeathed to his "ignorant physician" the disease which had tormented him so long, and to Françoise permission to re-marry: he believed she would do so soon because "I have forced her to fast, and that should have given her a good appetite; let her enjoy it then a little and let her prudent wisdom not have recourse to a paralytic. . . . On the other hand, let her not reproach her second husband with the virtues of the first."

But the widow Scarron did not re-marry. She was very poor until Anne of Austria, alarmed at "the danger of leaving so young and beautiful a woman in such dire need," gave her an annual pension of £700. She lived as a lady boarder in a Paris convent, and continued to make herself useful to friends. She was somewhat reserved but Madame de Sévigné managed to draw her out and found her talk "delicious." She was never idle; even in a lurching carriage she would work at her tapestry, and on summer holidays with Madame de Montchevreuil would be up at six to pick caterpillars off the rose-bushes.

When Madame de Montespan was expecting her first child by Louis, the question arose, who should bring it up? A mutual friend approached the widow Scarron, whose reaction is typical. Instead of snatching at a chance to advance herself, to enter the orbit of the Sun King, she consulted her confessor. Her confessor told her that she must not consent to bring up, even in secret, a child who was the fruit of the Montespan's adultery with an unknown father. But if Louis himself intervened, avowed his paternity, requested Madame Scarron to bring up the child of the King of France, then she as his subject could not claim any right to decline. That is what happened, and so Madame Scarron, a widow who had never really been a wife became responsible for a child, and later of children, who were not hers.

She considered the post an honour—but it involved hard work and worry. Even workmen had to be kept outside the house which served as a crèche. "I used to climb on a ladder to do their jobs myself. . . . The nurses would never put their hands to a thing, for fear they might be tired and their milk less good. . . . Often I would go from one nurse to the other, in disguise, carrying a basket full of linen and meat on my arm, and I would sometimes spend the whole night with one of the children lying sick in a house outside Paris. I used to get back to my home in the mornings by a back door, and after dressing I would get into a coach at the front door to drive to the Hôtel d'Albret or the Hôtel Richelieu, so that my friends should not even suspect that I had a secret to keep. People wondered why I was growing thin."

In 1675 Louis repaid Madame Scarron's discretion and care by giving her sufficient money to buy the estate of Maintenon, a moated castle with pepper-pot towers, and from that year the children's governess came to be called Madame de Maintenon. Sometimes she would take them down to Saint-Germain in a closed coach, to visit their father, who was becoming increasingly fond of them. The impression she made on the King was not very favourable. "I do not like your *bel esprit*," he would say to the Montespan; she was neither smart nor sophisticated, her black dresses seemed to him affectation, and worst of all she liked to discuss "sublime subjects"—which at this period Louis abhorred.

Madame de Maintenon made the eldest boy, the Duc du Maine, write extracts from ancient history, which she entitled *Oeuvres diverses d'un auteur de sept ans* and dedicated to Madame de Montespan with a discreet hint to mend her life: "I know his most secret thoughts, Madame, and the admiration with which he listens to what you say; I can assure you in all truth that he studies you much more closely than his books." In one of his letters the little Duc complained to his mother that she had not seemed sad at their last parting: again it was the governess giving a little lesson in maternal love. That seems to have been the Maintenon's way: perseverance in secret.

Her prudence was continually to the fore. Louise de La Vallière she had advised not to rush into austerities, but to make a "trial trip," as a lady boarder. Louise replied, "Would *that* be a penance? Such a life is very pleasant. That is not what I want." On a later occasion she advised Mademoiselle de Fontanges to give up the King. The favourite replied scornfully, "You speak of removing a passion as though it were a dress." Again, during a furious argument, the Montespan had once asked her acidly, "What keeps you at Court?" "The King's will, my duty, my gratitude and the interests of those dear to me." On all three occasions Madame de Maintenon had shown much good sense, but little feeling.

She was, indeed, a woman of duty rather than of warmth and affection: in this the grandchild of that Old Testament Calvinist who held in such abhorrence sins of the flesh. On her signet ring was inscribed the word "*Recte*" with a plumb-line. In her marriage with Scarron she had sought not love but a useful and sometimes dominant role; she had agreed to bring up Louis's children not from love but from duty. And yet she was not altogether a cold woman. Madame de Sévigné, who seldom made psychological mistakes, confessed that she could thaw. She seems, rather, to have been frightened of her feelings: perhaps with reason, for after all her father had served a prison sentence for treason, while one of her brothers was a heavy drinker who chased the girls, and the other a suicide. She was afraid, too, of the wrath of the Almighty. According to the courtesan Ninon de Lenclos, she "was virtuous out of weak-mindedness. I tried to cure her, but she was too much afraid of God."

Meanwhile, Louis was becoming interested in this unusual woman. For a woman to please the King she had to be good-looking; to hold him she had to have wit. Madame de Maintenon was still beautiful and looked scarcely more than thirty. As for wit, it was the first thing about her to strike Paul Scarron. Hers was quite a different kind of wit from the Montespan's: less imaginative and funny but more solid: a way of saying sensible things crisply. At first it had savoured to Louis of the Précieuses; it had seemed to him out of touch with life because it was out of touch with the Court. Gradually he recognised his mistake. Her tenderness to his children also pleased Louis. "Madame de Maintenon knows how to love," he was once heard to say. "There would be great pleasure in being loved by her."

Then, again, she had an admirable gift for detail: when her brother married she worked out his budget down to the last wax candle, and even reminded him to be sure and mark any linen he sent to the laundry. Now exactitude and thoroughness were traits which Louis much admired. Madame de Maintenon was a woman who got things done—and this too was something Louis admired. But the new thing for Louis was this—here was a highly attractive woman who lived not for herself but for others. All her life had been spent helping other people.

In the last years of the 'seventies Louis felt more and more drawn to Madame de Maintenon and gradually his feelings turned to love. Because of his Bourbon temperament, as soon as he was in love he wanted to sleep with her. It was just at this point that Madame de Maintenon showed herself unique among all the ladies of his kingdom. She declined! She who owed him her marquisate, her position as governess, her apartments in the royal palace, declined the honour of being loved by the Sun King. Moreover, she declined for the strangest of reasons—because sleeping with a man not her husband, even were he King of France, was sinful.

Doubtless Louis was very surprised, but he certainly was not repelled either by her sense of sin or by her rather cold temperament. Cold natures often act as a challenge to those who are sensual, and so it seems to have been with Madame de Maintenon and Louis. He began to spend hours at a time in her apartments. When "the affair of the poisons" had opened his eyes to the Montespan, he began to value even more Madame de Maintenon's moral rectitude. And she, believing it her destiny to turn Louis back to the path of virtue, pleaded with him (as once Mademoiselle de La Fayette had pleaded with Louis XIII) to be kind and loving and faithful towards his Spanish wife.

The circumstances were favourable. Louis had broken with the Montespan and had no wish to embark on another passionate love affair. He felt a new need for stability and moderation. Since Madame de Maintenon would not become his mistress, he took her advice and for almost three years proved himself an excellent husband to Marie Thérèse. The Queen was delighted: "she displayed so much satisfaction that it was commonly remarked. She had no objection to being joked about this subject, and upon such occasions used to laugh and wink and rub her little hands." She had her portrait painted and gave it to Madame de Maintenon as a token of gratitude.

So for the last part of her life the Queen was happy. She had a year to enjoy her marble and gilt apartments at Versailles, which faced south and got all the sun. She could not play a full part at Court, for she still had not mastered the French language; she divided her time between gambling and the oratory. Of her children, only the Dauphin survived: a fat, lazy young man but a dutiful son. In the summer of 1683, when only forty-five, the Queen fell ill of an abscess under her arm: "Instead of making it burst, Fagon her physician had her blooded; this drove in the abscess, the disorder attacked her internally, and an emetic, which was administered after her bleeding, had the effect of killing the Queen."

So ended twenty-three years of that curious hybrid, political marriage. There had been a happy honeymoon and a happy twilight, when Louis had begun to appreciate just how good a person his wife was, but in no circumstances could it ever have been a close union. "He loved her for her virtue, and for the sincere affection she bore him notwithstanding his unfaithfulness." In all their married life, Louis was heard to remark, she had never once caused him a moment's pain. He knew that he could not say as much of his own behaviour, though he had always shown consideration, and made his mistresses treat Her Majesty with all becoming respect.

In the months following the Queen's death Louis, wearing full violet mourning, alone now as he had never been before, took stock of his life. He had built up France, developed its industries, extended its frontiers: he had won a fair measure of military glory; he was unquestionably the most powerful man in the world. But what of his own self? He had always wanted to lead a regular personal life; long ago he had promised Marie Thérèse that he would settle down at thirty. This year he would be forty-five, and he felt that need more urgently than ever. Should he make another political marriage, say to the Infanta of Portugal or to a Tuscan princess? Such an alliance with a foreign power would certainly benefit France and, if it produced more children, would strengthen the succession. But would it lead to an orderly personal life? Hardly, for at forty-five Louis was beginning to be set in his ways, and being a Frenchman to his finger-tips would find it difficult to adapt himself to a complete stranger who was also a foreigner. On the other hand, there was no eligible Frenchwoman who possessed the blood royal deemed essential to a Queen of France. And yet he could not dispense with a woman. He was far too virile for that.

The woman Louis most loved and respected was Françoise d'Aubigné, Madame de Maintenon. Although she declined to become his mistress, he believed that she loved him too in that odd, unemotional way which was hers. But by birth she was a commoner. Although she had the particle *de* in front of her surname and possesed good connections, she was a complete nobody. For the Sun King to take as his Queen so pale a satellite was unthinkable, for it would shatter God's order in France, of which rank was believed to be an integral part. An example had occurred in 1670 when Mademoiselle, a princess of the blood royal, had

wished to marry the Comte de Lauzun. There had been such an
outcry from all classes that Louis, who privately favoured the
marriage, had been obliged to step in and stop it.

Ever since his love affair with Marie Mancini Louis had been
conscious, often painfully conscious, of this conflict of loyalties
between his private and public lives, between his own fulfilment
and the welfare of France. Surely even royalty had a right to a
happy marriage—not from mere selfishness but because without
some measure of domestic stability a Christian life became impossible? Yet to strike out now for personal happiness would be an
act of boldness almost as difficult as it would have been to marry
Marie Mancini in face of his mother and of Mazarin. A marriage
with Madame de Maintenon would have to be morganatic, and
no French king had ever contracted such a union. True, succession
to the throne would not be in question, for Madame de Maintenon
was past the age when she could hope to bear children. But even
so, since the King embodied his kingdom, this marriage with the
widow of a burlesque poet would make France a laughing-stock
before the world, it would undo all the glory for which he had
toiled so long. No, even a morganatic marriage was unthinkable.

But what if the marriage were kept hidden? One of the most
striking of Françoise de Maintenon's gifts was her capacity for
keeping a secret. Masked, she had entered the Montespan's bedroom to remove her new-born children, and never a whisper about
their birth or upbringing was heard at Court. And later, when
Louis so often went to her room, she never boasted, as every other
favourite had done, that the King enjoyed her company. Her black
dress was the very symbol of discretion. And so a plan began to
take shape in Louis's mind, a breathtaking plan. No one was told:
it had to be secret.

Secret it has remained. Only a phrase here and there allows us
to guess what was happening. On 7th August, 1683, eight days
after the Queen's death, Françoise de Maintenon wrote to her
brother: "The reason which prevents me seeing you is so useful
and so glorious that you ought to be full of joy." On 14th August
she wrote to Villette, her cousin: "The news you send me is false:
the King has no love affairs—you can say so without being afraid

of appearing ill-informed." On 14th September Cardinal Cybo wrote from Rome that the Pope had heard with keen satisfaction the account of Fr. de La Chaize's conversation about the King's "piety" and asked God to shower down on His Majesty abundant blessings. (Fr. de La Chaize was Louis's confessor.) A present to Madame de Maintenon arrived from Rome: she wrote about it at once to her confidante, Madame de Brinon: "With all my heart I wish I could have hidden the present I have received from Rome, for I am so glorified in this world on account of certain good intentions which come from God, that I have reason to fear I shall be humiliated and confounded in the next; there is nothing to reply on the subject of Louis and Françoise; those rumours do circulate—but I'd like to know why she would be unwilling? I should never have believed that difficulties in this matter would come from her side." ("Hide" and "fear" are words which recur often at this period.)

On 20th September, to her confessor: "Don't forget me in your prayers, for I greatly need strength in order to make good use of my happiness." On 11th October, to Madame de Brinon: "I am dying to see you. I haven't had time yet to get my bearings (*me reconnaître*)." On 5th December, to the same: "I beg you to speak to absolutely no one but me about that man"—meaning the King.

Six months later, on 18th June, 1684, in a letter to her brother: "Our positions in life are different, mine brilliant, yours calm, and perhaps sensible people would find it just as good. God has put me where I am, I must do as best I can. He knows that I have not sought my position; I shall never rise higher, that is something I know all too well." In other letters from this period: "my situation is of the kind which cannot be discussed" and "I am incapable of making any unreasonable demand to him to whom I owe everything."

What were the happiness and glorious position at which she hinted? That she had not become Louis's mistress is shown by her reference to the position being God-given. As for money and rank, these had little value for the Maintenon. And at this time, as is clear from other sources, neither she nor any of her relatives and protegées enjoyed striking success at Court. Her happiness lay elsewhere. Within months of the Queen's death Louis asked Françoise de Maintenon to be his wife but not his Queen, and she gave her consent, renouncing beforehand all the external signs of a greatness that was never to be made known.

When did the marriage take place? According to Saint-Simon's guess, in mid-winter 1683-4; according to the Abbé de Choisy's guess, in 1684—for in 1687, "three years after her marriage," Choisy gave Madame de Maintenon a copy of his *Journal du voyage en Siam.* The evidence of Madame de Maintenon's own letters suggests June, 1684. It seems likely that the marriage took place at night in the chapel of Versailles, that the altar was prepared by Bontemps, Louis's first *valet de chambre*: that Mass was said by Fr. de La Chaize, and that the nuptial blessing was given by Harlay, Archbishop of Paris. The witnesses were probably Louvois, Minister of War, and the Marquis de Montchevreuil, an old friend of Madame de Maintenon and now Governor of the Duc du Maine.

Louis was forty-five, Françoise forty-eight. It is possible that during the ceremony he gave her his left hand, instead of his right. This was the custom in morganatic marriages, hence their name: "left-handed marriages." It was usual for a contract to be drawn up and signed, and for an entry to be made in the parish register. Neither has been found, but neither was essential for the validity of the marriage.

Would it be possible to keep the marriage secret from all save the inner circle of five? Almost every action on every day of the King's life was and would have to continue public; he lived in a whispering gallery of five thousand people; he went to bed and got up watched by a score of courtiers, quick, brilliant men who knew how to interpret the least glance, the slightest nod. Somehow Louis and this woman whom he had learned to trust must lead, behind the public life, a secret private life, so secret that the Court which had always known when he took a new mistress, must never suspect that he had now taken a new wife.

The plan succeeded. Of course the amount of time Louis spent in Madame de Maintenon's company excited rumours, but they were never more than rumours. Some people guessed, but no one knew for certain. Even Louis's own sister-in-law Elizabeth Charlotte of Bavaria, who had married Monsieur in 1671, a year after Henriette's death, and knew most Court secrets, did not know whether the King had a wife. In 1686 she wrote to the Duchess of Hanover: "As long as there is no declaration, I find it difficult to believe. To judge by marriages in this country, if they were really husband and wife, their love would not be as strong as it is now, unless keeping it secret adds a spice lacking in publicly declared marriages." In 1687: "I have not been able to discover whether or not the King has married Madame de Maintenon. Many people say that she is his wife and that the Archbishop of Paris married them, in the presence of the King's confessor and Madame de Maintenon's brother; others deny it and it is impossible to know which view is correct. But what is certain is that the King has never had, for any of his mistresses, the passion that he feels for her; it is really curious to see them together. If she happens to be in the same place he cannot remain quarter of an hour without whispering something to her or speaking to her in secret, although he has spent the whole day with her."

For both Louis and Françoise it was a second marriage after an unsatisfactory first marriage; to both it brought happiness. Touching little notes are extant, in which Louis courteously requests the privilege of her company, of a walk with her, of a meeting, the hour and place being left for her to decide. At last he had been able in some measure to reconcile passion and reason, beauty and order. As for Madame de Maintenon, the tone of her letters reveals happiness—her own particular brand of happiness: believing herself in a position (at God's prompting) to achieve good. Born in a prison precinct, brought up penniless to become the wife in name only of a burlesque poet, then foster-mother to someone else's children, she was now mistress, though only half a dozen people knew it, of Versailles, its palace and gardens; united till death with the King of France. "Her position is unique in the world," wrote Madame de Sévigné, another who guessed the truth. "There never has been nor ever will be again anything like it."

CHAPTER 15

The Grandeur of France

HOW DID LOUIS GOVERN FRANCE? What did he achieve and what did he change? Here as so often his actions flowed from fixed principles. According to Bossuet, monarchy is the most usual, the oldest and the most natural form of government, being modelled on the family. It is also the best, because most opposed to division. Of all monarchies the most perfect is the hereditary, especially from father to eldest son, because this is the form God established among his chosen people. A monarch must be reasonable, but should he happen to yield to irregularity, inconstancy, inequality or eccentricity, the people must continue to practise obedience: instead of criticising the form of government they must profit from the security it affords to lead Christian lives.

Louis accepted these principles, but put more stress on his people's welfare. "A King," he wrote, "must bring all classes of his subjects to the perfection befitting their nature." "When a King labours for the State, he labours for himself; the welfare of the one constitutes the glory of the other. When the former is great, happy and powerful, he who is the cause of all these advantages is glorious."

Good government, Louis wrote in his Memoirs, stems primarily from the application of common sense to a sufficient number of facts. The King's common sense is less fallible than other men's, because God gives him special guidance. Bad government arises from natural predilections, from wanting to please this or that friend or from accepting advice without weighing it: that is why Louis advised his son to turn a plan over twenty times before carrying it out. These rules worked well in practice, for Louis's mind was analytical, not intuitive.

Louis ruled with the help of a Council of State, which met every week-day morning at a table covered with green velvet edged with gold. Louis chose the questions to be discussed: decisions were taken not by majority vote but by the King, who spoke last. In this sense Louis was responsible for all the achievements of his reign. The Council consisted of only four members, but these were joined in later years by the Dauphin and by the Dauphin's son. In 1672 the four members were Le Tellier, Pomponne, Louvois and Colbert. They were all from the middle class: such men, Louis believed, were less swayed by passion than powerful nobles, and since they owed everything to him would work more devotedly. Louvois was the son of Le Tellier; when Louvois died, Louis said to King James II: "I have lost a good Minister, but neither your affairs nor mine shall go the worse for it." He then appointed Louvois's son Barbesieux to the Council, telling him, "I trained your father and I will train you." He preferred to employ men with a family tradition of service. Colbert was succeeded by his son, Seignelay; Colbert's brother, Colbert de Croissy, became Foreign Minister, to be succeeded by his son Torcy. All were extremely able. Indeed, Louis had only three mediocre Ministers, the two Briennes and Chamillart. All three he disgraced. He also disgraced Pomponne, whom he considered slow and lacking in grandeur, but twelve years later, in 1691, reappointed him.

The four Ministers comprising the Council of State were chosen precisely because they were reasonable, balanced men, without dominant passions, and so their lives tend to be sober and lacking in incident. An exception is Louvois, who was cruel, bullying and sometimes brutal, for ever cracking his whip. Fossier the sculptor complains that his pension is in arrears: let him shut up or he will be thrown into prison. Workmen at a certain fortress are slacking; let them knuckle down or they will pay with their lives. Louvois's tone is unique in governmental correspondence, which was invariably firm but also moderate and polite. Louvois, who built up the army, did not get on with Colbert, who was a navy man; this gave rise to tension and rivalry: for example, Colbert would not commission the painter Mignard because Mignard was Louvois's protégé, and in 1688 Louvois dismantled a fortress in Cherbourg solely to annoy Seignelay, who had ordered it built. But the striking thing is not these small differences but the harmony in Council over fifty-five years, the Ministers' tireless devotion and loyalty to their King. This loyalty permeated all departments: during the whole reign only one case of treason occurred, in 1664, when an official named La Pause was discovered selling secrets.

In Louis's view monarchy could work only if the King had unquestioned authority, the authority which flows from a disciplined character and the possession of more power than any other body in the State. That had been the lesson of the Fronde. So the most important of Louis's reforms was to diminish privilege and to increase the power of the Crown. As regards the armed forc' in 1662 on the death of the Duc d'Épernon the post of col .cl-general of the French infantry was abolished, and in future Louis conferred all the appointments, hitherto the prerogative of the colonel-general. In appointing the Duc de Vivonne commander of the Mediterranean fleet in 1669, Louis took away his right to appoint captains to his galleys and to pay his men: a special Treasurer of the Galleys was appointed answerable to the King. By 1670 every French regiment and ship was under the control of civilians. Similarly Louis took away from provincial governors all authority over garrisons and control of public money. These functions, abused in the past, were given to intendants, Louis's own representatives, middle-class men with legal training answerable only to the King and his Ministers.

In other fields the need for reform was no less pressing. Louis's decisions in Council were transmitted to the provincial Parlements, whose duty it was to register them. Here, at the beginning of his personal reign, Louis came up against a tangle of privilege, injustice, corruption, local vendettas and vested interests. In 1661, at Toulouse, a councillor of Parlement murdered a man in the street in full daylight; he got off scot-free. Certain curés of Languedoc ill-treated a bailiff sent by the Secretary of State, La Vrillière. The Bishop of Lodève, informing Colbert of this, added: "If the matter is referred to the Parlement of Toulouse or to some local judge, to be reduced to the rules of parliamentary chicanery, it will never end, and the crime remain unpunished to the very great prejudice of the King's authority."

In June, 1662, Louis prescribed that in each town of the kingdom a hospital should be founded for the sick poor, beggars and orphans. This was plainly a beneficial measure, but the Parlement of Dijon obstinately refused to register it. When Colbert proposed a canal between Beaucaire and Aigues-Mortes, the intendant Besons reported: "The scheme is useful for the service of the King and the good of the provinces, but because of vested interests the States will not pass it; they do not understand the advantages of trade." Clearly in these conditions little could be done for the welfare of France.

It was one of Louis's major achievements to induce Parlements to co-operate with the Government without drastically curtailing their rights. First, he made clear that the provincial Parlements, like the Paris Parlement, must confine their discussions to judicial matters. Then, in order to cut short futile debates that dragged on from session to session, he imposed a deadline: if, in regard to any edict, Parlement wished to present the King with its "very humble remonstrances," it must do so within a week or, in the case of provincial Parlements, within six weeks. In another decree dated October, 1665, Louis took away from Parlements the title of *cours souveraines* and replaced it by that of *cours supérieures*. This change was less extreme than may appear: it merely allowed Louis greater freedom of action in certain cases. For example, in 1680, when the Parlement of Rouen condemned several sorcerers to be burned, Louis was able to step in and stop the execution.

Louis went on to reform municipal powers. Mayors of large towns often had their own cannon and gunners; in 1665 Louis directed that all such cannon should be handed over; they needed, he said, to be recast. In 1668 he reduced the number of aldermen from twenty to four, decreed that four years must elapse before a mayor or alderman held office a second time, and also laid down that any deputations travelling at public expense must be approved by the Government. To soften these blows in the same month Louis authorised mayors and aldermen to wear robes of violet satin and ermine mantles. This was a feature of his policy: while adding braid and tassels to the scabbard he quietly removed the sword.

Mayors, however, continued to be a problem. They were powerful men: the mayor of Dijon, for instance, was colonel of the local militia, 10,000 strong. He was elected for a term of years, but only about two per cent of the townspeople had a vote—in Dijon those who paid taxes of £1 or more a year. Continual complaints came in that mayors favoured those who had voted for them and penalised others. In 1692 Louis decreed that in future mayors would be appointed by the Government for life, to ensure that they exercised their functions with equity and "without passion." This was the most extreme of Louis's encroachments on local rights.

In certain provinces such as Languedoc, Brittany and Burgundy Louis had to get his measures passed not only by the local Parlement and municipality but by the States General. The States General of Burgundy, for example, was convoked every two or three years by letters patent of the King. It sat in June for twenty days and numbered some 450 persons of whom seventy-two were from the third estate.

For the first fifteen years of his personal reign Louis had to use tact, persuasion and even cajolery with this powerful body. Several of his measures aroused opposition: for example, the decree that all titles of nobility must be scrutinised, which meant that many self-styled nobles suddenly found themselves paying taxes, and the decree that all municipal debts must be paid off, which resulted in rich townsmen having to aid the poorer peasants. Again, in 1665, Louis proposed that industries should be started in Burgundy; the States retorted that that was impossible "because it was very expensive, difficult and useless." Only after a struggle did they agree to vote £10,000—two-thirds of the sum requested—over three years. Always the initiative came from the Government: new roads, bridges, a plan for making the Arroux navigable, a new canal from the Saône to the Loire, and each time Louis had to battle with privilege, inertia and often simply a spirit of independence in order to get his measures approved.

It was the States General which voted the sum payable by the province in taxes. In the first part of the reign a provisional sum was suggested by the King, which was then debated and usually lowered. But in 1677 for the first time the States made no fuss: indeed they said they would let Louis fix the sum, "begging His Majesty nevertheless to be content with £400,000." In 1679 even this humble reservation was lacking: "The States have at once unanimously granted the said sum with such deep feelings of respect and love for the sacred person of His Majesty that it would seem there is not one among them who would not give his goods and even his life to contribute to the glory and satisfaction of His Majesty." This remarkable language reflects popular satisfaction with what Louis was achieving at home and abroad. He had won his people's confidence. Right down to the end of the century the States General of Burgundy voted the sum asked for freely and without fuss: only with the disastrous War of the Spanish Succession did they again start making reductions.

The States General of Burgundy remained a free, independent body, and this can be illustrated by a curious incident. It was part of Louis's financial policy to create virtual sinecures and sell them to the highest bidder. One such sinecure was that of the royal dancing master, whose function it was for a set fee to register and control all dancing teachers in a given region. In 1680 the States General declined to approve the letters patent of the royal dancing masters assigned to Burgundy, pointing out that according to an edict of 1617 only surgeons, apothecaries, goldsmiths and locksmiths were obliged to register with "masters." Louis conceded the States' point and the royal dancing masters gracefully withdrew.

A guiding principle in any absolute monarchy is the desire to unify, but often Louis found unity difficult to achieve. One example is his attempt to reduce the weights and measures of France to uniform standards. Plainly this reform would have been beneficial, but the merchants and particularly the people raised an outcry: claiming, for instance, that the *trémic*, the new measure of salt to replace the shovel, kept back a goodly part of what it seemed to pour out. Louis did not enforce his system; he contented himself with standardising the measures used in naval arsenals.

These two typical examples chosen from many others point to a general truth. Usually his immense personal prestige was sufficient for the King to carry through his reforms. If not, he declined to impose them by force or by severe curtailment of existing rights. Louis never flouted majority opinion.

To sum up, Louis's administrative policy was fourfold: strong personal government, the substitution of middle-class intendants for powerful nobles (in other words, the replacement of armed force by law), reduction of privileges open to abuse, and co-operation with local bodies in implementing the countless public works planned by his Council of State. The striking success of the policy can be gauged from official correspondence. In the early 1660's letters from provincial intendants are an almost continual dirge; by 1670 complaints are rarer and by 1675 have almost ceased. The new machinery has begun to work and to work well. Prosecution for bribery or of contractors failing to honour their agreements is no longer a usual occurrence, money voted reaches its destination, violence has virtually disappeared, taxes are assessed impartially: at almost every level there is a new stability, efficiency and confidence.

Louis's second great civil achievement was in the field of law and public order. On 30th May, 1665, he told his Council that having put the finances to rights, he now intended to reform justice, and each Minister was to submit a memorandum on the things to be reformed within three weeks—the deadline is typical of Louis. The result was the new *ordonnance civile*, drawn up and registered in 1667. Among hundreds of small reforms the price of judicial posts was lowered; births, marriages and deaths had to be notified to a registrar; legal procedure was hurried up and made more uniform. As a corollary measure Louis also reopened the Paris law school, which had been closed for a hundred years, and founded chairs of law in all French universities.

In 1670 there followed a code of criminal law; among its reforms a prisoner had to be questioned within twenty-four hours of arrest, and prisons had to be inspected. The *ordonnance* relating to waters and forests and the edict regulating commerce completed the Code Louis, which was to control the legal system of France for a century and a half until replaced by the Code Napoléon. Again, the available records suggest that justice was better administered under Louis XIV than at any time since the thirteenth century. "Complaints and petitions," writes Louis, "arrived in great numbers but I did not allow that to put me off. . . . They enabled me to inform myself in detail about the condition of my people. . . . When cases of injustice came to my attention I made further inquiries and sometimes stepped in to rectify them. One or two examples of this kind prevented a thousand similar abuses."

On two famous occasions Louis decided law-suits against himself. The first case, in 1680, was an action between the King and certain private individuals in Paris who had erected buildings on his land. He gave judgment that the houses should remain to them, together with the land. The other case concerned a Persian named Roupli, whose merchandise had been seized by tax officials in 1687. The King's decision was that all should be returned to him, and he added a present of 3,000 crowns. Roupli carried back to his own country his admiration and gratitude: almost thirty years later, when a Persian ambassador came to Paris, it was discovered that he had long known of the incident and that it was still talked about.

In 1685 Louis published his Code Noir to improve the lot of slaves in the West Indies. Slaves were to be baptised if they wished, and not forced to work on Sundays and holidays. They were allowed to marry. Masters who abused their authority were in future liable to punishment. A scale of food, clothing and care during sickness was laid down. It was forbidden to sell separately a husband, wife and children under age. Emancipation was made easier, and a master over twenty might free a slave without formality. The Code Noir was an outstanding humanitarian measure far in advance of its time.

In the matter of public order, Louis's reforms were no less important. When he came to power, duels were the curse of France. In 1654 the Maréchal de Gramont reckoned that in the past twelve years 940 gentlemen had died in that way. It was a duel in 1663 between eight combatants which determined Louis to suppress the practice once and for all. He did so, thus succeeding where two previous kings had failed, and all Europe followed France's example.

In 1660 according to Boileau Paris at night was more dangerous than a dark wood. In that year Coysevox and his fellow students at the Academy of Arts were afraid to return to their lodgings at seven in the evening for fear of robbery and violence, particularly at the hands of armed lackeys. Louis took a number of measures to restore order. In 1660 and again in 1666 he forbade private individuals to carry arms. He took away the policing of Paris from the magistrates and created the new office of Lieutenant of Police. He chose as its first holder Nicolas-Gabriel de La Reynie, who for thirty years worked tirelessly to make Paris not only safe but cleaner and healthier. The number of police was quadrupled and the streets lit by 5,000 lamps, an innovation soon copied by every capital in Europe.

The third important part of Louis's home government was public works. Louis approved and sometimes himself initiated many hundreds of new projects ranging from the canal linking the Mediterranean and Atlantic to the planting of trees along main roads. Here Paris can serve as an example. At the beginning of his personal reign out of a total of 665 streets only thirty measured from five to eight yards wide. The others ranged in width from a yard and a half to three yards. It was Louis who planted the Champs Elysées in 1667 and three years later pulled down the old bulwarks between the Bastille and the Porte Saint-Martin to make spacious tree-lined "boulevards." It was he who laid out the Faubourgs Saint-Germain and Saint-Honoré, with wide streets and imposing houses. To reduce congestion he limited buildings to a height of forty-five feet. He completed the Tuileries, and to link it with the Left Bank replaced a tottering wooden bridge by the graceful Pont Royal. To improve the water supply fifteen new fountains were installed.

Louis gave Paris the Observatory, the Gobelins, the chapel of the Salpêtrière, and the Louvre Colonnade. In 1676 he inaugurated the Invalides, arcaded buildings round a series of courtyards, the whole covering thirty acres. The Invalides housed 7,000 wounded or old soldiers who would otherwise have had to eke out a living cleaning churches or as bell-ringers. Louis paid particular attention to hostels and to hospitals, which a German writer in 1700 declared to be the best in Europe. In Paris "there is one called the Hôtel Dieu, where gentlefolk and even great nobles come every evening to care for the sick and wounded. . . . The bed-curtains are all of white linen, very well made and embroidered in places with flowers."

It was in 1685 that Louis decided to build an arcaded square in Paris to rival Henri IV's Place Royale (to-day the Place des Vosges). Mansart drew up the plans, which were several times revised, and building began in 1699. The result was that masterpiece of restrained dignity, the octagonal Place Vendôme. Soon provincial cities—Poitiers, Marseille and Pau—were building similar squares to set off a statue of the King.

Stable and efficient government, the enforcement of law and order and a multitude of public works—it was by these achievements that Louis rendered France contented and thriving. He could not have done these things alone. He was helped at every stage by Ministers, intendants, jurists, architects, scientists and craftsmen; by men like Jules Hardouin-Mansart, who became Louis's protégé at the age of twenty-nine, and the honest lawyer Sieur de Novion, who in 1665 rid Auvergne of murder and plunder committed with the connivance of the nobility and even of the governor. In this gallery of Louis's assistants one portrait stands out in sharper detail than the rest: that of Sébastien Le Prestre, Seigneur de Vauban. Vauban was a builder who made France's frontiers strong and secure, thus guaranteeing security and order at home: so he is an apt symbol of the reign.

Vauban was born in 1633 of impoverished gentlepeople living in the wilds of Burgundy. Loyal to his provincial governor, he fought under Condé's flag in the Fronde and was taken prisoner. He was noticed by Mazarin and given a job as sapper, the most dangerous post in the army. It was in 1667 that Louis saw Vauban at work and took to him at once by that mixture of recommendation and personal choice which is found in nearly all the King did. He gave him a lieutenancy in the Guards and a pension of £400 from his private purse. For the next thirty years he employed Vauban unceasingly as foot-soldier, artilleryman, overseer, manufacturer of powder and saltpetre, mining engineer, builder of bridges and canals and roads, hydrographer and surveyor, tactician and strategist.

Peace, far from bringing rest, was the time of hardest work. It was then that Vauban designed and built fortresses to protect the frontiers of France, particularly the new-won frontiers on the north and north-east. These fortresses are among the most marvellous works of the reign. They resemble mammoth starfish, some the size of a small town, built of smoothest, shelving stone, banked with turf, defended by demi-lunes and ditches and glacises. Their ground-plans are like complex geometrical diagrams in which distances, trajectories and tangents determine the siting of each courtine and *place d'armes*.[1]   It was Vauban who made of the fortress a classical work of art: that is, he rationalised and streamlined, doing away with useless excrescences such as orillions of small diameter, enlarging the superficies of bastions and making the courtines rectilinear: "It is not the quantity of outworks that counts, but the arrangement." Thirty-three such fortresses Vauban built; 300 more he repaired and reorganised so as to be virtually new; and it was said that "whatever he invested, fell; whatever he defended, held."

Like Louis himself and all the leading figures of the classical age, whether poets or diplomats, architects or generals, Vauban was a master of detail. For buildings constructed in water and for the extrados of vaults exposed to rain he perfected a special cement: two-thirds crushed tiles, one-third lime, the whole to be diluted with linseed oil. Nothing was too trifling for his attention. At Dunkirk, which was his masterpiece, the glacis was being spoiled by moles: from the other end of France Vauban wrote recommending a particular mole-catcher, an excellent fellow who, he claimed, would also reduce field-mice.

Dunkirk, Strasbourg, the Ile de Ré, Toulon—his work took Vauban back and forth across France by steadily improving roads. In the past loyalties had been provincial; Vauban was one of the first to come to know and love the land of France—all of it, welded into a whole by the King's strong will—and to care deeply about its welfare. As he jogs on a tired horse through the scrub land of

[1] See page 375

Provence he thinks up a clever scheme for irrigating the soil and delightedly jots it down to tell the King. His notebooks are full of such patriotic plans.

Vauban was a robust, hefty man with a big jaw, strong mouth and surprisingly gentle blue eyes. These were the clue to his character. Hard with himself, he was kind and humane to others and hated the bombardments which Louvois favoured. He besieged fifty-six towns and each time he hoped to do it so skilfully that the enemy would yield without a shot being fired. "I would rather preserve 100 of Your Majesty's soldiers than kill 3,000 of the enemy." Events made him a soldier, but he was always dreaming of a quiet farm with cows and apple trees. He was generous to a fault and would share his pay with less fortunate colleagues, whose lot he did much to improve. In the 1660's an engineer was everyone's servant and would last at most five or six sieges before being wounded. Vauban changed all that and in 1675 persuaded the King to make the engineers a separate body, with a proper scale of payment.

Vauban married a Burgundy girl. He was continually begging for leave to go and see her. He rarely got it. "Blessed liberty! which I plainly perceive exists only among the Americans!" He seems to have been a lusty man, for in his will he named four women, including an Irish lass, all of whom claimed to have borne him a child. "I find their claims difficult to believe," wrote Vauban, "but all the same I will make provision for them."

Vauban and Louis were linked by mutual esteem and a deep personal friendship which lasted forty years, till Vauban's death. In a letter of 1706 Vauban says that "after God, the King means everything to me." But he was very outspoken to Louis and often grumbled of overwork. Louis, for his part, would not let a shovelful of earth be moved without Vauban's approval, and in a room of the Tuileries he kept scale models of all Vauban's fortresses, which played such a large part in his own glory. Louis to Vauban, 13th June, 1693: "I have received all your letters. I have not replied very regularly, and I am quite happy to profit by their contents, though my plans do not quite coincide with your thoughts. Continue to write to me what is in your mind, and do not be disappointed if I do not always adopt your suggestions, and if I do not answer very regularly."

One day when working together Vauban told Louis about a citizen of Saint-Malo, "a devout and generous man," and asked that he might be given a patent of nobility. "No," said Louis, "I cannot do that. Nobility is a matter of birth." Vauban took offence, picked up his plans and rose without a word. Louis asked where he was going; Vauban said he was not in the mood for work. For two days Louis did not speak to him and Vauban became uneasy. The third day he presented himself as the King was going to Mass. Louis drew him aside and said, "Vauban, I am not angry with you. I grant you a patent of nobility for your friend."

The incident is revealing, for Vauban was continually siding with the small man. In 1699 he presented Louis with a treatise entitled *La Dîme royale*, which advocated that all taxes should be replaced by a five per cent levy on the products of the soil, no one to be exempt. The system for all its merits was quite impracticable, for Vauban proposed payment in kind and a poor harvest would have left the Treasury with a serious deficit. Moreover, Vauban's proposals challenged the whole basis of Louis's financial policy, which was to create and sell at a high price tax-free offices. Louis, however, did not take the treatise amiss and less than two years later promoted Vauban to be marshal. Vauban died in 1707, modest to the end: "After forty years I find myself only half an engineer."

Vauban was merely one among hundreds of loyal hard-working men who vied with each other in their eagerness to assist the King. From wide interests they were able to make constructive suggestions. The details, indeed the whole execution, of their schemes was doubtless due to them, but the general organisation was the King's. As Voltaire well says, there can be no shadow of doubt that the magistrates would never have reformed the laws, the finances would not have been put on a sound basis, nor industries established, nor discipline introduced into the army, nor a regular police force instituted in Paris; there would have been no fleets nor thriving colonies, no encouragement of science and the arts;

none of these things would ever have been peacefully and steadily accomplished in such a short period and under so many different Ministers, had there not been a ruler to conceive of such great schemes, and with a will strong enough to carry them out. When to these enduring changes are added victories in war and the extension of France's frontiers, by the values of his age the King amply deserved the title bestowed upon him in 1678 by the municipality of Paris: Louis the Great.

CHAPTER 16

The King's Religion

RELIGION played a surprisingly large part in Louis's magnificently worldly reign. New Orders rose and flourished: Mère du Calvaire's Clairettes, Marcelle Germaine's Daughters of Providence, Venerable Françoise de la Croix's nursing sisters. Jean-Jacques Olier founded the Sulpicians to train priests, and the Duc de Ventadour the Company of the Blessed Sacrament, a secret group of laymen, to guard public morals (it was they who had *Tartuffe* banned). Visionaries included Marguerite-Marie Alacoque, the devotee of the Sacred Heart, and Marie des Vallées, a counsellor of St. Jean Eudes; it is a measure of popular interest that even the visions of a pseudomystic, Antoinette Bourignon, were recorded in nineteen volumes.

Belief was the normal attitude of both men and women. Even sacrilege was easier than disbelief, witness Madame de Montespan, and rare free-thinkers like Saint-Évremond packed their bags for London. The bedside books at Versailles were Fr. Suffren's *Christian Year* and Firmin Raissaint's *Meditations*. Madame de Sévigné, behind her worldly chatter, was a devout Christian: she enjoyed reading religious history, discussed sermons and explained all events as the work of Providence. Artists such as Le Brun, Puget and Girardon all spent part of their fortune building a chapel in their parish church. La Fontaine, for all his mockery, prayed like a child; so did Colbert and Turenne. Both Nicolas Fouquet and Anne's old enemy, the Coadjutor Archbishop of Paris, died as good Christians.

The tone of their religion had been set by St. François de Sales: it was mild, moderate and gay. "Do not desire crosses, save insofar as you have borne those that have already been sent you." One day Claude Perrault entered a rowdy inn: the hubbub was caused, not as he at first believed, by peasants or lackeys, but by six Fathers of the Oratory who were trying to practise the precepts of St. François, namely "to laugh and appear contented at all costs." It was a Christianity which enjoyed life: Lent was observed at Versailles but the soles were delicious and cooked in butter. Moderation was the keynote but to a few fervent men moderation appeared half-heartedness.

One of these fervent men was Blaise Pascal. He was born in 1623 in Clermont, the only son of a high official in the Board of Excise, and educated at home. When he was eleven someone at table accidentally struck a china plate with a knife, then silenced the ringing sound with his hand. This aroused Pascal's curiosity and he produced *A Treatise on Sounds*. At the age of twelve without books he rediscovered the first thirty-two propositions of Euclid; at sixteen he wrote a treatise on conic sections which astonished Descartes; at eighteen he invented the adding machine.

Pascal was frail and delicate, and during his adult life never knew a day without pain. When he was thirty, partly through the influence of his sister Jacqueline, a nun at Port-Royal, he decided to live only for God. He removed the tapestries from his room, made his own bed and ate in the kitchen. He gave up his favourite foods: sauces, oranges and fruit juice. The following year he had a profound religious experience which he likened to fire, after which he made a number of retreats at Port-Royal. During the last five years of his life he was an invalid who could absorb little but warm liquids, drop by drop. He was a good man, but lacking in warmth—he scolded his married sister for fondling her children —and easily given to impatience. He was curiously detached and before having a conversation which might give him pleasure put on a pointed iron belt. He thought a true Christian should never say "I" or "me," and his humility amounted almost to self-disgust. He died of a form of nervous convulsion at the age of thirty-nine.

Pascal made two discoveries which filled him with horror: first, that the God of his day, the "prime mover" dear to geometers and philosophers, bore no relation to the Christian God; secondly, that the religion practised by most men in society was not Christianity at all but a facile quasi-paganism evolved by smooth casuists. For instance, you might avoid perjury by saying, "I swear I did not do that," then adding in a whisper, "to-day." If you heard four different parts of the Mass simultaneously, that satisfied your Sunday obligation. If someone tried to rob you of more than £10, you were at liberty to kill him. These were some of the abuses Pascal denounced in *Les Provinciales*, a work which shook the established order and caused the choleric Chancellor Séguier to be bled seven times in five days.

Pascal, a genius racked by headaches and insomnia, was acutely aware of the misery of man. Man, he says, is only a reed, the weakest in nature; he is limited and can feel neither extreme heat nor extreme cold; his world can be wrecked by such tiny factors as the proportions of Cleopatra's nose or a grain of sand in Cromwell's ureter. Man is naturally credulous and incredulous, timid and reckless; he is neither angel nor beast, an "incomprehensible monster." He is not usually reasonable: he treats eternity as of small duration and life like eternity; he fluctuates between despair and pride; indeed every human action and emotion soon naturally entail their opposites. Duplicity and contrariety are so ingrained that even as he performs a humble action he puffs himself up.

Pascal feels himself miserable: but are all men miserable? What about the King? "Experiment," says Pascal. "Leave a king quite alone without any sensual pleasure, without any cares to occupy his mind, without squadrons or amusements, to think about himself at leisure, and a king without amusements will be seen to be a man full of miseries." As for a king's glory, Pascal considers it unnatural: we do not find the cart-horse yielding its oats to the race-horse. Glory is man's basest weakness, but it is also the surest sign of his excellence, for it shows what store he sets by the minds of his fellows.

A further paradox: man's greatness lies in the fact that he alone in all the world is aware of his misery. His greatness lies in his power to think. But Pascal the mathematician had found that even this power is seriously curtailed. Take the problem of an infinite number: however high the number we imagine, it can always be made higher by adding one: hence the "frightening" discovery that the universe is infinite and continually eludes man's efforts to grasp it. The cosmos is unintelligible, and therefore God can no longer be proved cosmologically.

Man, therefore, is miserable, unreasonable and riddled with antinomies. Religious truth must be able to explain man to himself. Is there such a truth? Yes, answers Pascal—the doctrine of man's fall and redemption. Only in the person of Christ can we understand our misery and hope to escape from it. True, the fall, the transmission of Adam's sin and the Incarnation seem vastly improbable, even contrary to justice, yet incomprehensible though these mysteries are, man without them is even more incomprehensible.

All this was quite new. Philosophers before Pascal had tried to prove the existence of God from reason; Pascal's originality lies in arguing from the whole personality: God must satisfy not chiefly reason but the human heart, and only a personal God, Jesus Christ, can fully do that. Love comes before belief (for which we must await God's grace) and Pascal's declared intention was "to make religion lovable."

Pascal is one of the glories of Louis XIV's reign. There is something deeply moving about this frail genius lying awake and in pain, alone with the stars and the Gospels, sketching the book whose very incompleteness would endorse its main theme. Yet Pascal's psychology, so perceptive and profound, remains one-sided. Man is more than a scholar with private means alone with God; he is a member of society. Louis, who so fascinated Pascal, might well have answered the philosopher: "You are right in calling my job the most difficult there is, but left to myself I do not brood—as you claim—on possible revolution, eventual sickness and certain death. On the contrary, I take a great deal of pleasure in being alive; in conceiving new roads, canals, industries, overseas trading posts and measures of justice. The man who works and builds for others is by no means miserable: he is the pride of creation and the image of God."

To Pascal goes the credit of having raised in its most fundamental form a key question of the reign: "Is Christianity primarily a religion of reason or a religion of love?" This question, although never openly stated, underlay all three of Louis's religious struggles: with Jansenism, Protestantism and Quietism.

Jansenism in the strict sense is a particular teaching about grace and free will. God is omnipotent; how then can man act freely or acquire merit? The answer is that we simply don't know, this is a mystery. But the mystery had been treated as a problem capable of solution ever since the fifth century when an ascetic from Britain named Pelagius so emphasised man's powers of self-improvement as virtually to deny the efficacity of grace. St. Augustine in refuting the Pelagians asserted that we are saved only by Christ's merits and that only a small number are predestined to be saved, those to whom God chooses to give the singular grace of perseverance. The Church adopted the African Doctor's teaching as her own but treated with extreme caution certain passages in Augustine's later writings in which he somewhat overstressed the role of grace. These writings had already been used to support Calvinism and in 1640 were made the basis of a new book entitled *Augustinus* by one Cornelius Jansen, Bishop of Ypres. A friend of Jansen, a fiery Basque named Saint-Cyran, taught Jansen's views in the influential abbey of Port-Royal-des-Champs, near Paris. They were hotly disputed and in 1650 a French bishop asked the Pope to condemn five propositions which he attributed to Jansen. These propositions stated that some of God's commandments are impossible to the just; that grace is irresistible; and that Christ did not shed his blood for all men. In 1653 the Pope condemned these five propositions, without however naming the author. In 1654 he specifically condemned the teaching of Jansen.

Jansenism, in the wider sense, was a movement of moral reform emanating from Port-Royal. If undue emphasis on man's free will engenders pride, undue emphasis on predestination leads to near-despair which by some psychological quirk fosters not laxity but austerity and strict observance of the commandment to love; and this was what happened at Port-Royal. Such practices answered a need, and many great men retired to live as solitaries at Port-Royal, which became renowned for holiness and an atmosphere of love. One of these solitaries, Arnauld d'Andilly, grew fine nectarines and pears which he sent to Anne of Austria's table, where Louis enjoyed them as a boy. His governess quipped that the fruit at least was quite free from taint.

Jansenism found a most determined opponent in the King. Louis's Christianity, like that of so many of his courtiers, was solid and immovable, moderate and optimistic, an affair of the head rather than of the heart. Louis was not a man who prayed for long stretches or thought a lot about God, but from both parents he had inherited a strong sense of religious duty. He tended to be scrupulous. Once when they were boys Philippe had offered him a spoonful of boiled meat on a fast day. Louis refused it and lectured his brother for eating meat while pretending to fast. He heard Mass every day of his life but one, even in the trenches. When he "took medicine"—that is, when he was purged at full moon and remained in bed—Mass was said in his room. Even during his love affairs he had a talk every week with his confessor.

Louis disliked Jansenism for a number of reasons. With con-considerable acumen he describes it in his Memoirs as the school "which teaches that knowledge is not necessary in order for a man to be saved." Its extreme pessimism jarred on his moderate, optimistic Christianity. It denounced and tried to ban the theatre, which Louis loved. During the Fronde Jansenism had proved a rallying point for his enemies, and he associated this "body without a head" with political disunity and division. Finally, as a heresy condemned by the Pope, Jansenism was a dangerous challenge to established authority. At the end of 1660 Louis told the bishops that he was resolved that "the pernicious sect should be utterly rooted out."

A formulary was drawn up to be signed by all ecclesiastics: "I condemn with heart and mouth the doctrine of the Five Propositions of Cornelius Jansen, contained in his book entitled *Augustinus*, the same not being the doctrine of Augustine, which Jansen had falsely expounded, contrary to the true meaning of that Doctor." The Port-Royalist nuns, for the most part ignorant of the history and merits of the dispute, refused to sign a statement of fact in regard to a book which they had not read and which was in any case too difficult for them.

The *Augustinus* is a very long Latin folio. Louis once asked the Comte de Gramont to read it through that he might really know whether the Five Propositions were there or not. "If the Propositions are there," reported Gramont, when his task was done, "they are there *incognito*." It seems likely that the Propositions can in fact be inferred from certain passages, but at the time even this was by no means generally agreed. Nevertheless because of their importunity some of the Port-Royalist nuns were imprisoned, others removed to more orthodox convents. In 1669 they agreed to sign the formulary "sincerely" instead of "purely and simply" —a piece of casuistry which permitted mental reservations.

Save for the period 1669-79, when a temporary truce was called, Jansenism continued to bedevil the reign. During Louis's boyhood the Port-Royalists had produced great men like Pascal and Arnauld, and the holy nuns in coarse grey habit and red cross portrayed by Philippe de Champaigne. But from 1670 onwards the movement became a narrow sect and the nuns "pure as angels and proud as devils." "To confess our family name," boasted Mère Agnès, "is tantamount to confessing God," while the Jansenist le Maître began a letter to his father like this: "God having made use of you in order to bring me into the world." Self-centredness showed itself in a desire to be in the news, to shock, even to be persecuted. As the Archbishop of Paris told Mère Angélique in 1679: "People are for ever talking about Port-Royal, about these Messieurs de Port-Royal: the King does not like anything that causes commotion."

What Louis really disliked was Port-Royal's refusal of a frank and open obedience to the Pope on a spiritual matter. It was this which decided him in 1679 to forbid Port-Royal to take boarders or receive novices. As a result the convent went into decline. In 1705 Pope Clement XI published a brief condemning those who, in signing the earlier anti-Jansenist formulary, used mental reservations: the nuns of Port-Royal refused to accept this brief and after a short persecution Louis finally dispersed them in 1709, razing their convent to the ground.

Meanwhile an Oratorian priest in exile, Pasquier Quesnel, restated Jansenist teaching in a book entitled *Réflexions Morales*. He emphasised the irresistible power of grace, the fruitlessness of human effort, the glories of persecution for righteousness's sake. In 1711 Louis asked Rome to condemn this book; two years later in the bull *Unigenitus* the Pope anathematised 101 propositions extracted from the *Réflexions*. By decisively vindicating human effort, *Unigenitus* was the death-blow to Jansenism.

Thus Louis's lifetime coincided with the birth and virtual extinction of the Jansenist heresy. It was he who took the lead in having the sect condemned. But Jansenism as a movement towards humility, self-doubt and affective love continued to be a very important force throughout the reign. Racine had a saintly aunt at Port-Royal and in his will asked to be buried there: the malicious said he would never have done such a thing in his lifetime. Madame de Sévigné was friendly with Jansenists like Nicole and Abadie: at the age of eighty-two Arnauld d'Andilly gave her a six-hour lecture, calling her "a beautiful pagan who adored her own daughter." Great ladies like Geneviève de Longueville and Madeleine de Sablé lived at Port-Royal, and it was there that La Rochefoucauld wrote his pessimistic *Maxims*. Jansenism was the unofficial opposition, challenging many of Louis's principles, particularly his legalistic concept of the Church. But it was a force for good, since it prevented smugness and provided a healthy corrective in an age of tremendous achievements. Lully once entered a worldly Paris church and, hearing one of his operatic airs being played on the organ, exclaimed, "Please forgive me, Lord—it was not written for you." Over against that image may be placed the black wooden crucifix which Jansenists favoured, with the body of Christ carved out of a single piece of bone or ivory, so that the arms are stretched almost vertical: a figure of intense suffering. The counterweight was needed and served its purpose.

Before considering the second religious problem of the reign—Protestantism—a word must be said about Louis as head of the

Church in France. This role he took very seriously. The bishops he appointed were usually excellent and he corrected a number of abuses: he no longer allowed any layman to possess a benefice under the name of a hired cleric, nor anyone not a priest to acquire a bishopric, like Cardinal Mazarin, who had been appointed to Metz though not ordained. With regard to Rome, he upheld the principle that the French Church had certain "liberties," that is to say rules, customs and privileges which the Pope may not infringe. Louis never forgot that he too was God's representative on earth. The Pope's infallibility had not yet been proclaimed, and Louis looked on the Pope not as a superior but as an ally, someone who knew theology and could issue bulls against any heresies that might disturb France.

Louis's policy towards Rome may be described as one of high tariffs. He found a long running battle with Innocent XI (1676-1689) over the *régale*, that is, the French king's right to draw revenues from vacant bishoprics and abbacies, and to appoint to benefices within their gift. This right, originally granted to François I for certain parts of France, Louis wished to extend to the whole kingdom. He first made the demand in 1673 and when it was rejected there was strong pressure on Louis to break with Rome and set up a separate Church. Louis, however, much as he prized independence, refused to purchase it at the cost of schism or any kind of disunity within Christendom. Largely as a result of moderation on the King's part and on the Pope's an open break was averted. In 1693 Louis won his point, when Innocent's successor extended the *régale* to all France.

Unity is the key to Louis's policy towards French Protestants, and since it is a complex word it becomes necessary to analyse it. First, at an abstract level the One was considered unconditionally superior to the Many. Monotheism, monarchy, monogamy were three prime examples. It was accepted, therefore, that one belief, whether in a family or in a kingdom, was somehow "better" than manifold opinions.

It was also more pleasing. Unity got rid of disorder. This was true not only of gardens, but of all art and indeed of all concepts. Therefore any image of France, or of Frenchmen, which showed them to be a unified whole was intrinsically more pleasing than one which showed diversity.

Thirdly, it had a practical value. Oddly enough, it was taken for granted that unity produced better results than diversity, monopoly than competition. The trading companies are one example. Another occurred in 1680 when Louis gave the Comédie Française exclusive acting rights in Paris, explaining that this would "make it possible for them to attain even greater perfection."

Fourthly, it had a historical basis. Just as classical columns were a feature of Versailles and the Louvre Colonnade, so the theory of the early Christian Empire underlay much of Louis's religious thinking. As heir to Constantine and Justinian, it was his duty to check religious "deviation." For centuries, until it fell into abeyance under Henry IV, French kings had solemnly sworn as part of their coronation oath: "I will seriously endeavour to extirpate all heretics, so branded by the Church, out of my land, and the government subject to me." Louis had inherited the spirit of that oath, and the underlying value placed on unity.

For these reasons it was a generally accepted principle in France that every effort should be made to achieve religious unity; in particular to convert the Protestants, who numbered about one million, a twentieth part of the population. During the first part of his personal reign Louis often exhorted his Protestant subjects to "embrace the King's religion"; time and again he asked Colbert to try to convert the foreign artisans who had settled in France. But he bore no grudge against Protestants: Turenne, his favourite general, had been most of his life a Protestant. There is no doubt that Louis as a young man wanted to convert—not to repress— the Protestants. He even seems to have envisaged concessions on the Catholic side. In 1672 he signed a letter proposing reunion, which was circulated to Protestant ministers: "Forty-two bishops have told the King that for the good of this design a retrenchment be made of: The Service of Images, the Invocation of Saints, the Doctrine of Purgatory, Prayers for the Dead, and that Divine Service be established in the vulgar tongue, and Communion in both species, and that for the Real Presence it be determined as divines of either side shall agree, and that if the Pope should oppose, he should be over-ruled therein, and that a patriarch in France should consequently be made." But this radical plan came to nothing and during the rest of the 'seventies, evidently as a result of war and the need for national unity, there was a hardening in Louis's attitude: laws against Protestants were enforced more strictly, though there seems to have been no deliberate policy of repression.

The next change in Louis's attribute to the Protestants occurred when he fell in love with Madame de Maintenon. Whereas Louis was a man of strong feelings—the morganatic marriage alone would be enough to show that—Françoise de Maintenon was a woman not of feeling but of duty. Seldom did she become deeply fond of people: rather, she thought that "she ought to help them," with the emphasis on the "ought." Moreover, the basic categories in which Madame de Maintenon ordered her experience were religious categories. As a child she had been torn between a Calvinist aunt and a Catholic aunt, and the strain of those years had left its mark. She had been rescued from "error" and in turn she felt a driving need to rescue others. "Helping," for Madame de Maintenon, meant converting.

Protestant peasants on her estate, relatives, friends, friends of friends—Madame de Maintenon catechised them all, and her efforts met with striking success. Thus, in the two years 1680-1 she converted one Villette, Comte de Mursay, the little Villette-Mursay girls and two other relatives. Apropos of Marmande, Villette's son, she wrote to her brother: "I am very pleased at the conversion of Monsieur de Vaux. Please remember me to him. Poignette is a good Catholic, Monsieur de Marmande also. Monsieur de Souché abjured two days ago. I am the only one to be seen, in the churches, leading some converted Huguenot." Another letter names more converts: "In a few days I shall have Mesdemoiselles de Sainte-Hermine, de Caumont and de Mursay; I hope I shall not miss one of them. But I like Minette [later Comtesse de Mailly], whom I saw at Coignac, and if you could send her to me, I should be delighted. There is no other way now but violence, for de Mursay's conversion will cause the family pain."

This sort of zeal in converting Protestants was something new at Court. What was Louis's reaction to it? There is no doubt that at heart he did not believe in trying to change people. The difference between Louis and Madame de Maintenon appears in their attitude to their wayward brothers: Louis accepted Philippe for what he was and did not try to change him, whereas Madame de Maintenon paid a priest to reform d'Aubigné: "he followed him about like a shadow and wore the heart out of him." On the other hand, Louis believed that it was his duty as King to extirpate heresy, and so he could not but applaud Madame de Maintenon's successes.

These successes also suggested an answer to another question: How in the seventeenth century might a King of France live up to his title of "Most Christian King"? In the old days it had been relatively easy. Thus in his Memoirs Louis notes with satisfaction that Charlemagne "defended religion against the Saxons, Huns and Saracens." But when the Elector of Mainz sent the philosopher Leibnitz to France in 1672 with a scheme for the conquest of Egypt, Pomponne replied in Louis's name that "projects for holy wars had ceased to be fashionable since the days of St. Louis." Ceased also to be feasible. Was there some other way of playing the glorious Christian King? Perhaps.

In the period immediately before 1680 a plan began to take shape in Louis's mind. It originated partly in genuine religious zeal, partly in a pagan thirst for glory, partly in the desire for religious unity which characterised Protestant no less than Catholic countries in the seventeenth century—it was a Protestant who declared, "Difference of religion disfigures a State." The plan was this: to convert his Protestant subjects—all of them. What Madame de Maintenon had done in one part of France he would accomplish throughout his kingdom. He would offer to God a wholly Catholic France. It would be spectacular and it would go down in history. This was the plan Louis began to carry out in 1680; the following April Madame de Maintenon wrote delightedly: "If God preserve the King there will not be one Huguenot left twenty years hence."

How did one go about converting one million Protestants? First of all, by preaching to them. Louis, like most Frenchmen, had great confidence in reason's ability to attain to the truth; he believed that the Protestant minority was opinionated, that they had only to apply their reason or be shaken out of their inertia to arrive at the single truth which gave unity. Louis himself was now a unified person: gone were the days when passion and reason had torn his soul apart, and passion had usually won.

In 1680 and the years following Louis sent missionaries into strongly Huguenot areas such as Normandy, Poitou and Languedoc, and he instructed the intendants to gather leading Protestants, harangue them and urge them to abjure. Unity was waved about like a banner: "the incontestable unity of God cannot allow multiplicity in religion, or in the worship inseparably attached thereto." At the same time new decrees excluded those who professed the R.P.R.—the so-called reformed religion—from holding certain public offices, and from becoming printers, librarians, lawyers or doctors. Pastors were forbidden to minister in any one place for longer than three years; in reprisal for a seditious sermon or the least infraction of the law, Protestant churches were razed. On the other hand, privileges and partial tax-exemption were promised to those who abjured.

At the beginning of the campaign of conversion one of the intendants, Marillac by name, visited Poitou escorted by dragoons. It had long been customary to billet troops with the local population; and by breaking the law or even, at the time of the Fronde, by siding with the King's enemies, a householder rendered himself liable to lodge more troops and for a longer period than his law-abiding neighbours. Marillac, a violent and ambitious man, took it on himself to billet most of his dragoons in Protestant houses; he himself bullied, threatened, shook his fist in people's faces, and encouraged his troops to do likewise. Unexpected results were obtained. The Bishop of Luçon noted that during 1680 instead of the usual thirty conversions in his diocese, there were four hundred. In Upper Poitou no less than 30,000 Protestants abjured during 1680. Louvois, the Minister of War, congratulated Marillac but sent him more precise instructions for 1681: "The King's intention is not that you should billet all your men in Protestant houses; but suppose you have a company of twenty-six horsemen and the

Protestants are liable to lodge ten; then mark them down for twenty. Billet them with the richest, on the grounds that when there are not enough troops in a district for all the inhabitants to lodge some, justice demands that the poor be exempt and the rich shoulder the burden."

But Marillac went beyond these orders. His dragoons beat up those who refused to heed the missionaries; drove men and women to church, sprinkled them with holy water and treated them as lapsed if they returned to their Bible-reading; committed what the official correspondence discreetly called "disorders." When news of the "dragonnades" reached him, Louis became very angry. He rebuked Marillac and presently dismissed him from his post as intendant.

Louis expressly forbade any kind of violence towards Protestants. As Madame de Maintenon put it: "One cannot precipitate matters; one must convert and not persecute." But the billeting of troops in Protestant regions continued, and this indirect pressure produced the desired result. Many of the wealthier Protestants abjured rather than have fine houses turned into barracks, many of the poorer in order to escape the heavy charge of feeding two or three soldiers for weeks or even months.

Conversions usually took place *en masse*, when the lead had been given by several influential families; for instance, the towns of Pau, Montpellier and Nîmes were converted in their entirety; all but two hundred of the four thousand in Orthez; twenty thousand in the generality of Montauban; sixty thousand in the generality of Bordeaux. By autumn, 1685, the Protestants had been reduced by three-quarters: most had become Catholics; some had emigrated; others, infringers of the law, had been sent to the galleys.

Those that remained were protected by the Edict of Nantes, whereby Henry IV had recognised Protestants as a "body" within the State and guaranteed their religious freedom. This edict ran counter to Louis's notion of unity and he resolved to strike it from the laws of the land. It was on 18th October, 1685, that he signed the Revocation of the Edict of Nantes. In the preamble he recalled that it had always been the intention of his grandfather, his father and himself to "unite to the Church those who had so easily strayed from it." The methods adopted had met with success "since the better and greater part of our subjects of the said R.P.R. have embraced Catholicism; and since for that reason the execution of the Edict of Nantes . . . remains useless, we have come to the conclusion that in order to wipe out all memory of the troubles, confusion and evil caused in our kingdom by the progress of that false Religion, we cannot do better . . . than to revoke the said edict entirely . . ." Louis's Revocation ordered Protestant churches to be demolished and services to cease; Protestant schools to be closed, and all children who might be born in Protestant families to be baptised as Catholics.

The Revocation strikes us to-day as an intolerable piece of interference in other men's spiritual affairs. But Protestants apart, almost everyone in France wholeheartedly approved. According to Madame de Sévigné, "Nothing is so beautiful as what it contains, and a king has never done and never will do anything more memorable," while that otherwise sensible man Bossuet became positively lyrical: "Let us spread the news of this modern miracle, let us pour out our hearts on the piety of Louis; let us raise our cheers to heaven and tell this new Constantine, this new Theodosius, this new Marcian, this new Charlemagne: 'What you have done is worthy of your reign; it gives it its true stamp; through you heresy is no more; God alone has performed this wonderful thing.'" Alas, as Pascal might have pointed out, once again reason had played fast-and-loose with love.

No one seems to have expected so many Protestants to choose exile rather than abjure. Within the next few years more than 200,000 left France. From the fields of finance, industry and science many leading figures left, including Christian Huygens, inventor of the pendulum clock and first to formulate the theory that light travels in waves. Silk-makers emigrated to England and Holland, glass-makers to Denmark. Six hundred army officers took service abroad. Not only did the Revocation cream France of some of its best talent, it hardened Protestant opinion abroad against Louis. More than thirty years later in Old South Church, Philadelphia, a boy named Benjamin Franklin heard the preacher thunder against "that accursed man, persecutor of God's people, Louis the four-teenth."

A third religious problem arose to disturb the latter years of Louis's reign. Quietism, like Jansenism, was a subconscious protest against the active, conceptual features of seventeenth-century Christianity: a reassertion of the feminine, passive aspect of the human soul. It contained much that was good, but like Jansenism it went to extremes. Its chief exponent was a pretty widow named Madame Guyon. Born of *petit bourgeois* parents in Montargis, as a child she had had visions "like St. Teresa" and had once sewed on her chest with ribbon and a darning needle a paper inscribed "Jesus." She was subject to hysteria, during which her body would swell up and turn marbled violet. The day after her marriage she burst out sobbing, saying that she had made a hateful sacrifice and wanted to be a nun. However, she bore her husband four sturdy children, and when Monsieur Guyon died found herself with an annual income of £16,000. She then announced that she was going to win souls: "Our Lord has made known that he has destined me to be the mother of a great people." She travelled round France with a Barnabite priest, wrote books—a commentary on the Canticle of Canticles took her only twenty hours—read works of mysticism and reproduced in her own body the states she found described there. She even declared that she was married to the Child Jesus, who had put an invisible ring on her finger.

In 1688 she came to the attention of Madame de Maintenon. At this time Madame Guyon was forty. She had a gushing voice and large, rather prominent eyes that sometimes wandered and became trance-like; her manner was supple and affectionate. She explained to Madame de Maintenon the method of prayer advo-cated in her books, *Spiritual Torrents* and *A short and very easy method of praying from the heart*: she was to come into the presence of her Maker with hands empty of good works, to abandon her-self to the pure love that despises all action, to cast away all hope of reward and fear of punishment, to be quiet and lose herself in God. This approach appealed to Madame de Maintenon, who found it a wholesome corrective to her own exceedingly active and rather dry temperament. She invited Madame Guyon to lecture to the girls of Saint-Cyr, a school which she and the King had founded for the daughters of impoverished noblemen, and to have her own room in the school.

Before long all the girls at Saint-Cyr were talking of nothing but pure love, holy silence, passive indifference and abandonment of the soul. It became the thing to rise from prayer eyes streaming with tears, to neglect a lesson—particularly a difficult lesson—in order to "go into ecstasy," to retire early to bed in order to cultivate "holy silence." Recently the girls had performed Racine's *Esther*; this was even better, they could act all the time.

Her confessor soon opened Madame de Maintenon's eyes to the dangers of such an extreme, if well-intentioned, doctrine. Recognising her mistake in the schoolgirls' affected behaviour, she immediately dismissed Madame Guyon, destroyed her writings and ordered complete silence on the subject. But the pretty mystic had meanwhile found a new ally in François de Fénelon, former tutor to the Duc de Bourgogne. Fénelon was a tall, thin priest of noble birth, with a pale face and burning eyes, sensitive, passionate and generous to a fault. His was a complicated nature which oscillated between self-assertion and self-doubt. "I cannot explain the basis of my character; it escapes me; it seems to change from hour to hour. Who am I? I simply don't know." But when he met Madame Guyon, he seemed to find himself: as Saint-Simon maliciously puts it, "leur sublime s'amalgama." Here at last was someone with the force and single-mindedness he lacked. He called her "Maman Téton," while she addressed him as "Bibi."

Fénelon was convinced of Madame Guyon's good intentions, and although he did not follow her blindly he resolved to come to her defence. He published a book entitled *Explication des maximes des Saints sur la vie intérieure*, which depicted Madame Guyon as belonging to that group of mystics who had astonished and at moments scandalised the world and the Church, and yet, as the Church herself confessed, had triumphed in the end. Fénelon went on to defend Madame Guyon's teaching. He declared that the soul can live in a habitual state of the love of God which is wholly pure and disinterested. In that state we desire salvation not as our deliverance or reward but simply as something which God is pleased to will and that He would have us desire for His own sake. In the passive state the soul exercises all the virtues without adverting to the fact that they are virtues; it desires even love, not as its own perfection and happiness, but simply insofar as love is what God asks of man.

Fénelon's book caused an outcry, and soon all France was taking sides. Louis was very angry indeed. Personally he disliked Fénelon's emotional brand of religion and believed it unorthodox: "He has the most fanciful mind of any man in my kingdom." This meant that the Duc de Bourgogne, heir to the throne, had been brought up virtually in heresy; what was worse, the young man openly sided with his former tutor.

Both Fénelon and Madame Guyon were his wife's protégés and on Madame de Maintenon the King's anger fell. In a terrible interview he scolded her for the havoc she had caused and thereafter for a long time he refused to visit her room. "Pray for me, I implore you," she wrote to a friend. "I had not sufficient strength to support my good fortune, judge what will become of me in adversity." "Never was I so close to disgrace." She who had so longed to do good had ended by hatching heresy within the King's palace. She almost wore herself out with weeping until the day when Louis, moved himself, gently said as he sat beside her bed, "Madame, are you going to die of this business?"

Fénelon's book also roused the anger of the greatest prelate in France, that pillar of the established order and reasonable religion, Jacques-Bénigne Bossuet. Physically and temperamentally he was the complete opposite of the delicate, refined Fénelon. The son of a Burgundy judge—the family motto was Bon bois Bossuet around a rugged vine stock—he was square-headed and broad-shouldered, with a thundering voice, an enemy of all that was vague, doubtful and idiosyncratic. Though Fénelon was thirty years his junior, Bossuet was the more energetic man: after a full working day he would wrap himself in a bearskin and spend half the night writing letters, sermons and books, all closely reasoned, syllogistic and

based on hard fact. The eagle of Meaux he was called, while
Fénelon was known as the swan of Cambrai.

The eagle attacked the swan's Quietism on two grounds:
psychologically it was mistaken because the basis of human nature
is the instinct for happiness, and dogmatically it was heretical, for
a soul favoured to such a degree by spiritual communion with God
would no longer require the Church's help in the form of the
sacraments: it would have attained to a private religion. Para-
doxical though it might seem, love, the very core of Christianity,
even the love of God, was interested and acquisitive; what is more,
it must be regulated and kept within bounds. Reason, even at the
moment of self-abandonment, must still retain control.

Fénelon answered this attack by charging Bossuet with destroying the pre-eminence of charity over hope—that is to say, over
hope of one's own salvation. Bossuet defended himself. Soon the
debate had degenerated into an unedifying quarrel in which private
confidences were violated and political rivalry asserted itself. Paris
sang:

> Dans ces combats où deux prélats de France
> Semblent chercher la vérité,
> L'un dit qu'on détruit l'espérance,
> L'autre soutient que c'est la charité:
> C'est la foi qu'on détruit et personne n'y pense.[1]

For two years the affair dragged on until Rome issued a brief
condemning Fénelon's book—a judgment to which the swan submitted with exemplary good grace. It was chiefly the psychological
basis of Quietism which the Pope condemned: he denied first that
we can love God with a love of pure charity, without any trace of
fear or of desire for reward, and secondly that we can will our salvation only for the glory of God.

If Fénelon was wrong according to the letter, according to the
spirit he may well have been right. Humble submission to God's
will, dying to oneself, mystical prayer, a love which is generous
to imprudence, the "folly of the Cross": these were aspects of

---

[1] In these battles where two prelates of France seem to be looking for the
truth, one says that Hope is being destroyed, while the other says that it is Charity:
in actual fact it is Faith they are both unwittingly destroying.

Christianity which found too little place in seventeenth-century religious practice and needed to be reasserted.

The religious ferment of the age inevitably left its mark on Louis. It obliged him to take an interest in theology and spiritual questions. It was the chief external force in his decision to put his private life in order and marry Madame de Maintenon. It tempered his extravagance in building and a tendency to luxury. It increased his compassion for the poor. It aroused an interest in Christian education and led to the founding, with Madame de Maintenon, of Saint-Cyr, which became the best girls' school in France. It made Louis place less stress on the externals of religion. It opened his eyes to the view that love and compassion might be just as valuable as knowledge, work and achievement.

"It seems to me," wrote Louis, "that we must be at the same time humble on our own account, and proud on account of the office we fill." That was Louis's dilemma in the second half of the reign. Was it even possible to draw the distinction? Had he revoked the Edict of Nantes as God's good servant or—more likely —to increase his own glory? The fact is that right up until the end of the century Louis had not achieved the desired balance. Pride, passion for glory, the desire to be first—these were still his dominant motives. Yet the very movements Louis had fought—Jansenism and Quietism—affected him more deeply than he knew. The principles of humility and submissive love of God's will had not been crushed, only driven underground. How they were finally to transmute the King's pride will appear later.

CHAPTER 17

Patron of the Arts

LITERATURE AND THE ARTS in Louis's reign reached a pitch of excellence seldom equalled before or since. Here the King played an essential part; indeed seventeenth-century classicism probably could not have existed without him. To start with, it was he who had created that political and civic order, that sense of stability and justice which, as once before, in fifth-century Athens, made it seem reasonable to believe in a moral order corresponding to the natural order. Then again, being a sociable person he had collected a large Court, mainly of intelligent and sensitive people, and this Court had certain accepted values and interests in common. Neither they nor their King travelled abroad, and this tended to strengthen their values while concentrating attention on their own particular tensions and conflicts.

In this community of some five thousand men and women it was Louis's actions and words which set the tone. Condé in his old age apologises for his slowness in climbing a staircase at Versailles; "Cousin," says Louis, "one who bears such a weight of laurels must needs move slowly." To Massillon, after a sermon: "I have heard several great orators, and I have been very much pleased with them; as for you, every time that I have heard you, I have been much displeased with myself." The tone which Louis set was one of realism tempered with kindness, and this is precisely the tone which pervades almost every work of classical literature.

Louis was himself a writer. In 1668 he began to edit and polish his Memoirs of the years 1661 and 1666. Their key words are order, glory and reason: they make one feel the charm there is in the exercise of good sense. The style is majestic, clear and spare. Louis had a liking for symmetry, particularly the balancing of two phrases. As regards language he was very particular, and Bossuet paid him this tribute: "The precision of his words is the image of the exactness of his thoughts." He favoured what was elegant, regular and noble. One day Boileau was reading aloud an account of the King's campaign: "After making a feint towards Flanders, he headed back ('rebroussé chemin') for Germany." Louis stopped him, saying "rebrousser" was not a very noble or elegant word. Racine and others present agreed, but Boileau declared it was the only exact word and ought to be used even if rather harsh. The incident shows that Louis preferred a pleasing sound even to precision.

All these tastes left their mark on classical literature, but the most important influence of all was Louis's interest in people. Perhaps his chief strength was judgment of character, what La Bruyère calls his infallible gift "for discerning men's minds, talents and character when choosing candidates for a post." His Memoirs are primarily psychology, even to the point of self-analysis: "My dominant passion is certainly love of glory." He liked nothing better than speculating about men's motives. One day he noticed Racine walking with the Marquis de Cavoie. "Those two are often together: I can guess the reason. Cavoie when he is with Racine thinks himself a wit; and Racine with Cavoie imagines that he is a courtier."

It is not surprising therefore that nearly all the writers of Louis's reign, wanting to win his approval and the approval of the Court which mirrored the King, should have chosen man as their subject, man's feelings, moods, passions, loves, his inner debates and outward extravagances, treating them in a spare, elegant, direct style. This was by no means as inevitable as may appear. Under Louis XIII, for instance, writers were bored by man as he is: their favourite subjects were cardboard heroes, the death of a parrot or the first white lock in their beloved's hair.

The writers of Louis's reign are all psychologists, and all ask a very special question about man. Each age puts its own question. Montaigne had asked, How can man guard against pain and misfortune? Voltaire and the Encyclopaedists were afterwards to ask, How can we further man's progress?, and the Romantics, How can man be happy? The question posed by the age of Louis XIV was this: How can man be good—good, that is, in relation to his fellows and to God; how can he lead a good life? The question was a psychological question, but it arose from moral anxieties.

For underneath the smooth, elegant, balanced phrases a terrible ferment was at work. On the one hand was man, a reasonable creature possessing in Revelation certain God-given rules for being good; on the other hand when it came to practice either man's will was too weak to apply the rules, or his passions got the better of him, or passion put on the mask of reason, even to the point of self-deception. Worse still, virtue itself could sometimes prove disastrous: a man practises meekness and self-sacrifice, only to lose his house and all his savings; a sweet Christian precept like sincerity can in certain circumstances blow up society. How is man to lead a good life?—that was the question, and none of the writers know the answer for certain. None provides an easy moral, nor do they agree even in their pointers. If they had known the answers, they would not have written such good plays or books, but the important thing is that they thought an answer was possible. They were making an attempt at a moral or social geometry: there *were* rules for the good life if only one could discover them. Because they lived in an age of order and assurance their anguish was tempered by hope.

The explosive discovery of the age was that reason does not create values or even choose them. Reason can see ideas clearly, carry an argument to its logical conclusion, distinguish a true from a false statement, but it is not a value-creating faculty as most people still thought. (How man does come to love this or that principle and hate another, no one asked or knew.) Reason in fact is merely a tool which can be turned to good or base uses, a mask for this or that passion. So it would be a mistake to view the classical conflict as Reason versus the Passions. Rather, it was a question of arranging passions, self-interest and the Christian virtues—these were the accepted data—into a pattern of the good life; somehow, within or without—even perhaps as the Jansenists claimed through direct illuminism—to find a regulative principle for leading the good life. If a principle happens to be recommended in the literature of the period, it is usually implicitly, not explicitly, and varies, as we shall see, from author to author.

Molière suggests that the regulative principle is society. Because the miser and the snob appear ridiculous, society laughs at them and, in certain cases, may correct them. In *Tartuffe* he provides an even more interesting answer. There the whole of society is menaced by the extravagances of devout hypocrites, and it is only the discerning action of the King himself who sets things to right: "Nous vivons sous un Prince ennemi de la fraude." Sometimes love, especially first love, may provide the regulative principle, but not always. At the end of *Le Misanthrope* Alceste invites Célimène to accompany him in his flight from society, "Pour trouver tout en moi, comme moi tout en vous," but Célimène declines this too exclusive love, and here as so often Molière suggests that woman's intuition is wiser than man's logical arguments.

Molière, of course, is not always so serious. With the lightest of touches he exposes the hypocrisy and affectation of the age of Louis XIV, succeeding in making us love his dupes, whether it be a man who had taken a wife above him and keeps reminding himself, "Tu l'a voulu, Georges Dandin" (again, the mystery, the unreasonableness of choice) or Monsieur Jourdain dismissing cosmology and physics as so much *tintamarre*, so much *brouillamini*, and asking his philosophy teacher for a lesson in spelling.

Many of the comic incidents came straight from Court: for example, the scene in *Tartuffe* when Orgon inquires about his devout friend. The maid tells Orgon that Tartuffe dined off a brace of partridge—"Le pauvre homme!" Orgon exclaims—that he slept soundly—"Le pauvre homme!"—that he had four glasses of wine for lunch—"Le pauvre homme!" It was Louis who had used those words, in an affectionate sense, in 1662 when a courtier was listing the succulent courses in a dinner eaten by Bishop Péréfixe on a fast-day in Lent; Molière overheard and five years later transferred the scene to the stage.

The King collaborated with Molière more than once. For example, a French business man named d'Arvieux back from Smyrna describes Turkish customs to Louis, who at once thinks of introducing Turks on to the stage. He puts d'Arvieux in touch with Molière and Lully; a play is written, Louis reads it, likes it and sends d'Arvieux to Baraillon, the royal costumier, where he spends eight days helping to design turbans, veils and scimitars. The result is *Le Bourgeois Gentilhomme*, given in September, 1670, "with a success which satisfied the King and all the Court."

Nicolas Boileau, who was a close friend of Molière, likewise ridiculed hypocrisy, pedantry and any flashy or hollow behaviour. He, too, saw the deceitfulness of reason—"Il est vrai, de tout temps la raison fut son lot, Mais de là je conclus que l'homme est le plus sot"[1]—but unlike Molière he believed that the best regulative principles are humility—"the wise man is the person who thinks he is not wise"—and friendship, for friends can criticise without giving offence. This blunt, good-natured Paris *rentier* was himself a loyal friend to many at Court, not least to the King himself. He remains important for his enunciation of the classical virtues—clarity, concision and verisimilitude; for his insistence on unflagging work—a poet must revise his lines twenty times at least; and for his influence on other poets, notably Racine, whom he may have persuaded to abandon Italian preciosity for the spare chiselled beauty of the Alexandrine.

Jean Racine was the third of Louis's close literary friends. As a young man Louis had played in Desmaret's witheringly anti-Jansenist comedy, *Les Visionnaires*: he had acted his role exceptionally well and in later life still knew the play by heart. Now Racine's Jansenist sympathies were as well known as the King's hostility to that sect, so Louis's patronage of the playwright is further evidence of his love of fine literature.

Racine formulates the classical conflict in somewhat new terms. Phèdre, for example, is already a prey to her passion for Hippolyte when the curtain rises, she is already past the point of return, and the pathos lies in the powerlessness of reasonable argument to draw her back. Not only reason but will also is shown to be less effective than most people imagine. *Phèdre* has been called a Jansenist work—proof that without grace man cannot act virtuously—but on unconvincing evidence. If any character in the play is a Jensenist it

---

[1] It is true that down the ages man has prided himself on reason, but from that I conclude he is the biggest ass.

is surely Hippolyte, not Phèdre—"J'ai poussé la vertu jusques à la rudesse"—and Hippolyte is presented in an unfavourable light. More important, Phèdre is made to sin by the gods—and no Jansenist taught that. The truth seems to be that Racine has chosen to submit himself to the values of Euripides, according to which the sentence of the gods on illicit love is one which no mortal can commute.

Phèdre is perhaps the most perfect example of the classical style under Louis XIV. Not only are the unities observed, but the play has compactness, singleness of purpose and simplicity of language: words are used in their original and strict sense, they are all in scale and related to each other harmoniously. Imagery is unusually telling because so restrained. When Phèdre says:

Quelle importune main, en formant tous ces noeuds,
A pris soin sur mon front d'assembler mes cheveux?[1]

for the rest of the scene her braided hair suggests unbearable mental anguish. Even alliteration is used to disclose character, as in the wonderful line where Phèdre describes Thésée and at the same time reveals her own tastes:

Mais fidèle, mais fier, et même un peu farouche.[2]

After *Phèdre* Racine abandoned the theatre for eleven years, until at the request of Madame de Maintenon he wrote two plays for the schoolgirls of Saint-Cyr, *Esther* (1688) and *Athalie* (1691). *Athalie* is an astonishingly original and daring work, perhaps the first true Christian tragedy. Heaven at last is on the side of the hero and working for order, not destruction. The spiritual turmoil is as complex and bewildering as in Racine's earlier plays and the questions are still moral questions—"La foi qui n'agit point, est-ce une foi sincère?"[3]—but now a regulative principle has emerged in the shape of the law, not only the Mosaic law, but all law, which is an expression of divine order, an absolute to which man in doubt can cling.

Most other writers of the reign also hint at a principle for

---

[1] What importunate hand has gathered my hair
And tied it across my brow in all these knots?
[2] But faithful, proud and even a little fierce.
[3] Is faith without works a sincere faith?

regulating human life. Pascal suggests grace, Bossuet obedience to the King and the Pope, Madame de Sévigné devotion to one's children, La Fontaine knowledge of the species one belongs to— and its limitations. As for Jean de La Bruyère, he evolved a curious regulative principle, which may be described as salvation by social mediocrity. From his experiences in the Condé circle he deduced that the small man of merit will be snubbed by great lords, never win the ear of a prince, never earn much money. But this very lack of success will canalise his energies, make him single-minded and give him that "character" which so many men in the second, somewhat relaxing half of the reign, Fénelon for example, were desperately seeking.

A word by way of conclusion about Racine and Boileau as historians of the King's reign. Louis appointed them in 1677. He expected them to celebrate his victories but drew the line at flattery. Racine had a tendency in that direction and after his Discourse before the Academy was told by Louis, "I'd praise you more if you hadn't praised me so much." Boileau, on the other hand, was not a man to pull his punches: "Sire, nothing is impossible to Your Majesty; having set out to write bad verses, Your Majesty has succeeded"—and he believed that kings had more need of poets' pens: "Sans elles un héros n'est pas longtemps héros"—than poets had need of patrons.

Curiously enough, Racine's appointment was criticised. Maréchal d'Estrades feared that coming from a humble provincial family he would attribute "plebeian sentiments" to Louis, as he had already done to the hero of *Alexandre*, but Racine was too much the smooth courtier to make any such blunder. Shortly after his appointment Louis met Racine at Court: "I'm disappointed that you didn't come on this last campaign; you would have had a taste of war, and your journey would not have been long." "Sire," replied Racine, "Monsieur Boileau and I had only town dress. We had ordered country clothes, but the places you were attacking fell before our clothes were finished." Boileau's wit was drier. In the same year, hearing that a cannon ball had missed the King by seven paces, he said to Louis, "Sire, I beg you as your historian not to finish my history so soon."

In 1678 Boileau and Racine bought themselves horses and with long swords at their belts, rode to war with Louis. They caused much amusement: Boileau, particularly, was all over the place in his saddle. They had to be near Louis at every moment which might prove memorable, and because they were writing for participants and their families they had to be scrupulously accurate. The "Messieurs du Sublime," as they were called, bothered generals, noted down military slang, observed the enemy through telescopes and were thrown from their horses in the mud. Having inquired of a general where they should stable their horses, they were met by the freezing reply: "Give them to me, gentlemen, I will hold them myself." At the siege of Ypres, the Duc d'Enghien wanted to lead them to the trenches, "to show them the danger." Mademoiselle de Scudéry believed they were too frightened to see anything; Bussy was probably nearer the mark when he says they found the danger less than they had imagined.

"Were you far from the cannon?" Louis asked Boileau.

"Sire, a hundred paces."

"Weren't you afraid?"

"Sire, I trembled greatly for Your Majesty, and even more for myself."

Their history, alas, was never written. Boileau found it impossible to justify that key event, Louis's invasion of Holland, and thereafter lost interest. Racine worked hard, translating a treatise on how to write history by the Greek sophist, Lucian, and amassing reams of notes on such subjects as the position of the planets at Louis's birth and the position of his regiments at the siege of Namur. Everything touching the King seemed to his contemporaries worthy of record, and that was Racine's undoing. He became bogged in a mass of detail and never succeeded in reducing his notes to narrative.

In the other arts too important work was being done on an equally extensive scale, particularly in architecture which Louis intended to express the glory of the age and, as Bossuet put it, "help to keep up respect for the majesty of kings so necessary to the rest of the world." The spirit of Versailles was catching. Noblemen abandoned family manors where they had lived in one room and commissioned fine houses, where each suite comprised an antechamber, a salon, a bedroom, a dressing-room and sometimes a study. Across the Ile de France château after château went up. Mansart alone was responsible for Clagny, Dampierre, Laigle and Vauves, and for the rebuilding of Saint-Cloud and Chantilly.

Beauty in architecture, as in literature, was held to reside not in the novelty of the elements but in their arrangement. Proportion is indispensable, for it alone imparts unity. According to the Academy of Architecture, while taste in decoration varies from age to age, the sense of proportion is innate in human nature, identical therefore in the ancients and in the moderns. (Similarly, Racine is delighted with the applause given to *Iphigénie*, for it shows that good sense is the same now as in classical Greece.)

The practical results of this theory were the use of the classical orders, considered an essential feature of every good building, and a general tendency towards simplicity, unity and the balance of equal parts. The new houses had a less divided façade, and a rhythm of masses replaced a rhythm of decorative elements. The commons were moved from the wings to separate buildings and the staircase from the centre to the side. The most important change concerned the roof. Under Louis XIII each part of the house had its own roof, often high, heavy and encumbered by dormer windows, lanterns and arrises: the series of roofs seemed to crush the building. In the new houses a single roof, unencumbered and reduced in height, crowned the house as a whole. Louis himself went a stage farther. He had a liking for long horizontal lines, and whether for that reason or because he was more logical in following the ancients, he usually commissioned flat or nearly flat roofs. The roof of Versailles was covered partly in lead, partly in copper, but the lead made the upper rooms unbearably hot: in a letter to Pontchartrain in July, 1695, La Bruyère says that he could have cooked a cake on the gutter of his room.

The churches of Louis's reign also aimed at unity and regularity. They are more sober and simple than their Italian or Spanish counterparts. Unity was often enhanced by suppression of the transept. Inside, the main feature was the colonnade, with rounded arches. Stained glass was usually replaced by ordinary glass, thus flooding the nave with light; sometimes Gothic pillars were rounded and given capitals. The dome was becoming popular, and so was the semi-circular apse, as used by Mansart for the chapel of Versailles. Indeed churches as a whole show a rounding of forms, even in minor decoration: this was the age *par excellence* of the monstrance. Among the notable churches of the reign are Mansart's chapel of the Invalides, the Conception and Saint Michel at Menton, and Notre Dame at Bordeaux.

The best painters of the age, Nicolas Poussin (1594-1665) and Claude Lorrain (1600-82), lived in Rome, and even Louis could not lure them back. Poussin was born near Evreux, where Normandy softens into the Ile de France. His self-portrait shows a stern, dynamic, rather anxious face with taut, indrawn lips, yet as far as is known his life was calm, regular and contented. As a young man he visited Italy and there discovered his inspiration in classical sculpture, which he copied directly, adding only a few details from life. Like Racine and the French architects he was extraordinarily humble towards ancient Greece and Rome: it would seem that this acceptance of the subject matter and many of the forms of his art released energy for that perfection of the whole, that "finish" which marks the classical masterpiece.

Poussin's genius lies in balancing a variety of natural features or of figures (more than fifty in his sketch for "The Taking of Jerusalem") so as to give the impression of unity and complete serenity. He does this most often by grouping the main elements or the figures in a circle or oval. The change Poussin wrought in painting is equivalent to the change wrought in gardens by the King when he turned streams into fountains: an image of transience was replaced by one of eternity. "A great narrator and creator of myths"—Bernini's opinion of Poussin is still the best. And since myth is built from order and control it would be unfair to seek in Poussin spontaneity of emotion: his Sabine women, for instance, seem to be screaming for help in faultless Alexandrines.

Both Poussin and Claude painted noble scenes and exalted objects—marble columns, temples, palaces, tall regular spreading

trees, fine ships. This was in striking contrast to the other great
school of painting, the Dutch, which made art out of humble
objects: brick courtyards, tiled interiors, fishing smacks, a servant
girl pouring a jug of milk. The still-life did not appeal to French
painters: they were much too interested in an ideal past and in
people, particularly people who realised certain difficult ideals.

Until almost the end of the century Poussin dominated painting
in France. His influence was beneficial in that it promoted excellence of draftsmanship. His chief disciple was Charles Le Brun,
who in co-operation with the King directed the arts from 1664 to
1683. Le Brun was primarily a decorator with a prolific imagination. He designed most of the statues at Versailles, as well as altars,
pulpits, catafalques, tombs, prows of ships, tapestries and Savonnerie
carpets. He also designed much of the furniture of the age: marble
consoles; gilded tables with scroll legs decorated with masks,
palms and foliage, whose crosspieces supported vases or baskets of
flowers; ceiling-high cupboards which shut with the precision of
a snuff-box, their doors divided into panels each with a gilt figure
in relief, the whole inlaid with ebony, brass, tortoiseshell, mother-
of-pearl or ivory; broad-backed chairs covered with damask,
brocade, tapestry and cut velvet: all that rich, solid, majestic, very
masculine furniture that to-day perpetuates the King's name.

The period of opulent, solid decoration and large-scale mytho-
logical paintings runs from 1661 to the time of Louis's second
marriage. Thereafter the most important form is the portrait.
Here again the contrast with republican Holland is striking. While
Rembrandt had sought out humble, suffering humanity, the French
Court painters imparted to each portrait an air of nobility, self-
assurance, pomp and swagger.

Among the leading artists Pierre Mignard excelled with women.
His portrait of one of Louis's daughters blowing bubbles, a spaniel
at her feet, looks forward to the elegant, decorative lighter portraits
of ladies which were to be France's particular achievement in the
eighteenth century. Hyacinthe Rigaud, on the other hand, brought
to the portrait Rembrandt's chiaroscuro and a new uncompromising
realism which succeeded better with men than with women. Once
he painted a lady who was heavily made up. When she complained

that he had not caught the freshness of her complexion, Rigaud replied dryly: "That's surprising, for your rouge and my red come from the same shop."

The best portraits of the reign have an unequalled majesty and power. If one compares Rigaud's likeness of Louis's witty courtier, the Marquis de Dangeau, with for example François Pourbus's "Henri IV," painted a century earlier, there is an astonishing increase not only in mass (broader shoulders, cascading periwig and embroidered silk mantle) but also in assurance. Henri IV is a brave little figure, jutting out his chin; Dangeau is so assured he does not need to parade his courage: he is the King's man and that is enough.

Just as the spate of new houses gave work to painters, so the spate of paintings gave work to engravers. The canvases of Poussin and Le Brun in particular were multiplied in this medium. It was Louis who raised engraving from an industrial to one of the fine arts when about 1670 he proposed that the monuments and art treasures of France should be recorded in a collection of engravings to be called the "Cabinet du Roi." Among those who took part in the scheme were first-rate artists like G. Perelle and Michel Hardouin. By the end of the century Paris had two hundred master-engravers.

Robert Nanteuil (*c.* 1625/5-78) is the best of the engravers from life. While Abraham Bosse depicted the bourgeois and the poor, Nanteuil portrayed only the nobility, chiefly men. In his seven portraits of Louis he achieves his declared aim of expressing the sitter's "mind and character." If psychological insight with economy of means was the ideal of the age, Nanteuil's engravings, so forceful and living, must be accorded a very high place.

Two other features of painting in the second half of the reign deserve notice. One is the triumph of the Rubenists over the Poussinists. The Poussinists held that painting was primarily design, that which can be reduced to geometric, therefore to intelligible forms. The Rubenists were partisans of colour. They held that painting should deceive the eye, and that colour does this more effectively than drawing. Some even said that colour represents truth, whereas drawing only represents an abstract of truth made to satisfy the reason.

The second change is the growth of religious painting, as Louis and the Court became more devout. In the Salon of 1673 about ten religious paintings were shown, in 1699 seventy-two, and in 1704 over a hundred. The two large-scale commissions of the later half of the reign were the dome of the Church of the Invalides, the painting of which was entrusted to a Rubenist, La Fosse, and the chapel of Versailles, the ceiling of which was decorated by Coypel, a Poussinist in the tradition of Le Brun. Louis was dissatisfied with Coypel's work and well pleased with La Fosse's, and this fact is interesting inasmuch as La Fosse's composition is markedly baroque. That Louis did not remain fixed in the tastes of his early manhood is further shown by his patronage, from about 1704, of Alexandre-François Desportes. Desportes, the son of a peasant from Champagne, was the first French painter of animals other than the horse. He accompanied royal hunts in order to sketch the hounds, and from these drawings Louis chose the best to become paintings.

In sculpture, too, the King's breadth of taste is evident. In 1683 a strange statue arrived at Versailles from the south of France by one Pierre Puget, who had long decorated churches in Genoa before taking employment in the arsenal of Toulon as a designer of ships' poops. Entitled "Milo of Cortona," the statue depicted the tortured figure of an athlete combating a lion, a writhing mass of straining muscles that recalls Michelangelo's "Slaves" and went clean against all the classical scupture of the reign. Louis, however, liked the "Milo" so much that he placed it in the most conspicuous place in the gardens, opposite the entrance to the *allée royale*.

The other leading sculptors of the reign are François Girardon, a close collaborator of Le Brun, who produced at least one fine work in the tomb of Richelieu, and Antoine Coysevox. It was Louis who commissioned Coysevox's statues of Fame and Mercury, now at the entrance of the Tuileries, rivals in spreading news of the King, "now of war, now of peace, but always of glory." For these statues Louis rewarded Coysevox with a pension of £1,300, the highest he accorded to any artist. Coysevox also did a dozen busts of the King, the best being that commissioned by the Hôtel de Ville in 1689, now in the courtyard of the Carnavalet. Like Nanteuil, Coysevox has left a whole gallery of character studies, notably of Le Tellier, Arnauld and the Grand Condé.

One aspect of life is so far missing in the arts: sensuousness, a spontaneous outpouring of joy, tenderness and pathos. It is lacking even in literature, where the one lacuna is lyric poetry. It found its expression in the music of the reign. In this art too the classical style prevails: line is preferred to colour, proportion to ornament. Both the leading composers of the reign, Jean-Baptiste Lully and François Couperin, were draughtsmen interested in tone-colour only as a means to making their linear structure clear.

Lully's chief compositions are operas, songs, military marches and motets; his tunes are memorable and easily hummed, they are full of fun and flirtation. On his death in 1687 Lully's mantle fell to François Couperin, whom the King chose in 1693 as one of the organists of the royal chapel and ennobled in 1696. Couperin composed Masses and motets, concert pieces for Versailles and—his chief title to fame—clavichord pieces, some for his pupils, the Dauphin's children. In contrast to Lully, Couperin excels at a kind of sensuous purity. Louis liked Couperin's music but to the end of his life preferred the more voluptuous violin to the clavichord.

Literature, architecture, painting, interior decoration, engraving, sculpture and music—during the reign every art reached a high pitch of excellence and the total achievement is colossal. The sheer quantity of work produced is astounding: Rigaud painted upwards of forty portraits a year, Bossuet's sermons, treatises and correspondence fill forty-three fat volumes, while Quinault is credited with more than 150 libretti. Here, as in other fields, the King's own energy seems to have stimulated those around him. As for the quality of the work, there can be no certain proof in such matters, but it seems reasonable to believe that had James II, the Emperor Leopold or even Louis XIII been ruling France there would have been no *Misanthrope*, no *Phèdre*, few of the majestic country houses and gardens, little of the beauty and serenity which stems from vigorous action within an accepted order. On the title page of almost every masterpiece in the reign is printed the official *imprimatur*, "With the King's privilege": a formula, yes, but one that suggests a general truth. Racine was the King's historiographer, Mansart the King's architect, Le Brun the King's painter, Lully the King's master of music; tapestries, carpets, engravings—all bear the royal crown. Directly or indirectly literature and the arts reflect Louis's tastes and character; at every point the classical age bears the unmistakable signature of the King.

CHAPTER 18

Domestic Pleasures

THE YEARS 1685 to 1700 were the period of Louis's middle age. Abroad, the King maintained France's glory, though at a lesser pitch, while at home he did much to foster notable advances in science. For Louis personally it was a period of domestic contentment.

In 1685 Louis was forty-seven. His health continued excellent. His body was naturally robust and stood up well to long hours of work, to pleasure and hard physical exercise. Yet since the age of eight Louis's scrupulous First Doctors had recorded a succession of headaches and spells of tiredness, pimples and rashes, chills and sore throats; by the year 1685 this *Diary of the King's Health* ran to several hundred pages. With only the *Diary* to go on, one would suppose that Louis had been what Scarron claimed to be: a walking textbook of ailments.

According to Vallot, his earliest doctor, Louis had a warm, bilious temperament. Like most of his courtiers he ate too much game and highly spiced sauces; for the consequent disorders there was one staple treatment: purging and bleeding, bleeding and purging. Medicine was still bedevilled by astrology—in 1658 Louis's surgeon-in-ordinary had advised that the King should be bled in the first and last quarters of the moon, "because then the humours have returned to the centre of the body"—and tended to ask interesting though misguided questions: "Can nature do more than education to make a hero?" "Are pretty women more fertile than others?" Doctors were treated as figures of fun, and in the presence of the King Molière once chaffed his physician, a certain Mauvillain: "We reason with one another; he prescribes the remedies; I omit to take them and I recover."

Louis himself, during his rare illnesses, did not much mind who treated him. Daquin, Vallot's successor, owed his post to Madame de Montespan (she made Daquin reward her with a "commission" of £660). He belonged to the Montpellier faculty, which used the Arabs' pharmacopoeia: earthworms against gout, bees' ashes to make hair grow, ant-oil against deafness. For toothache spirit of nicotine was usually prescribed, but Louis preferred essence of cloves. Toothache and smallpox were the two curses of the seventeenth century. Louis had his first experience of the former in 1685. Daquin extracted a number of teeth, but failed to remove a root in the upper jaw. This developed into an abscess, with osteitis and inflammation of the sinus. To relieve the pain it was decided to extract Louis's remaining upper teeth. During the operation (with nothing to anaesthetise the gum) the surgeon broke part of the jaw-bone and left a gaping hole, to which, on a single day, the cauterising iron was applied fourteen times by a certain Monsieur Dubois, "who appeared more exhausted than the King, such was his unflinching courage in moments of pain." The abscess healed, but Louis's sinus remained sensitive for the rest of his life, while the loss of his upper teeth made it difficult for him to chew.

Louis seems to have been susceptible to abscesses. Throughout 1686 he suffered from a very painful anal fistula. His surgeon, Félix, decided to perform what was called "la grande opération." For several months Félix perfected his technique on patients in the Paris hospitals and even devised a specially terrible-looking bistoury. On the evening before the operation Louis held a Council of Ministers, and immediately after the fistula had been removed, although his pain was such that sweat stood out on his brow, he received ambassadors in audience. "We are not like private individuals," he remarked. "We owe ourselves to the public."

Three weeks later Madame de Maintenon wrote: "He has suffered to-day for seven hours as if he were being broken on the wheel." But the operation had been a complete success and by the end of 1686 Louis was well again. He gave Félix £15,000, a country estate and a patent of nobility.

Apart from attacks of gout and the stone, Louis was to enjoy good health until the very end of his life. He was as active as anyone half his age. There was indeed something sun-like about his sheer physical energy, and it was this energy which played so large a part in his quest for glory, driving him even in middle age to continue to assert his power abroad.

His gains after the Treaty of Nijmegen—notably the "reunion" of the Alsatian cities and the annexation of Strasbourg—led Louis to believe that nothing could check France's expansion eastward. So when the Elector of the Palatinate died childless in 1685 Louis put forward a flimsy claim to that country, which lies north of Alsace on the French side of the Rhine, on the grounds that the Elector's sister, the Princess Elizabeth Charlotte (Liselotte), was Monsieur's second wife and therefore Louis's sister-in-law. This claim alarmed Europe and in 1686 William of Orange formed against Louis the League of Augsburg, consisting of Spain, the Empire, Sweden and various German princes. When Louis invaded the Palatinate in 1688 the League declared war against him, to be joined in 1689 by England, who in that year proclaimed William her new king. The War of the League of Augsburg was to last until 1697. Thus for the second time in the reign, as the result of an act of aggression, Louis was obliged virtually single-handed to fight a long war against the leading powers of Europe.

The immediate result of events in 1688 was an influx of English exiles to Saint-Germain. The Queen arrived first. Maria of Modena, the daughter of a cousin of Mazarin, was "thin, with fine dark eyes, a pale complexion, fine teeth, a good figure, very self-possessed and pleasing." On her dressing-table she found a little casket containing 6,000 pistoles (£20,000)—a present from Louis, always solicitous towards those in distress, particularly an attractive lady. According to Madame de Sévigné, "This Queen gives general satisfaction and has a pleasant turn of mind. Seeing the King [of France] caressing the Prince of Wales, who is a beautiful child, she said, 'I was envious of my child's happiness, because he does not understand his misfortunes, but now I pity him for not being aware of Your Majesty's caresses and goodness.' All she says shows judgment and courage."

James arrived the next day, and this appearance of a Stuart King in exile seemed to set the clock back thirty-nine years.

"There's a good man who has given up three kingdoms for a Mass," quipped the Archbishop of Reims, and Madame de Sévigné wrote: "He recounts all that happened in England with an insensibility that makes him look a fool." Louis took a kinder view and treated James amiably, declaring "that this King was the best fellow in the world, that he should hunt with him, that he should come to Marly and Trianon, and that courtiers would have to get used to it."

At the end of February, 1690, James set off for Ireland with a French fleet, and Louis bade him good-bye with one of his well-turned phrases: "The best thing I can wish you is never to see you here again." But the Battle of the Boyne put an end to Stuart hopes and the unfortunate James returned to France. Instead of curtailing his hospitality now that the English King and his followers were to be his guests for life, Louis continued to place Saint-Germain at their disposal and gave James an annual pension of £200,000. While her husband made long retreats at Rancé's Trappist monastery, Louis was particularly kind to Maria, organising stag-hunts, plays and concerts, "being always careful to give to the Queen every consolation great or small that was in his power."

Louis's working day was now heavier than ever. On the death of Louvois in 1691 Louis became his own Minister of War: he was at his desk for eight or nine hours daily and often held an afternoon as well as a morning Council. In 1691 he was present at the capture of Mons, and the following spring decided to direct in person the siege of Namur, one of the strongest fortresses in the Spanish Netherlands. Madame de Maintenon gallantly agreed to accompany him, but she lacked the Montespan's campaigning spirit: "the paving so sharp that it cuts the feet . . . four hundred steps to be climbed. . . . So far I have visited only two churches, where, in addition to atrocious music, there was a fog of incense which made me dizzy." Racine, too, accompanied the King, and he had troubles of a different kind. For his history he questioned officers in different parts of the field, but their reports seldom tallied: "I can see that the truth, which we are always being asked for, is more difficult to find than to write."

Louis, who had lost none of his old skill as a soldier, captured Namur after a month's siege. This important victory was his last personal success in battle, for after taking part in operations of the following year, 1693, for the rest of the reign he left command in the field to his generals. In his various campaigns he had shown himself a brave and competent commander, but not a brilliant one. He had the defects of his virtues: prizing carefulness, he lacked the reckless flair which swoops and darts and thrusts a sudden mortal blow at the enemy's heart. Besides, he seems to have disliked bloodshed. What he liked was besieging and capturing very strong towns, and at this he had excelled.

Desultory fighting was to continue for another four years and to end in an interim peace, whereby Louis gave up his claim to the Palatinate on consideration of a large payment to his sister-in-law. Both Louis and the League realised that until the death of the childless King of Spain—an event expected at any moment—no lasting settlement could be made in Europe.

In 1693, the year he decided to ride no more to war, Louis reached the age of fifty-five. He began to spend more time with his children and grandchildren, and to get to know them better. He also began to think of those who would succeed him to the throne.

Louis had only one legitimate child, the Dauphin, then aged thirty-two. As an army officer the Dauphin had proved disappointing. He had cleared the Paris region of wolves, but it was abundantly plain that he would never clear the Netherlands of France's enemies. He was a dutiful, obedient son, but dull and heavy: the Court found it discouraging to think that he was heir to the throne of France. As Bossuet sadly said: "With him we go forward, hoping against hope." The Dauphin's wife, a plain, melancholic Bavarian princess, gave him three sons before dying in 1690. The Dauphin then secretly married a certain Mademoiselle Choin, of whom Liselotte says: "She had the hugest bosom I ever saw; those enormous charms of hers were the Dauphin's delight."

The Dauphin rarely spoke. "Mademoiselle Choin once remarked upon his silence; he replied that the words of people in his position carried great weight and an ill-considered remark could do irreparable harm, and for that reason he would rather say nothing at all. To someone as indolent and as indifferent to all about him as he was, silence in any case came more easily, but, excellent as his precept was, he rather overdid it." The Dauphin and his wife lived quietly at Meudon and had little influence at Court or in the government.

Of the Dauphin's three sons, the eldest, the Duc de Bourgogne, born in 1682, was intelligent, handsome and strong-willed; he promised one day to become a good king. The second, the Duc d'Anjou, inherited his father's heavy, slow disposition. According to Liselotte, he was "a thorough Austrian in appearance, with his mouth always open. I have told him about it hundreds of times, and being of a docile nature he always shuts it when he is told, but as soon as he forgets he opens it again." The third, the Duc de Berry, was much livelier, "a charming youngster and always so gay." But he was very stupid, and spent his time playing shuttlecock, skating in winter or making himself useful to the ladies: "one makes him bring her a table, another needlework, a third gives him some other order"; meekly he would oblige, then perch himself on a stool to await their further good pleasure.

Besides these four legitimate descendants, Louis had five surviving natural children: a daughter by Louise de La Vallière; two sons and two daughters by Madame de Montespan. Louise's daughter, Mademoiselle de Blois, born in 1666, was "beautiful as Mademoiselle de Fontanges, agreeable as her mother, with the figure and air of the King, her father." She had married a Prince of the Blood, Louis de Conti, nephew of the Grand Condé, who left her a widow at nineteen: an exceedingly gay, amusing widow, whose love affairs were much discussed. She was a favourite with Louis, but she had a cruel, mocking side to her nature and made fun of the new pious atmosphere at Court introduced by Madame de Maintenon.

Louis's eldest child by Madame de Montespan was Louis-Auguste, Duc du Maine. Infantile paralysis at the age of three had left him with a limp. This limp, poor health and his bastardy gave him a sense of inferiority. Like the King's other natural children, he had been legitimised and ranked immediately below the Princes of the Blood, but he constantly felt the need of justifying that position; he longed to impress the King with feats of bravery. "Have I ambition?" he wrote from the battlefield to Madame de Maintenon, who loved him like a son. "I overflow with it, Madame, and also with submission to the King's commands." War proved him more submissive than triumphant: he never really succeeded in standing on his own feet. In 1692, at the age of twenty-one, he married a grand-daughter of the Grand Condé —a tiny doll-like creature whose jewelled headdress weighed almost as much as her body—and came completely under the domination of this bold, lively little creature, nicknamed from her explosive temper Dona Salpetria.

The second surviving child of Louis and Madame de Montespan, Mademoiselle de Nantes, was the cleverest of Louis's children. She was beautiful and amusing, but completely heartless. Her chief diversion was playing spiteful jokes. The King married her, also, into the Condé family—to Louis, Duc de Bourbon; by this triple marriage alliance he ensured that after his death the ambitious Condés would remain loyal to the crown. The third child, Françoise-Marie, who in 1692 became the wife of her first cousin, Philippe, Duc de Chartres, was an incarnation of pride and laziness. Nicknamed Lucifer, she believed that she, a Daughter of France— although of illegitimate birth—was doing her husband, a mere Grandson of France, an almighty honour by marrying him. Her pride alienated him to such an extent that he fell in love with his own daughter and, according to Liselotte, Françoise-Marie got drunk as a fiddler three or four times a week. Finally, the youngest of Louis's children, the Comte de Toulouse, was a good fellow, but unintelligent, curt and cold.

Thus, of Louis's children and legitimate grandchildren only one, the Duc de Bourgogne, seemed likely to achieve much good for France. Louis trained him at Council meetings as once he had been trained by Mazarin. Most of the legitimised children squabbled and caused scandals: Louis constantly had to make peace or rescue them from scrapes. Incidentally, although Louis himself spoke distinctly, all his children pronounced their r's in an odd way: Pahi for Paris. Louis saw them often and liked to have them at Court, but he could not be really close to them. As he grew older, there was a danger that under Madame de Maintenon's influence Louis might cut himself off from the younger generation, become pompous and severe. That this did not happen is largely due to the arrival in France, one autumn day in 1696, of a ten-year-old Italian princess.

Marie Adélaïde of Savoy was the daughter of the Duchess Anne, who in turn was the daughter of Monsieur, Louis's brother, and of his first wife, Henrietta of England. She had come to marry Louis's grandson, the Duc de Bourgogne, thus setting the seal on an alliance between France and Savoy, a country which had formerly adhered to the League of Augsburg.

Louis was hoping much from this grand-daughter of the charming Henrietta whom everyone but her husband had loved, and to meet her travelled as far as Montargis.

I arrived here before five [Louis wrote to Madame de Maintenon] but the Princess did not come till nearly six. I went to receive her in her coach. She waited for me to speak, and then replied very well but with a slight embarrassment which would have pleased you. I led her to her room through the crowd, allowing her to be seen from time to time by lighting up her face with the candelabra. This she supported with grace and modesty.

"Grace," incidentally, was the fashionable word in the 'nineties. Samuel Prior noted that "a man is called gracious, that is to say honest; a woman is gracious, that is, beautiful; people sing, eat and gamble gracefully."

Finally we reached her room, where there was a crowd and heat enough to kill one. I presented her from time to time to those who approached, and watched her from every point of view in order to tell you what I think of her. She has the best air and most beautiful figure I have ever seen, perfectly dressed and her hair also, eyes bright and magnificent, eyelashes black and admirable, complexion very even, white and red, all that could be desired; the most beautiful black hair possible and in abundance. She is thin as is proper at her age, mouth very red, lips thick, teeth white, long and irregular; hands well shaped but of the colour of her age. She speaks little, at least as far as I have seen, and is not embarrassed when she is looked at, like one accustomed to the world. She curtseys badly in rather an Italian way. She has something Italian in her face, but she pleases, as I saw in everyone's eyes. To speak to you as I am in the habit of doing I find her perfect, and should be sorry if she were more beautiful. I repeat, I am pleased with everything except her curtsey. I will tell you more after supper, for I shall notice many things that I have not yet been able to see. I forgot to tell you that she is small rather than tall for her age.

Then comes two phrases very revealing of Louis the man:

Up to now I have behaved wonderfully. I hope I shall maintain a certain easy manner till we reach Fontainebleau.

At Fontainebleau Madame de Maintenon was able to judge Marie Adélaide for herself. "She has a natural courtesy which permits her to say nothing but what is pleasant. Yesterday I tried to prevent her caressing me, saying I was too old. 'Ah, not so old as that!' she exclaimed, and did me the honour of embracing me." The little princess came like a breath of spring to the ageing Court. She was wonderfully lively and loving. She played blindman's buff and spillikins with the courtiers, sang at table, even danced on her chair. She used the informal "tu" to Louis, rumpled his clothes and mussed his wig. When the post arrived, she would open his letters and sometimes sit on his knee while he read them. "Everybody here has become a child again." And everybody loved her, save perhaps the little Princess of England, aged four, who had set her heart on the Duc de Bourgogne and announced in tears that "she would go into a convent and never marry all her life."

Not since Louise de La Vallière had such a delightful person come into Louis's life. He loved Marie Adélaide as his own daughter and for the next dozen years she was to bring him much happiness. Nothing was too good for her. Here is the otherwise austere Madame de Maintenon arranging dinner on a fast day: "She must have a prawn soup in a silver bowl, a roll of bread such as she always eats, a piece of brown bread, fresh butter, fresh poached eggs, a sole on a small dish, currant jam on a plate, a flask of wine, a china jug full of water, small enough that she may be able to help herself, and a china drinking cup." After her marriage in 1697 (the young couple were allowed to live together only two years later) Louis gave a ball in the Hall of Mirrors, with four orange trees bearing hundreds of oranges conserved in sugar. Because she loved dancing, masquerade followed masquerade, in which she appeared as Flora, the Queen of Hearts or a Chinese princess. Sometimes a fortnight would pass without her seeing daylight. In 1698 Louis made her a present of the menagerie at Versailles and its farm, where she sometimes played the dairymaid and churned butter for the royal slice of bread. Almost anyone else would have become atrociously spoiled, and the really astonishing thing is that, no matter how many compliments and jewels were showered on her, Marie Adélaide never did become spoiled.

It was still Madame de Maintenon who played by far the most important part in Louis's life. Though she now had what she wanted, the power to do good, Madame de Maintenon was not completely happy. Her temperament would not allow that. "Pray God," she wrote to her director, "to give me strength to support the pleasures of the Court." She found fault with the younger ladies for their "immodest" dress, their laziness, their habit of taking snuff. She had few close friends. As Fénelon told her: "When you discover some defect in those you hoped to find perfect, you grow too disgusted and carry your dislike too far." She loved the King as much as she could love any person—yet she disliked the sexual side of marriage. Her atavistic Calvinism seems to have been repelled by the pleasures of the flesh for which Louis had such an appetite. She wrote to her spiritual director about "painful occasions"; he replied that it was a great grace "to be the instrument of God's counsels and to do out of pure virtue what so many other women do without merit or from passion." She was keeping His Majesty from sin and was to think of heaven where soon "the subjections of the present life will be over."

Despite Madame Guyon and Fénelon, Louis still trusted his wife's sound common sense. Working in her room, he would sometimes ask her: "What does Lady Reason think about this?"

"Qu'en pense la Raison?" There is no doubt that he continued to love her deeply. There exists a touching little note written from army headquarters in 1691: "However much you love me, my love for you will always be greater."

In middle age Louis continued to indulge his taste for building. The domestic pleasures and informal atmosphere which increasingly appealed to him demanded a smaller kind of house. In the park of Versailles Louis pulled down a small blue and white faience Trianon in Chinoiserie style which years ago he had built for Madame de Montespan and replaced it with a beautifully proportioned single-story, flat-roofed pavilion with a portico supported by columns in pairs. In the flower-beds grew thousands of tuberoses: so heady was their scent that sometimes the King and his suite, out for an evening stroll, were obliged to leave the garden. At the new Trianon Louis would dine informally, allowing ladies to sit at his table and even to recline on canapés afterwards, which would have been unthinkable at Versailles. Once the princesses let off fireworks outside Monsieur's door and the Duchesse de Chartres even lit a fire under his window; the noise and dense smoke caused Monsieur to jump out of bed and take to his heels in a nightshirt.

But the Trianon was too close to Versailles to be really informal and private. Louis felt the need of his own little country estate.

At last [writes Saint-Simon], weary of magnificence and throngs of people, the King convinced himself that he wanted a small place where he could sometimes be alone. He looked about near Versailles for a site to satisfy this new taste. Among other places he studied the slopes surrounding Saint-Germain and the extensive plain which lies below, where the Seine, as it winds out of Paris, waters so many flourishing towns and rich estates. He was urged to choose Luciennes, where Cavoie later built a house with an enchanting view; but he replied that such a lovely site would ruin him and that since he planned a mere trifle he wanted a site which would allow him to build that and no more.

Behind Luciennes he found a valley, narrow and deep,

with sheer sides, rendered inaccessible by marshes, with no view at all, shut in by hills at every point, extremely confined, with a wretched village on the side of one of these hills called Marly. The chief merit of this enclosed space was that it lacked a view or any possibility of a view. The narrowness of the valley, which seemed to preclude large-scale building, was also greatly in its favour.

Finally the hermitage was built . . . and gradually it grew; as one addition was planned here and another there the hills were cut away to make more room for building, while most of the hill at the end of the valley was removed in order to provide some sort of view, though a very imperfect one. More buildings began to take shape as well as gardens, lakes, aqueducts and the well-known truly extraordinary "machine of Marly"; parks were laid out, the forest trimmed and enclosed, statues and valuable furniture moved into place. . . . Tall trees were continually transported there from Compiègne or even further and replanted as dense, ready-made forests. Three-quarters of the trees died but they were replaced immediately. Vast stretches of thick wood, threaded with shadowy paths, were suddenly changed into immense lakes on which people glided in gondolas, then turned back into forests which excluded the light from the moment they were planted. I am speaking of changes I myself have witnessed in a space of six weeks. Ornamental lakes were altered a hundred times, waterfalls also, each time being given quite a different shape.

Marly consisted of one medium-sized château, called The Sun, dominating twelve smaller buildings, each named after one of the signs of the Zodiac, six in line on each side of a pool of water. In this and the other pools swam Louis's favourite carp: Dawn, Golden Sun, Flax Grey, Beautiful Mirror, the Dauphine, Pearl, Topaz and Proserpine. The chief glories of Marly were its water —fountains, falls and cascades—and its flowers. Louis was still fond of Spanish jasmine, tuberoses and orange blossom but in middle age he became a Rubenist in his taste for brighter coloured flowers, notably tulips. Lister, a visitor in 1698, says that eighteen million tulips, including other bulbs, were sent to Marly in the space of four years: "Such a show . . . in the broad beds, of a 1,000 paces long, everywhere, all this garden over, in their full beauty, was a most surprising sight."

Louis grew fonder and fonder of Marly. Often he spent Wednesday to Friday there every week. Because he took with him only a few guests, an invitation became the most sought-after honour at Court. On Wednesday morning the courtiers would approach Louis and say simply, "Sire, Marly!" Later in the day a list of guests was issued. Racine, himself a frequent guest, remarks that those on the list felt so honoured that they were always in a very good mood: so Marly was gay. Occasionally distinguished visitors such as Cardinals were invited: according to Madame de Maintenon, "their scarlet shows up perfectly against the green of Marly."

In this beautiful retreat etiquette was relaxed. Louis got up in the morning, ate his meals and went to bed without hundreds of eyes watching every move he made. When he went walking, all the men were allowed to wear their hats and in the salons everyone was allowed to sit down. Despite this, precedence bulked as large as ever. The desire to be in touch with the King, to be spoken of or considered favourably by him reached extraordinary lengths. For example, when Louis moved to a new palace or to Marly, pages chalked on the doors the name of the person who was to occupy this or that room. Sometimes "Pour" was put before the name. The "Pour" was theoretically reserved for Princes of the Blood, but it could be given to anyone as a mark of special favour. When the Princesse des Ursins—merely the wife of a minor Italian nobleman—arrived at Marly and found a "Pour" chalked on her door, she nearly swooned with joy. Another example: in 1699, after the death of Racine, Boileau reports in all seriousness that "His Majesty spoke to me of Racine in a way to make every courtier long to die, if they thought that the King would speak of them in those terms after their death." One last incident which borders on the fantastic. The Abbé de Polignac was following the King in the gardens of Marly when it began to rain. The King made a friendly remark to him about his coat, which was ill-suited to withstand the elements. "It is nothing, Sire," he replied, "the rain at Marly is never wet."

Louis's chief diversion in the sixteen-nineties was hunting the deer and stag. Since the year of the Queen's death, when he had broken his arm, he followed the hounds in a four-horse *calèche*, driving very fast. Louis's enthusiasm for hunting was shared by the dumpy, kind-hearted German princess, Liselotte, who saw more than a thousand stags taken, and had in all some twenty-five falls from her horse. Liselotte, incidentally, adored Louis, to whom she refers in her letters as the Great Man, and was exceedingly jealous of Madame de Maintenon ("the old whore," "the witch," "goody Scarron").

Louis's other diversions were shooting pheasants, music, opera, plays, gambling at lasquenet, pall-mall[1] (he taught Marie Adélaïde how to play) and billiards, for which a short, flat cue was used, curved at the end, and a table on which stood a skittle and hoop. Louis was very fond of billiards. One day he was playing before a group of courtiers when a quarrel arose over a disputed shot; Louis called the Comte de Gramont, who was seated nearby, to settle the difference.

"Sire," replied Gramont, without moving, "you are in the wrong."

"What, sir!" said Louis. "But you didn't even see the shot."

"If there had been the slightest doubt about the shot, Sire, the gentlemen watching would have cried that you were in the right."

At Marly Louis lived as a family man, at Versailles he again became a public figure. Versailles at this period was the centre not only of Europe but of a steadily expanding world. In 1682 an embassy of Moroccans—devout Muslims—arrived with four ostriches for the royal menagerie (Louis tactfully ordered all tapestries with the human figure to be removed from the ambassadors' Paris lodging). In 1684 envoys from Siam in tall pointed hats brought gifts to the French King—they prostrated themselves for so long that Louis wondered whether they would never rise—to be followed in 1685 by Russians: at a performance of *Amadis*

[1] A game in which a ball was driven through an iron ring suspended in a long alley.

they were much alarmed by the stage effects until Louis explained that these were not produced by witchcraft.

There was a steady increase of interest in far-off countries. In 1698 Louis formed a highly profitable Company to trade with China, which set a fashion in porcelain, screens and lacquered cabinets. From Senegal French explorers penetrated to the fringes of the Sahara, while Canada was enlarged by the territory of Hudson's Bay and extended as far as Lake Superior. In 1682 Cavelier de La Salle, a fur-trader, sailed down the Mississippi to its mouth, where he erected a column with the arms of France and in a splendidly boastful speech claimed possession of all the land between the Rocky and Allegheny Mountains, an area more than three times that of France, "in the name of the most high, mighty, invincible and victorious Prince, Louis the Great . . . upon the assurance we have had from the natives of these countries, that we are the first Europeans who have descended or ascended the said river Colbert, or Mississippi." In 1699 French settlers arrived in the new colony, which in honour of his king La Salle had named Louisiana.

These embassies and discoveries led to an interest in map-making and it was under Louis's patronage that scientific cartography was born. It was he who encouraged Jean-Dominique Cassini to send expeditions to Cayenne and the West Indies to gather material for a huge planisphere twenty-four feet in diameter. Edward Halley's observations on the Cape of Good Hope were used, as well as reports from Madagascar and Siam. The telescope and pendulum clock had made it possible to determine longitude: as a result land masses and islands were rearranged like so many pieces of furniture, Asia reduced in bulk and the Mediterranean given its proper length of forty-one degrees. On the basis of tri-angulation and topographic surveying Gabriel La Hire was com-missioned to draw a new map of France. The map showed France to be smaller than people imagined—on the Brittany coast smaller by more than a degree and a half. Louis remarked to La Hire: "You have taken from me more of my kingdom than I have won in all my wars."

The other sciences, too, benefited from Louis's patronage. In the Observatory which Louis had built at the beginning of his personal reign—"to surpass in beauty and utility even those of Denmark, England and China," Cassini discovered four satellites of Saturn, to which he gave the name "Ludovici." Roemer, a Danish astronomer subsidised by Louis, calculated the velocity of light from the satellites of Jupiter; Roberval and Frénicle studied the problems of free fall; Mariotte discovered the compressibility of gases. Joseph Pitton de Tournefort classified 8,000 species of plants in a system generally adopted until the time of Linnaeus. In 1699 Louis enlarged the Académie des Sciences from sixteen to seventy members and appointed Fontenelle secretary. Among the Académie's inventions were a machine for sawing planks, a fire engine, and a device for preventing anchor cables snapping. Nehon invented a technique for casting large mirrors. Printing methods were perfected: in 1694 the Imprimerie Royale began to produce *Médailles sur les Evénements du Règne de Louis le Grand*, which after eight years in the press emerged as the most splendid book ever printed.

Descartes's theories, which Louis had been brought up to accept, were now, after half a century, being challenged from two directions. First, Christian Huygens's experiments in the collision of elastic bodies and in accelerated motion showed that there were more properties than mere extension. Huygens replaced Descartes's "geometric" world with one of energy and work. Secondly, advances in anatomy were winning respect for inductive methods. The leading figure here is Claude Perrault, the physician who designed the Louvre Colonnade. Perrault found that the salamander was not, after all, incombustible, that the pelican did not nourish its young with blood: in short, that experiment, and particularly dissection, were the only sure way to truth. He himself dissected many animals, including camels and elephants, and his experiments indirectly led to improvements in surgery. The operation on the King had been no isolated success, and in 1699 Louis declared that surgeons, who had formerly belonged to the barbers' corporation, should be styled "practitioners of a liberal art."

Geometry had had its day of glory and now a new picture of

the world was emerging in which a more complex, less rigid order was discovered not from syllogistic deductions but through inductive methods. Towards the end of the century these methods became all the rage. Louis's nephew, the Duc de Chartres, had his own well-equipped laboratory. The ladies of Paris attended lectures in mathematics by Carré and applied Roberval's computations to games of roulette. Nicolas Lémery, a self-taught apothecary, conducted courses in chemistry for large audiences of working people. In the provincial academies odes and madrigals gave way to scientific notes or *mémoires*.

Amid these changes the century drew to its close. On 4th January, 1699, Liselotte wrote to the Duchess of Hanover:

There is a great discussion going on at Court in which everyone takes part from the King down to the lackeys. This is the subject of the dispute: Does the century begin with the year 1700 or with the year 1701? Monsieur Fagon and his party are for 1700 because, they say, the hundred years are then completed: but the others maintain that they are not completed until the year 1701. I should love to hear Monsieur Leibnitz's opinion about it; to tell the truth, I agree with Monsieur Fagon, but the King, the Dauphin, the Prince de Conti, Monsieur and all the Court are for 1701. ...

No matter when precisely it ended, Frenchmen began to take stock of what was already beginning to be called the Grand Siècle. The "Quarrel of the Ancients and the Moderns" had been decided in favour of the moderns, championed by Fontenelle and Charles Perrault. First in his *Poème sur le siècle de Louis le Grand* (1687), then in 1688-96, in his *Parallèles des Anciens et des Modernes*, Perrault, applying his brother's inductive methods, concluded that the century of Louis equalled or even surpassed the centuries of Pericles and Augustus. Surpassed—this was a bold claim. In the first half of his reign even Louis had hardly hoped to be worthy of the traditions of classical antiquity. But much had been achieved since then. Frenchmen had before their eyes Paris—a city of domes, arches, new churches and houses, clean-cut stone quays; the palace of Versailles, the gardens of Marly, the splendour of the Court; the works of Lully, Molière, Racine; of Coysevox and Puget; a well-run, orderly system of government and taxation; frontiers extended; an army capable of fighting on five fronts. Since 1661 there had been twenty-four years' peace—well above the average for the past three centuries. Surely this was superior to anything antiquity had achieved. Instead of sighing for the classical past, Frenchmen confidently confronted the present and decided to enjoy it. Some, such as Fontenelle, even began to look hopefully forward. And so, at the turn of the century, from an inspection of what had been achieved in Louis's reign, perhaps the most revolutionary of all ideas was born: the idea of progress, the belief that civilisation had made definite advances, and that more were to come.

CHAPTER 19

An End to Glory

ON THE MORNING of the ninth of November, 1700, a horseman galloped into the courtyard of Fontainebleau with an urgent dispatch. It was decoded and handed to Barbezieux, Minister of War, who read a message from Blécourt, French ambassador in Spain. Barbezieux hurried to Louis and told him the contents. Louis cancelled his hunting for that afternoon and ordered that during the winter no plays or festivities should take place. Then he called a Council meeting for three o'clock.

It had happened at last: the event which every chancellery in Europe had been awaiting for forty years. Charles II of Spain, only child of a marriage between Philip IV and his own niece, Mariana of Austria, had been born in 1661: stricken with inherited syphilis, with dropsy and epilepsy, he had been expected to die in childhood. But somehow Charles the Sufferer, "more a medical curiosity than a man," had suvived. He had taken first a French and then a German wife, but had no children. During the last three years it had become obvious that he was dying. Blécourt's dispatch contained two pieces of news. Charles had died, thus bringing the Hapsburg line in Spain to an end. And three weeks before his death Charles had signed a will bequeathing Spain and Spanish dominions—the Netherlands, possessions in Italy and the remnants of the world-wide Empire—to the second of his great-nephews, Louis's grandson, the Duc d'Anjou, and to the Duc's successors. (The eldest great-nephew, the Duc de Bourgogne, was in direct line to the French throne, and Spaniards felt averse to a union of the French and Spanish crowns.)

Three trusted advisers attended the Council meeting that afternoon in Madame de Maintenon's room. Madame de Maintenon and the Dauphin were also present. One thing was obvious to all, and that was the glory of the Spanish King's offer. It was an extraordinary tribute both to Louis and the new status of France that a Hapsburg, ruler of a country which for three centuries had been France's deadly rival, should have turned to Louis for a new king, asked for Bourbon blood and Bourbon protection. Spain had said in effect: "We want to be like you. Give us your grandson, so that he may make us great."

The question to be decided was the gravest that had yet arisen during the fifty-seven year reign: Should France accept the legacy? Before the arrival of Blécourt's dispatch the situation had stood like this. Louis had proposed to the powers of Europe that Spain and the Spanish Empire should be divided between the two closest heirs: the Archduke Charles of Austria was to get Spain, the Spanish Netherlands and Spanish possessions overseas; the Duc d'Anjou the Two Sicilies, the Tuscan ports and the Milanese. England and Holland had accepted this proposal, but the Emperor had rejected it: he wanted the whole inheritance to go to his son, the Archduke Charles. The virtue of Louis's extremely moderate proposal was that it would guarantee the balance of power in Europe: Austria would get the lion's share of the inheritance, but neither she nor France would become more powerful than any league that could be formed against them. Now came the legacy: an offer to France of far more than Louis had proposed.

At the Council meeting in Madame de Maintenon's room Beauvillier, governor of the children of France, advised Louis to reject the legacy and stand by the partition treaty signed with England and Holland. Beauvillier was a virtuous man but no politician. He evidently believed that England and Holland would take up arms in order to rob the Emperor of much of Italy, and then hand their conquests over to France, thus installing her as mistress of the Mediterranean. Pontchartrain, the Chancellor, merely summed up the difficulties on both sides without casting a vote. Torcy, Secretary for Foreign Affairs, said that since the Emperor would clearly never agree to partition Louis should accept the legacy, all the more so since under the terms of Charles's

will, if Louis declined it, Spain and her possessions were to be
offered to the Archduke Charles. This was also the Dauphin's
opinion. When the meeting broke up at seven, Louis had not yet
taken his decision.

On 13th November, after supper in his own rooms, Louis
playfully asked Madame and the Princesse de Conti what they
thought of the Spanish difficulty. Both said that they would send
the Duc d'Anjou to Spain. "I am sure," replied Louis, "that
whatever I do will be blamed by a good many people."

Two days later the Court moved to Versailles, where on
Tuesday, 16th November, after his *lever*, Louis gave an unprecedented order. The double doors of his study were to be opened
wide and all the courtiers invited to enter. "Then," says Saint-
Simon, "he ran his eyes majestically over the numerous company.

" 'Gentlemen,' he said, showing them the Duc d'Anjou, 'here
is the King of Spain. Birth called him to the crown, the late
King also, by his will; the whole nation wants him and has asked
me for him urgently: it was an order from heaven. I have granted
it with pleasure.' He turned to his grandson. 'Be a good Spaniard,
that is your first duty now; but remember that you were born a
Frenchman, and so maintain union between the two nations; that
is the way to make them both happy and to keep the peace in
Europe.' "

It was perhaps the most dramatic moment of the reign. The
Spanish ambassador fell on his knees and kissed the Duc d'Anjou's
hand. "The Pyrenees," he exclaimed, "have ceased to exist."

The newly proclaimed King was a youth of nineteen. He had
a long heavy face and a drooping lower jaw which Liselotte had at
last taught him to keep closed, but he was generous, truthful and
brave. No one had noticed him before but now he and Louis
were suddenly equals: arriving in the tribune for Mass, the Most
Christian King offered his cushion for the Most Catholic King to
kneel on, but he, red with confusion, would not accept it. And so
the velvet cushion was put aside and both knelt on the bare carpet.

The formal parting took place at the Duc du Maine's house,
Sceaux, on 4th December. Two thousand carriages, three deep,
lined the main avenue. In groups according to rank Philip's

family kissed him good-bye. "Sobs were heard everywhere, and nothing could be seen but handkerchiefs drying wet eyes." Even Louis wept as he gave his grandson last-minute advice: "Whatever happens, you must be the master. Never have a favourite nor a Prime Minister. Consult your Council and listen to what they have to say, but decide for yourself. God, who has made you a King, will give you the necessary wisdom, so long as your intentions are good."

The emblazoned coaches with their escort of Life Guards—ostrich plumes, banners and the inevitable ribbons waving in the wind—clattered out of the courtyard and down the tree-lined avenue out of sight. Two months later they would reach Madrid. And one by one the Governments of Europe—all but the Empire and Holland—recognised Philip V as the lawful King of Spain. Since neither England nor Holland had declared war, Louis had every reason to be satisfied with his acceptance of the legacy. True, the Emperor, as expected, had ordered an attack on the Milanese, which was a Spanish possession, but Louis immediately sent sixty battalions to help in its defence. Fighting there continued through the first part of 1701. But it seemed probable that this limited war could soon be ended—if only England and Holland kept out of it.

Now as never before was the moment for tact and self-effacement, but the whole course of Louis's career made it almost impossible for him to practise these virtues precisely when they would most have benefited him, and in that sense Fénelon was right when he dated France's disasters to Louis's invasion of Holland in 1672: "Since then you have always insisted on granting peace and imposing your conditions as the master instead of conducting them with equity and moderation." On several separate occasions Louis now behaved towards Europe as though he were the master.

Wishing to help his grandson take possession of his legacy, in February, 1701, Louis seized from the Dutch the towns of Antwerp, Luxembourg, Namur and Mons, as well as the seaports of Nieuwpoort and Ostend; he announced that he would hold them until the arrival of Spanish troops, and having handed them over, all French troops would then leave Spanish soil. Louis's action naturally angered and alarmed the Dutch, who regarded these towns as an indispensable barrier protecting the United Provinces from France. However, for the moment they disguised their feelings and recognised Philip as King of Spain.

Louis's second piece of tactlessness was this. After a brief flurry of activity, the new King of Spain relapsed into a state of torpor similar to that of his father the Dauphin. Nothing, not even Louis's forceful letters, could make him take decisions. The result was that Spain, poor, demoralised and riddled with internal rivalry, was virtually falling to pieces. Only a man of authority could save her—and the Spanish Junta asked Louis to be that man. Louis accepted, he could hardly do otherwise, but instead of limiting his influence to bare essentials he began to reshape the country at every level—quite openly, regardless of English and Dutch nervousness. He created a Supreme Council, known as the Despacho, composed of four persons. He started reorganising Spanish finances. He even drew up the list of the Gentlemen of the King's bedchamber. Abroad, he ordered French squadrons to guard Spanish American possessions, while French merchants took in hand the wilting colonial trade.

The prospect of a strong, united Spain under Louis's indirect control alarmed England no less than seizure of the Netherlands towns had alarmed Holland. On 7th September the two maritime powers formed a Grand Alliance with the Emperor. They declared their intention of recovering the Spanish Netherlands for Holland, of securing the Milanese and Spanish possessions in Italy for the Empire and of forbidding French traders to enter the Spanish colonies. But there was no declaration of war. England, at least, still hoped to achieve these goals peacefully.

At this moment a new factor entered the situation. Paradoxically, just when Louis's political influence seemed greater than ever, his actual power was being threatened at quite another level—the ideological. The very advances in knowledge which had contributed to the idea of the Grand Siècle, the very successes Louis had achieved, were now shaking the whole basis of kingship. The French monarchy presupposed certain absolute values, and absolute values were steadily losing ground. It was observed, for instance, that the Siamese turned their backs to a woman as a mark of respect, that the Turks shaved their hair and let their beards grow, that Mohammed was not, as had once been thought, an impostor, but the founder of an estimable religion, and that the Chinese philosopher, despite his atheism, was virtuous. Was the Bible after all a unique book of revealed truth? It taught that there were 4,004 years from the creation of the world to the birth of Christ—Bossuet even specified that on 18th February 2305 B.C. Noah had released the dove from the ark—but now an Egyptian chronicle had been discovered which dated back the Egyptian dynasties more than 10,000 years. Everyone in Louis's youth had believed in Romulus; Romulus it was now held had never existed. A mood of criticism and doubt was gaining ground and even crept into Versailles: Louis's own nephew, the Duc de Chartres, believed neither in Christianity nor in the divine right of kings.

But it was England that embodied the main threat to Louis's idea of kingship, indeed England and France now stood for two opposed principles of government. Locke, the apostle of the Revolution of 1688, looked coolly at the French system and found it wanting: he argued that parental power is temporary and does not extend to life or property, and he laid stress on the injustice of primogeniture to the ruler's other sons. Civil government, he taught, was not something established by divine authority but was the result of a contract, and was an affair purely of this world. Locke's ideas had been put into practice. True, England, valuing compromise, still kept a king, but he was dependent upon legislative sanction and so upon Parliament; similarly the hereditary principle, though not rejected, was made dependent upon Parliament's will.

Frenchmen who thought like Louis answered Locke in this way: What grounds were there for believing that men in the remote past had lived according to reason in a happy "state of nature," and then made a contract to create a government? Impossible to conjure the notion of "right" out of such shadowy facts. French logic was wary of English compromise: if you make the basis of the State the individual's enlightened self-interest, then you strip the monarch of his functions and he ceases to have any grounds for existing.

This was the ideological background, in September, 1701,

when James II fell gravely ill in the palace of Saint-Germain and presently lay at the point of death. Louis called a Council to discuss an important political step which was also a question of principle: whether France should recognise James's son, the Prince of Wales, as the new King of England. The Council pointed out that the English Parliament had recently decided that the Crown, on William's death, should go to the House of Hanover. It would be a mistake, said the Council, further to offend England by recognising the Chevalier de Saint-Georges, as the French called the Prince of Wales.

Louis, however, thought differently. On 13th September he went to visit for the last time his old friend, kinsman and pensioner of nearly twelve years. James lay pale and gaunt, his beard grown long "like a Capuchin friar." In a weak voice he thanked Louis for all his past kindness. Louis replied:

"Sir, that is but a small matter. I have something to acquaint you with of greater consequence"; upon which the King's servants, imagining he would be private (the room being full of people), began to retire, which his Most Christian Majesty perceiving, said out aloud, "Let nobody withdraw," and then went on: "I am come, sir, to acquaint you, that whenever it shall please God to call Your Majesty out of this world, I will take your family into my protection, and will treat your son the Prince of Wales in the same manner I have treated you, and acknowledge him as he then will be King of England"; upon which all that were present, as well French as English, burst into tears, not being able any other way to express that mixture of joy and grief with which they were so surprisingly seized; some indeed threw themselves at his Most Christian Majesty's feet, others by their gestures and countenances (much more expressive on such occasions than words and speeches) declared their gratitude for so generous an action, with which his Most Christian Majesty was so moved, that he could not refrain from weeping himself.

What prompted Louis to disregard his Councillors and recognise young James Stuart as King of England? More than chivalrous feelings, more than friendship for Maria of Modena, more than close ties with the Stuarts going back to childhood. Louis was ageing: in a few days he would be sixty-three. In giving his grandson to Spain he had achieved an enviable triumph. But what, after all, did his reign amount to? What did Louis the Great stand for? Surely not merely for growth and prosperity and patronage? A principle underlay these things: the principle of God-given authority. To be precise, the principle that Kings were originally chosen or marked out by God, that they possessed special powers and gifts, that these were transmitted from father to eldest son, and that if a King were childless, then the King alone might designate a successor from among his relatives. But in this choice he would be guided by God. This was the principle that had been challenged by the English Parliament in 1688 and again in February, 1701. If the parliamentary theory of kingship or the republican doctrines applied in the United Provinces were allowed to spread, then the days of the French monarchy, and perhaps of monarchy everywhere, would be numbered.

It was one thing to recognise James Stuart, quite another to declare the fact openly at this particular moment. Instead of drawing a distinction between King by right and King in fact, Louis threw down the recognition like a challenge. Englishmen, already suspicious of Louis's intentions, received the news as an insult. Did Louis intend to bully England into taking a Catholic king, as he had once bullied French Protestants into abjuration or exile? Anger swept the country. William recalled his ambassador and dissolved Parliament. The new elections filled the House with enemies of France and subsidies were voted for war.

Holland, meanwhile, reiterated her grievances at Louis's seizure of the Netherlands towns. She pointed to this act and the recognition of the Stuart line as proof that Louis intended to make himself master of a Catholic Europe. At this period, paradoxically, nothing could have been further from Louis's mind. He seems to have had no intention of extending the frontiers of France. His aim, rather, was to help his grandson bring order to Spain and her Empire as he in his younger days had brought order to France. But despite the skill of the shrewdest ambassadors in Europe Louis now found it impossible to convince England and Holland of his good intentions. Religious and national sensibilities had been too deeply wounded. Louis had played the master once too often.

On 15th May, 1702, in London, the Hague and Vienna, war was declared against France: the War of the Spanish Succession.

Louis did not want this war which he had largely brought on himself. He faced stronger enemies than ever before: England, Holland, the Empire and their allies, including Denmark, nearly all the German princes, the Elector of Hanover, the Elector Palatine, the Duke of Lüneburg, the Duke of Mecklenburg-Schwerin, the Bishop of Würzburg and the Bishop of Münster. In 1702 England contributed 50,000 soldiers and sailors, a number quadrupled by the end of the war; in the same year the combined armies numbered a quarter of a million men. Against this powerful coalition Louis had 40,000 cavalry and 160,000 infantry; eighty ships of the line against England's 170, and only three allies, Portugal, Savoy and Bavaria, of whom the first two deserted him before the end of 1703. Moreover, for the first time he had to defend not only France but Spain, whose army was small, ill-equipped and poorly led.

Louis decided to concentrate his armies against the Empire, in the hope of knocking her quickly out of the war. In 1702 he sent his best general, Villars, to cross the Rhine; at Friedlingen the French won an important victory. The next year Villars again crossed the Rhine and marched as far as Riedlingen, on the Danube. There he waited for the Elector of Bavaria's army, hoping to make a joint march on the Imperial capital, Vienna. "The Emperor Leopold thought Vienna was so certain to fall that he was about to leave it. . . . The only troops available to defend the city were a few recruits on the way to join their regiments." But at the last moment the Elector, a timid man, backed out. Villars had trouble extricating his army and in disgust temporarily resigned his command.

In 1704 Louis again sent a French army against Vienna, this time under Marsin. But by now the Allies realised the seriousness of the threat. The English general, John Churchill, later Duke of Marlborough, marched to the Danube, devastated Bavaria and at Blenheim captured, scattered or killed 30,000 of the French army of 50,000. The crack regiment of Navarre buried its banners in shame before surrendering, and on the battlefield the Emperor erected a statue with this inscription: "Let Louis XIV know that no man before his death should be called either happy or great." When the dispatch reached Versailles, no one dared hand it to the King: "it was left to Madame de Maintenon to tell him that he was no longer invincible."

The French defeat at Blenheim destroyed Louis's hopes of quickly knocking the Empire out of the war, but in the long run its effects were less grave than the capture of Gibraltar, in the same month, by the English. Henceforth English ships were to sail the Mediterranean "like swans on the river at Chantilly." It was from an English ship that the Archduke Charles landed in Catalonia in 1705; he captured Barcelona on 9th October and made it his capital; shortly afterwards he was proclaimed king throughout Valencia and Murcia. England and Holland had already recognised him as such and declared that one of their aims was to install him in his possessions. Thus both sides now admitted that on the outcome of the war would depend whether the Bourbons or the Hapsburgs dominated the Continent of Europe.

Philip made a brave attempt to regain Barcelona, but on 11th May, 1706, a powerful Anglo-Portuguese army raised the siege. A total eclipse of the sun which darkened the earth on that day was believed to portend the disasters which now began to overtake France.

News of Philip's failure at Barcelona reached Louis on the same day as reports of Villeroi's defeat by Marlborough at Ramillies, which cost France her strongholds in the Netherlands and left her north-east frontier exposed. In October another French army under Orléans and Marsin was defeated at Turin and the French cause in Italy ruined. These were three disasters of the utmost gravity and they shocked Louis deeply. Madame de Maintenon compared his tribulations to those of Job: "God wants to give him the same patience."

During 1707 France suffered no further losses, but a party of Dutch scouts pushed almost to Versailles and on the bridge of Sèvres captured Beringhen, the Dauphin's First Equerry. Later he was rescued. "Although the King was very fond of Beringhen, he was not at all pleased to learn that the Small Stables were *en fête* in honour of their master's return, and he sent a message forbidding the projected firework display or any special marks of rejoicing: occasionally he had these fits of jealousy, and thought that every mark of distinction should be reserved for himself and himself alone."

The following year, 1708, brought the fall of Lille: Louis "was stricken to the heart to see one of his own first conquests in enemy hands; this beautiful town, so French, pillaged by all the nations which had entered it."

A series of very different disasters began quietly enough on 5th January, 1709, eve of the Feast of Kings, which once before had been a decisive date in Louis's life. That night it froze and continued freezing for seventeen days. After a twelve-day thaw snow fell, followed by a cutting wind and hard frost till mid-March. Not for 101 years had there been such a winter. On 13th January the Paris thermometer fell to the equivalent of minus 21½ degrees Centigrade. Even Provence had minus 16 degrees. The Seine froze at Paris and ice snapped the mooring ropes of forty barges. The sea round the coast froze firmly enough to bear a horse and fully laden cart. A half-finished letter still exists dated 14th January: the ink had frozen at the end of the writer's pen. At Versailles bottles of liqueur with a high alcoholic content burst with the frost even in rooms where a fire was blazing. One evening Villeroi entertained Saint-Simon to supper in his small room, and though he had put the wine on the mantelpiece to warm, lumps of ice fell out into their glasses when they poured the decanters.

Louis personally never suffered from cold but he cancelled his afternoon walks out of compassion for his courtiers. Schools and law-courts had to be closed. In the south thousands of olive and orange trees were frozen, in Périgord all the walnut and chestnut trees. Vines everywhere were ruined. Cows and goats died in their barns. Sheep were frozen to death, as well as chickens, game and even rabbits. Altogether France lost half its livestock. A number of people died at Versailles from effects of the cold, including the King's confessor and one of his former mistresses, the Princesse de Soubise. In Paris the mortality rate doubled and on the frontiers soldiers were frozen to death at their posts.

There was fear in French hearts in 1709, fear at Versailles, because spring, far from bringing relief, brought new misfortunes. It was found that all the corn had either been frozen or, because of the twelve-day thaw, rotted in the ground. "The earth seems dead," wrote Fénelon; "it promises neither fruit nor harvest." The harvest of 1708 had already been poor: half the usual yield, and in Brittany corn was fetching five times its normal price. "Could you believe that anything would have afflicted me more than the war?" wrote Madame de Maintenon. "The famine with which we are threatened makes me even more afraid."

In the past there had been occasional food shortages, but always Louis had been rich enough to help, distributing "the King's bread" to upwards of 20,000 Parisians daily. Now he was too poor to do this. But he immediately ordered a special tax to help the hungry, from which no one was exempt (his own six months' contribution was £1,400, and the Dauphin's half that sum; as a result each poor person in Versailles received a 5-lb. loaf weekly). He lifted all taxes on transport between provinces, ordered wholemeal bread to be baked for rich and poor alike, and prohibited hoarding or speculation. But the food simply was not there. In Burgundy and the Vendômois bracken had to be used to make flour; in the centre and west couch-grass and roots such as asphodel. Going wolf-hunting, the Dauphin found his way barred by women clamouring for food. Into the country towns crowded starving skeletonous figures "as at the Last Judgment." "Children live on boiled grass and roots," wrote the Attorney-General of the Parlement of Burgundy. "Some even crop the fields like sheep."

Louis had always looked on himself as the father of his people. In brighter days he had taken joy in their prosperity, and now he shared to the full their grief and the pain he was unable to assuage. He suffered in a way he had never suffered before, in the person of each of his subjects. In April barley and buckwheat were sown, but for the moment famine grew worse. Never in living memory had a country been so shattered by the elements—or only once, in 1672, when Louis's invasion had caused the Dutch to flood half their land, ruining their crops and drowning their livestock. Something would have to be done, and done soon. Louis, "touched to the quick by the state of his kingdom," decided on a step which cost his pride dear: at the end of April he sent Torcy to the Hague to beg the Allies for peace.

On 27th May Heinsius, the Grand Pensionary, after consulting Marlborough, Prince Eugène and the Emperor's legate, handed Torcy "the preliminaries of the Hague," the Allies' minimum conditions. The forty articles demanded the cession of Strasbourg to the Empire and of Newfoundland to the English, the recall of French troops helping Philip and the abandonment of Spain to the Archduke Charles. To thirty-nine of the articles, painful though they were, Louis was ready to consent. But a fortieth article demanded that Louis should declare war on his own grandson, that he rather than the Allies should be the instrument of Philip's expulsion from Spain. These were humiliating terms such as had never in living memory been proposed to an enemy—or only once, by Louis himself in 1672 to the Dutch. "Since war there has to be," Louis replied, "I prefer to wage it against my enemies than against my children." He broke off the peace talks.

France's situation was now very serious indeed. Louis, anxious to help in however small a way, at once sent his gold plate to the Mint. Princes and courtiers followed his example. In future they ate off faience, while the King used vermeil or silver. The King's gold plate weighed 554 marks and brought £81,000 to an Exchequer heavily burdened by famine relief. For months at a time now it could not pay the army. Soldiers sold their muskets, officers their linen in order to buy barley-and-bean bread. Villars, appointed commander-in-chief on the northern frontier, had to return to Versailles to plead for a few dozen sacks of flour. As they awaited the next allied blow the men's morale was low: "they were ready to take off their hats at the name of Marlborough."

Shortly before dawn on 11th September, 1709, Marlborough and Prince Eugène attacked the French army on the Franco-Netherlands border near Malplaquet. At noon Villars got a bullet through his knee and had to be carried off the field. Boufflers, a seventy-year-old marshal who had offered his services in a junior post, now took command and fought with exemplary courage.

But at three o'clock the French centre gave way and Boufflers sounded the retreat. Despite severe losses the Allies were left in possession of the battlefield and went on to seize the key stronghold of Mons, from where they stood poised to invade France whenever they chose. Marshal de Villars, meanwhile, was carried to Versailles in a litter. The surgeons wanted to amputate his wounded leg; the Marshal refused. Villars's condition was virtually the condition of France.

Eleven thousand Frenchmen died at Malplaquet, the flower of that army which had once been the King's pride. This was a side of war Louis had not experienced before. War in the past had meant glory and conquest; he had seldom spared a thought for those it had killed, wounded or bereaved. Meanwhile Frenchmen recalled that Marlborough, the victor of Blenheim and Malplaquet, had learned soldiering under the fleurs de lys. When precisely? During Louis's Dutch campaign of 1672. It was striking how each successive disaster recalled the Dutch war, the first years of glory.

These were not pleasant thoughts. Louis began to suffer from depression and nerves: "sometimes," says Madame de Maintenon, "he has a fit of crying that he cannot control, sometimes he is not well. He has no conversation." The old pride and absolute self-confidence were steadily waning and it was by sheer force of will that he controlled himself in public and observed with sunlike regularity his daily routine: *lever*, Mass, Council, dinner, hunting, dispatches, *coucher*, exactly as in the days of peace.

Madame de Maintenon suffered too but in a different way. Anonymous letters reached her, repeating Dutch libels that she was buying up all the wheat. All the defeats were blamed on her:

> Au Dauphin irrité de voir comme tout va:
> "Mon fils, disait Louis, que rien ne vous étonne,
> Nous maintiendrons notre couronne";
> Le Dauphin répondit: "Sire, Maintenon l'a."[1]

One day she confided to a friend: "I feel the sorrows of the King, the Princes, and the State, to a degree that is known to God alone.

---

[1] The Dauphin was irritated at seeing everything in decline. "My son," Louis said, "don't be put out. We shall maintain our crown." The Dauphin replied, "Sire, Maintenon has it" (or "Let us maintain it").

... It is because I am not great. I have only been raised up." How was it, she wondered, that Louis, converted to a moral life, should be suffering far more than in the wild days of the Montespan? "The designs of God are incomprehensible. Three great Christian kings [the third was James Stuart] seem to be abandoned. Heresy and injustice triumph."

With his armies shattered, his people hungry and peace denied except on intolerable terms, Louis prepared to enter another winter. It was at this stage, almost of desperation, that he appealed directly to his people in a letter circulated in every town and village:

... Now that all sources of revenue are virtually exhausted I come before you to ask your advice and your assistance at a moment when our safety is threatened. By our united efforts we shall show our enemies that we are not in the condition they would like to believe and by the help that I am asking of you because I consider it indispensable we shall oblige them to make a lasting peace, honourable for us and satisfactory to all the princes of Europe.

As a result of the King's appeal valuables were given to the Exchequer and new recruits joined the colours. But still more money was needed. Louis's advisers proposed the *dixième*, a ten per cent special levy. Louis disliked the idea. He was tormented by compassion for his suffering people and by scruples about his right to touch their property. One day that autumn Maréchal, his surgeon, found the King so sad that he feared for his health. Yes, Louis confessed, "I am infinitely miserable." He imposed the *dixième* in October despite himself and despite pleas: "The King will soon be reigning over ghosts, and his country will be one vast cemetery."

There had been some question of putting the Dauphin at the head of the Flanders army, but Louis decided against it. The life of the next king was too valuable to risk. So Monseigneur continued his wolf-hunting. At Marly he would sit in a corner whistling and tapping his snuff-box, or scanning the births and deaths column in the Gazette. He attended Councils regularly. Louis could not have wished for a kinder, more straightforward or more respectful son. He was popular, especially with servants, but somehow curiously detached, as though he believed the horoscope cast thirty years earlier: *fils de roi, père de roi, jamais roi.*[1]

On 8th April, 1711, Monseigneur, who had just left his Château of Meudon on his way to hunt the stag, saw a priest go by carrying Communion to a sick man. He dismounted to kneel in respect, then asked what was the matter with the sick man and was told that he had smallpox. Monseigneur had had smallpox slightly as a child but he was still afraid of it, and that evening he said to Boudin, his doctor, that he would not be surprised if he caught it again. Next morning he got up as usual, intending to go wolf-hunting, but turned faint while dressing and was put to bed.

As soon as he heard the news Louis moved to Meudon, although he never felt at ease in any but his own houses. He saw his son morning and evening, spending a long time at his bedside. On the 14th Monseigneur seemed better; fishwives arrived from Paris in a hired coach, kissed his bed and promised to have a *Te Deum* sung. "When I'm really better," he said. He ordered them to be given a good dinner and some money.

On the afternoon of the 17th Louis noticed with alarm that his son's face and head had swollen considerably. He asked Fagon, his own doctor, to examine him. During supper Fagon came in and said gravely that there was little hope. Louis hurried downstairs but for fear of infection the Princesse de Conti made him remain outside the bedroom. He sat on a canapé for an hour "shivering and trembling from head to foot." About midnight Fagon came out, bent sadly over his cane, and Louis knew that his son was dead.

He was led by Madame de Maintenon into the courtyard, where Monseigneur's berlin stood waiting, Louis signalled another coach, then drove to Marly. Nothing was ready: no keys, hardly a stub of candle. Louis sat for an hour in Madame de Maintenon's antechamber without a fire, weeping in the dark for this only son, the only one of his six legitimate children to have grown to adult life. Until now he had been spared personal loss. France had suffered, and he had suffered with her, but only now in the dark cold room

[1] Son of a king, father of a king, but never a king.

did he know the intense grief experienced by so many of his subjects.

Next morning Louis called his Chancellor and other Ministers. In a broken voice, each word cut short by tears, he asked whether the title of Dauphin should be given to the Duc de Bourgogne, Monseigneur's son, although strictly it should be applied only to the King's eldest son. Yes, thought the Chancellor, since the young duke was now his immediate heir. And so it was decreed. Louis then ordered 3,300 Masses said for the repose of his son's soul, and a whole year's mourning. Coaches were draped in black, servants wore black livery, courtiers removed lace and buttons from their cuffs, wore dark batiste cravats, attached pieces of dark material to droop from their sleeves, put crêpe on their hats and black buckles on their shoes. Wherever he turned at Versailles Louis came upon these black images of his grief, reflected back and forth, back and forth endlessly down the rows of crêpe-hung mirrors.

The new Dauphin was a handsome, conscientious young man not yet thirty, the sort of hard worker Louis liked. He had a good knowledge of Latin, philosophy and science, and joked that he would be known as Louis the Learned. He attended all Council meetings, "relieved the King as much as he could and was sympathetic and charitable. He had sold all his mother's jewels to give help to impoverished wounded officers." Louis offered him £12,500 a month, but he was content with £3,000. He said he wanted to be called not Monseigneur, but simply Monsieur.

On this grandson and his wife, the Italian princess Marie Adélaide, Louis's hopes were now centred. They represented the younger generation, the bright future which made bearable the disasters, bloodshed and humiliations of war. Marie Adélaide was as gay, charming and informal as ever; only she knew how to rouse the King from his army maps and dispatches. One evening she heard Louis and Madame de Maintenon speak in friendly terms of the English Government, which seemed disposed to make a separate peace. Marie Adélaide broke in: " Aunt, it cannot be denied that England is better governed under a Queen than under a King; and, Aunt, do you know why?," fluttering and frisking about the room as she spoke; "because under a King the country

is really governed by women, and under a Queen by men."
Louis and Madame de Maintenon could not help laughing and
said they quite agreed.

Marie Adélaide now had her own Court and gave intimate
dinners *à la cloche*, with no servants present. After losing several
babies she was the mother of two sons, both pretty as a picture,
the Duc de Bretagne, born in 1707, and the Duc d'Anjou, born
in 1710. For all her spirits, Louis considered her "capable of difficult
and important things."

As the months passed Louis became even more attached to his
new heir and the Dauphine. Towards his own son Louis had been
somewhat reserved, and in the past the Duc de Bourgogne had
tended to be timid, but now a new intimacy grew up between
them. When a captain of the bodyguard had to be appointed
Louis surprised everyone by allowing the Dauphin to make the
choice: "At my age it is not for me to choose men who will serve
me only a short while, but will serve you all their life." Towards
the Dauphine he was continually showing kindness. He ordered
his musicians to play regularly at the Mass she attended—a favour
for which she had not asked and which touched her deeply. Everyone felt sure that the young couple would make an excellent king
and queen.

On 18th January, 1712, Louis moved his Court, still in mourning,
to Marly. The Dauphine, who had toothache and an inflamed
cheek, went to bed when she arrived but got up at seven to preside
over the salon, "her head swathed like a lay sister. She had supper
in bed. Next day her husband received a letter from Philip, King
of Spain, warning him and his wife to beware of poison. Vague
though the warning was, the Dauphine took it rather seriously.
She was twenty-five and a Turin astrologer had predicted she
would die before she was twenty-seven. She often spoke about the
prediction. One day she had said to her husband, "The time's
getting near. Whom will you marry when I'm gone?" "Should
that ever happen," he answered, "I'd never remarry. In a week
I'd follow you to the grave."

Next day the inflammation had subsided, and the Dauphine felt
better. She was newly pregnant, and pregnancies brought on these

inflammations, particularly as now when the weather was cold. On the first day of February the Court returned to Versailles, and on the 5th the Duc de Noailles gave her a beautiful snuff-box full of Spanish snuff. She liked snuff, took a pinch and found it very good. That was towards noon. She put the snuff-box on her dressing-room table, then had dinner at which she ate a lot of a cake she had cooked herself. It contained white cheese, sugar and maize flour, and she drank hot liqueurs to help her digest it. That evening she began to shiver with fever and felt a pain in her lower cheek. She went to bed and could not get up even to go to the King's apartment after supper. She was given "English drops" and opium, and bled twice, but nothing eased her pain or fever. Remembering the snuff-box, she asked one of her ladies to fetch it. It was not on the dressing-room table nor was it ever seen again.

On the 9th red marks appeared on her skin. The doctors suspected measles, fatal cases of which had been notified in Versailles and Paris. Louis was at his wits' end. He repeatedly visited her and even ordered the reliquary of St. Geneviève to be exposed, which was done only for public calamities. On the 11th she was given the Last Sacraments, and bled from the foot. She was unexpectedly resigned: "To-day a princess, to-morrow nothing." She spoke of certain gambling debts, and these Madame de Maintenon promised to pay. When the doctors gave up hope, ordinary people pressed through the guards and crowded her apartment. A naval officer begged the doctors to try a sudorific he had brought back from abroad. They examined it and gave it to her, but it did not help. At 8.30 that evening she died.

Again Louis, accompanied by Madame de Maintenon, drove straight to Marly to be alone with his grief. No one at Court had been so loving or so lovable as Marie Adélaide. For years she had brought joy and warmth into his life. And now no more games of pall-mall, no more masked balls, no more drives together after the deer. "I have lost my daughter the Dauphine," he wrote to the King and Queen of Spain, "and although you know how dear she has always been to me, you cannot imagine what sorrow I feel at her loss. . . . There will never be a moment in my life when I shall not regret her."

The new Dauphin, at the King's orders, had been kept away from his wife's bed for fear of contagion. On the 14th at Marly he looked so pale and drawn that Louis had his pulse taken. On the 15th he attended a Council meeting and worked for three hours with Torcy. Next day he felt very ill and a rash appeared. "So be it! So be it!" he murmured. Heart-broken by the death of Marie Adélaide he had lost all desire to go on living. "He was extraordinarily fond of his wife, and it was sorrowing for her death that gave him his fever. For several days the fever ran an irregular course, but it returned severely on the fourth day. They bled him. . . . His skin became discoloured with many purple stains and spots, which were larger and quite different from the ordinary measles rash. They gave him stimulants and tried to make him sweat, but the perspiration would not flow freely."

Louis refused to believe that he who had suffered two such tragic losses could now suffer a third. When on the 17th the Dauphin asked to have Mass said in his room next morning so that he could receive Communion as early as possible, Louis almost defiantly wrote to Parlement to explain that this was merely a pious wish, and that they should not jump to tragic conclusions. On the 18th shortly after midnight Mass was said by the King's almoner. Five hours later the Dauphin lost consciousness. At 8.30 he raised his joined hands above his breast and a few moments later was still.

"The King had a very bad cold, so they did not rouse him, but on his awakening he was told the terrible news, and as soon as we knew that it had been broken, we all hurried to him. The sight was a truly harrowing one. . . ." This death was perhaps the worst shock of all to Louis. He had become deeply attached to his grandson, but also this loss jeopardised the kingdom as a whole. His heir now was no longer an intelligent, energetic young man trained by working closely with Louis, but the late Dauphin's son, a mere child of five.

While the bodies of the Dauphin and his wife in the same carriage were escorted to Saint-Denis, Louis returned to Versailles. There on 5th March he went through a new ordeal of grief as the lives of the young couple he had just lost were retold, stage by stage, in traditional condolatory speeches, first from Parlement, then from the Audit Office, the Board of Excise, the city of Paris; and next day from the Great Council and the Académie Française.

The final flowery peroration ended with a flourish. It seemed that at last some respite had come, and that Louis could begin the slow process of adjustment to his triple loss within a year. But the very next day the Sons of France, the children of the late Dauphin, developed a measles rash. Not just one, but both. They had been baptised privately at birth. Louis was seriously alarmed and ordered their governess, the Duchesse de Ventadour, to have them christened immediately with every care: both were to be called Louis.

Next day, the 8th, Fagon called in five doctors from Paris. They examined the purple rash and prescribed bleeding, just as had been prescribed for their parents. Their governess thought the younger boy, not yet weaned, too small to be bled. She took him to her own apartment, kept him warm, gave him a biscuit and a little wine. Slowly the purple rash subsided. But the older boy, Louis's heir, who had a raging fever, was duly bled. It did not seem to help. "No, no," he cried, "I don't want to go to Saint-Denis. That's a horrible journey, horrible." Shortly before midnight he died, the third dauphin within a year.

All eyes turned to the King. Louis was broken-hearted and crushed. Never before had a King of France had to bear such a string of losses, and Louis was so attached to his family, to tradition, to the handing on from father to son. But somehow he managed to keep control. Though he wept in private, he continued his public performance without wavering: dispatches, councils, receptions, reviews. Now as never before, says Saint-Simon, he deserved the title of Louis the Great. As for the Court, it was swept by panic. People were convinced there had been foul play. First the Dauphine's mysterious snuff-box, and now two heirs to the throne removed in less than a month—evidently by someone bent on the throne himself. Their suspicions fell on Louis's own nephew Philippe, formerly Duc de Chartres and now Duc d'Orléans, a free-thinker who read Rabelais during Mass, spent whole nights in the quarries of Vauves trying to communicate with the devil, and what is more, was known to dabble in chemistry. Now, went the rumours, Orléans had only to poison the little one-year-old heir and the Duc de Berry: then he would be the next king of France.

Louis, however, declined to take these suspicions seriously, even though after autopsies some of his doctors declared they had detected symptoms which might suggest poison. Louis knew Philippe through and through, as he knew all the members of his family: a lazy pleasure-seeker of thirty-eight, he had inherited not his mother's sense of responsibility but his father's ineffectiveness. Louis knew he had no desire for the crown; he was not a poisoner, merely "someone who boasted of crimes."

Overwhelmed with grief, the King was working towards quite a different explanation. The military defeats, the famine, the loss of four of his closest family within a year—were these things a coincidence? The religious ferment of the age had left its mark on Louis and where as a young man he might have seen only a series of chance events, he now became aware—gradually, not abruptly—of a definite pattern, more than a pattern, a drama, the sense of which was this: the terrible events were punishment—personal punishment. He, the King, had innocent blood on his hands, particularly the blood shed in 1672, and it was for this blood that he was making expiation.

For a man as proud as Louis this was not an easy admission. And even when it was made, several attitudes were open to him. He might pit himself in revolt against punishment so cruel or he might disclaim his guilt, shift responsibility for the Dutch war on to his advisers. A third course lay open, one which had been taken by a great king more than two thousand years before, a king in so many ways like Louis that his name kept cropping up in sermons and in Papal letters.

David the dancer, David the player on stringed instruments, David the warrior, David the lover, David the builder of a great cedar-wood house—he, too, had become puffed up with glory and made war too often, so that the Lord resolved to punish him, sending a plague that killed 70,000 of his people, and embroiling his kingdom in a disastrous war which cost the life of his favourite son. And through His prophets the Lord explained these disasters to the king: "You are a man of war and have shed blood."

Louis had special reason to remember this predecessor, for a painting of King David hung in his bedroom beside his plumed four-poster. At night when the candles were snuffed the two kings were alone together and perhaps it was during these nights that Louis came to realise how disastrously he had gone amiss. He was guilty of more than the Dutch war of 1672. For fifty years he had dedicated his life to political and military glory: to more and more fortresses surmounted by the white standard with golden lilies, which all other flags must respectfully salute. Now the fortresses lay in ruins, the flag of glory shot to pieces and, since he was growing old, past repair. It was borne in upon the ageing King that his pursuit of glory had been a terrible mistake—worse than a mistake, a sin which even such grandiose schemes as the conversion of French Protestants could not cover, and for which he was now paying with the lives of those he loved best.

In this sudden, otherwise total, darkness there was one glimmer of light. Louis recognised his sin, recognised that he was the one to blame, and that the punishment was just. He did not revolt, he accepted. It was too late now to put things right. For the moment all that remained was to plead that France might not be taken from him, to plead for mercy, as once David had done: "O God, how numerous are my enemies! What a multitude rises up against me. . . . Like silver you have tried me in the melting pot. . . . Heal me, God, for my bones are trembling. . . . I am exhausted with weeping, every night my couch is bathed in tears. . . . Until when, O God, will you forget me?"

CHAPTER 20

Death of a King

IN APRIL, 1712, Louis entrusted the Flanders army, and with it the hopes of France, to his most experienced general, Marshal de Villars, a big, well-built handsome man of fifty-eight, with a bluff back-slapping manner, boundless optimism and unwavering self-assurance. Villars liked panache—in moments of danger he would quote Corneille—and the good things of life. While raising war contributions in Germany, he declared unblushingly that a third part would be used "to fatten my calf," "*pour engraisser mon veau*"— a pun on Vaux, the beautiful house he had bought from Fouquet's widow for £170,000. When informed by a critic that Villars "does good business," Louis replied, "True, but he also does good business for me, and for the State."

Villars had married an heiress, Angélique de Varengeville, and his passion for this girl, thirty years his junior—he even wanted her to accompany him on campaign—was the subject of jokes. Louis liked Villars for his uprightness and frankness. He knew how to handle him in his moods of touchiness and did not mind the vanity which made him enemies at Court.

Villars arrived at Marly brimful of optimism and ambitious to win further laurels—"my reputation is a thousand times dearer to me than my life." The waters of Bourbonne had healed his knee, though it was still stiff. On 16th April, the eve of his departure for the front, Villars took leave of the King. "On that day," he wrote, "the self-control of the monarch yielded to the feelings of the man. The King shed tears, and said to me in a voice that went to the heart. 'You see in what state I am, Monsieur le Maréchal. Few have known what it is to lose, as I have lost in the space of a few weeks, a grandson, a grand-daughter-in-law and their son, all of great promise and tenderly cherished. God punishes me, and I have deserved it. I shall suffer less in the next world.

" 'But now let us leave sorrowing over my domestic misfortunes and see what can be done to avert those of my kingdom. I have shown clearly what confidence I have in you, since I have entrusted you with the armed force and the security of the State. I know your own zeal and the worth of my soldiers. But in the end fortune may desert you. If that should happen, what is your opinion as to the course I should take?' " Before Villars could reply, Louis resumed: "My courtiers urge me to retire to Blois, but I shall never consent to let the enemy approach my capital. . . . I shall collect all the troops I can muster at Péronne or Saint-Quentin, and there will make a last stand, to perish with you or to save the realm."

Next morning Villars set off to rejoin his army, which was based on Cambrai and Valenciennes. The surrounding country, flat and open, was Europe's battlefield. Almost every farm had billeted troops and every spinney had rung to bugle calls. A day's ride away lay places already famous or one day to be famous as battle honours: Fleurus, Ramillies, Malplaquet, Fontenoy, Waterloo, Mons and Ypres. And here the decisive battle of Louis's reign was about to be fought.

In early July, three months after the farewell at Versailles, Le Quesnoy, a town on the Sambre fifteen miles down from Landrecies, fell to the Allies, and a pincer movement threatened. On 17th July Louis, who had originally told Villars to take the defensive, changed his strategy: he ordered Villars "to march against the enemy and launch an attack in order to save Landrecies."

The geography was this.[1] The Rivers Escaut and Sambre flowed north-east, roughly parallel and twenty miles apart. Valenciennes blocked the Allied advance up the Escaut, Landrecies the Allied advance up the Sambre. Between these two towns, in the village of Bermerain, Prince Eugène had his headquarters. Beyond the Escaut, to the north-west, stood the fortified town of Denain, a link between Valenciennes and the main Allied base, seven miles away, in Marchiennes.

[1] See p. 195

On 22nd July Villars moved his army to new positions, directly opposite Landrecies, but on the other side of the river. On the evening of that day Villars crossed the Sambre and made a reconnaissance, but everywhere he found the Imperial army solidly entrenched. Returning to his headquarters at noon on the 23rd, Villars pondered the ground and took a characteristically bold decision. Instead of crossing the Sambre, he would make a quick march twenty miles west, cross the Escaut and launch a surprise attack on Denain. If he could capture Denain, the Allied supply lines, already perilously long, would be cut, and the army at Landrecies isolated; on the other hand, he must not fail, for then Landrecies would certainly fall, and with it France's last hope.

Secrecy was essential. Villars told only three of his staff and that afternoon sent no dispatch to Fontainebleau. At dusk the army began to march east, elated at the prospect of action at last. But after half an hour they were turned about. At first there was murmuring; then a whisper spread that Villars was up to some trick.

The night march passed without incident. Villars had hoped to be across the Escaut by dawn, but not until seven were the pontoon bridges in place. Since his presence seemed undetected Villars decided to cross.

Prince Eugène, meanwhile, on his morning reconnaissance between the rivers, observed in the distance the bulk of the French army massed near the Escaut. He assumed they were withdrawing on Cambrai. It never occurred to him that Villars would dare attack a camp as well fortified as Denain with his back to a river. Calmly he turned to his escort; "Gentlemen, let us go back for lunch."

The French advance guard crossed the Escaut, drove off a scouting party of Dutch cavalry, then cut the road between Denain and Marchiennes. Meanwhile, the French garrison of Valenciennes was hurrying south to threaten Denain from the other direction. The commander at Denain, the Dutch-born Earl of Albemarle, sent an urgent courier to Prince Eugène, which brought him to Denain about noon. Prince Eugène ordered Albemarle to hold out to the last man, then rode off to bring up the bulk of his army, camped twelve miles away. The French had three hours in which to capture Denain.

Villars drew up his army like this: forty battalions in fourteen columns, twenty-five paces apart, preceded by companies of grenadiers with fascines—bundles of faggots—to bridge the ditches, and followed by twelve battalions in reserve. Villars took up a position on the right. When an aide pointed out that the grenadiers were short of fascines, Villars replied, "The men who fall first will be our fascines."

The troops knelt and said a short prayer, to the boom and zing of ranging shots from light artillery. Then at a signal they began to advance. Villars had imparted some of his own optimism and they shouted *"Vive le roi! Vive le roi!"*—"gladly as though going to a wedding." Elbow to elbow, to the beat of five hundred drums, in columns straight as the avenues at Versailles, the twenty-six thousand French soldiers advanced at a quick walk, bayonets gleaming in the sun.

Ahead lay the camp of Denain, guarded by entrenchments and parapets three times the height of a man. Twenty paces from the entrenchments, the French were met by three volleys of musketry in succession, and by grapeshot from six-barrelled guns. Twelve hundred men crumpled to the grass. For a few moments three battalions wavered, then soldiers pressed forward to fill the gaps and the advance continued. The first lines of infantry jumped into the ditch and "climbing like cats" scaled the twenty-foot parapets. Grenadiers hacked at the palisades with axes.

The twenty-four battalions of Dutch infantry manning Denain had put their trust in fortifications and guns. When they saw the French, despite their losses, continue to advance, many deserted their posts. The Earl of Albemarle tried to rally them, but as the French infantry broke through the pallisade and swarmed into the town most of them fled. After a last brave stand in Denain Abbey Albemarle surrendered his sword, while the Dutch infantry in their hurry to escape crowded on to the one remaining bridge: the bridge gave way, and hundreds fell into the Escaut and were drowned.

From a distant observation post Prince Eugène watched what he could not prevent. Hours later, when fourteen Allied battalions arrived by forced march on the right bank of the Escaut, they were met and turned back by heavy French fire from the left bank and the newly arrived French garrison from Valenciennes. After several fruitless attempts to cross, Prince Eugène sounded the retreat.

At Fontainebleau the Court was living from hour to hour. The King repeatedly asked whether there was fresh news from Flanders. It was rumoured that the Court, though not the King, would withdraw to Chambord in case of defeat, and some families had already packed their trunks. For two days no dispatch had arrived and nerves were near breaking-point when at six o'clock on the morning of the 26th, having ridden all night, a messenger galloped into the palace courtyard. Anxious faces appeared at the windows. Tell us! Victory or . . . ? Victory! The greatest of the war! Louis was awakened early and told the news: Denain captured, twenty-four enemy battalions killed or made prisoner. He went immediately to the chapel where a *Te Deum* was sung. After Mass he wrote to "his cousin" Villars, congratulating him and his men: "I have been giving striking proof of the nation's gallantry."

Villars had a maxim that the worst mistake in war was not to follow up a victory. He acted on it now, sending part of his army to attack Marchiennes, which fell on 30th July. A hundred guns were captured and so many Dutch cheeses that the soldiers used them to play bowls. Without a supply base, Prince Eugène was obliged to raise the siege of Landrecies. The Allies, however, still retained Douai, which commanded another approach to the heart of France, up the River Scarpe. On 8th September, after a series of French attacks had captured three bastions, Douai surrendered with all its garrison: fifty-two enemy standards were sent to Versailles. On 10th October Bouchain, a town commanding the Escaut, also fell. Prince Eugène, having lost a total of fifty-three battalions in six weeks, retreated with the remnants of his army to Brussels. By then Villars had liberated all French soil.

After so many sufferings and losses—the terrible winter and the ensuing famine—Villars's string of victories had saved France.

Villars was the hero of the hour, and this time Louis's thanks were touched by no shadow of jealousy. At Versailles he embraced Villars publicly and appointed him Governor of Provence, loaded him with presents and allowed him to keep six enemy guns as trophies. An anagramist turned Louis-Hector de Villars into Le Héros de la Victoire, and the Académie Française made him their first warrior member.

As a result of Villars's victories Louis was able to negotiate an honourable peace. Separate treaties with England, Holland, Portugal, the Duke of Savoy and the King of Prussia were signed at Utrecht on 11th April, 1713. As regards the main issue of the war, Louis may be said to have emerged victorious, for his grandson was to remain King of Spain, acknowledged as such by all the powers. On the other hand he was obliged to cede his important point of principle, and to recognise the rights of the House of Hanover to the English throne. James Stuart was asked to withdraw to Lorraine.

As regards territory, the kingdom of France was to keep her frontiers intact, retaining Alsace and Strasbourg. England made important gains, including Gibraltar, Minorca, Newfoundland and Acadia (New Scotland and part of New Brunswick). The Netherlands passed to the Empire. By the treaty of Rastadt (6th March, 1714) Holland was to garrison the barrier towns and the Scheldt was to remain closed: in other words, the Emperor was not free to develop Antwerp as a rival to the Dutch ports. Since the interests of Holland and the Empire were unlikely to lead them again into alliance, France's weak northern frontier was now much less vulnerable than at any time during the reign.

The Milanese, Naples and Sardinia also passed to the Emperor, but the Spanish colonies overseas remained in the dominion of the King of Spain. Spain in fact benefited from the war, for the loss of so many possessions made her concentrate her efforts at home. Moreover, from 1705 to 1709 Louis had virtually ruled Spain from Versailles and instituted sweeping reforms, curtailing the powers of the Church and grandees in order to strengthen the central government. These reforms and the Bourbon dynasty were to make the eighteenth century a golden age: the enlightened monarchy of his great-grandson, Charles III, was not the least of Louis's legacies to Europe.

The war had played havoc with France's hard-won prosperity. Industry was crippled by taxes, food scarce and the poor suffered intense hardship. Between 1683 and the end of the war the purchasing power of the livre declined by twenty-five per cent, while in the same period the funded and unfunded debt rose from £50 million to something like £1,000 million. The position would have been even worse but for a large influx of silver from Spanish South America.

Peace, therefore, came as a deliverance. "What glory," writes Madame de Maintenon, "for our King to have carried on a ten years' war against all Europe, endured all possible misfortunes, suffered a famine and a kind of plague [typhoid], which has carried off millions of souls, and to see it end in a peace which places the monarchy of Spain in his family." But Madame de Maintenon's use of the word "glory" is a survival, almost unique at this period. The quest of glory meant war; war meant national suffering and virtual ruin. The word "glory" no longer figures in official acts. It had disappeared from Louis's vocabulary, except as an attribute of God.

This is one small sign of a deeper moral change in Louis. He had entered the war a proud man, believing himself bound to succeed as he had always succeeded in the past. In 1700, according to Madame de Maintenon, "The King will never miss a service or fail to observe a day of abstinence; but he refuses to understand that he must humble himself and learn the spirit of true repentance."

The first glimpse of humility appeared after the disasters of Ramillies and Blenheim. "Some days ago," writes Madame de Maintenon in 1707, probably referring to Louis's cancellation of the firework display to welcome Beringhen, "I said to the King frankly, 'Sire, you have done wrong and are very much to blame.' He accepted it wonderfully, even with humility. The next day, as it was necessary to speak of what he had done, I wanted to pass over it lightly and said, 'It is done, Sire, we must think no more about it.' He replied, 'Do not excuse me, Madame, I was very wrong.' . . . He has no opinion of himself, does not think himself at all indispensable and is persuaded that another would do as well as he, in many things better. He attributes none of the marvels of his reign to himself but regards them as the effects of God's providence. In a whole year he does not show as much pride as I do in a day."

A further change took place in 1709 when Louis sacrificed his own glory to his people's welfare and sent envoys to beg for peace. That cost him, he says, "a violent effort"; caused him to act "against the whole bent of my nature." Then came the humiliating Dutch terms, and Louis's awareness that he was expiating the invasion of 1672. What is remarkable is that a man of seventy, after a lifetime of adulation, should have reacted not with Stoical resignation nor with bitterness, but in a spirit of self-judgment. He realised that "Louis the glorious warrior" was a mistaken part, and therefore that much of his life had been misdirected. Instead of shutting his eyes to the unpleasant past, he faced up to it: he regretted now much of what he had done, he was touched with sorrow and repentance.

As time went on, his humility became more marked. In 1711 he presented the Duc de Bourgogne to a deputation of bishops: "Here is the prince whose virtue and piety will bring yet more prosperity to the Church and greater happiness to the kingdom. He will do everything better than I." After trying repeatedly to heal a dispute between the Gallicans and Jesuits regarding the liberties of the French Church, Louis says: "Perhaps this important matter will come to a quicker and more successful conclusion in other hands than mine." A nun at Saint-Cyr shows him a learned book by one of her relatives; Louis confesses that he cannot read Latin: "I am just an ignorant fellow."

The war had also given Louis a deeper compassion for his people, whose burden he tried to lighten by curtailing his own expenditure. Because public opinion considered it an extravagance, in 1710 he stopped providing board for the forty or fifty court ladies and their suites who came to Marly. Though luxurious meals were all the fashion, Louis cut his table expenses and became "one of the soberest men in his kingdom." He stopped building altogether, confining himself to planting trees. Gone were the days when he covered himself in diamonds, "so that his whole body radiated light"; he dressed simply, usually in brown, with less embroidery and a shorter wig.

The change of heart is no less evident in State affairs. Immediately peace was signed Louis demobilised the bulk of his armies, so that by 1715 the price of corn and bread had begun to fall. Believing that it would help the poorer classes, in eleven successive stages he restored the value of the coinage, which had been devalued by thirty per cent in 1709. His last diplomatic act, in January, 1715, was to send the Comte du Luc to try to negotiate an alliance with the Emperor, thus signifying his intention that France and the Hapsburgs should henceforth live in peace.

The sense of loss and regret which partly underlay Louis's change of heart was constantly brought home to him by the memory of Marie Adélaide. It was she who had "brought the whole palace to life," and on her death "darkness descended on the face of the earth." No balls were given now; there was no one to slip into Louis's room at seven in the morning to tell of masquerades and moonlight boating; no one with quite the same warm, spontaneous, giving nature. It is noteworthy that Louis did not try to efface her memory as he had once effaced those of Marie Mancini and Louise de La Vallière: at fêtes beside the Versailles canal he always drove alone and would not let any other princess take Marie Adélaide's seat in his four-horse calèche.

Versailles was becoming a palace of memories. Louis's brother Philippe had died in 1701. Lully, Molière, Racine, Boileau, and Mansart; Seignelay and Vauban; Bossuet and Louis's confessor, Fr. de La Chaize, all were gone. So too was Madame de Montespan, her hair in old age a beautiful snowy white—"the thought of her death frightened her so much that she paid several women to sit in her room at night with candles lit and the curtains drawn so that if she woke up she could be reassured by seeing them playing cards or eating." Louise de La Vallière had died in her Carmelite cell.

So many losses brought Louis closer than ever to Madame de Maintenon, his wife now for almost thirty years. Liselotte writes:

"Although the old woman is my bitterest enemy, I nevertheless wish her a long life for the King's sake, because everything would be ten times worse if the King were to die at this juncture, and he is so devoted to the woman that he would assuredly not survive her."

While Louis's health, even in his seventies, continued robust, Madame de Maintenon suffered from rheumatism.   Against draughts she had invented what she called her *niches*, small sentry boxes lined with red damask which enclosed her elbow-chair and sheltered her on three sides.   But Louis liked lots of doors and windows in his houses, all of course arranged with geometrical exactitude, one plumb opposite the other.   So even in her *niche* Madame de Maintenon shivered, writing from Marly: "Symmetry, symmetry, if I stay much longer here I shall become paralytic. Not a door or a window will shut, and one is lashed by a wind that reminds me of the hurricanes of America."   Even in old age, when she was deaf and bleary-eyed, Louis was happy with Madame de Maintenon.   There was just sufficient tension between their characters to make for piquancy: she for ever trying to reform not only the King but everyone at Court; he more loving and tolerant, accepting people as they were, with their defects and foibles, bringing out the best in them by example and leadership and incentives, not by preaching; she turning her back on the world, he still enjoying his music and hunting and gardens.

Of a new black dress embroidered with a little gold, Madame de Maintenon remarks: "The personage must be dressed up, though the person has no longing for anything but a tomb," whereas one of Louis's pleasures towards the end of his life was to review the French and Swiss palace guards in their brilliant red and blue.   Again, Madame de Maintenon writes that the opera "is the only real pleasure the King has, where one hears nothing but maxims utterly opposed to the Gospel and Christianity.   It seems to me it would be better to suppress or change it, but if I say a word the King replies at once, 'It has always been so.   The Queen my mother and the Queen, who went to Communion three times a week, thought as I do about it.' "   It is true, she adds, as though this were very odd indeed, that the immorality makes no impression on Louis personally, and he is interested only in "the beauty of the music, the sounds and harmonies."

During his seventies Louis's day was as crowded as ever. In the morning he held a long Council; after lunch he hunted or went shooting on foot. His eye was still sharp, and it was not unusual for him to bag thirty-two pheasants with thirty-four shots. In the late afternoon and early evening he would work in Madame de Maintenon's room with one of his Ministers. She would read or embroider, while the Minister sat on a stool. After supper he would receive members of his family in the same room. Orangeade and lemonade were served, and the violins played. The princesses told him of changes in their country houses; Liselotte made jokes against herself. About twelve-thirty Louis would say good night and go to his bedroom for the formal public *coucher*.

From the end of hostilities until his death Louis was a happy man. Again and again in her letters Madame de Maintenon remarks on it: in 1713 "he seems to me gayer than ever before." The truth is that Louis had at last abandoned his desire to be first in everything; he was now at peace with the world and with himself.

In May, 1714, Louis's youngest grandson, the Duc de Berry, died childless as the result of a hunting accident. This left Louis with only two direct legitimate descendants: Philip V of Spain, who had renounced the French crown, and his great-grandson, Louis, Duc d'Anjou, only surviving child of the Duc and Duchesse de Bourgogne. The Duc d'Anjou was a pretty but very delicate child of four, and it seemed doubtful whether he would live long. Next in line was Philippe, Duc d'Orléans, he who had been suspected of poisoning the heirs to the throne.

He had been born in 1674, the son of perfumed, bejewelled, chattering Philippe, whose good looks he inherited, and his second wife, Liselotte. His father had not been a religious man, and his mother, who slept through the sermons in Versailles chapel, had evolved her "own little religion," based on her Bible reading. Their son grew up without any religion at all. He felt contempt not only for the Church but for every kind of authority. He was brilliantly gifted—acted, sang, painted, made engravings, distilled perfumes, composed five-voice motets and even an opera, *Panthée*

—but he could not remain interested for long in any one subject. He who hated authority seemed to lack authority over himself: the offspring of such oddly assorted parents, he had inherited no line of direction, no guiding principle. As a result he drifted into debauchery. Behind locked doors in the Palais Royal he gave orgiastic suppers, with nude girls in silver dishes. His behaviour with his daughter gave rise to rumours of incest. "*Loteries* held here," the Parisians chalked on his walls, in allusion to Lot.

The character of Philippe, Duc d'Orléans, mattered a great deal to the King, as he began to grow old and looked to the future. If tradition were to be followed, it was Orléans who should be appointed Regent. But the prospect of entrusting the orphan Duc d'Anjou and the destinies of France to such a person filled Louis with dismay and Madame de Maintenon, who naturally disapproved of Orléans, with horrified anguish. It was partly at her repeated request that Louis, on 2nd August, 1714, drew up a will to bar Orléans from effective power. Louis instituted a Council of Regency composed of fourteen noblemen, among them the Duc du Maine and the Comte de Toulouse, Louis's legitimised sons by Madame de Montespan: both well-meaning though somewhat ineffective. The Council would decide all matters by majority vote; Orléans, though he would bear the title of Regent, would merely preside. The boy King's personal safety and education would be in the hands of the Duc du Maine. Under the Duc du Maine's authority Louis's only surviving boyhood friend, the Maréchal de Villeroi, would be the young King's governor.

On 27th August Louis handed his will, with its seven seals, to the First President of Parlement. He ordered it to be hidden in the wall of one of the massive towers of the Palais de Justice, and closed with an iron door behind an iron grille, with three keys for each, to be kept by the great officers of Parlement.

As a boy Louis had been present when his mother had broken his father's will before Parlement. He knew that of the two key figures, Orléans and Maine, the former was by far the stronger and the abler politician. To Maine Louis said, "However great I may make you during my lifetime, after I am gone I can do nothing for you. Then it will be up to you to hold on to your new position

—if you can." To Maria of Modena he confided, "I have made my will. But I know just how little it is worth. While we are alive we can do as we please, but we are worse off than an ordinary citizen so far as making arrangements for the future is concerned." As he suspected, the future of France lay with the Duc d'Orléans. But at least the kingdom was united: there would be no second Fronde.

The summer of 1715 Louis spent at Marly. It was a happy summer. In addition to his regular Councils Louis hunted the deer several times a week, sometimes staying out until half past eight; reviews were held and plays performed—notably Molière's *Le Mariage Forcé* and *Le Médecin malgré lui*. One May morning Louis and the Court observed an eclipse of the sun through telescopes. The five-year-old Dauphin was showing a graceful turn of phrase and an interest in geography. In the evenings the violins played in Madame de Maintenon's room.

That summer, however, it began to be noticed that Louis's appetite was falling off. Also, he suffered from constipation, for which Fagon, his first doctor, made him eat iced over-ripe fruit at the beginning of his meals, and from attacks of gout, for which Fagon would make him sleep heavily covered. As a result he perspired freely and this constant perspiration weakened him. On top of that he continued—against Fagon's orders—to eat highly spiced soups, which were bad for his blood. He lost weight, his cheeks began to sink, the spring went out of his step; he looked what he was, a man of seventy-six in indifferent health.

The news spread and began to be discussed in foreign capitals. In London bets were laid as to whether Louis would still be alive by the beginning of September. "He usually had the Dutch newspapers read to him by Torcy, after the Council of State. Torcy did not have time to look over the papers beforehand, and one day as he was reading them he suddenly came upon these bets in the London letter; he stopped, stammered, and passed on to something else. The King saw that he had skipped something, and wanted to know what it was; Torcy turned red, and said it was only some impertinent remarks not worth noticing. The King, however, insisted on knowing what they were, and Torcy had to read the paragraph about the bets from beginning to end. The King pretended not to mind, but he felt it acutely; so much so that, when he sat down to dinner shortly afterwards, he could not refrain from alluding to the subject, though without mentioning the newspaper."

The first signs of illness appeared on 10th August. After dinner on that day Louis suffered slightly from a pain in his stomach. He was dosed by Fagon with spirit of amber. Afterwards, feeling better, he went out for a breath of air. As usual in his last years he was pushed in a three-wheeled chair which he steered himself. He watched white marble statues from Rome being set up in the gardens. In case his indisposition grew worse, he decided to return to Versailles that evening.

That night in his room at Versailles he was kept awake by thirst. However often he drank, he remained thirsty. Next morning, feeling weak, he cancelled his hunt, but worked as usual. That night he went to bed looking pinched and tired.

On the 13th at six in the evening Louis felt a stabbing pain in his left leg. His surgeon, Maréchal, diagnosed sciatica and rubbed it with hot cloths. After supper Louis had another attack of pain and was obliged to go to bed. He spent a restless night, suffering almost continually from his leg, and next morning, the 14th, no *lever* was held: the King stayed in bed. For once that sun-like uniformity and regularity were broken, and the Court knew that the King was ill, more ill than he had been since the fistula of 1686. Time seemed to slow down. His doctors and those attending the King began to record the daily minutiae which had suddenly become of tremendous importance. One of these diaries was kept by a certain Antoine, Louis's gun-bearer, who had the right to enter the King's apartments. It is his simple, misspelt, tender record which provides the clearest picture of events.

On the morning of the 14th a group of doctors arrived from Paris. In order of seniority they felt the King's pulse, agreed that he had fever and prescribed ass's milk, "to dampen the chest." A few hours later they held a second consultation and on Fagon's advice countermanded the ass's milk, which had not yet been administered. Louis, meanwhile, sat propped up in his white-plumed four-poster in the white and gold panelled bedroom, gleaming with Boulle furniture, overlooking the Marble Court-yard. Above his bed was an arch decorated in gilded stucco with figures of fame holding trumpets; in the centre France watched over the King with a crown and trophies. Here that morning Louis held a Council: he dined off panada—boiled bread and butter; in the afternoon he was visited by Madame de Maintenon.

Next day, the feast of the Assumption, Louis was carried to hear Mass and Vespers in the tribune of the chapel. He returned by way of the Galerie, where so many courtiers crowded to glimpse him that he had difficulty in passing. On the 16th he went to Madame de Maintenon's room to listen to motets and Italian songs.

On the 19th Maréchal noticed on Louis's left foot a small black discoloration. He hid his alarm and treated the mark by rubbing it with hot cloths. The following day Louis's leg was bathed for an hour in a hot bath of Burgundy wine filled with aromatic herbs. After the bath he said he felt much better.

On the 22nd ten doctors arrived from Paris to examine the King. They prescribed ass's milk, which was administered next morning for the first time. When the ten doctors asked him whether it had done him good, Louis replied, "Yes, but it has not calmed the pain in my leg." He realised that none of the doctors had yet found a remedy for his swollen, burning left leg, which Maréchal unbandaged, rubbed and rebandaged without easing the pain.

During the night of the 23rd-24th Louis suffered from dizziness. The doctors blamed the dizziness on the ass's milk, which was immediately stopped. They again examined his leg and found another black discoloration, this time below the garter. They began to suspect that these discolorations were gangrene. They wrapped the leg in cloths soaked in camphorated brandy, "to bring back its natural heat."

After a cup of bouillon for dinner Louis held a Council in his bedroom. His old friend Maréchal de Villeroi presided. Villeroi was pleased when the first surgeon interrupted the meeting to change the bandage on Louis's leg, for he wanted to see its con-dition for himself. So far he had heard only reports. The surgeon gently unrolled the bandage. To Villeroi's dismay the leg was completely black, right down to the foot. "It hurts me less now," said Louis, but Villeroi felt certain it was incurable and returned to his apartment in order to hide his tears. Louis was helped into an armchair. Although in less pain, for the first time he felt extremely sad and worried. Nothing could rouse him from this mood; at four o'clock he sent for his confessor, Fr. Le Tellier, and asked him to prepare his soul for death.

This news spread through the Court and beyond, drawing crowds of ordinary people to Versailles. Everyone realised now that the King was going to die. Would he show regret, as Cardinal Mazarin had done, at leaving so many possessions? Would he cling wildly to the life he had loved so much? Had he really learned humility and resignation? They would know presently, for Louis was going to die as he had lived, in public.

Next day, the 25th, was the feast of the King's patron, St Louis, and a national holiday. Though he felt much worse, Louis insisted that the drums and hautboys should play beneath his window as soon as he awoke, and the orchestra of twenty-four violins should play in the next room during dinner. In the evening he was asked whether he wished to receive the Last Sacraments. "With all my heart." His body, grown very thin, was anointed with holy oil, as once before on his Coronation Day.

After adding four or five lines to his will, giving the Duc du Maine control of the civil and military household, he received the Duc d'Orléans, asking him to serve the Dauphin as loyally as he had served him, and the Duc du Maine, telling him that he would have charge of the Dauphin's education. He slept for an hour and woke to find Madame de Maintenon beside his bed. "He asked me to forgive him for not having been kind enough to me and for not having made me happy, adding that he had always loved and esteemed me. He wept, and then asked if anyone was in the room. I said, 'No.' 'But even if they saw me weep,' he said, 'no one would be surprised that I was moved to tears with you.'"

He made plans for after his death. "As calmly as if he were ordering a new fountain for Versailles or Marly," he ordered the Comte de Pontchartrain to carry his heart to the Professed House of the Jesuits. The Dauphin was to be taken to Vincennes, where the air was healthier than at Versailles. Then, remembering that the Court had not been there for fifty years, he explained exactly where the plan of the castle was deposited and ordered it to be taken to the grand master of the lodgings.

Next morning, the 26th, he was so weak that his head had to be supported when he wished to drink. He received the Princes and Princesses, kissing them all in turn. Later, he ordered the officers of the household to be admitted. The curtains of his bed were then drawn back and Louis told the kneeling figures how satisfied he was with their services, and that if he had given them any reason for vexation or complaint, he asked their pardon.

He sent for the Dauphin, who was lifted by his governess on to an elbow-chair beside the bed. The boy had very dark big eyes, a chubby face and a pretty rosebud mouth. A lifetime ago Louis had been just such a small boy brought to a king's bedside. Louis gazed at him with tears in his eyes. He was aware that this was an important moment. The last message of a French king to his heir was taken very seriously; it was the summing-up of a lifetime.

"Soon," Louis said to the boy, "you will be King of a great kingdom. I urge you never to forget your obligations to God; remember that you owe Him everything. Try to remain at peace with your neighbours. I have loved war too much. Do not copy me in that, or in my overspending. Take advice in everything; try to find out the best course and always follow it. Lighten your people's burden as soon as possible, and do what I have had the misfortune not to do myself." After these words of deep and even astonishing humility he gave the boy his blessing.

That night the King went through "unimaginable" pain, except in his leg, which had become insensible. On the morning of the 27th Maréchal tried a remedy proposed by the master-surgeons of St. Cosmas: scarification. Although he made incisions in the lower part of the leg, the King felt nothing. This led him to probe deeper in order to discover the seat of the gangrene. As he cut to the quick, the King cried, "Maréchal, you're hurting me a lot," That gave the surgeons hope that the leg would sup-purate: it was again bandaged in corrosive and swathed in linen soaked in camphorated brandy.

In the afternoon Madame de Maintenon came to see the King. It was the last time they spoke together. He told her he was anxious about her future. "I am a mere nothing," she replied. "Don't worry about someone who is nothing." But she did ask him to put in a good word for her with Orléans. This Louis promised to do. Later he said that he had always been told it was difficult to compose one's mind for death, but he did not find it so. Madame de Maintenon said that it must be difficult for a man of wordly attainments, with hatred in his heart, or owing anything to anyone. "Ah," said the King, "as a private individual I owe nothing to any man; if I owe anything to my kingdom, I throw myself on the mercy of God."

In the presence of the Chancellor and his trusted first *valet de chambre* certain caskets were now carried into the bedroom from the study and the papers they contained were burned. Later the surgeons again examined the leg and found the gangrene worse. Louis passed a very bad night and was seen to clasp his hands repeatedly as he said his prayers.

On the morning of the 28th, as Fr. Le Tellier was speaking to him about God, he noticed in the mirror that two attendants seated at the foot of his bed were weeping. "Did you imagine that I was immortal?" he said. In the evening Fr. Le Tellier asked him if he was in great pain. "No," said the King, "and I am sorry for it; I should like to suffer more, as some expiation for my sins."

On the 29th hopes were raised. A rough Provençal peasant named Brun arrived from Marseille and told Orléans that he had a medicine which purified the blood and cured all kinds of gangrene. Orléans told the King's doctors, but they refused to allow their patient to take a medicine whose "nature and effects" they did not know. However, the Princes of the Blood, seeing that the royal doctors had given up hope, agreed that the medicine should be tried, and Orléans took Brun to the King's bedroom.

Brun found the King's pulse very weak but said that even at this late hour his elixir might effect a cure. Producing a bottle he poured four drops into a small glass of Burgundy wine. Orléans gave this to the King, who drank it. Two hours later a second dose was administered. It seemed to do the King good: he began to look much better; he spoke more easily and in a stronger voice. Brun then had special bouillons cooked, one of which the King drank every hour. He even took a little solid food: "If the King eats again," said Orléans, "my apartment will be empty of courtiers." Next morning, however, Louis relapsed and again became unconscious for short periods. The royal doctors then began to call Brun a charlatan and muttered that by giving the King an unknown remedy he had laid himself open to criminal prosecution. Brun became terrified, left the palace and was not seen again.

At two in the afternoon Madame de Maintenon arrived from Saint-Cyr. She found Louis unable to speak, his eyes wide open and set. After spending a short time beside his bed she returned to Saint-Cyr, "my retreat and my tomb." Meanwhile, at news that the King was in his last hours more and more people had gathered outside the palace, all discussing the illness. Why had the surgeons not amputated the leg? Why had the good Dr. Brun been dismissed? Public prayers were being said throughout the kingdom; the Blessed Sacrament was exposed in the palace chapel, in the parish of Versailles and at Saint-Germain.

On the 31st the King appeared calmer. In the hope of speaking to him a last time, Madame de Maintenon again hurried to the palace, only to find him unconscious—motionless as the paintings on either side of his bed, "King David" by Domenichino and "St. John" by Raphael. In the afternoon Cardinal de Rohan, Grand Almoner of France, son of the red-headed beauty, Anne de Rohan-Chabot, Princesse de Soubise, who had once been the King's mistress, entered Louis's bedroom to recite the prayers for the dying. These penetrated his fading mind, and he said the responses so loudly that he could be heard above all the attendant priests. He recognised the Cardinal and said, "This is the last favour that the Church can do for me," and that was the last time he spoke to anyone. Several times he was heard repeating, "*Nunc et in hora mortis.*" Then he said, "Help, O God, help me quickly!" Those were his last words. He was unconscious through the night. At a quarter to nine on Sunday, after a number of short sighs and two gasps, without any agitation or convulsion, he died.

Such was the death of King Louis XIV on 1st September, 1715, aged seventy-seven all but four days, having reigned seventy-two years three months and eighteen days. All the windows of the apartment were opened wide while two *garçons de chambre* closed the King's eyes. His face was yellowish and pinched, but not greatly changed. When fresh linen had been put on the bed, the royal family, courtiers and household servants filed in to pay their last respects. They could hardly believe that "the man whom they had so recently seen full of glory and majesty could now feel and stir no more." Outside, in the gardens, Neptune and the bronze Tritons continued to pour their foaming streams of water into the marble basins, where floated the first autumn leaves.

On the 22nd, after an autopsy and the removal of the heart, the King's body was embalmed and placed in a lead coffin, which, in turn, was enclosed in an oak coffin. On a copper plaque was inscribed the King's name, age and length of reign. On 6th October the heart, which the doctors described as of normal size and in excellent condition, was carried by Cardinal de Rohan to the church of the Jesuits' professed house in that same Rue St. Antoine where Louis XIII used to visit Sister Angélique in her Visitandine convent. A eulogy was made, one of many with the same theme: Louis the Great had lived as a hero and died as a Christian.

On the evening of 9th October the hearse, drawn by six black horses, set out with its armed escort for Saint-Denis, by way of Paris. The new boy King had left that afternoon for Vincennes, so that the palace of Versailles stood empty and silent, in the care of a few servants. Next morning the cortège arrived at the Abbey of Saint-Denis, where the coffin was laid under a catafalque hung with black velvet, surrounded by pictures evoking the reign: duels forbidden, regular attendance at Councils, patron of arts and sciences, rivers crossed under enemy fire, frontiers defended by new fortifications, famine relief, a king given to the Spaniards.

On 22nd October solemn High Mass was sung in the Abbey church. After the *De Profundis* Louis's body was lowered into the Bourbon vault, to lie with his ancestors. Then a traditional ceremony took place. The King of Arms, removing his hood and tunic, threw them into the vault. Taking two steps forward into the mortuary chapel, he called in a loud voice, "Heralds of the arms of France, come and perform your duty." The heralds approached and they too threw their hoods and tunics into the vault. Then the King of Arms called on the great officers in turn to surrender the emblems in their keeping.

"Bring the standard of the Hundred Swiss." It was brought, and lowered into the vault.

"Bring the standard of the Hundred Archers." It was brought, and lowered into the vault.

Regimental standards that had accompanied Louis on his many campaigns, as a boy during the Fronde, as a young man in Holland, and later in the war against the League of Augsburg, one by one they were brought and lowered into the vault. When all the standards had been ceremoniously lowered according to tradition until the coffin was covered with embroidered silk, with the glory Louis had loved and learned to love no longer, the King of Arms turned to the congregation: "The King is dead." He repeated this three times, adding, "Let us all pray God for the repose of his soul." Then the vault was closed.

SOURCES AND NOTES

APPENDICES

INDEX

Sources and Notes

Dates are given New Style. In the seventeenth century the New Style calender used on the Continent was ten days behind the Julian or Old Style calendar used in England. In the eighteenth century the discrepancy was eleven days.

Sums of money. The sterling equivalents used throughout the book are based on the value of the pound in 1964, when three livres = £1 sterling. For equivalent values today (January 1990), the reader should multiply these sterling figures by ten (i.e. three livres = £10 sterling (US$16). The purchasing power of the livre fluctuated considerably throughout the reign. Three livres = 1 écu; 10 livres = 1 louis d'or or pistole.

Memoirs. Most are to be found in two nineteenth-century collections, one edited by Petitot, the other by Michaud and Poujoulat. Where other editions have been used I have indicated them. Among the more important are the King's Memoirs, edited by C. Dreyss (1860), *Mémoires de de la Duchesse de Montpensier*, edited by A. Chéruel (1891), *Mémoires de Madame de Motteville*, edited by F. Riaux (1886) and *Mémoires de Saint-Simon*, edited by A. de Boislisle (1879, etc.).

Chapter 1: *Birth of a Dauphin*

For the meeting with Louise de La Fayette and other events that day, V. Siri, *Memorie Recondite* (1677-79) and the Memoirs of La Roche-foucauld; also H. Griffet, *Histoire du règne de Louis XIII* (1758) and Le Vassor, *Histoire du règne de Louis XIII* (1700-13). For seventeenth-century Paris and routes, Jacques Hillairet, *Evocation du Vieux Paris* (1952-4). For Louis XIII's character, Jean Héroard, *Journal du Roi* (Héroard, who was the King's physician until 1628, recorded telling conversations and behaviour in such detail as to make his diary virtually a case-book). For Louise de La Fayette, the Life by Madame de Genlis (1813). The most intimate portrait of Anne of Austria is that by her lady-in-waiting, Madame de Motteville; biased, however, against Mazarin. See also Montpensier, *Divers Portraits*, and E. Herbillon, *Anne d'Autriche, reine, mère, régente* (1939). For Louis XIII's married life, L. Vaunois, *Vie de Louis XIII* (1936). For Louis XIII in ballet, H. Carré, *Jeux, sports et divertissements des rois de France* (1937). For Louis's birth and rejoicing, the *Gazette* and *Le Mercure François*. For Louis's first months, Motteville. The medal in Anne's honour is reproduced in Ménestrier, *Histoire du Roy Louis le Grand par les Médailles*. For Louis XIII's last days, the accounts by his *valet de chambre*, Dubois, and his confessor, Père Dinet (in *Cabinet Historique*, vol. xii).

Chapter 2: Anne, Regent of France

For the clash between Beaufort and Condé, the Memoirs of La Châtre and of Monglat, and the Journal of Olivier d'Ormesson (ed. Chéruel, 1860). The breaking of the will is described in the Memoirs of Mathieu Molé and the Journal of Olivier d'Ormesson.

Mazarin is portrayed by nearly every memorialist of the day. There is no satisfactory biography. His career can be followed in his Letters, edited by Chéruel and d'Avenel (1872-1906).

Walter Montagu (1603 ?-1677) was the second son of Sir Henry Montagu, first Earl of Manchester. While attaché at the British Embassy in Paris he went to Loudun to witness the exorcisms of the Ursuline nuns. What he saw there led him to become a Catholic. Later he settled in France, where he had the ear of two queens, Henrietta Maria and Anne of Austria.

For Beaufort's plot and arrest, the Memoirs of Henri de Campion. The valuable reports by Venetian ambassadors are collected in Berchet and Barozzi, *Relazioni degli ambasciatori Veneti* (1860).

For Louis's education, the Memoirs by La Porte and Motteville. Péréfixe's Life of Henry IV describes at length a scheme for a united Europe under the aegis of France; the scheme was Sully's but Péréfixe attributes it to the King and doubtless made much of it to his royal pupil.

For events leading up to the Day of the Barricades, the Memoirs of Cardinal de Retz, of Omer Talon and d'Ormesson. For attempts to win over Condé, the *Carnets de Mazarin* (appendix i to vol. iii of Chéruel's *Histoire de France pendant la minorité de Louis XIV*), Retz and Omer Talon.

Chapter 3: *The School of War*

For the last months of 1648, Retz, Omer Talon and Motteville. For events on Twelfth Night, Motteville and Montpensier, *Mémoires* (ed. Chéruel, 1891). For life at Saint-Germain, Montpensier and La Porte. For Louis's boyhood, La Porte, Olivier d'Ormesson and Dubois. Also H. Carré, *L'Enfance et la Première Jeunesse de Louis XIV* (1944). Certain details come from Madame de Maintenon.

Louis's translation of Caesar's Swiss campaign, part of the first book of the *Commentaries*, was published in Paris in 1651. It is a luxurious folio volume of 18 pages, with 4 illustrations.

The Grande Mademoiselle has been the subject of two excellent biographies: V. Sackville-West's *Daughter of France* (1959), which catches to perfection the tone and values of the Court, and F. Steegmuller's entertaining portrait (1955). The incident about the pigs is quoted from Steegmuller, p. 48. For the meeting between Charles and Mademoiselle, Montpensier.

For the *Fronde des princes*, *Registres de l'Hôtel de Ville pendant la Fronde*, Omer Talon and the Memoirs of Brienne, *père*. For Mazarinades, C. Moreau, *Choix des Mazarinades* (1853) and Monica Sutherland, *Louis XIV and Marie Mancini* (1956) from which the translation of *Le Passe-Port* is quoted. For the night of 9th-10th February, 1651, Motteville. Mazarin's correspondence with Anne of Austria was published by the Société de l'histoire de France (1836).

For the Battle of the Porte Saint-Antoine, Montpensier, Conrart and Navailles. In her Memoirs Mademoiselle says that after ordering the guns to be swung round, she left the Bastille. Later "they fired three or four volleys, as I had ordered when I came away." But in a letter written the next day (now in the Bibliothèque Nationale) she says that twenty volleys were fired. In later life she seems to have tried to minimise her role, and once definitely told Madame de Motteville that she had not ordered the cannon to be fired. However, almost all the contemporary writers (Retz, for example) say that Mademoiselle was actually present at the firing of the cannon, and that she gave the order. (Louis himself believed Mademoiselle gave the order.) Their account has been followed here. Mademoiselle was thorough and a dutiful friend: only by being present herself could she be certain that the cannon would fire when Condé needed them most.

Chapter 4: Crowned King

The order of Louis's coronation is given in N. Menin, *Traité du Sacre et Couronnement* (1723). See also Godefroy, *Ceremonial* (1649). The story of unction being brought from heaven by a dove is first told by Hincmar, Archbishop of Reims, d. 882. The notion of inheriting the legacy of the Emperors was not confined to France. Henry VIII, for example, traced a similar claim through King Arthur, and through Constantine, whose mother, Helena, was believed to have been English. As late as Diocletian (245-313) the Roman Emperor claimed descent from the gods: "diis genitus."

The King's healing powers are discussed in R. Crawfurd, *The King's Evil* (1911). The verse quotation is from *Macbeth*, Act IV, sc. 3. French kings did not always show reverence for the ceremonial: at Ivry, cleaving down a man with his sabre, Henri IV growled, "Le Roi te touche, que Dieu te guérisse."

Louis's curriculum is given in H. Carré, *L'Enfance et la Première Jeunesse de Louis XIV* (1944). For events on 13th April, *Journal d'un bourgeois de Paris pendant la Fronde*, Monglat and Guy Patin, *Lettres* (ed. Reveillé-Parise, 1846). Locatelli, a Bolognese priest who visited France in 1664-5, writes: "Happy the man who can make his son a councillor in the Parlement of Paris! though it is true that the King has declared that he himself is the Parlement"—so the legendary phrase was already taking shape. (*Voyage de France: Moeurs et Coutumes Françaises* (1664-1665): Relation de Sébastien Locatelli, tr. Adolphe Vautier, 1905.)

For events subsequent to 13th April, *Journal d'un bourgeois de Paris*, the Memoirs of Turenne, and the letters quoted in Chéruel, *Histoire de France sous le ministère de Mazarin*, ii (1882), (pp. 257-62).

Chapter 5: First Love

For Mazarin's offices and wealth, *Etat des biens, revenus et effets appartenant à Monseigneur, la presente année 1658*, in P. Clément, *Lettres, Instructions et Mémoires de Colbert*, i (1861). His paintings and other works of art are listed in *Inventaire de Meubles* (1861). Although his family name was Mazzarini, he signed "Mazarini."

For Louis's relations with Madame de Beauvais, Boislisle, *Madame de Beauvais et sa famille* (1878). I have been unable to trace any evidence other than street songs for the story that Anne arranged Louis's *dépucelage*.

For Marie Mancini, her *Memoirs* (1678), and the biographies by F. C. Mackenzie (1935) and Monica Sutherland (1956).

For Christina of Sweden, Montpensier and *Mémoires des intrigues. . . . de la reine Christine de Suède* (1710).

Mademoiselle's visit to Sedan and meeting with the royal family are described in her Memoirs.

The murder of Monaldeschi is discussed in M. Rat, *Christine de Suède* (1959). For Louis's changed attitude to Christina, Montpensier.

Chapter 6: A Marriage is Arranged

For the Battle of the Dunes, the Memoirs of Turenne and Bussy-Rabutin. In 1662 Louis was to buy back Dunkirk and Mardyck for five million livres. For Louis's illness, Motteville, *Journal de la Santé du Roi* (ed. J. A. Le Roi, 1862), and Montpensier. The journey to Lyon is described by Mademoiselle, who accompanied the King. At Dijon Louis was greeted by an armed parade; Mademoiselle remarks (with evident pleasure) that martial ways were a tradition in Burgundy because Caesar spent so much time in the region. No one seems to have lost a chance of emphasising the continuity between the French kings and Caesar. Events in Lyon are described in Montpensier.

For Marie's exile and the King's pleas, Motteville, Madame de La Fayette, *Histoire de Madame Henriette d'Angleterre*, the Memoirs of Brienne *père* and *fils*, and the Memoirs of the abbé de Choisy. For the last meeting between Louis and Marie, Hortense Mancini's Memoirs (1675). The text of the Treaty of the Pyrenees is given in Vast, *Les Grands Traités du Règne de Louis XIV* (1893-9). For the wedding and its preliminaries, Montpensier, Motteville and Monglat. Louis's attitude to Spanish customs can be gathered from the instructions he gave to Philippe in 1700. The entry to Paris is described in the official *Gazette* (103) published on 3rd September, 1660. Racine's début is discussed in G. Brereton, *Racine: a critical biography* (1951). Madame Scarron's letter is given in Langlois, *Correspondance de Madame de Maintenon*, i (1933).

Chapter 7: Annus Mirabilis

Molière's career is discussed in J. Palmer, *Molière: his life and works* (1930). The French equivalent of the Baconian theory holds that Louis was the author of the plays attributed to Molière. See J. M. Garçon, *Sous le masque de Molière* (1953).

Préciosité did of course play an important positive role in the forma-
tion of Classicism: Bossuet and Racine, to name only two, started their
careers using precious imagery. In an early sermon before Anne of
Austria Bossuet could assert: "Our Saviour's life was a feast at which all
the dishes were torments"—a far cry from his lament for Henriette in
1670, where the phrases undulate with sober magnificence like the folds
in violet mourning: "O nuit effroyable! où retentit tout à coup comme
un éclat de tonnerre cette étonnante nouvelle: Madame se meurt!
Madame est morte!"

Mazarin's will is printed in vol. vi of *Oeuvres de Louis XIV*, ed.
Grimoard. For Council meetings in 1661, *Mémoriaux du Conseil de 1661*,
ed. J. de Boislisle (1905). For devastation caused during the Fronde,
A. Feillet, *La Misère du temps de la Fronde* (1862). For the condition of
France in 1661, Lavisse, *Histoire de France*, vol. vii (1905).

The fullest studies of Philippe are by Montpensier, Saint-Simon, and
the Princess Palatine (*The Letters of Madame*, trans. G. S. Stevenson,
1924-25). For his early transvestism, the Memoirs of the abbé de Choisy.

For Louise de La Vallière, the biographies by J. Lair (1935) and
J. Saunders (1959). The incident of the portrait is described in Brienne's
Memoirs.

Chapter 8: Fouquet's Challenge

For Fouquet, *Recueil des Defenses de M. Fouquet* (1665-1667), the Lives
by U. V. Chatelain (1905) and J. Lair (1890). For the manœuvres against
Fouquet, P. Clément, *Letters . . . de Colbert*, vol. ii. The celebration at
Vaux is described in a letter by La Fontaine to M. de Maucroix, 22nd
August, 1661. Vatel was later to take his own life at Chantilly, because
the fish failed to arrive in time for a dinner at which Louis was guest of
honour. Fouquet's arrest is described in the Memoirs of Brienne. This
d'Artagnan is Dumas's hero; but the *Mémoires de M. d'Artagnan* on
which Dumas drew were written by Courtilz de Sandras in 1700,
twenty-seven years after d'Artagnan's death; they are partly fact, partly
fancy. Fouquet's trial is discussed in G. Mongrédien, *L'affaire Fouquet*
(1956).

Chapter 9: Louise de La Vallière

P. Visconti, *Mémoires sur la Cour de Louis XIV*, ed. Lemoine (1909). For
the Comte de Guiche, W. H. Lewis, *Assault on Olympus* (1958). The

schemes to separate Louis and his mistress are discussed in J. Lair, *Louise de La Vallière* (1935). For Bossuet, A. Gazier, *Bossuet et Louis XIV* (1914). As Saint-Simon remarks, Bossuet often spoke to Louis "with a freedom worthy of the first centuries and first bishops of the Church." In a sermon on Easter Sunday, 1681: "Sire, vous-même, vos victoires, votre propre gloire, cette puissance sans bornes, si nécessaire à conduire un Etat, si dangereuse à se conduire soi-même, voilà le seul ennemi dont vous ayez à vous défier." The Duc de Mazarin's protest is recorded by Saint-Simon, Choisy and Olivier d'Ormesson.

The chief sources for the two diplomatic incidents are d'Estrades, *Lettres, mémoires et négociations* (1743) and Créqui's report, dated 21st August, 1662, in *Revue des questions historiques*, vol. x. Pepys gives a vivid account of the London incident, noting that the Spaniards had lined their harness with chains of iron that could not be cut.

The traveller who watched Louis in church was Locatelli, *op. cit.* The sun-image and motto were the subject of a long book: C. Ménestrier, *La Devise du Roy Justifiée* (1679).

Les Plaisirs de l'Ile enchantée is included in Molière's works (Pléiade edition, vol. i, 1956). The episode of the madrigal is recounted by Madame de Sévigné. Louis's gifts to writers and savants are listed in P. Clément, *Lettres . . . de Colbert*, vol. v. The banning of *Tartuffe*, which is discussed in J. Palmer, *Molière: his life and works* (1930), shows how anxious Louis was not to go against public opinion, even in small matters. Louis's relations with Lully are discussed in H. Prunières, *Vie de J.-B. Lully* (1929) and with Philippe Quinault in biographies by E. Gros (1926) and J. Buijtendorp (1928).

For artistic theories under Louis XIV, H. Lemonnier, *L'Art français au temps de Louis XIV* (1911). Bernini's visit to Paris is described in R. Wittkower, *Bernini's Bust of Louis XIV* (1951). For Claude Perrault, his brother's Memoirs, ed. Lacroix (1878).

Chapter 10: The Rebuilding of France

For Colbert and France's economic development, P. Clément, *Lettres . . . de Colbert*, vols. ii and iii (1863-65), and C. W. Cole, *Colbert and a Century of French Mercantilism* (1939). For the navy, C. La Roncière, *Histoire de la marine française*, vol. v. (1920). Louis's letter to Colbert is given in P. Clément, *Histoire de Colbert*, 3rd revised edition, vol. ii (1892), pp. 463-4. For the West Indies, S. L. Mims, *Colbert's West Indian Policy* (1912). For Canada, Francis Parkman, *The Old Régime in Canada* (1875).

SOURCES AND NOTES

Chapter 11: Athénaïs de Montespan

The description of Louis at the army review in the spring of 1665 is by Locatelli, *op. cit.* Madame de Montespan was born 5th October, 1640, and baptised Françoise; she seems to have adopted the name of Athénaïs shortly after her marriage when she mixed with Précieuses at the Hôtel d'Albret. See J. Lemoine, *De la Vallière à Montespan* (1902) and, for her appearance, Visconti's Memoirs. Her character is described in Visconti's Memoirs, Spanheim's *Relation de la Cour de France en* 1690 (ed. E. Bourgeois, 1900), by Saint-Simon and the Princess Palatine.

In 1663 Colbert wrote: "The two things which please His Majesty most are works of gold and silver filigree from China and jasmine."

For the Marquis de Montespan, Montpensier, the *Souvenirs* of Madame de Caylus and Bussy-Rabutin, *Histoire amoureuse des Gaules* (ed. A. Poiterin, 1857).

For Mademoiselle de Fontanges and Louis's other mistresses at this period, the notes by A. de Boislisle to *Mémoires de Saint-Simon*, vol. xxviii (1916). For Madame de Montespan's fall, G. Mongrédien, *Madame de Montespan et l'affaire des poisons* (1953). La Reynie's summary is in Bib. Nat, MSS. *fonds français* 7608, 477 *et seq.*

Chapter 12: In Search of Glory

Louis claimed the Spanish Netherlands as his wife's property, invoking the Law of Devolution, a local custom in force in some provinces of the Netherlands, whereby if a man married twice the succession went to the children of the first wife to the exclusion of those of the second. Marie Thérèse was the daughter of Philip's first marriage, while the Infanta and Charles II, the sickly boy who was the new King of Spain, were children of the second marriage.

For Dutch libels on Louis, P. van Malssen, *Louis XIV d'après les pamphlets répandus en Hollande* (1936). For the importance of Dutch banking, V. G. van Dillen, "The Bank of Amsterdam," in *History of the Principal Public Banks*, ed. Van Dillen (1934).

In 1670 Louis danced for the last time on the stage, as Apollo in a Court ballet, *Les Amants magnifiques*, arranged by Molière. It was the King's farewell to merely allegorical victories.

For the reorganisation of the army, L. André, *Michel le Tellier et l'organisation de l'armée monarchique* (1906). The Rhine crossing is described by the Comte de Guiche in his *Relation du Passage du Rhine* (Michaud et Poujoulat vii). For the flooding, M. C. Trevelyan, *William III and the Defence of Holland* (1930). For the new system of parallels, *Vauban, sa famille et ses écrits. Ses oisevetés et sa correspondance* (ed. Rochas d'Aiglun 1910). For Louis's diplomatic moves during the war, L. André, *Louis XIV et l'Europe* (1950), William Temple, Memoirs (1700-9) and *Letters* (1700-3). For the "Reunions," David Ogg, *Europe in the Seventeenth Century* (1959), ch. vi. For the chastisement of Algiers and Genoa, Voltaire, *Le Siècle de Louis XIV*, ch. xiv.

Chapter 13: *Versailles*

A comparison of Versailles, Marly and the Trianon with Hardouin-Mansart's other buildings suggests that Louis played an important part in designing the royal houses. Both Charles Perrault and Colbert maintained that keeping Louis XIII's hunting lodge would ruin the new buildings; Louis told them that if they pulled it down, he would put it up again "exactly as it is now." Fantasy relieved the interior of Versailles from vulgarity. For example, a circle becomes a crown, and the crown a ring of dancing children. Surprises like this and the *trompe d'œil* paintings on the Staircase of the Ambassadors stemmed from Italian stage design.

The King's day at Versailles is described by Saint-Simon. Louis's supper menu is given by the Princess Palatine. Louis's attitude to the nobility appears, for example, in his will: speaking of the ban on duels, he says that this ban should be retained "in order to preserve the nobility, who form the main strength of the State." "Liberté française" struck nearly every visitor to France. "La facilité de l'aborder [le Roi] de luy présenter toutes sortes de requestes et de placets est tout entière, la foule des Gardes et des Courtisans qui sert auprès de la plupart des Souverains bien moins pour les garantir du danger que pour empescher la vérité d'approcher de leurs personnes est plus employée à favoriser l'accez aux suppliants de quelque condition qu'ils soient, qu'à les repousser." (*Relation de la conduite présente de la cour de France adressée à un cardinal à Rome par un seigneur Romain de la suite de Son Eminence Monseigneur le Cardinal Flavio Chigi, Légat du Saint-Siège vers le Roy Très Chrestien*, Leiden, 1665. This relation is dated Paris, 11th August, 1664). For several of the anecdotes relating to life at Versailles, W. H. Lewis's excellent *Louis XIV: an informal portrait* (1959).

Louis's booklet, *Manière de montrer les Jardins de Versailles* (1690-99) has been edited by R. Girardet (1951). Jean Cotelle (1642-1708) was elected to the Academy in 1672. His paintings of the gardens now hang in the Versailles museum. La Fontaine's lines are from *Les Amours de Psyché* (Pléiade edition, Oeuvres Diverses, p. 185). This work and Quinault's libretti are indispensable to an understanding of the gardens of Versailles.

Chapter 14: *Madame de Maintenon*

The chief sources for the life of Madame de Maintenon are her own letters, edited by Langlois (the total number is estimated at 60,000), the *Souvenirs* of the Comtesse de Caylus, the Memoirs of Mademoiselle d'Aumale, and the letters of the Princess Palatine. Saint-Simon is very biased against her and extremely unreliable. See also the biographies by M. Cruttwell (1930) and M. Taillandier (1920). For Paul Scarron, Naomi Phelps, *The Queen's Invalid* (1951). During her first marriage Madame de Maintenon was strongly influenced by the Précieuses. If a Précieuse is one who uses her beauty to gain power, Madame de Maintenon may be described as a Christian Précieuse, seeking power to do good.

For the Queen's death, the Princess Palatine and Saint-Simon. For Louis's attitude to marriage between royalty and the lesser nobility, see Montpensier. "Kings," he told her, "must satisfy public opinion." The most curious feature of the Lauzun-Mademoiselle affair is that both loved the King more than they loved each other. Lauzun, for example, suggested that after the marriage they sleep apart, "so that he should not be late for the King's *lever*."

For the date of Louis's marriage, Saint-Simon, the Abbé de Choisy and the Memoirs of La Fare. Voltaire discusses the problem. Langlois believed the marriage took place in October, 1683, and this date has been adopted by Jean Cordelier in his *Madame de Maintenon* (1955). Sixteen eighty-three seems to me unduly soon after the Queen's death. The latest scholar to discuss the marriage is Louis Hastier in *Louis XIV et Madame de Maintenon* (1957). Hastier believes the marriage took place as late as 1697. In the spring of that year a blacksmith named François Michel, "the visionary of Salon," paid a visit to Versailles and had a private talk with Louis. What they discussed no one knows. Hastier believes that Michel was urged in a vision to speak out against the King's life of sin with Madame de Maintenon, that Madame de Maintenon, through her friend Madame Arnoul, persuaded Michel to go to Versailles and speak to the King himself, and that as a result the King decided to regularise his union. Hastier's evidence is too circumstantial to be con-

SOURCES AND NOTES

vincing. In support of the date 1697 Hastier produces testimony in the form of two marriage contracts. On 14th March, 1686, when Mademoiselle de Mursay married the Comte de Tubières de Caylus, Madame de Maintenon signed well down the page, whereas on 24th August, 1699, when Marie-Charlotte de Tubières married the Comte de Saint-Chamans, she signed in the same paragraph as the King and Princes of the blood, and immediately after them. It is true that precedence in such matters was strictly laid down and as strictly observed, but the evidence may mean no more than that by 1697 Louis was less careful to keep his secret and more inclined to show openly his favour towards "the very high and very powerful lady, Mme Françoise d'Aubigné, marquise de Maintenon," as she is already called in a contract dated 1695. For example, in 1694 when Pierre Mignard painted Madame de Maintenon's portrait and represented her as Saint Francesca Romana, he asked the King whether he should show Madame de Maintenon wearing a cloak lined with ermine, which was generally considered an attribute of royalty. Louis gave his consent: "St. Françoise richly deserves it."

Chapter 15: The Grandeur of France

Bossuet's political theory is powerfully argued in his *Politique tirée de l'écriture sainte*. Louis's principles are stated in his Memoirs and in the advice given to his grandson Philippe in 1700. For governmental correspondence, G. B. Depping, *Correspondance administrative sous le règne de Louis XIV* (1850-5). For Louvois, the biography by C. Rousset (1866) and *Letters of Louvois* (ed. J. Hardré, 1949). The classical account of the Government redressing wrongs and abuses is V. E. Fléchier, *Mémoires sur les Grands Jours d'Auvergne* (1665). For Louis's relations with municipal bodies and with provincial bodies such as Parlement and the States General, Depping, and Alexandre Thomas, *Une Province sous Louis XIV* (1844). In *An Introduction to Seventeenth-Century France* (1954), J. Lough takes a less favourable view of the King's politics at home, partly on the evidence of John Locke.

For Louis's legal reforms, Isambert, *Recueil des lois*, vols. xviii and xix. For public order, P. Clément, *La police sous Louis XIV* (1866). For improvements and building in Paris under Louis XIV, J. Hillairet, *Evocation du Vieux Paris* (1952-4). For Vauban, the biographies by Halévy (1923), Lazard (1934) and Drecq (1933). Louis's letter to Vauban is cited in C. Petrie, *Louis XIV* (1938), p. 251. It was Vauban who invented the socket bayonet (Martinet's bayonet had to be jammed down the muzzle) and the technique of destroying fortifications by ricochet fire; and it was he who got the army to adopt the flintlock instead of the musket, which required a match and was therefore unreliable in wet weather. In 1675 at Valenciennes he inaugurated the daylight assault: for then the soldiers "will be able to fight without confusion and tumult," and "the King's eye will make them surpass themselves."

Chapter 16: The King's Religion

For religion in seventeenth-century France, Daniel-Rops, *L'Eglise des temps classiques* (1958). For Jansenism, Sainte-Beuve, *Port-Royal*; H. Bremond, *Histoire littéraire du sentiment religieux en France*, vol. iv (1920); Pierre Pascal, "L'abbé de Saint-Cyran, les Chartreux et les solitaires de Port-Royal" (*Revue Historique*, CXCI, April, 1941). The raised arms of the Jansenist crucifix also, of course, possess a theological significance: that grace is not given to all. For the régale, E. Michaud, *Louis XIV et Innocent XI* (1882). As regards the ideal of unity, in politics no less than in the arts if nature did not follow the perfect lines believed to have been laid down by the past, then nature was held to be wrong.

The circular signed by Louis and Colbert is cited in a letter dated 31st October, 1672, from a Professor of Divinity at Sedan to Monsieur Herault, Minister of the French Church in London (*C. S. P. Domestic* 1672-3, p. 68). Public opinion was strongly opposed to a religious minority. For many years Ministers, clerical assemblies and Parlements had urged the King "to do something for God, who had done so much for him." A similar attitude to minorities prevailed in Protestant Geneva, Holland and England, where throughout the reign of Charles II Catholics were excluded from local and national government, while nonconformists suffered intermittent but severe persecution. Because heresy was still believed to damn a man eternally, tolerance had not yet come to be considered a virtue, except by a few enlightened thinkers such as Pierre Bayle. For mass conversions and the dragonnades, Lavisse, vol. vii, pt. ii (1906). Vauban's figures of the loss to the French armed forces and to industry are untrustworthy. In general, the adverse economic effects of Protestant emigration have been overestimated, even by David Ogg. See Warren C. Scoville, *The Persecution of Huguenots and French Economic Development* 1680-1720 (Berkeley, 1960).

For Quietism, Mme Guyon's *Autobiography* (Eng. trans. 1897) and Daniel-Rops, *op. cit.*

Madame de Maintenon's one lasting success was the founding, with Louis, of Saint-Cyr, a free school for the daughters of impoverished noblemen. There were 250 girls, a number increased during the War of the Spanish Succession, with its losses in wealth and lives. The girls had to have four quarterings and be free from scrofula, epilepsy and chronic "vapours"! Louis chose the teachers' black dress and black silk cap. He also insisted that each girl should have her own goblet, spoon and fork, and that these should be of silver. Coloured ribbons were awarded for good work and conduct: as at Versailles the system was one of incentive by trifles. During the latter part of the reign there was a demand from all over France for "girls trained under Madame de Maintenon." Saint-Cyr may be said to have inaugurated sensible lay education for girls.

Chapter 17: Patron of the Arts

Molière expounds his idea of comedy in the placets to the King concerning *Tartuffe*. These, like Racine's prefaces, must be read in the light of strong Church opposition to the theatre; both authors tend to exaggerate their moral purpose. The making of *Le Bourgeois Gentilhomme* is described in d'Arvieux's Memoirs: see W. H. Lewis, *Levantine Adventurer* (1963). Incidentally Louis's taste for stage farce is very un-French: the Turkish scenes in *Le Bourgeois Gentilhomme* come closer to Shakespearean jesting than almost anything else in French dramatic writing.

For Racine, the study by G. Brereton and Professor Knight's *Racine et la Grèce*. *Esther's* unparalleled Court success is described by Madame de Sévigné, who was given seats for 19th February, 1689.

The development of style in the twenty years between La Rochefoucauld and La Bruyère is quite extraordinary. Voltaire speaks of La Bruyère's "totally new use of the language which did not, however, break the rules." His style is a brilliant but unsatisfactory attempt to make more precise the largely abstract language he had inherited. Saint-Simon was more successful because he made much greater use of concrete words. In his analysis of character, however, Saint-Simon tends to abstraction, and therefore to vagueness: his portrait of Fénelon, for instance, is unsatisfactory on this account.

For the historiographers' adventures, Bussy-Rabutin's letters to Madame de Sévigné and des Maizeaux, *La Vie de Boileau Despreaux* (1712). The MS of Racine's unfinished history was destroyed in a fire.

For architecture, L. Hautecoeur, *Histoire de l'architecture classique en France*, ii (1948). Le Brun invented a fifth order: the column decorated with *feuilles d'eau*, capital made of palms and fleur de lys, cornice decorated with dolphins' heads, but lacking the authority of Vitruvius it was rarely employed.

Le Brun's theory of art, like most French theories at that time, rested on the doctrine of authority; the human mind must be led, directed and dominated by rules that are certain, such as "Good Taste" or "Reason." Blondel asks why when we see a crowd of soldiers scattered on a battlefield we suffer this confusion with disgust, and is able to answer only that our soul, finding there nothing stable and constant, grows uneasy and anxious. So, although they did not know it, for this generation which had experienced war and wanted to feel secure "Reason" often amounted to "Stability." Le Brun believed that art should depict objects either noble or hallowed by tradition. In this he was the spokesman of Court opinion: Molière had been roundly abused for introducing into one of his plays so lowly an object as a cream tart.

While Mazarin had employed chiefly Italian painters, as early as 1659 Louis recalled Pierre Mignard from Rome to paint his portrait for the Infanta: a work which took Mignard only three hours. For the engravers, E. Boury, *Robert Nanteuil* (1924). It was Roger de Piles, a Paris art theoretician (1635-1709) who started the movement in favour of Rubens in his *Dialogue sur le coloris* (1673). The Poussinists' defeat became official when Piles's friend, the painter Charles de La Fosse (1636-1716), a determined Rubenist, was elected Director of the Academy. For Puget, the life by P. Auquier (1903), for Coysevox, the life by L. Benoist (1930). For François Couperin, the study by Wilfrid Mellers (1950).

Chapter 18: Domestic Pleasures

The two questions cited in the text were contemporary examination questions at the Paris faculty of medicine. Louis's operation is described in the *Journal de la Santé du Roi*.

For the War of the League of Augsburg Lavisse, *op. cit.* vol. viii, pt. i (1908). The most important French victory came on 29th October, 1688, when the Dauphin received the submission of Philippsburg, on the right bank of the Rhine, commanding the chief route between France and Germany. When French troops withdrew they dismantled the fortresses and devastated the countryside so that the Palatinate could not be used as a point of attack against France. For this Louvois was chiefly responsible, though the King must also take a share of the blame. When Louis discovered that his Secretary of War had secretly ordered the burning of Trier, he lost his temper (a very rare occurrence) and went for Louvois with a pair of fire-tongs. It was Madame de Maintenon who separated the two men. Louis then commanded Louvois to despatch a counter-order, warning him, "If a single house is burned, you will pay with your life." "When I think of all the places they have blown up," writes the Princess Palatine (Liselotte), "I am filled with such horror that each night, just as I am falling asleep, I seem to find myself at Heidelberg or Mannheim, gazing upon the ravages they have committed, then I wake up shuddering and cannot sleep again for two or three hours. I recall these places as they were in my time, and imagine to what a pass they have now been brought. That reminds me of the state my own affairs are in, and I cannot help weeping bitterly. . . . But they think it wrong of me to grieve." Liselotte's long homesick letters, in which she sighs for a good beer soup and black sausage, are an important source for the period 1682-1715. Their style has nothing of Versailles: after hunting all day, "I come back red as a lobster." No French courtier would have mentioned so "ignoble" a beast.

Madame de Maintenon's description of Dinant, from which the quotations are taken, is typical Précieuse writing: "frightful rocks apparently of iron and absolutely precipitous. . . . All the coaches bumped as though their springs must break and the ladies clung on to everything within reach."

For Louis's children, Saint-Simon and the Princess Palatine. In one of her letters Mademoiselle de Blois complained: "The King often drives out and I am placed between Madame de Maintenon and the Princesse d'Harcourt. You may imagine how amusing it is for me!" The letter came into Louis's hands and caused him a good deal of pain. For the Duc du Maine, W. H. Lewis, *The Sunset of the Splendid Century* (1955).

It was "the mole," as Villeroi called Madame de Maintenon, who got Louis-Antoine de Noailles appointed Archbishop of Paris in 1695, and he, too, caused the King much trouble with his Jansenist leanings. Madame de Maintenon was more successful as an educator: it was she who took charge of Marie Adélaide's lessons, the staples being Roman history, classical myths, the clavichord and dancing.

The description of Marly is from Saint-Simon. Typical of changes in

fashion at the end of the century was the alteration in the royal mono-
gram: the L's now curve and are interlaced.

For the progress of science, M. Ornstein, *The Role of Scientific
Societies in the Seventeenth Century* (1928). M. Brown, *Scientific Organisa-
tions in Seventeenth Century France* (1934), and A. E. Bell, *Christian
Huygens and the Development of Science in the Seventeenth Century* (1947).
It was Bernard de Fontenelle, appointed by Louis's secretary to the
Académie des Sciences, who popularised the idea of progress, in the name
of which political thinkers of the next century were to call in question
the divine right of kings and so prepare the French Revolution.

Chapter 19: An End to Glory

Documents for the Spanish succession are given in F. A. M. Mignet,
Négociations relatives à la succession d'Espagne sous Louis XIV (1835-42) and
in A. Legrelle, *La Diplomatie française et la succession d'Espagne* (1888-92).

Louis's precepts to his grandson, virtually a primer of kingship, are
given by Voltaire. Philippe married Marie Adélaide's sister, who died
young of consumption, and secondly Elizabeth Farnese, who dominated
him and pursued an aggressive foreign policy.

For the growth of relative values, Paul Hazard, *La Crise de la conscience
européenne 1680-1715* (1935). James II's death is recorded by James
Clarke. Voltaire believes that it was Maria of Modena who persuaded
Louis to recognise her son; but throughout his life Louis had made it
an invariable principle never to take a State decision at someone else's
suggestion, least of all at a woman's.

For events in the War of the Spanish Succession, Lavisse, *op. cit.* vol.
viii, pt. i (1908). The Beringhen incident is related by Saint-Simon.
The deaths in the royal family are described by Madame de Maintenon
in her letters to the Princesse des Ursins and by the Princess Palatine.
Louis's interpretation of the deaths appears most clearly in his farewell to
Villars: "God punishes me, and I have deserved it."

Chapter 20: Death of a King

Louis's farewell words are recorded in Villars's Memoirs. The plan for
attacking Denain was first mooted by a civilian, one Lefebvre d'Orval,
a councillor in the Flanders Parlement.

Prince Eugène was the son of Eugène-Maurice de Savoie and Olympe
Mancini, "the Snipe," who had fled France at the time of the "affair of

the poisons." Like Marlborough, he had learned soldiering in the French army.

The terms of the treaties of Utrecht and Rastadt are given in Vast.

France's financial position after the war is discussed in Warren C. Scoville, *op. cit.* See also Boislisle, *Correspondance des Contrôleurs Génereaux des Finances* (1874-97). In 1701 the Treasury began to issue bank-notes; by 1706 those in circulation amounted to £60 million. The experiment was a failure and by 1709 they had all been changed into State bonds or coinage of the realm. Between 1700 and 1720, according to Lavisse, silver worth £83 million entered France from South America. By 1717 France's economic recovery was well under way, and she was to remain prosperous for most of the century.

The chief witness for the changes in Louis's character is Madame de Maintenon, whose indulgence did not increase with age. For further evidence, see the important article by M. Giraud, "Tendances humanitaires à la fin du règne de Louis XIV" (*Revue Historique* CCIX, April, 1953). The best portrait of Orléans is by Saint-Simon, his intimate friend.

In 1714 Louis proclaimed his legitimised sons, the Duc du Maine and the Comte de Toulouse, and their descendants, in default of princes of the blood royal, heirs to the throne. This was a necessary precaution in view of the Duc d'Anjou's delicate health. Here Voltaire's comments provide a corrective to Saint-Simon's diatribe against Louis.

The eclipse on Friday, 3rd May, 1715, is noted by Dangeau and provides yet another example of the growing interest in science. The decline in Louis's health and the incident with Torcy are recorded by Saint-Simon. For Louis's last days I have followed Jean and François Antoine, *Journal de la mort de Louis XIV* (1849), supplemented by Dangeau, Saint-Simon and Caylus, *Souvenirs.* For Louis's words to the Dauphin, I have followed Voltaire, who copied them from Louis XV's bedroom, where they were inscribed.

Madame de Maintenon did not desert Louis in his last days, as Saint-Simon claims. She considered that the King died "like a hero and a saint." She led a retired life at Saint-Cyr until her death in 1719.

Voltaire says that Louis was mourned less than he deserved. After so long a reign many Frenchmen welcomed a change, particularly the younger courtiers, who hoped to make their fortune quickly under a boy king. The warmest tributes came from Louis's former enemies, those who had vilified him in his lifetime. The Emperor, for example, went into full mourning and Prince Eugène likened the King's death to the uprooting of a mighty oak.

Saint-Simon and the Reputation of Louis XIV

The first serious study of Louis XIV was Voltaire's *Le Siècle de Louis XIV*. Voltaire, who had known the last fifteen years of Louis's reign, took a favourable view of the King. He praised Louis's judgment, generosity and taste, and regarded him as a great man. Voltaire published his book in 1751. He did not know Saint-Simon's *Mémoires*, which began to appear in 1788.

Whereas Voltaire was able to take a fairly dispassionate view of Louis, Saint-Simon had been deeply involved in Court life and domestic politics during the last years of the reign. His personal pride had suffered when Louis decided (quite rightly) that he was not cut out to be a soldier and declined to promote him, his ducal pride when Louis legitimised his own bastards and gave them precedence over dukes. Moreover, as an intimate friend of Philippe, Regent of France, only with Louis's death could Saint-Simon begin to play an important political role. These are some of the reasons why objectivity was not to be expected of Saint-Simon. And in fact his *Mémoires* created a new, very unsympathetic Louis: cold, proud, arbitrary, a monster of egoism.

In nineteenth-century France Saint-Simon's portrait was found very convenient in justifying the French Revolution. "Look," said the historians, "what a dreadful man this Louis was! What a good thing for France the Bourbons were sent to the guillotine!" In his *Histoire de France*, a highly tendentious but much read work, Ernest Lavisse (1842–1922) perpetuated Saint-Simon's "monster of egoism"; this was the heyday of the Third Republic, and Lavisse wrote off Louis the absolute monarch as a political failure as well.

In England also Louis's reputation stands low, but for different reasons. For several decades Louis was England's arch enemy and as such naturally hated. During his lifetime pamphlets appeared blackening the King's character. For example, *The Most Christian Turk* (1690) informed Englishmen of Louis's relations with Mademoiselle de La Vallière: "After a long caressing of this Mistress (by whom he had some Children, and is said, in a great Immergency, to play the Man-Midwife to one of them himself,) and Entertaining her with all the Glory and Gallantry of his Kingdom, he grew weary of those Beauties himself had sullied, and searched for those that were fresher." Saint-Simon's verdict tallied in a most satisfactory manner with Englishmen's traditionally hostile view and was adopted by all but a very few historians. More recently, our experience of dictatorship has made us particularly sensitive to anything savouring of arbitrary or tyrannical rule; again Saint-Simon has been combed to good purpose and with a bewildering lack of the historical sense Louis XIV has been lumped together with certain modern dictators.

How trustworthy is Saint-Simon's portrait of the King? Even in the nineteenth century certain scholars were disturbed by grave inconsistencies between Saint-Simon's *Mémoires* and the authorities on which he drew, such as Dangeau and Sourches. For example, Saint-Simon places Madame de Maintenon at the very hub of political events, a black spider weaving a web of doom around all who happen to incur her wrath: a view flatly contradicted by all other available evidence. He declares that Jansenism was little more than a scarecrow set up by the Jesuits in order to distract attention from their own Molinist heresy: again a simply fantastic statement. But only in 1928, when Boislisle had completed his 41-volume annotated edition of the *Mémoires*, did the extent of Saint-Simon's unreliability and, in particular, of his bias against the King become abundantly clear. In passage after passage Saint-Simon falsifies facts to the detriment of Louis.

The building of Marly, for instance. Saint-Simon says that it cost several billion livres, that Versailles, for all its size, did not cost as much as Marly "—and that is an understatement." Then he concludes: "Such was the destiny of a haunt of snakes and carrion, of toads and frogs, chosen solely to avoid expense. Such was the King's bad taste in everything; neither the most crushing war nor his religious feelings could blunt an appetite for proudly bending nature to his will." Now we happen to know that Marly cost only four and a half million livres, therefore a small fraction of what Versailles cost, that the site was marshy and wooded but exceptionally beautiful, and that the buildings Louis commissioned were among Mansart's finest. Such examples of distortion could be multiplied many times.

Louis himself is cut down to the measure of the author: Saint-Simon is plainly fascinated by the King but cannot forgive him for choosing his Ministers and intimate friends from the middle class. Villars and Mansart, to name only two estimable men, are presented in the blackest terms because their pedigree was found wanting. Saint-Simon actually ventures to assert that Louis mercilessly disgraced Vauban in his old age— again a serious distortion of known facts.

Despite Boislisle, Saint-Simon's unfavourable image of the King is still current because of his brilliance as a writer, the sheer bulk of the *Mémoires* and, above all, because of their superb artistry. The paradox is that Saint-Simon made his book a work of art precisely through these distortions, conscious or unconscious; only by showing Louis, Madame de Maintenon and the Duc du Maine in a dark light could he win the reader's sympathy for that ineffective figure, Philippe, Regent of France, and to a lesser degree for the author himself.

Plainly one can be fair to Louis only by treating with extreme caution the writings of a man so hostile to the King and wherever possible turning to more reliable sources. This I have tried to do and if the portrait that emerges differs from current notions of the King it is worth remembering that Saint-Simon, who wrote twenty-nine years after the King's death, differs even more radically from Voltaire and from Louis's contemporaries, such as the Grande Mademoiselle, the Venetian ambassadors, and the Princess Palatine.

APPENDIX B

French Fortifications in 1685

Above, two ground-plans to illustrate typical features

A, ravelin; B, demi-lune; C, tenail; D, double tenail; E, swallow's tail; F, priest's bonnet; G, ravelin or demi-lune with counterguard; H, hornwork; I, hornwork with indented flanks; K, crowned hornwork; L, crownwork

Left, detail and section

A, level of the earth; AB, distance from the houses to the rampart; BCED, rampart; FD, height of the rampart; BD, inner slope; EC, outer slope; NOEI, parapet; KN, height of the parapet (usually six feet); NO, slope of the parapet; PHI, banquette; PD, earth platform; CR, berm, or ledge; RST, parapet of the faussebraye; TV, narrow berm; VYZX, ditch; X4, covered way; 673, glacis of the covered way

From *Les Travaux de Mars ou L'Art de la Guerre*, by Manesson Mallet (vol. I, 1685)

375

Index

INDEX